THE SCOTS IN FRANCONIA

PLATE I. Tombstone of Abbot Trithemius
By Tilman Riemenschneider
(in the Neumünster, Würzburg)

The Scots in Franconia
A Century of Monastic Life

MARK DILWORTH

1974
SCOTTISH ACADEMIC PRESS
EDINBURGH AND LONDON

Published by
Scottish Academic Press Ltd
25 Perth Street, Edinburgh 3
and distributed by
Chatto & Windus Ltd
40 William IV Street
London W.C.2

ISBN 0 7011 1934 9

Printed in Great Britain by
Lewis Reprints Ltd.
member of Brown Knight & Truscott Group
London and Tonbridge

Contents

Illustrations

Thanks are due to the Rector of the Jugendheim Don Bosco (formerly St. James's) for Plates 4, 5, 8, 9, and to Rev. P. Wunibald Kellner, O.S.B., Münsterschwarzach for the remaining photographs. The cover is from Merian's View of Würzburg, 1648, and is reproduced by courtesy of the Mainfränkisches Museum, Würzburg.

Preface

Circumstances leading to the publication of the present work go back over a dozen years. I had already spent a sabbatical term investigating source material for the history of the Scottish abbeys in Germany and had published some preliminary articles establishing the personnel of the monasteries, when the opportunity was given me to do a more limited study in depth. My choice was the Würzburg abbey in the seventeenth century. It was an attractive subject in many ways but one offering particular difficulties as most of the Würzburg archives had been destroyed in 1945.

When the monastery was secularised in 1803, its archives were transferred to the Würzburg state archives, where they were split up and distributed among the various repositories. The early deeds were later transferred to the central archives in Munich. During the last war the Würzburg archives were taken to a country house for safety, but this was bombarded as a reprisal by the advancing American army and great damage done. Thus all that survives of the monastic archives for the later period is scattered material which escaped destruction. The manuscript volumes in St James's not of an archival nature were, however, given in 1803 to Würzburg university library and have survived. There is no trace of certain essential records (clothings, profession sheets, and so on). What happened to them in 1803 is not known, unless for some reason they were transferred to, or already formed part of, the episcopal archives.

The episcopal archives were put into a church crypt for safe-keeping in the war but molten lead during an incendiary raid in 1945 incinerated them almost entirely. Since Würzburg was a prince-bishopric, the episcopal archives were also the local government archives; the total destruction of the material in them relating to St James's is therefore a double loss, only slightly offset by the survival of some transcripts made in 1877-79 by Alexander Reid (now in Mount Stuart library) and by the use made of the archives by Michael Wieland. His extended article on St James's, published over a hundred years ago, is antiquarian in nature and not entirely reliable.

The writing of the history of St James's is thus very largely the piecing together of isolated items from other sources, particularly the archives of the sister-abbey at Ratïsbon, as a substitute for the use of the main archival sources destroyed. Inevitably, therefore, the narrative is less coherent than one might like. It is the story of one particular institution, related to the wider context in Germany and Scotland whenever this seemed called for, but a larger and more complex work would have been required to provide a continuous assessment of the abbey's place in the counter-reformation as it affected Germany and Scotland. In general, comment has been avoided on such matters as the attitudes of Propaganda to missionary monks, or the disputes over church property involving the Scots. Nevertheless, the book is intended to be a serious contribution to the history of the Scottish mission and of Benedictine monasticism. It is also to some extent a pioneer effort at cross-fertilisation of sources usually kept separate: Benedictine, local German, post-reformation Scottish. I hope to edit one source, the duke of Bavaria's letter-book, for the Scottish History Society; it provides important new information on Ninian Winzet and shows John Lesley in more favourable light than is usual.

This book is in substance a thesis offered to Edinburgh university in 1968. The word 'thesis' rightly strikes a warning note, so perhaps I should say that it was always my intention to publish the present work and that, although presented as a thesis, it was written as a straightforward narrative, with a view to publication later. Items requiring textual criticism or detailed investigation were dealt with in separate published articles so that the flow of the narrative would not be unduly impeded. In addition a fair amount of detail has been eliminated from the completed thesis or relegated to an appendix, and discussion of documents has been reduced to a minimum. Full use has also been made of an important new source discovered since the thesis was presented: the original *Indiculus Monasteriorum*, which had been lost for thrity years.

It is my pleasant duty to thank those who have helped towards the writing of this book: my superiors, who gave me the necessary leave of absence; the supervisors of my thesis, Professor Gordon Donaldson and Mr. A. J. A. Malkiewicz; the Leverhulme Trustees for a generous Research Award which enabled me to make two journeys to Germany and Rome and have documents photocopied; the Rev. William James Anderson, who gave encouragement and practical help from the beginning. To Dr. Ludwig Hammermayer (Munich) I am grateful for a fruitful and happy collaboration, and in particular for the use of his material from East Germany when I was unable to travel there. My thanks are due to the staffs of the libraries and archives where I worked, especially in Edinburgh, Würzburg, Ratisbon and Munich, for their unfailing courtesy and assistance; to all those who brought relevant material to my notice; and to those who accorded me personal kindness and hospitality when I was away from home. Unfortunately they are too numerous to mention by name. In its final form the book owes much to the Rev. B. FitzGibbon, S.J. and Dom Francis Davidson, who read the script and made valuable suggestions, and to Miss P. Turner, who did the necessary re-typing. Lastly, I am grateful to my mother, who looked after my material needs when the thesis was being written in Edinburgh; but for her it could never have proceeded so smoothly.

Fort Augustus Abbey
April 1971

CHAPTER 1

The Scotic Abbeys in Germany

Würzburg, the principal town in Lower Franconia, lies on both sides of the river Main, a tributary of the Rhine. The chief part of the town stands on low-lying ground on the east bank; the bank opposite climbs abruptly and is crowned by the Marienberg fortress, in whose shadow lies the church of St James, the *Schottenkirche* or Scottish Church. This ancient monastic establishment, founded in the twelfth century by Irish monks, was handed over to German monks in 1497. A century later it was given to Scottish Benedictines and remained in their hands until 1803.

It is thus quite possible that before 1595 no monk from Scotland had ever set foot within the monastery of St James of the Scots in Würzburg. Certainly until that time the monastery had never belonged to or been inhabited by monks from Scotland. And yet it had been called the monastery of the Scots, or *Schottenkloster*, since its foundation. To understand how it got its name one must go back to the early centuries of Irish Christianity when it was the custom for monks to go into voluntary exile and preach the Gospel as they went.[1] The Irish Church was organised on a monastic basis, a fact which greatly influenced their missionary work. Besides evangelising the neighbouring island of Britain they preached and settled in France, Belgium, Germany, Austria, Switzerland and Italy; to this day the memory of their missionary zeal persists in many parts of Central Europe. The name by which they were known and which they used for themselves was *Scoti*.

About the middle of the seventh century were founded the first monasteries on the Continent for Irish monks exclusively. It is not certain how long they survived or remained Irish: perhaps a matter of a generation, in some cases perhaps for a period running into centuries. Nor is it clear what rule they followed: no doubt the Rule of Columbanus to begin with, then either the Benedictine rule or some mixture of the two. But the stream of monks leaving Ireland for their *peregrinatio*, or voluntary exile,[2] though it may have slackened at times, never dried up. By the middle of the eleventh

11

century the chief scene of their activities was what we now call Germany, and here, at Ratisbon on the Danube, was founded the Irish monastery of Weih-Sankt-Peter in 1075-76.[3]

Its founder was an Irishman from Donegal named Muiredach MacRobartaig, usually known as Marianus Scotus, who is to be distinguished from the better-known contemporary Marianus Scotus, celebrated for his *Chronicle*. After the death of the Ratisbon Marianus in or shortly after 1080,[4] the monastery he had founded flourished to such an extent that a larger monastery, St James's, was built in Ratisbon about 1110. There were certain peculiarities about the original foundation of Weih-Sankt-Peter: it was subject in some way to the German abbess who had donated the property, and it is not clear that the rule followed there was Benedictine. The new foundation, however, was very different. It was an abbey, it certainly followed the Rule of St Benedict, and it was an independent community. More than that, it received in the first years of its existence the privileges of exemption from the bishop's jurisdiction and from all temporal overlords save the emperor himself.

A most remarkable period of expansion followed, in which no fewer than seven foundations were made in German lands alone in the space of fifty years from about 1135: St James in Erfurt, St James in Würzburg, St Giles in Nuremberg, St James in Constance, Our Lady in Vienna, St Nicholas in Memmingen, Holy Cross in Eichstätt. Irish monks from Vienna established themselves in Kiev, and probably the houses in Ireland which are recorded later as connected with the Ratisbon group of monasteries were likewise founded during this period of expansion. In Ratisbon itself Weih-Sankt-Peter continued in being but was a mere priory dependent on the new abbey of St James's. Bulls of favour and privilege from the holy see, letters of protection from the emperors, and benefactions from lesser personages continued to be bestowed, showing the favour in which the Ratisbon abbey was held. In fact, St James's in Ratisbon deserves to rank as one of the important founder abbeys of the middle ages.

All the houses grouped round Ratisbon observed the Benedictine rule, which by this time, thanks to its qualities of orderliness and moderation, had supplanted its rivals. This Irish Benedictine vitality also absorbed or channelled into itself all the zeal for peregrination of the *Scoti*. Henceforth these were the only Irish monasteries in Europe. They were, however, an end as much as a beginning.[5] They represented the last burst of vitality, before it petered out, of the Irish missionary movement which had begun several centuries previously and had been one of the most potent factors in the evangelisation of Europe. It was not mere chance

12

which determined Ratisbon as the centre of this monastic activity. The first missionaries in the region had been *Scoti*, and Ratisbon was a centre of Irish activity in the early missionary period. It was a town with a continuous Irish tradition.[6]

Würzburg also had a continuous Irish tradition perhaps even more striking.[7] The apostle of Eastern Franconia was St Kilian, an Irishman who was martyred there with his two companions about 689. In 752 his relics were translated by the first bishop of the see to the cathedral, which was dedicated in his honour. Würzburg became a place of pilgrimage for the *Scoti* as well as being a centre of their literary activity. The famous eighth-century codex of St Paul's epistles, with its glosses in Old Irish, belongs there, besides a number of other manuscripts. A well-known scholar, Clemens Scotus, worked at Würzburg in the early ninth century. Marianus Scotus the Chronicler went to be ordained priest at the tomb of St Kilian, and there is reason to believe that Marianus of Ratisbon likewise visited his tomb. In 1085 an Irish bishop, who was apparently head of a small community of monks, died at Würzburg. David Scotus was master of the cathedral school in the early twelfth century and was said to be still living there in 1137. It is also possible that when the Benedictine abbey was founded in Würzburg it was intended to serve as a hostel for Irish pilgrims to the tomb of St Kilian.

The founders and benefactors of St James's in Würzburg regarded the Benedictine monks as continuing the Scotic tradition and declared that it was out of devotion to their own patron Kilian that they made over their gifts to his compatriots. The position of the Irish monks in Würzburg, and of their Scottish successors after the Reformation, cannot be understood except against the background of this tradition going back to the eighth century and the apostle of Franconia, St Kilian.

Würzburg, therefore, was a natural place for founding a daughter-house of Ratisbon, but it should be borne in mind that the town had Irish connections, and within living memory also an Irish monastic community, independently of Ratisbon. The accounts of the founding of St James's in Würzburg vary according to whether they emanate from Ratisbon or not. In Ratisbon, towards the end of the twelfth century, the monks composed the *Vita Mariani*, which was more than a life of their founder as it contained an account of the foundation of their daughter-houses. According to this the bishop of Würzburg, Embricho, made grants of land on the outskirts of the town to the Ratisbon monks, whose fame had spread to Franconia. Christian, abbot of Ratisbon c.1133-51, sent a group of monks with Macarius, a well-known scholar, as abbot. The holiness and austerity of Macarius are described, and in

13

particular his habit of never drinking wine. Once, when visiting Bishop Embricho and being pressed by him to take a glass of wine, he changed it into water and so drank it, to the great edification of his host, who made a solemn public pronouncement on the miracle. The death of Macarius was later heralded by a tower of fire rising from the gate of the monastery into the sky.[8]

A later account is found in the *Libellus de Fundatione Ecclesiae Consecrati Petri* (the usual Latin for Weih-Sankt-Peter), a late thirteenth-century compilation made at Ratisbon containing much apocryphal material but based in part on some genuine earlier Irish source. This too makes Macarius out to be a Ratisbon monk, although the account is a product of the Celtic imagination at its most vivid and can be disregarded. The only help it gives is in associating Macarius with both Embricho and the emperor Conrad, which demands a date between 1138 and 1146.[9]

One of the abbots of the Würzburg monastery in the early sixteenth century, shortly after it had been taken over by German monks, was the celebrated scholar Trithemius. In one of his historical works Trithemius gives the date 1139-40 for the founding of the monastery,[10] but in another version of the same work he has 1134.[11] It is, however, in his *Compendium* of the history of St James's in Würzburg that Trithemius deals explicitly with the foundation. He gives an account very different from that of the *Vita Mariani*. Instead of Macarius being sent from Ratisbon, he came, already a Benedictine, from Ireland to Franconia with two companions and was blessed as abbot by Embricho in 1139. Trithemius also gives the text of a deed of Embricho in 1140 in which the bishop relates how he went to Mainz and was accosted by a Scotic monk named Christian, who begged him publicly to establish a house for *peregrini Scoti* in Würzburg. This was done, and the first abbot, Macarius, changed water into wine in the presence of witnesses, as a result of which a prebend in the cathedral was made over to the monks as an endowment. All this is in the deed. Trithemius then narrates three other miracles, one of which was worked in the presence of Pope Eugene III (1145-53) in Rome. Then, in 1153, Macarius died.

Apart from the names of Macarius and Embricho and the miracle of the wine and water, this account differs completely from the Ratisbon one. Trithemius can be suspected of bias in his silence regarding the Ratisbon abbey, for at the time of writing German monks had been occupying the Würzburg monastery for only a dozen years and he would not want to draw attention to its apparently unjust severance from the Ratisbon group of houses. He was also writing almost four centuries after the event, while the Ratisbon account dates from 1184-85, and he does not reveal his source for the other miracles of Macarius. On the other hand, he quotes documents which are still extant[12] and gives names and dates for Macarius's successors which can be checked in them, while the chronology of the Ratisbon account is quite unsound. Therefore, leaving aside his silence as regards Ratisbon, Trithemius's is by far the more reliable narrative. The foundation deed of 1140 is a forgery perpetrated in the years 1170-80 but the next document he cites, concerning a grant of land by Embricho in 1142, is genuine.[13] The name of Macarius, however, is not mentioned in it. We are thus left with two or three indisputable facts. The Scotic monks were in Würzburg in 1142. Within less than fifty years there were accounts of the first abbot, Macarius, and the miracle of wine and water, emanating from both Ratisbon and Würzburg but differing in other respects. By 1184-85, when the *Vita Mariani* was compiled at Ratisbon, the Würzburg monastery was linked to Ratisbon (whether or not it had been before), otherwise it could not have been claimed as a daughter-house.

It might be as well at this point to comment on the word *Scotus*.[14] No scholar nowadays disputes that *Scotus* in the early middle ages signified an Irishman — for the Romans even, Irish wolf-hounds were *Scotici canes*; its most accurate translation would be Gael or Gaelic-speaker. The term was thus also used to denote the Gaels who had left Ireland to settle in Dalriada (what is now Argyll). Scotus signified a native of the Gaelic-speaking area of Ireland and North Britain, and Scotia denoted the area itself. Primarily the latter term would refer to Ireland and secondarily to the colony or extension of the fatherland — call it what one will — in North Britain. After the Norman Conquest, however, a change in meaning took place: men began to distinguish between *Scotia* (North Britain) and *Hibernia* (Ireland). The Dalriadic settlement from Ireland gave its name to the country north of Forth and Clyde and eventually to the whole of present-day Scotland.

In Ireland the tradition remained that they were the original *Scoti* even though by the end of the twelfth century the term was no longer applied to anyone but a Scot from North Britain. On the continent, however, the Irish monks of Ratisbon and its daughter-houses continued to use the old name; they called themselves, and were called, *Scoti* in their legal documents throughout the middle ages. To this day their monasteries are known as the *Schottenklöster*. There was naturally a certain degree of confusion. As early as the twelfth century, for instance in the *Vita Mariani*, these monks who continued to call themselves *Scoti* used the name *Hibernia* to designate their homeland.

The remarkable expansion of the Irish monasteries centred on Ratisbon was followed by a process of consolidation which may

15

have begun from within but was certainly reinforced from without. In 1185 the pope decreed that the abbots were to visit Ratisbon annually and there receive instructions concerning regular observance. Thirty years later, in 1215, the Lateran Council issued a decree from which the present-day organisation of Benedictine monasteries into groups (called congregations) originates. It ordered that the black monks of each kingdom or province should unite and should hold general chapters every three years to legislate for all their houses. The Scotic abbeys, however, were provided for separately by a special bull of Innocent III: instead of belonging to the local congregation, they were formed into a congregation according to nationality, irrespective of locality. Each abbot was to be under the direction and authority of the Ratisbon abbot, who as abbot general had considerable powers of jurisdiction and discipline, and all were to attend a general chapter at Ratisbon every three years. It is worth noting that Benedictine monachism was never strong in Ireland itself (hence the gibe that Benedictines never did well in Ireland because their motto was Pax) and this congregation based on Ratisbon was by far the most important body of Irish Benedictines there has ever been. After the founding in 1232 of a priory at Kelheim on the Danube not far from Ratisbon, there were ten monasteries in German lands and at least two dependent priories in Ireland.

This Irish congregation remained in reasonably good condition for almost two hundred years.[15] The Ratisbon abbot maintained his position as *abbas matricularius, visitator et corrector* of the other houses. His abbey was exempt from all spiritual and temporal rulers except the pope and emperor, while the other houses were, in theory and to a large extent in practice, subject to the Ratisbon abbot. There is evidence of a general decline in the fourteenth century but it was not until after 1400 that the congregation began to break up. The recruits coming from Ireland were fewer in number and poorer in quality. Probably by this time the smaller Irish houses in Germany had hardly any community or none at all. The houses at Memmingen, Eichstätt and Kelheim ceased to be monasteries, while the abbeys at Nuremberg and Vienna were handed over to German monks in 1418.

The general chapter held at Ratisbon in 1479 established the situation within the congregation for the following decades: it enacted that all elections of superiors were to be held at Ratisbon and that no German could be made a superior unless all the Irish abbots consented to it and no Irishman was available for appointment. Clearly the monasteries with no community were meant. By now only the Ratisbon abbey had a community, from which superiors of the various houses were chosen.

The congregation suffered a further blow when in 1497 the Würzburg abbot died leaving no monk behind him and the bishop brought in German monks instead. At the dawn of the sixteenth century the once flourishing congregation of Irish monasteries had dwindled to the three abbeys of Ratisbon, Erfurt and Constance and the priory of Weih-Sankt-Peter in Ratisbon. Only the first-named had a community, and a very small one at that, from which was chosen a man to live as titular superior without any subjects in each of the other three houses. Probably the unsatisfactory state of the temporalities was as much to blame for this situation as was lack of recruits.

During the previous three centuries the Würzburg abbey had been at times the most flourishing of all the communities.[16] It had received a bull from Celestine III in 1195 confirming it in all its privileges and property, and it received other favours and privileges, although not such as would infringe the rights of the Ratisbon abbot-general. Würzburg was one of the more important Irish monasteries, possibly because it lay beside the resting-place of St Kilian and was the one nearest to the English Channel. The fifteenth century, however, brought trouble for the Würzburg monastery as it did for most of the others. The buildings were largely devastated in the feud between townspeople and bishop in the years 1397-1400 since they lay so near the bishop's fortress-residence. Conditions in the episcopal city continued to be unsatisfactory, with the result that the monastery's observance and economy both declined,[17] although there is evidence at times of a quite large community and of repairs made to the buildings. From about 1460 on, however, the abbot lived practically alone in the monastery.

The priory of Roscarbery in County Cork seems to have been founded from Würzburg and was thus directly dependent on it. In 1354 the prior and monks of Roscarbery swore obedience to the abbot of Würzburg and in 1378 they thanked him for visiting their house in person when he could have sent a delegate instead. We again find the prior of Roscarbery asking the Würzburg abbot for a visitation in 1454. In the fifteenth century the abbot of Würzburg made the presentations of superiors to the Irish monasteries in Memmingen and Constance but, in the case of Memmingen at least, this was probably due to the decline in its fortunes.[18] The general chapter of 1479 already mentioned declared that the Würzburg abbot had the right of presentation to the abbeys of Constance and Memmingen and the priory of Roscarbery though with certain restrictions. A letter of the abbot of Ratisbon a month later makes the position clearer: Constance and Memmingen are dependent on Würzburg, and the Würzburg abbot can make

17

visitations, appoint administrators and so on, but this is without prejudice to the rights of the abbot general as superior over Constance and Memmingen. There was evidently, at least at this period, some sort of hierarchical order in the congregation, and Würzburg stood high in it.

Undoubtedly there had been times when the abbot of Würzburg was an important churchman. He was nevertheless subject in matters of discipline to the Ratisbon abbot and was obliged to attend general chapters there. The houses distant from Ratisbon naturally fell to some degree under the domination of the local bishops. This was perhaps nowhere more so than in Würzburg, where the bishop was also the temporal ruler, being duke of Eastern Franconia and thus one of the princes of the Empire. Not only that, but the prince-bishop resided in the Marienberg fortress a few hundred yards away from the abbey. From 1268 on, it was he and not the Ratisbon abbot who carried out visitations, while the oath taken by Würzburg abbots after election entailed comprehensive submission to him. It was the bishop who was largely responsible for introducing German monks into the abbey in 1497.

Throughout the centuries from their foundation all these monasteries had Irish communities. It is so strange a situation that one might be inclined to doubt it, but the evidence for it is continuous and overwhelming. In spite of being on German soil they did not accept German recruits, and in spite of their continued use of the name *Scoti* all their links were with Ireland. It became more and more common to add some phrase like *vel Hiberni* as a sort of gloss to *Scoti* in documents, and occasionally one finds *Hiberni* or a similar word used alone, but right to the end they retained and used the title of *Scoti*. It is perhaps too much to say that no German was ever a monk in one of these houses, just as it is too much to say that nobody from Scotland ever was. As long as there was linguistic unity between Ireland and the Scottish Highlands — and such unity persisted into the seventeenth century at least — a novice from anywhere in Gaelic-speaking territory would surely be acceptable. Examples are known of *Scoti* from North Britain going to the Continent before the Ratisbon houses were founded; others from Scotland could equally well have entered those houses later. But although possible it is unlikely, since Roscarbery, the recruiting centre, was right at the south of Ireland.[19]

The retention of the title of *Scoti* by the Irish monks was to have fateful consequences. When the abbot in Ratisbon was involved in a dispute with the bishop in 1514, both parties appealed to the pope, and the outcome was a bull the following year deposing the Irish abbot on the ground that he was not a Scot and appointing as abbot in his place a Scottish secular priest named John Thomson.[20]

18

The affair becomes less surprising when it is realised that Scots traders were numerous in the town and district. They had been receiving citizenship of Ratisbon since 1493, which meant they had influence and an assured position. In 1500 they had entered into an agreement with the Irish abbot for the erection of a confraternity of Scots with an altar dedicated to St Andrew; fourteen Scots, of whom four were secular priests and one of these a graduate, signed or were mentioned in the deed. One must surely credit the Scots resident in Ratisbon with some influence in the affair, especially since a version of history claiming these monasteries as founded for Scots was circulating in manuscript and was soon to appear in print. Undoubtedly the Ratisbon Scots were in good faith, for the very name of the monasteries proclaimed their supposedly Scottish origin.

The significance of the situation in the Irish congregation can now be appreciated. The canonical position of the abbot of Ratisbon as abbot general gave the new Scottish abbot control *de jure* over the whole congregation, while the lack of any community in the other houses meant that there was no opposition to his assuming this control *de facto*. Indeed the only opposition came from interested parties in Ratisbon who had hoped to gain possession of the abbey themselves. It was not until 1520 that Thomson was in undisputed possession, by which time he had appointed Scots to be superiors of the other three houses in the same way as the Irish chapter used to do. Everything continued as before except that the nationality of the monks was different, the Germans being apparently quite indifferent as to which particular island in the Atlantic was the homeland of the Scotic monks.

For a number of years the Scottish community at Ratisbon flourished, but the new congregation thereafter fell on evil days. Two of the four houses were destroyed by war, leaving only the abbeys of Ratisbon and Erfurt. The former of these was in great measure destroyed by fire, the latter was without any Scots monk for many years. When the reformed religion was approved in Scotland by act of parliament in 1560, the Scottish Benedictine Congregation was all but extinct and various interested parties endeavoured to obtain possession of the Ratisbon abbey. A new dawn was about to break, however. A Scot was appointed abbot by Rome, and once again the traditional position of the Ratisbon abbot was to be of vital importance, for he saw himself as the rightful superior general of all the monasteries which had belonged in former times to the *Scoti*. No matter who had them now, they were considered to belong by right to the Scots and if justice were done would be restored to them. One such monastery was the abbey of St James in Würzburg.

The history of the Würzburg abbey in the meantime had hardly been brilliant. We are fortunate in having an almost contemporary account by Abbot Trithemius of the transfer to German monks which, after allowing for his bias in regarding the transfer as justified, we can easily accept as accurate.[21] In this the transfer is not depicted as a removal of the monastery from the Irish but as an introduction of German monks to initiate reform. Suitable *Scoti* were also to be admitted if any were found. The bishop, Laurence von Bibra, brought in three monks of the abbey of St Stephen in Würzburg, which belonged to the Bursfeld observance. No new abbot was appointed, and they were subject to the abbot of St Stephen's. The revenues, adds Trithemius, barely sufficed to support two monks, the buildings were ruinous, and necessary furniture was lacking. Bishop Laurence was very generous to the monastery, renovating the church and making donations of necessary gear.

In spite of protests from Ratisbon the German monks remained. They had only a prior there until 1504, when a monk of St Stephen's became their abbot. He attended the general chapter of his congregation as abbot of St James's in 1506 but resigned the same year and returned to his own monastery. Trithemius, who had already been abbot of another monastery for twenty-three years and was a scholar of exceptional influence, was brought in to succeed him and ruled until his death in 1516, conferring real distinction on St James's, as he was the paragon of his age and country. Indeed, so remarkable were his attainments that he is said to have been the prototype of Dr Faustus. In 1513, towards the end of Trithemius's rule, the monastery was joined to the Bursfeld Union, which meant that it bound itself to accept the discipline of this German reforming congregation's general chapters and visitations. Bishop Laurence confirmed this the following year in a document which shows that the move was made with his consent if not at his instigation.[22]

We can trace the subsequent decline in the abbey's fortunes in some detail. Trithemius's successor had four monks from St Stephen's but only three attended Bishop Laurence's funeral in 1519. In the Peasants' War of 1524-25 the monastery was plundered and burned. It is probably after this that the monks of St Stephen's found the effort to keep up the Scotic monastery as well as their own too much for them. When the abbot died in 1535 a temporary superior came for a year, then there was an abbot who ruled until 1542. His successor, who belonged to the abbey of Michelsberg in Bamberg, died five years later in May 1547, leaving no monk in the monastery. One was sent from St Stephen's but remained only some months. This was the end of St James's as a German monastery.

In 1548 George Flach, the suffragan (i.e., auxiliary) bishop and incidentally a Benedictine, was made administrator, not in the sense of being a temporary religious superior, for there were no monks, but to look after the property and derive an income from it for his own use. Part of the revenues was also applied to other purposes. Flach died at the end of 1564 and was succeeded by the deposed abbot of the neighbouring abbey of Schwarzach. Finally, in 1566, the new suffragan bishop, Anton Ress, was given the monastery to provide him with a residence and an income.[23]

This was the state of affairs when a new and capable Scots abbot was appointed to Ratisbon. It is really no surprise if one considers the upheaval undergone by Germany during this time. It has been calculated that in the Reformation period monastic life came to an end in no fewer than 416 Benedictine houses in Germany, 130 of them being monasteries of black monks.[24] Würzburg diocese like others had suffered from the religious strife, but in 1573 was appointed the great reforming bishop, Julius Echter, who set out to revitalise the religious life of his territory. With him ruling the diocese, the restoration of the Scotic monastery was a feasible project.

Notes

[1] For Irish monks on the Continent in general, see F. O'Briain, "The expansion of Irish Christianity to 1200: An historiographical survey", in *Irish Historical Studies*, iii, 241-66, and iv, 131-63; L. Gougaud, *Christianity in Celtic Lands* (London, 1932), chap. 5: The Irish abroad; Kenney, 187-89, 224-25 and chap. 6; J. P. Fuhrmann, *Irish mediaeval monasteries on the Continent* (Washington, 1927).

[2] See also J. Leclercq, "Mönchtum und Peregrinatio im Frühmittelalter", in *Römische Quartalschrift*, lv, 212-25.

[3] For this foundation and the monasteries which stemmed from it, see also Kenney, 605-06, 616-19; *Vita Mar*, 368-71; Gwynn, "Notes", 6-20; Renz, xvi; W. Wattenbach (ed. Reeves), "The Irish monasteries in Germany", in *Ulster Journal of Archaeology*, vii, 227-47, 295 ff; D. A. Binchy, "The Irish Benedictine congregation in mediaeval Germany", in *Studies*, xviii, 195-210.

[4] The evidence for Marianus's known dates is given in "Marianus", 126, 138.

[5] The works listed in note 1 consider it in this light.

[6] See also J. Hennig, "Irish monastic activities in Eastern Europe", in *IER*, lxv, 394-400.

[7] See Kenney, *passim*; Gwynn, "Notes", 7; Gwynn, "Continuity", 57-64.

[8] *Vita Mar.*, 370.

[9] Libellus, f. 71v ff.

[10] *Chronica Mon. Hirsaugiensis*, in *Opera Historica* (1601). No page reference is needed as it is a year-by-year chronicle.

[11] *Annales Hirsaugienses* (St Gallen, 1690). For Trithemius as chronicler, see Arnold, 144 ff.

[12] In Mun. HSA, KU Würzburg, 6470 ff. Many are transcribed in Copialbuch and calendared in Wieland, 135 ff.

[13] A. Brackmann, *Germania Pontificia* (1911-35), II, 3, p. 193-94; A. Wendehorst, *Das Bistum Würzburg*, Teil I (Berlin, 1962), 146.

[14] See Gwynn, "Notes", 12-13; Gwynn, "Continuity", 70-71.

[15] See also U. Berlière, "Les chapitres généraux de l'Ordre de St. Benoît, V: Ecossais d'Allemagne", in *Revue Bénédictine*, xix, 68-75. The important documents are transcribed in Baillie and Copialbuch or calendared in Renz.

[16] For Würzburg in particular, see Gwynn, "Ireland", 407-10; Gwynn, "Continuity", 68-81; Wieland, 12-14, 119-24, 145-78; Copialbuch.

[17] Oegg, 358-60.

[18] For Memmingen, see F. L. Baumann, *Geschichte des Allgäus* (Kempten, 1881-90), II, 420-23.

[19] "Marianus", 131-33.

[20] For the dispute and the early Scottish period, see K. T. Gemeiner, *Regensburger Chronik*, IV (Regensburg, 1824), 1514-20; M. Dilworth, "The Schottenklöster at the Reformation", in McRoberts, 241-44; *idem*, "The first Scottish monks in Ratisbon", in *IR*, xvi, 180-98; "Necrologies", 178-82; Hammermayer, "Reformation", 149 ff.

[21] Compendium.

[22] Wz. SA, Urk. 124b/125; printed in Gropp, I, 168-69.

[23] For the German period at Würzburg, see Wz. SA, Admin. 477/10499, f. lrv; *AU*, xviii, 173, 193-98; Chronicon; Wieland, 15-16, 124-27, 179-81; addition to Compendium (Ludewig, 1004). Fcr the period of rule of Trithemius himself, see Arnold, 208 ff.

[24] B. Danzer, "Die Benediktinerklöster und die Glaubensspaltung des 16. Jahrhunderts", in *Benediktinische Monatschrift*, xi, 399-404.

CHAPTER 2

Attempts to regain the lost abbeys
1576—83

The train of events which led to the occupation of St James's in Würzburg by Scottish monks can be said to have begun in 1575 when John Lesley and Ninian Winzet went to Rome together.[1] Lesley had held various important offices in Scotland under Queen Mary, finally becoming Bishop of Ross; he followed Mary into exile in England and acted as her ambassador to both Elizabeth and the regent Moray. In 1571 he became involved in the Ridolfi plot, was imprisoned in the Tower of London and under threat of torture betrayed his associates. His credit destroyed, he was released in January 1574 and went to France, where he renewed acquaintance with Winzet and tried to serve Mary's interests in such a way as not to harm Elizabeth's. Although he never succeeded in winning back entirely his former credit with Mary and his fellow Scots, and probably did not deserve to, she appointed him her ambassador to the papal court of Gregory XIII. In autumn 1575 he set off for Rome, and in his retinue was Ninian Winzet.

Winzet, possibly the most outspoken and most successful of the apologists for the old faith in Scotland, was a learned man, a secular priest and the schoolmaster in Linlithgow. Obliged to flee from Scotland in 1562 because of his controversial writings, he proceeded to enjoy a distinguished academic career at the Sorbonne, where he was the president of the German nation. Most of 1571 he spent in England, serving Queen Mary in some confidential capacity, and during this time he revisited Scotland. He returned to Paris, then in 1575 took a degree in theology at Douai in Flanders, a town which was already becoming known as a counter-reformation centre for English-speaking exiles. Later that same year he went with Lesley to Rome.

The pope, Gregory XIII, was eager to launch a counter-reformation offensive against Scotland and England by all and any methods, political, military, missionary. Here Lesley and Winzet were neighbours of the English Catholic exiles who planned to found a second seminary in Rome after the model of the one which was already so successful at Douai. In 1576 Scottish Catholics were making efforts to found a similar establishment; this was the seminary founded at Paris a few years later, which eventually moved to Douai and remained in existence until the late eighteenth century.

In the same year, 1576, Lesley and his friends in Rome had their attention drawn to the Scottish abbeys in Ratisbon and Erfurt, both of which were in critical circumstances. The Erfurt abbey had had no Scots abbot for fifteen years and was being administered by an official of the diocese, while the Ratisbon establishment had been the subject of very unflattering reports in 1574-5 from the legate Ninguarda and the Scots Jesuit, John Hay. They criticised both the canonical position of the abbot, Thomas Anderson, and his personal life. In the spring of 1576 Anderson died, leaving only one professed monk and one novice in the house, most probably his own nephew and son respectively. The town senate undertook the administration of the abbey, but the Scottish citizens and traders in Ratisbon appealed to Rome to entrust the administration to them and appoint a Scottish abbot in order to ensure that the abbey stayed in Scottish hands. Nor were their fears groundless, for various interested parties wished to possess it, the most formidable of these being supporters of the Jesuits who planned to set up in Ratisbon one of the colleges which they were establishing all over Europe.

A memorial was drawn up by Lesley, apparently before the news of the latter developments reached him, in which he petitioned the pope to have the Scotic monasteries in Germany restored to his nation. The information which Lesley provided was a curious mixture of reasonably accurate facts and very inaccurate hearsay, and although the details about Ratisbon and Würzburg were correct, he also listed monasteries that had had no Irish connections for centuries. Lesley wanted the monasteries in order to provide livings for Catholic Scots in exile and educate young men for missionary work in Scotland. He had discussed the matter with Cardinal Morone, who left Rome at the end of April 1576 to act as papal legate at the forthcoming diet in Ratisbon, and had asked him to intercede with the emperor, the elector of Mainz and the duke of Bavaria to get the abbeys handed over to the Scots. Should this prove difficult, Lesley wanted at least part of their income to be allotted to Scottish students or a Scottish seminary, and when the present German occupiers died, the monasteries could then be handed over.[2]

The vicissitudes in Ratisbon need not be described. While the Diet continued its course and the various parties struggled to gain possession of the Scots abbey, Lesley was working in Rome for the appointment of Ninian Winzet as abbot. He produced another memorial for the German congregation of cardinals[3] and at the end of 1576 formally petitioned the pope to appoint Ninian Winzet to the abbacy in Ratisbon. By a bull of 13th June 1577 Gregory XIII did so. Winzet received the Benedictine habit and abbatial blessing at the hands of Thomas Goldwell, the Marian bishop of St. Asaph's resident in Rome, and set off for Ratisbon, where he arrived on 9th August. The unsuccessful claimant supported by the Scots citizens, one William Chalmers, likewise a secular priest, was appointed abbot of Erfurt soon after. He too had acted on behalf of Lesley and had investigated for him the state of the Erfurt abbey. The recovery of the two abbeys for his nation must be considered an outstanding diplomatic success of John Lesley.

Within less than a year Lesley and Winzet were making systematic efforts to obtain possession of other *Schottenklöster*. Lesley was the principal in the affair, and at this point events in Scotland itself influenced the activities of the exiles. On 12th March 1578 the resignation of Morton from the regency was proclaimed in Edinburgh, whereupon the pope decided to send Lesley to Scotland to make use of the opportunity. Lesley intended to travel through the German lands and work for the recovery of the Scotic abbeys before continuing on his way to France. Mary Stuart supplied him with letters for the emperor and the duke of Bavaria, asking for their help and commending in particular Ninian Winzet, whom she styled her confessor, while Gregory, having made Lesley his ambassador to James VI, gave him letters of recommendation addressed to various monarchs. It is apparent throughout the negotiations, now and later, that full use was made of the expressed desires of the unfortunate Mary, the position of Lesley as her ambassador, and the prestige of Winzet as her confidant.

In August, his History of Scotland completed, Lesley set off northwards. He visited the Archduke Ferdinand at Innsbruck on the way, and in Bavaria was kindly received by the duke, who likewise gave him letters of recommendation. By the end of September he was in Prague, where on his own admission the recovery of the abbeys was not his sole business with the emperor Rudolf II on Mary's behalf. Lesley's claims to the *Schottenklöster* were based on their title of 'Scottish'; no doubt he was entirely convinced that they had belonged to his nation since their foundation, and few of the men with whom he negotiated were in a position to know he was mistaken. Rudolf accepted his arguments, promised Mary that he would help, and on 8th October issued a document calling on those concerned to see that the monasteries were returned to the Scots. The most desired abbey was that of Vienna, where German-speaking monks were still in possession.

Lesley delegated the negotiations for this to a Scot, Thomas Guthrie, then set off westwards to Bavaria.

By 1st November Lesley was in Ratisbon, and he and Winzet set out for Eichstätt together. The difficulty they met with here was that Abbot Anderson in 1568 had agreed to accept an annual sum, since most of the income of the Scotic monastery had been allotted to the diocesan seminary founded two years previously. Lesley did not even succeed in obtaining free places for one or two Scottish students in the seminary but had to be content with a small sum payable annually to the Ratisbon abbot. In his negotiations at this time over the Nuremberg abbey, which had been German since 1418 and in Lutheran hands since 1525, Lesley met with no success whatever. It was his declared intention to proceed from Eichstätt with all speed to transact the pope's business in France, but he visited various German bishops on the way, notably the prince-bishops of Würzburg and Mainz.

The bishop of Würzburg, Julius Echter, was not unaware of these plans and activities. The nuncio Delfino had apparently approached him on behalf of William Chalmers in 1577, and Echter had duly interceded for him. Now Lesley arrived to petition for the restoration of the abbey in his own town and for his help in regaining two abbeys in Cologne which had belonged to Irish monks centuries before. Echter received him kindly and showed himself favourable to the idea of restoring the Würzburg abbey. Lesley then proceeded on his way, leaving it to others to carry on the negotiations for the realisation of the project, as he had done in the case of the Vienna abbey several weeks previously.

A list of the *Schottenklöster* was drawn up by the Scottish monks of Ratisbon, at some time in 1578, for the benefit of Lesley.[4] It included all the houses of the old Ratisbon congregation except Kelheim, and a few apocryphal ones in addition. The notes on Vienna and Würzburg are interesting. The Vienna abbot had only four or five monks, so the Scots wished to gain possession when he died, and the emperor Maximilian (who died in 1576) had promised restitution. The Würzburg monastery was in the possession of the auxiliary bishop, but would not be difficult to acquire as the prince-bishop desired to have labourers for the Lord's vineyard. This was probably a fair summing-up of Julius Echter's apostolic outlook even if the writers were over-sanguine about the ease with which they could gain possession. The list mentioned William Chalmers as being in Erfurt, but in fact Chalmers was unable to endure conditions there and was obliged by poverty and the hostility he encountered to leave the town towards the end of September 1578. Indeed Chalmers and Lesley probably arrived in Prague about the same time. It is possible, though hardly likely, that Winzet protested against Chalmers's appointment — certainly the later Scottish monastic historians thought he did — as Chalmers had not been elected from and by the Ratisbon community and had not acknowledged the rights of the Ratisbon abbot-general. Already in December 1576 a memorial to the pope had emphasised the Ratisbon abbot's superior position.[5] Nevertheless Chalmers performed a useful function in going to Erfurt and showing that the traditional occupants of the Scotic abbey still claimed their property.

After the departure of Lesley from Germany, Ninian Winzet was left with the task of pursuing the negotiations. His own abbacy in Ratisbon was successful from the start. Within a short time he had won the confidence of the ruling duke of Bavaria and of his son who succeeded him, and had struck a firm friendship with Erasmus Vendius, the secretary of the dukes. Their help and patronage tided him over many of the initial difficulties, as his letters to them show. Ninguarda, the nuncio in South Germany and, for a time, administrator of the Ratisbon diocese, was his firm supporter and helped him to recover the alienated property of the monastery. The Jesuits were likewise his friends and allies. By March 1580, according to a visitation report of Ninguarda, there were six monks besides the abbot in St James's, and they had established some form of college for the instruction of Christian youth. The monastery was poor but the religious observance was good, adds the report.[6]

In 1581 Winzet was once more actively engaged in the work of regaining the lost abbeys. His own monastery was still the only one in the possession of the Scots. Nobody had succeeded Chalmers at Erfurt, while Lesley's delegate had been unsuccessful in Vienna and an imperial decree of April 1580 had decided against the Scots. In the autumn of 1581 Winzet set off on journeys which lasted two months and took him to the north and west to visit the prince-bishops of Würzburg and Mainz and the authorities in Nuremberg and Erfurt. Ninguarda supplied a letter to take to Bishop Echter, saying that Winzet, as abbot of the Ratisbon mother-house, now had the duty of continuing the work begun by Lesley. Both Ninguarda and Echter were zealous Catholic reformers, and accordingly the letter praised Winzet's achievements in restoring monastic life and sound studies in Ratisbon and begged Echter to help him to regain the Würzburg abbey. The most interesting thing in the letter is the mention of a plan of Winzet's which would please Echter and be useful to his diocese.

What this project was we do not know. Possibly it concerned putting the Würzburg abbey to some educational use. By 5th November Winzet was back in Ratisbon and writing to Vendius about the limited success of his mission. He had been impressed by

Echter's learning and character and heartened by his favourable reception, for the bishop professed himself willing to restore the abbey to the Scots on the death of his auxiliary, provided there was sufficient revenue to support a community. At Nuremberg, on the other hand, the case was hopeless. In Erfurt there seemed to be no obstacle although the monastery itself was desolate; the Ratisbon community had just elected their senior monk as abbot of Erfurt and he would shortly set out on his mission. This was John Hamilton, a former monk of Paisley Abbey who had become Winzet's prior in Ratisbon.[7]

The traditional relationship between the Scottish abbeys in Ratisbon and Erfurt was now restored. A year later, in January 1583, the auxiliary bishop of Würzburg died.[8] Echter thereupon transferred the financial administration of the abbey to his own exchequer.[9] Winzet too went into action. Already by early April he was in Würzburg and discovering that difficulties still lay ahead. The chief obstacle was the rival claim of the German Benedictine monks of the nearby abbey of St Stephen's. Winzet discussed the matter with his rival fellow-abbot, who pointed out that the Scots had voluntarily abandoned their abbey almost a hundred years before, since when all its abbots had been German and most of them had been from St Stephen's. Winzet returned home and in Easter week asked the duke of Bavaria for letters of recommendation to the emperor and Bishop Echter, to help him in his efforts.

The duke did not provide the desired letters immediately, and three months later Winzet sent Vendius an urgent reminder about them. Meanwhile, on 8th June, the abbot of the Vienna monastery had died and an Augustinian friar in Vienna had written to Winzet, evidently by arrangement, to tell him the news at once and saying that now was the moment to realise his plans. Ninian set off for Vienna, leaving his prior, John James Whyte, who will play a prominent part in this narrative later, in charge at Ratisbon. At the end of July Whyte wrote to Vendius that Winzet was desperately awaiting the necessary letter at Vienna, while he himself hoped to have the letter for Bishop Echter very soon. Evidently, too, the Scots had not given up all hope of success in Nuremberg, for Winzet had sent copies of documents issued in their favour by emperor and nuncio, to help the duke to draw up letters to Julius Echter and the town senate of Nuremberg.

The duke's secretary drew up the letter for Echter on 1st August and sent it to Prior Whyte the next day. It was no merely formal document; after mentioning the desire of pope, emperor and Scottish queen for the restitution of the abbey, and recalling the evangelisation of Germany by Scottish saints and the plight of their

28

exiled successors, it spoke at length of Ninian Winzet's achievements in Ratisbon. At once Whyte had the letter taken to Würzburg, where the bishop showed it to the abbot of St Stephen's. On 7th August the abbot penned an energetic rejoinder to Echter, which the latter despatched to Ratisbon with his own reply the following day. The messenger was delayed and did not deliver them to Whyte until 5th September.

The two letters are long but most informative. The gist of the abbot's is that the Scots — it did not enter his head that the previous *Scoti* were not Winzet's countrymen — had of their own free will and through their own fault lost St James's. It had been incorporated into St Stephen's, which had thereupon spent considerable sums of money to enable it to house a small German community. It was now a German monastery, and the abbot could not agree to any change in its status without the consent of the other abbots and communities in the province. Echter is therefore begged not to inflict injury on his own people by handing St James's over to foreigners.

One can see the abbot's point, that his predecessors had spent money on St James's to repair the ravages of neglect by the *Scoti*, although in fact the German period of occupation had hardly been more inspiring than that of the Irish; and no doubt he was right in saying he could not agree to give up the house without consulting his fellow abbots. It is clear that St Stephen's had lost no time in establishing its claim to the Scotic abbey, even if the bishop were to control its revenues. We know too that the German monks had advanced their claim even before Bishop Ress died[10] and that after his death they used St James's as a place of recreation.[11]

The bishop's letter likewise accepted that the *Scoti* in Würzburg were identical with the present Scots in Ratisbon, for he acknowledged the debt of gratitude owed to the Scots by Franconia. Echter, however, dealt mainly with the financial aspect. He stated clearly that the monastery had been badly administered by the *Scoti* and therefore had been handed over to St Stephen's so that at least the church services would continue. The shrunken revenues had been insufficient even to keep the church in repair, and the income, which was scarcely 200 florins a year, would have to be used for rebuilding the church. For several years to come, it would not support a community. Echter therefore suggested that the Scots should occupy other *Schottenklöster* where the finances offered more scope; they could then transfer part of the income for use in Würzburg. He would see to it that the abbot of St Stephen's was not opposed to the acceptance of some Scots in St James's.

Echter's letter marks an important step forward in the negotiations of the Scots to occupy the Würzburg abbey, even though twelve years were to elapse before the plan became a reality. It only remains to say that Winzet himself was unsuccessful in Vienna. He had composed his eleven reasons why the Scots should have the Vienna abbey, and he had received the desired letter from the duke, signed 23rd July, praising among other things his educational establishment in Ratisbon.[12] But all was in vain. Then, in August or early September, when he was on the point of setting off homeward to Ratisbon, he fell seriously ill and was at death's door for some time. Indeed he was not fully recovered by the following May. As far as acquiring monastic premises for the Scots was concerned, Erfurt was Winzet's only success, and in this he merely consolidated the position already gained in principle by Bishop Lesley. Nevertheless, and more important, he also prepared the way for the recovery of the Würzburg abbey.

Notes

[1] For events up to the winter of 1578-79 see Hammermayer, "Reformation", 176-221, 229-45. Much use has been made of Letter-book, f. 231-331 for the years after 1577. Many of the documents concerning Winzet and Ratisbon are printed in Hewison, I, cix-cxviii; II, xxi-xxiii; *Cal. State Papers Scotland*, V, 289-90. Other references are intended to be supplementary to these.

[2] VA, Arm. 64, Tom. 11, f. 484-85.

[3] VA, Arm. 64, Tom. 28, f. 196.

[4] Copy in Germ. Sancta, f. 15-17. See "Trilogy", 128.

[5] VL, MS Vat. Lat. 12159, f. 6r.

[6] Hammermayer, "Reformation", 245-46.

[7] For him see "Necrologies", 183, corrected by Reg. BOA, Sch., Urk. 79.

[8] *AU*, xviii, 194.

[9] Ser. Abb; Gropp, II, 419.

[10] Wz. SA, Admin. 477/10499, f. 1; also catalogue description of Wz. SA, Misc. 1146.

[11] Indiculus, f. 36r.

[12] Hübl, 16-19; Chronologia, 86-92.

CHAPTER 3

Success in Würzburg

1584—95

In the years following 1584 Ninian Winzet was in his late sixties. There is no evidence that he continued his efforts for the recovery of any of the *Schottenklöster*. He had the task, despite continued ill-health and financial worries,[1] of ruling his slowly growing community in Ratisbon and of keeping watch over the monastery in Erfurt. His college, which at the end of 1583 had up to a hundred students, also occupied his energies, for he himself taught the higher courses in it,[2] although in 1588 the Jesuits removed at least some of its scope when they founded their college in Ratisbon.[3] In 1585 Abbot Hamilton of Erfurt died and in his place the Ratisbon chapter elected Richard Irvine. Then in July 1592 John James Whyte was elected coadjutor abbot of Ratisbon, with the right of succession to Winzet. The election documents speak of Winzet's serious ill-health;[4] he was seventy-three that year and in fact died two months later, in September. Clearly he wished to hand over the reins of government before he died, and his epitaph in the abbey church speaks of him 'legitimately and canonically' providing a successor. Thus in the years after 1592 Whyte was abbot in Ratisbon, and Irvine abbot in Erfurt. These two men and a third, Francis Hamilton, were to play the leading part when the Scots finally gained possession of St James's in Würzburg. It is worth noting that all three were learned men.

John James Whyte was born at Ardlawhill, near New Aberdour in Buchan. In January 1574 he was admitted to the German College in Rome at the age of twenty-two, left in November 1576 and was already a monk at Ratisbon in 1578.[5] Thus he must have known Winzet in Rome and he became one of the first members of Winzet's community. He was already prior in 1583, having no doubt succeeded John Hamilton in this office during the winter of 1581-2, and he held it throughout the remaining ten years of Winzet's abbacy. Evidently, too, he enjoyed a reputation for theological scholarship, for when it was decided to hold a public disputation between Catholic and Protestant champions in the

31

episcopal residence in Ratisbon, the expatriate Scot, Whyte, was chosen to represent the Catholic side. In July 1592 the community elected him to be Winzet's coadjutor and successor; then, on Winzet's death two months later, he duly succeeded as abbot.

Richard Irvine was born near the Irvine burn in Dumfries-shire, into the border clan of Irvine of Bonshaw. The date was probably some time before 1560. He matriculated at St Andrews in 1574 and graduated as master four years later. In February 1579 we find him in Paris being given written leave by Archbishop James Beaton to receive the sacrament of confirmation and all holy orders from any bishop. He must have gone straight to Ratisbon and in 1584 was novice master there. In June the following year the community elected him abbot of Erfurt.

Francis Hamilton entered the Scots college at Pont à Mousson in Lorraine in 1587.[6] The register describes him as being 'of Steanhouss' and belonging to Edinburgh, which must mean that he belonged to the well-known family of Hamiltons of Stonehouse in Lanarkshire, since the Stenhouse at Liberton near Edinburgh had no connection with the Hamiltons, and in fact he used the Stonehouse arms.[7] His first appearance in a Ratisbon document is at Whyte's election in July 1592.

At this election five monks took part in addition to Winzet and Whyte, while Irvine was at Erfurt. This does not indicate any notable increase in numbers, but probably all were priests and there may have been student monks and novices in addition. The most serious obstacle to an increase in the community was no doubt the limitations of the revenues. The same obstacle stood in their way at Würzburg, while the revenues at Erfurt were too small to allow any residue for Würzburg as Echter had suggested. In the years 1586-88 an account was drawn up of what the monks of St Stephen's in Würzburg had spent on the Scotic abbey and had received in return.[8] One gets the impression from the documents that it was not so much a vindication of their rights to the abbey as a calculation of what they were due in compensation, and this seems to be confirmed by the action of Bishop Echter's officials, who in 1587 began to copy the most important documents in St James's into a register,[9] a proceeding which incidentally has proved of inestimable value to the later historian. During this time the new auxiliary bishop was living in St James's and had been carrying out his ordinations there since December 1584, but when he died in 1590 no new suffragan was appointed.[10]

One can surmise that this is why Winzet wrote two letters, in 1591 and the following year, about the restoration of the monastery to the Scots.[11] Unfortunately no details of the letters have been preserved. Nothing more is known after this until 1594, when, according to the traditional version of the abbey's history, occurred a semi-miraculous happening which resulted in the return of the *Scoti* to Würzburg. A Diet was held in Ratisbon, which Echter as prince-bishop of Würzburg attended. He lodged in St James's with the Scots monks, where naturally Abbot Whyte spoke to him about the Würzburg abbey. Then the bishop fell ill of so violent a fever that the doctors were unable to do anything and his life was in danger. In his extremity he vowed to God and St James to restore the Würzburg *Schottenkloster* to the Scots if he recovered. Recover he did and kept his vow. In early 1595 Whyte sent him some Scottish monks, who on St George's day were solemnly installed in St James's.

Such a story is naturally to be regarded with suspicion, even if one is hardly justified in rejecting it out of hand. A Diet was in fact called in 1593 to deal with the Turkish menace and lasted well into the summer of 1594. But if one accepts the story it must not be divorced from what preceded and what followed. The traditional version contains no hint of the negotiations of Lesley and Winzet, yet, as we have seen, Echter had proposed eleven years previously that Scots monks should be received in Würzburg if they could provide means of support for themselves. The chief effect of his visit to Ratisbon, granted that this was in fact the decisive factor, was to induce the bishop himself to make notable financial benefactions. Nor did the incident sweep Echter off his feet; on the contrary, he acted very much in character and with considerable deliberation.

There are, however, good grounds for considering the story to be a later invention. Trithemius's *Compendium* of the abbey's history was adapted and continued by the Scottish monks. The first version extant, completed shortly after July 1680, does not contain the story of the illness but merely says that Echter restored St James's to the monks of the nation that had brought the faith to Franconia. A second adaptation of the chronicle, written in 1690, includes the story. It should be noted that the reason for the Diet, the Turkish menace, and even the name of the Turkish ruler, Murad III, are correctly given. Nevertheless it seems incredible that the chronicler of 1680 would have omitted the story if he knew it, so we can conclude tentatively that it came into being between 1680 and 1690, almost a hundred years after the event. It was certainly not current in 1631 when someone, presumably a Scots monk, drew up a summary list of abbots of St James's and remarked that Echter restored the monastery to the Scots in 1595 at the request of the pope and the Ratisbon abbot,[12] nor in 1655 when a Scot declared that Echter only acted under threat of censure from Rome.[13]

The first certain intimation of renewed efforts in this direction does in fact concern the pope. It comes from a brief of Clement VIII to Julius Echter, dated 8th October 1594, which to all appearances is a reply to a communication from the bishop. Clement expressed approval of Echter's plan to restore the Scottish monastery, but since there was such a lack of Scottish priests and monks, he wanted the revenues for the next eight or ten years to be used to support a seminary for young Scots of noble birth, who on completion of their studies would become monks and would also do missionary work in Scotland.[14] Like so many documents illustrating the history of the Scots in Würzburg, its significance is difficult to assess since it has survived in isolation and, as it were, out of context. All we know is that six months later monastic life began once more in St James's with three monks, which is hardly enough for any community life.

A curious episode about the same time is probably connected with the plans of the Scottish monks. The ancient abbey of St Gallen was, like St James's in Ratisbon, a consistorial abbey, which meant that an abbatial election was confirmed by being announced by the pope in a consistory of cardinals. On 12th November 1594 its newly elected prince-abbot was informed by Cardinal Paravicini that the agents of the Scottish nation in Rome had petitioned to have part of the abbey's revenues assigned to their college. The reason given, of course, was that St Gall, founder of the abbey, was a Scot. Paravicini said that it would be enough if two Scottish students were subsidised by the abbey at the Jesuit university of Dillingen in South Germany. The new abbot's agent in Rome warned him that Paravicini would delay his confirmation in consistory until he replied but that the pope would not expect him to give money except of his own free will. The nuncio, for his part, advised him to reply that he would see about it after his election was confirmed. The abbot, however, wrote angrily to his Roman agent refuting the Scottish claims and saying, among other things, that if he did start subsidising students they would be German secular priests, not Scots.[15] The matter had not been settled by the end of the year, for on 4th January a laconic minute of the monastic chapter stated that the Scots in Rome wanted five hundred ducats yearly, then wanted two Scots to be supported at Dillingen, and the abbot had written to Rome.[16]

Had this anything to do with the refounding of the Würzburg monastery? Ratisbon and Scottish monks are nowhere mentioned, except when the abbot denies that if a Scot is professed in St Gallen he is to be preferred as abbot rather than the others.[17] Evidently someone had been making such a claim. It was only eighteen years since John Lesley's memorial at Rome had claimed St Gallen for the Scots, but Paravicini's letter does not explicitly say that the Scots college to be subsidised was in Rome. The Scots College in

Rome was founded by bull of December 1600, and the efforts to preserve its forerunner, the Scottish *hospitium*, are said to have begun with the arrival of Bishop William Chisholm in Rome in 1596.[18] It is thus not certain that the Roman college is meant, especially when two subsidised places at Dillingen, many hundreds of miles away, were reckoned a satisfactory substitute.

It is plausible to suggest a connection with the Scottish plans for Würzburg. The cardinal's letter was written only a month after the papal brief to Echter, and Dillingen was within comparatively easy reach of Ratisbon. The time, the place and the implications of the Scottish version of *Schottenklöster* history all point to the Scots monks in Germany. On the other hand, the brief to Bishop Echter can be interpreted as an attempt to deflect the revenues of St James's away from a monastic foundation. The Roman documents to Würzburg and St Gallen could then be parallel attempts to obtain subsidies for Scottish clergy and might well be connected with the intense intrigues going on in Rome among English and Welsh priests. In fact these intrigues came to a head with the death of the English Cardinal Allen at this very time, in October 1594. The refounding of the Würzburg abbey may have been Echter's reaction against this pressure from Rome. In the absence of evidence, however, we can only surmise.

To place the new foundation in its Würzburg context, one must consider the achievements of Julius Echter as prince-bishop of Würzburg. When he took charge of the see in 1573, half of it had become Protestant, while the half that had remained Catholic was sunk in laxity and ignorance. He took the spiritual interest of his territory as his primary aim in life, and set out both to restore Catholicism and to introduce necessary reforms. Having made alliances with Catholic princes, he inaugurated a programme of winning back those who had fallen away from the old faith and forcing those who preached or professed Lutheranism to leave his territories. His vast scheme comprised reform of clergy and religious, re-education and re-building. It was Echter who founded the University, which quickly gained an international reputation and is still flourishing, as well as the famous Hospital in the town. Churches, seminaries and religious houses owed their origin or reconstruction to him. At his own expense, in his forty-four years of rule, he built or rebuilt over three hundred churches.[19]

Thus, Echter in 1573 found a territory that was going over to Lutheranism or dissolving into religious chaos. He was at once the spiritual and the temporal ruler, being bishop of the diocese of Würzburg and duke of Eastern Franconia (the title of all the bishops), and four decades of energetic reform and strong action against objectors, with the temporal arm in perfect accord with the spiritual, transformed the situation. He has deservedly been known by such titles as 'the Great' and 'the Solomon of Franconia'. The refounding of St James's took place at the exact mid-point of his long rule and cannot be viewed in isolation from Echter's reforming activities. It is clear that he wanted to have another monastery which would provide fitting divine worship and sound theological study. The standard biography of Echter says indeed that the bishop's kindest care was for the Scottish abbey, but the force of the statement is greatly reduced by the author's devoting precisely eleven lines out of 667 pages to St James's and wrongly calling it St Andrew's abbey.[20]

A word should also be said on the procedure for founding a new monastery. Benedictines differ from other religious orders in that their communities are usually more or less independent of each other. The novice when making his profession binds himself to a particular community, for in fact Benedictines are not a religious order, technically speaking, but a confederation of communities. When a community undertakes the establishment of a new monastery, a certain number of monks are sent to inaugurate monastic life there. The traditional number is six or twelve; the traditional metaphor is that of a swarm of bees leaving the hive and establishing a second hive elsewhere. The new foundation accepts novices, who include allegiance to it when they make their vows. After a time, when it is decided that the new foundation is viable, it is given its independence, and the founding members either return to the mother-house or transfer their vow of stability or allegiance to the new monastery. Until this cutting of the umbilical cord the mother-house and its foundation form a composite unit, with a fair amount of come and go between them.

This general description, considerably modified however by the traditions of the old Scotic congregation and by the position of Benedictines in the diocese of Würzburg, gives a picture of the Scots abbey in Würzburg in the two decades after 1595. It is, at least nowadays, not usual to elect an abbot in a new monastery until it is seen to be viable, yet one was given to Würzburg immediately, presumably because the Ratisbon Scots were used to electing abbots to houses, such as Erfurt, in which there was no monastic life at all. This also happened, incidentally, elsewhere in post-Reformation Germany where disputes over church property between Catholics and Protestants were common; a titular abbot with one or two monks would be put into a monastery to keep it from falling into Protestant hands.[21] It is not usual either to make or accept conditions such as the Scots (as we shall see) agreed to in 1595; they are to be explained by a determination that the sad state of the later Irish period should not recur, and by the unusual degree of control exercised by bishops of Würzburg over monasteries in their diocese.

On 30th April 1595, in the presence of the notable persons of Franconia and the cathedral canons, the monastery of St James was solemnly restored to the Scottish monks. The newly appointed prior, Francis Hamilton, delivered an oration in Latin,[22] interlarded with long passages from authors and Greek quotations. His text, taken from the Vulgate 103rd Psalm, concerned the cedars of Lebanon in which the sparrows make their nests. The founders and restorers of St James's were the cedars, the Scots monks the poor sparrows driven from their own nests by heretics. In 1134, said Hamilton, Bishop Embricho had sent to the Ratisbon abbot for Scottish monks, and now Bishop Julius had sent for the same to Abbot Whyte.

The first Scottish chronicle merely cites Hamilton's printed oration as testimony of the ceremonies on the last day of April, then states that Richard Irvine was appointed the first abbot. The later chronicle, having recounted the story of Bishop Echter's illness, gives a much more elaborate account, according to which three Scottish monks went to Würzburg in 1595: Richard Irvine, Francis Hamilton and John Stuart. They were to wait for other Scots due to arrive very soon from Ratisbon; then, when there were enough monks to hold an election, they chose Irvine as abbot. These three were in fact the foundation members, but the rest is almost certainly guess-work on the part of the compiler, who was unaware that Irvine was abbot of Erfurt and refers to him as a simple monk. We shall also see that the three Scots remained alone for at least a year. The election no doubt took place in Ratisbon, where the chapter had elected all abbots since 1479. For some unknown reason, too, the compiler of this chronicle changed the date of the ceremony from 30th April to St George's day, which is the 23rd.

Delivering an oration twenty years later, on one of the most solemn occasions in the whole history of the monastery, the suffragan bishop described the return of the Scots. The monastery, he said, was rebuilt from its ruins and elegantly equipped with cells, refectories and libraries; a new roof and twin towers were given to the church; then finally a new colony of monks was brought in; and all by the generosity of Julius Echter.[23] This is probably the most accurate summary of the train of events. Having rebuilt the monastery and church of St James's Echter offered it to the Ratisbon Scots who had been petitioning for its restitution. Perhaps he did so while attending the Diet at Ratisbon or as a result of his visit there, but the Scots came on his terms and not on theirs.

In a solemn deed drawn up on 2nd May 1595[24] John James Whyte, abbot of Ratisbon, and Richard Irvine, abbot of Würzburg, bound themselves to stringent conditions. After acknowledging that but for the care and benefactions of Julius Echter in rebuilding the church and augmenting the income the monastery would be in hopeless case, the two abbots decreed as follows, in order to prevent any recurrence of the former sad state of affairs: Five Scottish monks as well as the abbot must reside in the monastery. If the full number is lacking, and not made up within six months, the bishop and his successors will be free to make up the six by introducing German monks, and in an abbatial election the most suitable person shall be elected, be he German or Scots. In order to perform choir office fittingly and provide for the instruction of novices, all six monks will be priests or at least in major orders or ready for ordination within a year. All will be good and useful men, and one is to teach theology publicly in the university. The bishop will be free to carry out a visitation of the monastery each year, either personally or by delegate, with full powers of jurisdiction and correction, in the same way as he is wont to do in all the monasteries of his diocese. Both the bishop and the dean and chapter affixed their seals to the document, which can be regarded as the foundation charter of the new community. The condition regarding number of monks to be made up regardless of nationality has echoes of the papal document of 1497 introducing German monks into St. James's, and it is noteworthy that Whyte[25] styles himself merely abbot of Ratisbon and not abbot-general of all the Scottish monasteries in Germany. The new foundation was clearly made on Echter's terms.

A visitation of some kind was in fact carried out that first year, 1595, and a horarium laid down for choir duties and study.[26] The brethren were to rise at 3 a.m. for Matins; this would be over by 4, and they were then to study until 5.30. Lauds, Prime and what the horarium terms first Mass (no doubt to allow all to receive communion and to provide for the neighbouring townspeople) took them to 6.30. From then until 8.30 they were to attend lectures and so forth, and return to the monastery for the sung conventual Mass at 10. Dinner, the main meal of the day, followed. The next duty mentioned is Vespers at 2. From 3 p.m. to 4.30 there was a second period of lectures, then they said the Office of the Dead, and supper was at 5 o'clock. Compline was said, and all retired to rest. A final note adds that on Sundays and feast days when the brethren did not attend lectures outside, the whole office was to be sung solemnly and Vespers were to be at 3 instead of 2.

These regulations show Echter's concern for two things, the public choir offices and clerical studies, for they legislate for nothing else. The monks would have their own customs or constitutions, as well as regulations made by the ruling abbot for other monastic duties. There would be periods of private prayer and spiritual reading, while in a small community each member would have many things to see to. On the other hand, one can presume that dinner was about 11 a.m. and was followed by an hour or so of compulsory recreation. The horarium was drawn up to fit in with the public lectures at the university, just across the Main from the Scottish abbey. There is no doubt that it was a severe enough regime by modern standards.

A small folio volume, beautifully neat and clean, has also survived from this time. It contains a list of the property handed over to the Scots and constituting the revenue of St James's, and the list is introduced by a copy of a deed of gift by Julius Echter, dated 11th September 1595.[27] It reminds posterity that the abbey and its property had been all but annihilated by bad administration and that the monastery has been restored so that divine worship may once more be carried out there. The sealed register of property and revenue has been handed over to the abbot and community, who in turn have bound themselves and their successors not to alienate, sell or mortgage any of the property but to look after it well, so that it may increase rather than diminish.

This brings us to the end of 1595. The first Scots were in residence and everything had been carefully tied up. Little seems to have been left to chance by the three regulating documents: the conditions accepted by the two Scottish abbots, the horarium established by the bishop, and the detailed list of property with the promise not to alienate. Together they effectively dispose of the myth that Julius Echter, under the influence of his semi-miraculous recovery from a dangerous illness, simply threw open to the Scots the gates that had been closed to them for so long. On the contrary, there was much careful legislation, and Echter was to continue his benevolent despotism until the early vicissitudes of the foundation were over.

Notes

[1] Letter-book, f. 366; Mun. GSA, K.s. 3292, 4.8.1590.

[2] Letter-book, f. 316; Mun. GSA, K.s. 3292, 11.7.1590; Hewison, II, xxiv; Indiculus, f. 59v.

[3] Letter-book, f. 375.

[4] Reg. BOA, St Jakob, Fasz. 5.

[5] M. Dilworth, "Scottish students at the Collegium Germanicum", in *IR*, xix, 17-18.

[6] The biographical details in Ziegelbauer, IV, 190 must be rejected.

[7] His seal on Wz. SA, Urk. 50.24.

[8] Wz. SA, Admin. 477/10499, f. 3 ff.

[9] This is Copialbuch.

[10] *AU*, xviii, 196-200.

[11] Reid, f. 127r.

[12] BRB, MS 7827-74, f. 327; printed in *Scottish Notes and Queries*, ii (1888-89), 20-21.

[13] Indiculus, f. 62r.

[14] VA, Arm. 44, Tom. 39, f. 309.

[15] SG, Bd. 359, f. 43, 57-80.

[16] SG, Bd. 303, f. 343.

[17] SG, Bd. 359, f. 59.

[18] *IR*, xii, 9-14, 143.

[19] A. Hofmann, "Julius und das Reformationsrecht", in *Julius Echter von Mespelbrunn*, ed. C. V. Hessdörfer (Würzburg, 1917), 117-27.

[20] G. Frhr. von Pölnitz, *Julius Echter von Mespelbrunn* (Munich, 1934), 344.

[21] Volk, 378-79.

[22] Later printed; reprinted in Gropp, I, 516-24.

[23] Gropp, I, 687 (from which the MS account in Wz. SA, HV f. 178, fo 520v is derived).

[24] For full text see Appendix A.

[25] In Compendium.

[26] Reid, f. 118v.

[27] Wz. SA, SB 548, f. 8-9.

CHAPTER 4

Linked with Ratisbon
1595—1614

In April 1596, within a year of the Scots' arrival in Würzburg, a Presbyterian minister, Master David Anderson, sent a report to his brethren in Scotland on the dangers threatening the Kirk from the plans of Scottish Catholic expatriates on the continent, and in it he gave a prominent place to the three abbeys in Germany.[1] His information about these, impressive in its accuracy, adds important details about the Scottish background of the monks, although it also has some puzzling features. The information about Ratisbon and Erfurt can be passed over briefly. Anderson correctly names abbot, prior and at least three other monks at Ratisbon, while for Erfurt he correctly gives John Walker, Irvine's successor in the abbacy, as the only monk.

At Würzburg the three monks are correctly named and expressly mentioned as being the only three in residence: a striking and confidence-inspiring case of agreement with the monastic chronicle. The birthplace of the abbot is correctly given as near Dumfries, while Anderson's statement that he was a servant to the old Lord Herries and attended his son Edward at St Andrews is corroborated by the appearance together of the two names Richard Irvine and Edward Maxwell on the matriculation roll of St Salvator's.[2] The report also correctly links Irvine with Archbishop Beaton, saying that the latter sent him to Ratisbon. It is equally accurate as regards Francis Hamilton, who is termed prior. The remarks about John Stuart, however, are puzzling, for he is called a boy of about eighteen, born near Glasgow. If this is correct he later received high office at an extraordinarily early age.

The degree of trustworthiness of Anderson's report is important, because his is the first clear reference to relations of the monks with Scotland and to their counter-reformation plans. He says that the Scots abbots were seeking leave from Rome for some activity in Scotland, including the bringing of boys back to Germany, for which purpose a meeting was held in April 1596 with Bishop Echter. Echter and the bishops of Ratisbon and Salzburg, adds

41

Anderson, had all promised to educate a number of these boys, who would do missionary work in Scotland or become monks and enable the Scots to recover other lost *Schottenklöster*. Whatever the truth of this part of Anderson's report, the ambitious project was never put into effect, though it probably does show in which direction the thoughts of the Scots monks were turning.

In these early years Francis Hamilton attended Würzburg university and was awarded his bachelor's degree. John Stuart also matriculated in 1598, the year when there is the first mention of other monks besides the three founder members, namely John Bog and William Ogilvie.[2] The Douai register offers both corroboration and a measure of perplexing contradiction as regards the Scots monks. The list which has survived from this time is not a roll in which students entering the Scots college were inscribed on arrival. In 1598, when the college was more or less wound up through lack of funds, the rector, Fr William Crichton, compiled a list of students accepted in the earlier period at Pont à Mousson and later under his own rectorship in Flanders. The comments he added were intended to show the status of the students at the time of writing in July 1598. No fewer than five concern the Scots abbeys; two of these were John Ogilvie, sent very recently to the Ratisbon abbey, and Alexander Bog, said to be either a soldier or a monk in Germany. The question arises whether they are to be identified, in spite of the difference in forename, with the Ogilvie and Bog at Würzburg. In the case of Ogilvie the evidence will have to be considered later as the matter is of some importance and he was to be the greatest abbot of Würzburg.

In spite of receiving new recruits, however, the Scots community had not got off to a good start. On 7th July 1598, after three years and two months of rule, for the sake of solitude and monastic quiet (so the chronicle puts it) Abbot Irvine resigned his office into the hands of the bishop. Certainly he left Würzburg and for the next thirty years lived as a simple monk at Ratisbon or Kelheim, the former priory which still belonged to the Ratisbon abbey.[4] We know that Bishop Echter and Abbot Whyte were on good terms, and the previous November Echter had asked the abbot to give board and lodging to some of his officials attending the Diet in Ratisbon.[5] Whyte now took on the administration of the Würzburg abbey himself. Where he lived during the next four years, when he was abbot of Ratisbon and administrator of Würzburg, we do not know; all the Würzburg chronicle says is that he had the wine-press constructed. He also laid a foundation stone in the Würzburg monastery in 1600.[6]

In 1602, shortly before Whitsun (26th May), Whyte resigned the administration, and Francis Hamilton was elected abbot on 6th

July. Probably the election took place at Ratisbon as the Würzburg community was still very small and it was Whyte who commended Hamilton to the bishop.[7] Hamilton was no more successful than Irvine had been. He ruled the abbey for about two years according to his own testimony, and according to other testimony he did not do it very well.[8] This puts the end of his rule in the summer of 1604, but it was not until a year later that Echter promulgated his settlement of the abbey's affairs. Possibly some monk appointed by the bishop acted as administrator in the intervening year.

The original of Echter's settlement of June 1605 has survived. Since the monastery was in debt and with no prospect of becoming solvent, it was arranged that Hamilton should depart until the debts were paid. Only three monks were to remain; the other three monks and all other persons were to go elsewhere. John Stuart was appointed to be the superior of the monks who remained and to see that the church services laid down ten years before were kept up. To save the monks from having to absent themselves from their monastery, the care of their properties was entrusted to the bailiff of St Stephen's, who was to provide the three Scots yearly with a hundred florins and a tun of wine; with what remained he was to pay bills, keep fifteen florins a year for himself, and repay a loan of three hundred florins from the bishop's exchequer at the rate of a hundred a year. Another of the monks who stayed, William, was to take charge of domestic affairs and help the bailiff as much as possible.[9]

This declaration bears the seals of the bishop and Abbot Hamilton, and it is fairly obvious that Bishop Echter's guiding authority was behind the arrangement. No doubt the other monks went back to Ratisbon where they belonged. A year later Whyte, who was in Würzburg, gave Hamilton leave to reside in any monastery he chose or in any Catholic locality where he could wear the religious habit. As Echter had freed Hamilton from all obligations to Würzburg, so did Whyte free him from all obligations to his community. Indeed, in the document giving Hamilton his freedom, Whyte not only called himself abbot-general but said he had power over the other Scottish abbots even to the extent of removing them and spoke of his two communities in Ratisbon and Würzburg.[10]

Thus, ten years after its foundation, there were still only three monks in St James's and its state was very unsettled. Now begins a period in which the fortunes of the Ratisbon and Würzburg abbeys were inextricably tangled, with Whyte residing in Würzburg once more and leaving his own abbey in Ratisbon in the care of others. At this time, too, an effort was made to obtain the restoration of the former Scottish abbey in Constance, which had been demolished in

1530. The proceedings show clearly that the two Scottish communities were not separate bodies.

The negotiations over Constance will only be touched upon insofar as they throw light on the Scots in Würzburg. In September 1607 Abbot Whyte, writing from Ratisbon, said that he had sent two monks to negotiate: Adam MacCall, who had been prior at Ratisbon for some years, and John Stuart, a man of noble birth but nobler still for learning and piety. Thus Stuart, a founder member of Würzburg and later superior there, was now a delegate of the Ratisbon community. One reason given by the Scots for opening the negotiations was that there were more monks professed at Ratisbon than the revenues would support.[11] That numbers had increased was undoubtedly true, while the finances were not altogether sound, to judge from a papal document of July 1608 regarding the recovery of illicitly alienated monastic property.[12]

The negotiations were in full train when Whyte, on 2nd May 1608, appointed Fr Adam MacCall administrator in Ratisbon. This seems an extraordinary step, and indeed one does find Whyte doing extraordinary things. He gave as reasons his age and infirmity and the fact that he was compelled to live at Würzburg. He himself retained the power of visitation and correction and of deciding in cases of dispute between the administrator and community, but MacCall was to hold office as long as Whyte was abbot. A month later John Stuart was given full powers to negotiate in Constance.[13] Stuart completed the negotiations, which resulted not in the restoration of the abbey but in compensation for its loss. On 4th March 1609 the Ratisbon Scots approved what he had done and appointed Adam MacCall to take his place. MacCall as administrator then concluded a formal agreement that same month with the approval of the nuncio.[14]

There is one very strange feature of the Constance affair, which has little connection with Würzburg but should be touched on briefly as it sheds light on Abbot Whyte's behaviour as a superior and goes far to explain why his projects seldom prospered. In March 1609 one Patrick Stuart appears suddenly, signing himself as subprior; moreover, he acted with MacCall in the final negotiations with the Constance town authorities and the nuncio and signed the formal agreements. Improbable though it may appear, this Patrick was a novice at the time and was refused admission to profession when his year's probation was completed; otherwise we must accept the even less likely explanation that two different Patrick Stuarts appear in St James's, Ratisbon in 1608-9 and neither is ever heard of again. Patrick, a priest already, took the habit at Ratisbon on 5th September 1608 and Whyte wrote to him from Würzburg exhorting him to persevere. The following August, when the year of noviciate was almost over, six monks at Ratisbon were in favour of accepting him and three against, but Adam MacCall, the administrator of the abbey, considered that these three opposed Patrick's admission out of prejudice.

Not so Whyte: in a letter from Würzburg to the three he said harsh things about most of the other six and ordered Patrick to be dismissed. A month later he wrote an open letter to the community at Ratisbon in which he complained of MacCall's audacity and impudence in trying to circumvent his authority and accused MacCall of conspiring with Patrick against the abbot and some of the brethren. Patrick promptly appealed to the papal legate, who instituted an official process. The end of the affair, in November 1609, was rather an anti-climax. After resounding salvoes of charge and countercharge, both those who favoured and those who opposed Patrick's profession agreed that the revenues could not really support an extra monk. Accordingly he decided to depart in peace, the community testified to his good character, and Patrick Stuart's brief appearance on the Ratisbon stage was over.[15] But sinister light is thrown on Whyte's prudence and qualities of leadership. He had written harsh things about half his monks and had openly quarrelled with and denounced the administrator whom he had installed only a year previously. The impression is given that he was a man who acted first and thought afterwards, and that he was the sort of superior who delegated duties without defining them and then interfered in his subordinates' execution of them.

In or around 1609, and possibly as a result of the quarrel with MacCall, Whyte took the first steps in a matter which was to involve Ratisbon in untold trouble for twenty years. He petitioned Rome saying that after seventeen years of rule he was worn out with age and wished to have, before his death, a coadjutor with right of succession or else to resign and let a real abbot be elected at once.[16] It should be noted that Whyte was in his late fifties and was to live for twenty years longer and be involved in Ratisbon affairs for ten of them.

The proceedings would not be of much relevance for the history of Würzburg, had this not happened at a time when the two monasteries were still very much interconnected. The abbot of Ratisbon was also the abbot-general of the congregation. It would therefore be as well to say a word about coadjutor abbots. A coadjutor abbot today, unlike a coadjutor bishop, has almost complete control of his monastery; the abbot himself retains merely a few more or less honorific functions. Then, when the abbot dies, the coadjutor takes the title of abbot and continues to exercise the control which he has in fact assumed some time previously. A coadjutor can be elected when the abbot feels himself unequal, or is

45

considered by higher authority to be unequal, to the burden of office. It is in reality much the same as resignation or deposition but preserves the outward semblance of delegation. On 10th March 1611 the Scottish monks of Ratisbon and Würzburg elected Fr Benedict Algeo (nowadays written Auldjo) coadjutor to Abbot Whyte,[17] but that it was not a normal election of a coadjutor abbot, at least according to modern norms, is evident from later events.

We have no information about the Scots in Würzburg at this time, except that we can be reasonably sure their number was less than six. The community had, however, one outstanding man, William Ogilvie, who had taken his vows for the Würzburg abbey, a fact which is explicitly mentioned in several documents.[18] He was prior and cellarer in Würzburg when on 28th November 1611 the Ratisbon chapter elected him abbot of Erfurt to succeed James Winzet, nephew of the famous Ninian.[19] Abbot Whyte presented him to the archbishop of Mainz for confirmation by a letter which reveals a great deal about himself.[20] He says he had instructed his coadjutor and monks at Ratisbon to hold the election, and the tone is of one acting a part and enjoying it. Whyte evidently saw himself as the grey eminence controlling the affairs of the congregation through his deputies while himself remaining out of the battle line because of his advancing years. One meets the same tone in several of his effusions.

Ogilvie was confirmed as abbot of Erfurt on the last day of January 1612,[21] and the following autumn he was carrying out a visitation in Ratisbon, where Algeo's appalling misrule was already having its effect. Whyte, in virtue of his office as Visitor General of the Scottish monasteries in Germany, had delegated Ogilvie to perform the task. On 19th October Ogilvie declared that the alienation of the former priory at Kelheim by Algeo was illicit and therefore revoked.[22] Twelve days later Whyte issued a declaration, which he promulgated in chapter on 7th December. There was unanimous agreement at the visitation that Algeo should be removed from office, so Whyte deposes him, sentences him to imprisonment and appoints Ogilvie administrator of Ratisbon in his place. There are touches of Polonius in the document, and indeed one of Algeo's offences was calling Whyte a silly old man.[23]

This arrangement did not last long. Ogilvie went to live at Würzburg and Algeo was restored to office. Little more than a year later, on new year's day, 1614, William Ogilvie and the combined communities at Ratisbon and Würzburg addressed a letter to Abbot Whyte saying that they had warned him when Algeo was restored as coadjutor the previous year and that they would appeal to Rome if he did nothing about it. The following May the Ratisbon monks delivered a letter of their own to Algeo, which does not concern the history of Würzburg directly but throws light on the background against which the Würzburg affairs must be seen. There had been dissension in Ratisbon ever since Algeo's election; apparently no monk in priestly orders apart from Whyte himself had voted for him and there had been underhand dealing over his confirmation as abbot. We can judge what they complained about in Algeo's rule by their demands that he should himself obey Whyte and keep within the limits of the authority allowed him by Whyte, and should render an account of the revenues during the past months.[24]

The relations between Ratisbon and Würzburg at this point are worth examining. The joint election of Algeo and the joint protest about his misrule show that the abbacy of Ratisbon was a matter affecting their common interests. Five monks of each house signed the protest, and it is an indication of their involvement that the document had to be taken 140 miles to let both communities sign. The same document has the words: 'We . . . who are members of the Scottish congregation', while Whyte in a letter a year later to the archbishop of Mainz affirms that the three Scottish abbeys constitute one congregation and work together.[25] In writing that in 1615, Whyte was reckoning without Julius Echter, although it was no doubt an accurate statement of the feeling among the Ratisbon monks.

We do not know where Whyte resided until the end of 1614 but it was probably, for part of the time at least, in Würzburg.[26] The communities were largely interchangeable. The Ratisbon monks went to Würzburg to do their theological studies before priesthood.[27] William Ogilvie, a monk of Würzburg, was abbot of Erfurt and for a time, administrator of Ratisbon. Richard Irvine, having been abbot of Würzburg, was living in Ratisbon. John Stuart, having been prior of Würzburg and then the Ratisbon delegate to Constance, was prior at Ratisbon in 1612 and prior again at Würzburg in 1614. The Ratisbon monk, Alexander Armour, who had been prior at Würzburg in 1612, was back at Ratisbon as prior in 1614, and another Ratisbon monk, Hugh Wallace, had gone to Würzburg to be cellarer. All this was no doubt Whyte's arrangement, stimulated by an understandable desire on the part of his monks to get away from Algeo.

The protest against Algeo has the names of five monks at Würzburg, followed by the words 'and the rest of the community'. This may be merely added as the examination candidate who has run out of facts adds 'et cetera', but it suggests that there were others, perhaps novices or aspirants, in the house. At any rate Bishop Echter's patience ran out and on 3rd November 1614 he issued peremptory orders to the Scots in his town. He said he had instructed them nineteen years previously, when the monastery was rebuilt from its ruins, to have six professed monks in St James's, of whom three were to be priests, and that his predecessors in the see had ordered the number to be made up by German monks if no suitable Scots were available. In spite of this there were not enough monks to provide the masses and choir office as he had arranged, nor had the community an abbot. So he delivered the ultimatum that they were to elect an abbot capable of seeing to the choir offices and temporal administration, and if no competent Scot was available they must elect a German. And until the number of monks increased they must follow a different horarium, which he proceeded to lay down. The chief differences were that Matins and Lauds would be at midnight, and the duties following the morning period of lectures were to be an hour later.[28]

It is difficult to see how midnight office, with a period of sleep before and after, helped to make up for a shortage of numbers. One is at liberty to speculate on the bishop's motives: is the whole document to be taken at its face value or not? Was he merely concerned about having six monks, or did he want to free the monastery from the unfortunate Whyte, whom he must have known well by this time, and his successor, the even less prepossessing Algeo? Did the Würzburg Scots themselves instigate the bishop to intervene so that they could free themselves from Whyte and Algeo? Whatever the truth of the matter, everything worked out most conveniently. Hamilton, who for years had not been living at Würzburg but was, as far as one can judge, still technically abbot, resigned in 1614;[29] Echter gave his ultimatum in November of that year; and two months later William Ogilvie was elected abbot by the Würzburg monks and not by the Ratisbon chapter. He had been living in Würzburg since 1613, seemingly to allow the Erfurt revenues to be used for paying off debts in Erfurt while he resided elsewhere.[30] Precisely what his status was in Würzburg is difficult to make out. He does not seem to have been superior, for three other monks in turn were prior during these years. With his election at Würzburg as abbot of Würzburg, however, the monastery became independent of the Ratisbon mother-house and entered on a period of prosperity and progress.

Notes

[1] NLS, Adv. 45.3.10 (Folio XLII, no. 34). Printed in T. McCrie, *Life of Andrew Melville* (Edinburgh, 1819), 524 ff. and in Hammermayer, "Reformation", 246-53.

[2] *Early Records of the University of St. Andrews* (Scottish Hist. Soc., 1926), 285, 175, 179.

[3] Wieland, 105; "Necr. Suppl.", 174.

PLATE 2.   Tombstone of Abbot Macarius
(in the Marienkapelle, Würzburg)

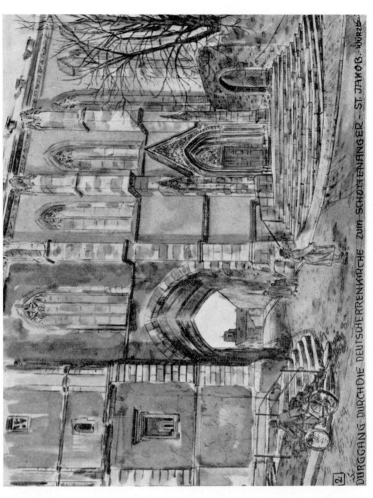

PLATE 3. Deutsch-Haus and road to St. James's showing the route followed by bishops' funerals

4 Reg. BOA, Sch., Urk. 568; VL, Barb. Lat. 8627, f. 5, 17.

5 SCA, Rat. C 7, 19a.

6 "Necrologies", 194.

7 Chronicon; Reid, f. 112r.

8 Wz. SA, MRA, Stift 2613 / K.735, p. 55, 35.

9 Wz. SA, Urk. 50.24.

10 Wz. SA, MRA, Stift 2613 / K.735, p. 7.

11 Con. St., KS, Fasz. 13, 5b, f. 3, 20.

12 Mun. HSA, KUSJR, 84.

13 Con. St., KS, Fasz. 13, 5b, f. 91, 27.

14 Con. St., Urk. Neu 11,688; N.Sp.A. 728-30; Renz, xvi, 79-80; K. Rieder, "Urkunden und Regesten zur badischen Kirchengeschichte", in *Freiburger Diözesan-Archiv*, N.F. xi (1910), 309-11.

15 Reg. HV, R 91, f. 76-81; Mun. HSA, KLSJR, 13;Reg. Regens.

16 SCA, Rat. C 9, 1.

17 Mun. HSA, KUSJR, 85; Black, 17, 38.

18 E.g., Wz. SA, MRA, Stift 2613 / K.735, p. 43-46.

19 ibid., p. 29 ff.

20 Erf. DA, GG VIe, f. 93.

21 Wz. SA, MRA, Stift 2613 / K.735, p. 21-34.

22 Reg. BOA, St Jakob, Fasz. 33.

23 VL, Barb. Lat. 8627, f. 4.

24 SCA, Rat. C 8, 5.

25 Wz. SA, MRA, Stift 2613 / K.735, p. 43.

26 VL, Barb. Lat. 8627, f. 9r; Erf. DA, GG VIe, f. 93.

27 Reg. BOA, St Jakob, Fasz. 33.

28 Wz. SA, Urk. 50. 24.

29 Chronicon; Reid, f. 112r; Wieland, 127.

30 Scholle, 39; Wz. SA, MRA, Stift 2613 / K.735, p. 35-38.

CHAPTER 5

Independence and growth
1615—23

On 22nd January 1615 the community elected William Ogilvie abbot of Würzburg and at once requested Bishop Julius to confirm his election. This is a formality attendant on abbatial elections, and one can gain an idea of the status of the abbey from the name of the confirming authority. Six members of the community requested the confirmation: Hugh Wallace, Adam MacCall and William Gordon, priests; Gabriel Wallace, a laybrother; Robert Forbes, a professed monk not yet a priest; and Thomas Duff, a novice.[1] This is almost the same community as had protested against Abbot Algeo's misrule twelve months before, except that John Stuart, the prior, had died, Adam MacCall had come from Ratisbon, and Thomas Duff had entered the noviciate. These six and Ogilvie can be regarded as the foundation members of St James's as an independent abbey.

Another event took place at this time, which gave the Scots a great deal of publicity and renown, at least locally, and no doubt had considerable effect on their morale. In fact it must have been a contributing factor to the period of progress and fervour which began with Ogilvie's election. The event was the re-discovery of the body of Abbot Macarius, the founder of the monastery. The grave was discovered in February 1614, and some time later the bishop decided to transfer the remains to a place of honour in the abbey church. Accordingly, on 1st February 1615, only ten days after Ogilvie's election, they were exhumed. Echter, who had prepared for the event by following spiritual exercises together with the monks, marked the occasion by presenting the monastic library with some books. It has been suggested that the election of Ogilvie was due to the desire to give fitting honour to Macarius,[2] but the terms of the ultimatum delivered by the bishop two months before hardly bear this out.

On 31st May the solemn translation of the body to the choir of the abbey church took place. Probably popular devotion to Macarius as a saint began to grow at once, although we have no contemporary evidence of it, and went hand in hand with the growth of the community under their new and competent abbot. Julius Echter in his declining years must have felt himself recompensed for his trouble and his benefactions to the Scots; they in their turn must have felt themselves called to play an important role in the church. A monastery is as susceptible to influences of leadership and esprit de corps and sense of purpose as any other human institution.

There were six monks besides the abbot in January 1615. The laybrother, Gabriel Wallace, died the following year but the novice, Thomas Duff, persevered and made his profession, followed by another novice, Alexander Baillie. The bishop attended the choir office on the patronal feast-day, St James's, 25th July 1616. Noticing that the monks were using the Roman breviary, he procured copies of the newly published Benedictine breviary and presented the professed monks, six in number, with one apiece.[3] A year later Julius Echter, having ruled his diocese and duchy for forty-four years, died on 13th September 1617. More than anyone else, he had made it possible for the Scots to establish themselves in Würzburg, and when his body lay in St James's before burial according to the age-old custom, a vigorous and growing community attended the obsequies. Thomas Duff, who wrote Latin verse on each and any occasion, composed two poems which appear to be a dialogue between himself and Ogilvie: he wanted to be professed but the abbot was replying that the monastery supported seven poor men and could not support an eighth.[4] This apparently trivial bit of verse illustrates the most important truth that the size of the community depended directly on the state of the monastery's economy.

Echter's successor, Johann Gottfried von Aschausen, had been provost of Würzburg cathedral before becoming bishop of Bamberg in 1609. With the encouragement of his friend in Rome, the famous Cardinal Bellarmine, he made consistent efforts to reform his diocese, which needed it badly.[5] On being appointed to Würzburg he retained his former see, so that he was prince-bishop of two contiguous territories, and he convoked a synod of the Benedictines in his two dioceses in the week 12th-18th December 1618. Ogilvie, having been summoned like the other abbots,[6] duly attended with his prior, Hugh Wallace. The synod proceeded to legislate in considerable detail for the various aspects of monastic life, then those present accepted the decrees for themselves and their absent brethren. The Scots were not singled out in any way. They too accepted the horarium (in which, incidentally, matins began at 3 or 4 according to the day and not at midnight) and much detailed legislation on monastic observance and even on the habit they wore. In fact the statutes have survived in a manuscript book of spiritual exercises written by the recently professed Thomas Duff for his own guidance and benefit.[7] The Würzburg Scots were now integrated into the German Benedictinism of Franconia.

In January 1615 when William Ogilvie was elected abbot of Würzburg, he was abbot of Erfurt but had been living for some time in Würzburg. Hugh Wallace was also present at the election. Two or three months later there was a rather peculiar dispute going on over the Erfurt abbacy.[8] The first we know of it is a petition from Ogilvie and two Germans to the archbishop of Mainz, in whose diocese Erfurt lay, saying that the abbey revenues could not support any monks and asking him not to appoint Francis Hamilton, now in charge of a parish near Erfurt, to the abbacy as he had not been a good administrator while at Würzburg. Instead they wanted Ogilvie to continue as before, retaining the title but living at Würzburg and so allowing the Erfurt finances to improve. On 23rd April the archbishop agreed and said there was to be no election.

This makes what followed rather grimly humorous. The very next day the Ratisbon chapter elected Hugh Wallace abbot of Erfurt,[9] and Abbot Whyte presented him to the archbishop for confirmation. The letter of presentation explained that the three Scottish monasteries constituted one congregation and it was considered desirable for Ogilvie to resign the abbacy at Erfurt and take on that at Würzburg as it was his monastery of profession and the monks there were young. Anyone who knows of Julius Echter's ultimatum to the Scots in Würzburg must smile at this; and the hollowness of Whyte's language is demonstrated even more forcibly by subsequent events.

In January 1616 three German abbots petitioned for Hamilton's appointment. The archbishop asked his officials in Erfurt if they considered it expedient to have a new abbot appointed; they replied firmly in the negative. Hamilton appealed again in August, and this time Ogilvie was asked for his opinion, which naturally was unfavourable. Hamilton waited a year before appealing yet again. This was in September 1617, and two months later the new bishop of Würzburg wrote on Ogilvie's behalf to the archbishop of Mainz asking for a new abbot to be appointed to Erfurt. The election of Wallace two and a half years before was evidently considered still valid, and he was promptly installed as abbot. One notes with amusement that the proceedings were instituted on 25th November, the day before Ogilvie wrote his letter of resignation.

Francis Hamilton now disappeared from the history of the Scots abbeys. Wallace, however, clearly preferred to be a real prior in a real monastery under an effective abbot rather than to assume abbatial dignity with no monks and next to no income. At any rate he remained in Würzburg, where he attended the synod of abbots in December 1618, signing himself as Hugh Wallace, abbot designate of Erfurt and prior of St James's, Würzburg. He was to be abbot of Erfurt for a further fifteen years but spent most of the time away from Erfurt, and in 1626 had been absent for so long that the diocesan officials put in an administrator.[10]

When Hamilton made his last appeal he produced a remarkable document, a notarial copy of an agreement signed and sealed by William Ogilvie and dated 5th October 1613, to the effect that Ogilvie would resign the Erfurt abbacy into Hamilton's hands as soon as he himself was confirmed as abbot of Würzburg. The copy was dated 30th August 1617, five days before Hamilton's final appeal, in which he pointed out that such an exchange was not simoniacal and was common practice in Italy. It is hard to see why Ogilvie should have made this illicit agreement unless he had a shrewd idea that he would be elected abbot of Würzburg but thought that Hamilton's status as still technically abbot impeded an election. In other words, Ogilvie might have been bribing Hamilton to resign. But why did Hamilton not produce the document before? If the document is genuine, Ogilvie is guilty of Machiavellian double-dealing, which does not seem in character. If, as seems more likely, it is a forgery (it has, incidentally, no notarial docquet), then Hamilton, and possibly also a notary, were conspiring to defraud. As to Hamilton's resignation, most probably he did so in 1614. The most likely explanation is that Julius Echter induced him to, or simply decided that Hamilton's previous request for letters of freedom constituted resignation. An absentee abbot like Hamilton would not have stood in Echter's way for long.

While the Würzburg abbey was growing in numbers and prestige, and the single Erfurt monk, the abbot, was living in Würzburg, the mother-house in Ratisbon was getting further and further involved in a series of troubles and upheavals. The documents are innumerable[11] — a striking illustration of the recognised truth that in the history of monastic life the scandals assume an undue significance because of their documentation. Algeo's election as coadjutor abbot in 1611 was puzzling enough. Only Abbot Whyte himself, of those who were priests, had voted for him; the notarial instrument of the election was signed by only four of the eleven electors;[12] and Algeo had managed to have the election confirmed by the bishop of Ratisbon without obtaining authorisation from Rome. He was deposed at the end of 1612 but reinstated the following year by Whyte. By February 1615 Whyte was again siding with his monks against Algeo and speaking of the need to elect a new coadjutor.

The key to much of the trouble, now and later, is the desire of the aristocratic bishop, Albert von Törring, who ruled the diocese of Ratisbon from 1613 to 1649, to gain control of St James's. At some point the nuncio in Vienna had delegated his own papal jurisdiction over the abbey to him. In March 1615 the bishop tried to force the monks to accept Algeo and when they resisted he imprisoned five of them, seemingly the whole community apart from Whyte. One escaped and called in the Lutheran town authorities, who released a second monk; the latter attacked Algeo and stabbed him, and the town senate refused to surrender the culprit.[13] At some point, too, the abbey had been mortgaged to the Protestant senate.

The nuncio now intervened to threaten the monks with excommunication; they appealed to the emperor on behalf of their imprisoned brethren. Then in May Rome ordered a visitation, which does not seem to have taken place. At any rate the community instituted a process against Algeo at Rome in June 1615. Ratisbon was an imperial free city but the territory outside it — including Stadt am Hof, the town at the other end of the bridge across the Danube — belonged to the duke of Bavaria. He now sided with the bishop and seized any monk found in his territory. He also arrested all the monastery's goods and revenues outside the town, with the result that the monks were soon in desperate straits.

In May 1616 sentence was passed in Rome against Algeo, but the nuncio and the bishop prevented its execution. Alexander Armour, the prior, who had been in Rome to further the case (and seemingly also to obtain confirmation for himself as the new coadjutor) returned to Ratisbon; where the arrest of the goods continued as before. Scottish monks had been forced to leave Ratisbon as they had no means of support, while Algeo was living nearby in Stadt am Hof and receiving all the income for himself. He was willing to hand over the abbey to the bishop in return for his support, reserving only a liferent for himself.

As the situation dragged on and got worse, an observer in Ratisbon described the principals. Whyte, he said, was a good man but senile and had always lacked firmness as a ruler. His monks were badly trained, unstable, and quite possibly not even really Catholics. Algeo was a good and intelligent man — when sober; in his cups, as he often was, he acted foolishly and would give away anything. Algeo had lost his case at Rome because of his uncanonical status, but this was something which could be remedied. A bull was eventually issued on 23rd August 1617 in his favour[14] and was put into execution on 30th January 1618. It confirmed that Algeo had been elected coadjutor and was to become the ruling abbot when Whyte demitted office. The latter now made a formal declaration of his resignation and handed over his keys. Algeo was thus abbot for life, and the monks present accepted him as such; among them on this occasion was William Ogilvie. On the following Trinity Sunday Algeo received the solemn abbatial blessing and was invested with crozier and mitre. The ceremony took place in the Franciscan church in Ratisbon, and the assisting prelates and ministers were all Germans.

A settlement was thus reached in Ratisbon, although hardly a peaceful one, nor did it prove to be a lasting one. The nuncio Carafa carried out a visitation of the abbey in February 1623, and from the acts he issued it is clear that monastic observance had deteriorated sadly. One enactment concerned the Scots in Würzburg: Alexander Baillie of Würzburg was to be prior and cellarer at Ratisbon and render an annual account to the nuncio.[15] A papal document of 1623 lets us see the state of the abbey finances. It had mortgaged monastic property to Protestants (no doubt the town senate) for 8000 florins, and the creditors were threatening to foreclose, so leave was given to borrow the sum from Catholics at a rate of interest of not more than 6 per cent.[16]

There was still some coming and going between the two abbeys. Adam MacCall, who held the office of cellarer at Würzburg when Ogilvie was elected, was back in Ratisbon as cellarer in 1619,[17] while Alexander Armour, Algeo's prior, had expressed to Carafa his wish to live at Würzburg and now changed places with Baillie. Alexander Baillie, born in 1590 into the family of Carnbroe in Lanarkshire, had gone abroad for his further education like many another young Protestant. Having enrolled in the Protestant university of Helmstedt in North Germany in 1612, he made his way that same year to the Scots College in Rome. In November 1615 he took the monastic habit in Ratisbon, then in the throes of the dispute with Algeo, and on Abbot Whyte's advice went instead to Würzburg, where he made his profession in November 1617 and became prior within less than five years.[18] He was certainly a competent administrator, as his later career shows.

Onlookers at Würzburg were interested in Ratisbon. Thomas Duff's muse was usually kindly, but his compositions on Algeo are vitriolic. One poem consists entirely of pejorative words beginning with the same initial letters as Algeo's name; another considers his names and declares that Algeo ('I freeze' in Latin) fits him, but Benedict (meaning 'blessed') is the direct contrary of the truth; a third effusion informs us that Algeo, like Judas, had red hair, but Judas sold his master for money while Algeo had done so for wine.[19]

As we have seen, Whyte finally ceased to be abbot of Ratisbon in 1618. A letter to him from Ogilvie belongs to this time. Whyte had written announcing his arrival in Franconia, and Ogilvie replied that he had to support ten monks in Würzburg and could not receive him, even for one night, nor could the abbot of St Stephen's. It is evident that Whyte was *persona non grata* in Würzburg. The letter also throws light on one aspect of the troubles in Ratisbon, for Ogilvie says it is dishonourable for the bishop of Ratisbon to cast out Whyte in his old age after Whyte had given him authority over the abbey against the wishes of the brethren. This probably signifies that Whyte, in order to end the sequestration of the abbey revenues, yielded to the bishop's pressure to acknowledge him as superior.

The letter is slightly softened by Ogilvie's advice to the old man to find a fixed lodging before winter, in which case he himself will make some contribution. Another letter on the same subject, this time from Whyte to Algeo, has also survived. The old man is saying that the bishop of Würzburg does not want him in Franconia and that Ogilvie denies ever promising unconditionally to take him in.[20] We know one particular grievance entertained against Whyte by the Würzburg monks: it was that he had, as superior general, foolishly squandered the compensation for Constance and not given any of it to their house. According to a Würzburg writer, Whyte was learned, he lectured, wrote and conversed exceptionally well and so was well thought of abroad, but at home he did harm with his maladministration and was disliked for his arrogance.[21] Whyte eventually retired to the abbey of Frauenzell in the Oberpfalz, where he died in 1629. One notes with pleasure that Duff wrote a sympathetic poem to the old abbot in his declining years.[22] The comment on Whyte in the Ratisbon necrology sums up the tragedy of his career: *doctior quam felix* — a gifted but unfortunate man.

The sad state of the Ratisbon house in 1623 is very much relevant, because it was in that year that the two monasteries embarked on a joint missionary enterprise. The ascendancy among the Scots had clearly passed to Würzburg, and the leadership and initiative came from Ogilvie; the events, too, were linked with a celebrated namesake of his. John Ogilvie, the Jesuit priest who is the only Scot in the post-Reformation period officially honoured by Roman Catholics as a martyr, was hanged at Glasgow Cross on 10th March 1615, seven weeks after William Ogilvie's election at Würzburg. Two questions must be asked. Why did persons associated with the martyr in Scotland become Benedictines at Würzburg and not Jesuits? and who was the John Ogilvie sent from the Douai college to Ratisbon in 1598?

The first question includes within itself the question of whether the martyr and the abbot were related, as has been suggested. No answer to this seems possible, however, since the family background of both is unknown; indeed, doubt has been effectively cast on the assertions usually made about the martyr's family and even on whether his real name was Ogilvie.[23] The martyr's biographers have also assumed that he was the John Ogilvie at Douai, whereas this too is very doubtful.

Briefly, there was no reason for the Douai student to go to the Ratisbon abbey in 1598 except to become a monk, since Winzet's college had ceased to exist, yet there is no hint that the martyr had any Benedictine background. Secondly, if the Douai student was the martyr, one would expect some comment in the register, especially since comments were added to other entries, yet there is none.[24] Was the student, then, William Ogilvie? It is the fallible Wieland, citing documents no longer extant, who lists William Ogilvie under the year 1598. To identify the latter with the Douai student, one must assume that William was a religious name, although the first clear case of a novice assuming a religious name was Peter Algeo becoming Brother Benedict in 1604. On the other hand, the mention of Ratisbon and not Würzburg as the destination of the student is not a difficulty, granted the interdependence of the two houses.

The identification of William Ogilvie with the Douai student must therefore be regarded as a possibility and nothing more. We know a few facts about William's background. Abbot Whyte, in presenting him as abbot elect of Erfurt, described him as being of noble birth and as having earned the regard of princes and prelates in Franconia.[25] Since both Würzburg and Mainz were prince-bishoprics in which bishop and canons were scions of the local nobility, and social position was inextricably entangled with ecclesiastical office, one's birth and social accomplishments were important. The Latin *nobilis*, however, did not necessarily imply possession of a title; a son of the smallest laird was described as *nobilis* at Würzburg or Ratisbon. Ogilvie used the arms of the Ogilvies of Deskford both on a new building he had erected and in the university roll when he was elected Rector. This, too, is inconclusive as all Scots abbots used arms connected with their family name. The martyr, incidentally, likewise described himself as being of noble birth. Francis Hamilton claimed that he had converted William Ogilvie to Catholicism and been the instrument of his becoming a monk;[26] the Douai student was also described as a convert from Calvinism.

All the early mentions of William Ogilvie at Würzburg are uncertain. After Wieland's unverifiable reference under 1598 comes the testimony to the election of an abbot of Erfurt in 1603, signed by William Ogilvie among others.[27] But the original is lost and there is something wrong, because another signatory is Benedict Algeo, who was not professed until 1605. Ogilvie may be the William given charge of domestic affairs at Würzburg in 1605, or the William at

Erfurt in 1608,[28] but William Gordon may be meant in either case. He may have been prior at Würzburg in 1606, since a document attributed to him as Whyte's prior in 1618 (a quite impossible date) belongs perhaps to 1606.[29] It is rather strange that the background and early career of the greatest Scots abbot of Würzburg should be so obscure. Until his election as abbot of Erfurt in December 1611 there is no incontrovertible fact of his monastic career, while all we can say of his background is that he was not of lowly birth, had been a Protestant and probably belonged to the north-east, where Deskford is.

The first associate of John Ogilvie the martyr to come to Würzburg was John Mayne,[30] who was born in 1583 in Glasgow, was brought up a Protestant, took the matriculation oath at Glasgow university in 1598 and was awarded his degree the following year. At some subsequent point he became a Catholic. When Fr John Ogilvie began his ministry in Glasgow in September 1614, Mayne received the sacraments from him; when Ogilvie was captured in October, Mayne along with others was likewise arrested and condemned to death. As they were in the same prison, it was to Mayne that Ogilvie sent the narrative he had composed about his own imprisonment, together with a covering letter for the Jesuit provincial in Austria. Mayne, having collected what information he could from eye-witnesses about Ogilvie's sufferings, added it to the narrative. Ogilvie was hanged, the others had their sentences commuted to exile. Mayne went to Bordeaux and delivered the narrative with his own continuation to the Jesuit authorities, who promptly had the whole thing printed. With him Mayne also had a letter from Ogilvie commending him to all Catholics on account of his condemnation and sufferings for the faith.

It is not clear if Mayne was a practising Catholic before John Ogilvie arrived in Glasgow. The indications are that he was, but he was himself to declare later that Ogilvie reconciled him to the Catholic church. One difficulty of all missionary accounts in Scotland during the early seventeenth century is the ambiguity of such terms as 'reconciliation' and 'conversion'. An account by one who lived with Mayne later (unfortunately known only through the Scottish Benedictine historian, Marianus Brockie, who was not above fabricating his sources) says that he was married and a Protestant but was converted by John Ogilvie. His wife died and he began to study for the priesthood, doing his philosophy at Douai and his theology in Rome. After becoming a monk he brought his only daughter from Scotland and she entered the Cistercian abbey of Himmelspforten near Würzburg.[31] The story is highly suspect but the Douai lists are defective for this period and there is partial corroboration of his family circumstances. On 10th November 1616

John Mayne in Flanders appealed to the archduke for financial help. Among the circumstances of his imprisonment and exile he recounted that he had had to leave his country with his wife and children and had now used up all he possessed, so that he and his family were reduced to great necessity. The treasurer was instructed to make him one payment of 150 *livres*.[32] Mayne was certainly at Rome for a short period in 1619, then he entered Würzburg, where he assumed the religious name of Silvanus and made his profession, probably in 1620-21.

When Mayne first went to receive Ogilvie's ministrations in September 1614, he was in the company of one Robert Hegate, who was also imprisoned and sentenced. Hegate had a young brother, James, aged twelve, who had not been brought up a Catholic, for fear that he might unwittingly betray the family. James frequently visited his brother in prison; he also ran messages for Ogilvie and was present at the latter's execution. When he was fifteen, that is, in or around 1617, he went to Douai to be educated as a Catholic.[33] Another student at Douai was the young Richard Tod, who was taken there by his father; and the father carried with him a letter of introduction from John Ogilvie, written in Edinburgh in August 1614, asking the rector to admit the boy.[34]

In January 1623 Mayne was in Douai, where he had fruitful contact with two institutions, the Scots College and the English Benedictine monastery. The Douai register says succinctly that a certain James Scott went with Hegate and Tod to become a monk at Würzburg at the beginning of January 1623. They travelled with Mayne. A few months later two more seminarists, Edward Maxwell and Robert Maclean, left for Würzburg, saying that they had been granted entry when Mayne passed through Douai and had now been told to come by Abbot Ogilvie. The rector asked for some proof of this, which they produced. Maclean was about eighteen, Maxwell perhaps three years younger.[35] The whole affair is a little strange, especially since the Jesuit authorities in Douai were not pleased. On the face of it the most obvious explanation would seem to be that William Ogilvie's rule at Würzburg attracted men like Mayne, and that Mayne's persuasiveness and reputation as a confessor of the faith were added to the renown of Würzburg to induce the students to go there.

There was, however, another important result of Mayne's stay in Douai, even more important than the obtaining of five promising novices, of whom four persevered. This was contact with the English Benedictines of the priory of St Gregory's in Douai. Unlike the Scottish abbeys, which had existed on German soil for centuries and had become Scottish almost by accident, the English monasteries had been founded in the early seventeenth century and with the specific purpose of engaging in missionary work in England. Douai, being an important counter-reformation centre, was a natural place for such a monastery. When Mayne went to Douai he lodged with this mission-minded Benedictine community, and when he returned to Würzburg with the three students he also took with him three letters from the English monks, all dated 16th January 1623.

The first of these was an open letter from Fr Rudesind Barlow, president of the English Benedictine Congregation, to all the Scots monks, the next was a letter from the prior of St Gregory's to Abbot Ogilvie, and the third was a formal document admitting the Scots to fellowship and a share in all spiritual benefits. The most important of the letters is the first, which outlines a plan for organising missionary work in Scotland under the aegis of the English Congregation. Briefly, the Scots monks were offered the same faculties and privileges as the English possessed, and they would be subject to the English superiors while on the mission but could be recalled at any time by their own abbot.

The second letter is perhaps significant in being addressed to Ogilvie personally, thereby emphasizing who among the Scots was providing the motive force. The remaining document, the *Fraternitatis Charta*, as it styles itself, establishes a close union of fellowship between the monks of the two nations and promises fraternal help and hospitality in all English houses to any Scots monk furnished with letters of credence. The Scots replied with two documents signed by all three abbots: by Algeo at Ratisbon towards the end of June, then by Ogilvie at Würzburg a month later. Hugh Wallace also signed at one of these places, no doubt Würzburg. One document accepts the English proposals gratefully, the other extends a similar Charter of Confraternity to them.[36] The Scots had now committed themselves to definite missionary activity involving Ratisbon as well as Würzburg, and Algeo was, at the very least, co-operating with the plans.

Notes

[1] Reid, f. 112r; Wieland, 105-06; "Necr. Suppl.", 174-75.

[2] Schott, 103-04.

[3] Copialbuch, f. 153r.

[4] Duff, f. 16.

[5] J. Brodrick, *Robert Bellarmine* (London, 1961), 323-35.

[6] Wz. SA, G.S. 2929/120.

[7] Wz. UB, M.ch.q.51, f. 136-41.

[8] Unless otherwise stated, the source is Wz. SA, MRA, Stift 2613/K. 735, p. 3-134.

[9] Reg. BOA, Sch., Urk. 89.

[10] Scholle, 39.

[11] Unless otherwise stated, all material comes from SCA, Rat. C8, C9; Reg. BOA, St Jakob, Fasz. 33; VL, Barb. Lat. 8627, f. 3-43.

[12] Mun. HSA, KUSJR, 85; VL, Barb. Lat. 8627, f. 39.

[13] Gumpelzhaimer, 1062. For the subsequent process see Mun. KA, GL 3347/30, f. 88-231.

[14] Mun. HSA, KUSJR, 87.

[15] SCA, Rat. C 9, 7; Baillie, f. 26-27.

[16] Mun. HSA, KUSJR, 89.

[17] Mun. HSA, KUSJR, 88.

[18] Ziegelbauer, IV, 129; *Scottish Hist. Rev.*, xxiv, 237.

[19] Duff, f. 20-21.

[20] Reg. HV, R 91; Reg. BOA, St Jakob, Fasz. 33.

[21] Indiculus, f. 50rv.

[22] Duff, f. 60r.

[23] W. J. Anderson, "A Jesuit that calls himself Ogilvy", in *IR*, xv, 56-65.

[24] Douai Reg. f. 140-41.

[25] Erf. DA, GG VIe, f. 93.

[26] Wz. SA, MRA, Stift 2613/K. 735, p. 81 ff.

[27] Erf. Tent.

[28] Reg. HV, R 91, f. 76.

[29] "Necr. Suppl.", 174, 175; Wieland, 61.

[30] For Mayne see Brown, *passim*; *Munimenta Alme Universitatis Glasguensis*, III, 62-63,8. The spelling Mayne is preferred as being the southern form (Black, 574, 590).

[31] Brockie, *ad* Ratisbon, 1639.

[32] Brussels, AGR, Papiers d'Etat et Audience, 2646, 2582.

[33] Brown, *passim*.

[34] Brown, 305.

[35] Douai Reg., f. 148v, 150r. The texts printed in *Colleges*, 15, 17, 18 are less full and give Mayne's name wrongly as Magnus.

[36] The whole correspondence is edited in "First Mission".

CHAPTER 6

Achievements and disaster
1624—36

In his letter to the Scottish abbots in January 1623, the president of the English Benedictine Congregation had said that the influx of aspirants from Douai would enable the Scots to spare monks for the Scottish mission. The numbers at Würzburg have been quoted already: there were six professed monks in 1617, to each of whom Bishop Echter gave a breviary, and there were ten at some time after 1618 when William Ogilvie refused to take in ex-Abbot Whyte. In June 1625 Ogilvie decreed that the edition of the breviary donated by Echter was to be the one used in the Scots abbey, and he bought seven more copies of it as the number of monks had doubled since Echter made his gift.[1] There were thus a dozen Scottish monks in Würzburg in 1625; as the new entrants advanced towards the priesthood Ogilvie could spare half a dozen monks and still fulfill the requirements laid down in the foundation charter of 1595.

The Würzburg Scots did in fact continue with their missionary plans, but no longer under the auspices of the English Benedictines. They had enthusiastically accepted the offer of their English brethren in the summer of 1623 and then, less than a year later, had both the pope and the cardinal protector of Scotland exerting themselves to promote a purely Scottish scheme. On 17th April 1624 the congregation of cardinals called *Propaganda*, founded not long before to take charge of all missionary work, gave very favourable consideration to a request from the Scots monks to form their own missionary body.[2] Ten days later the pope, Urban VIII, supplied Silvanus Mayne with a letter to Emperor Ferdinand II asking him to restore the Vienna *Schottenkloster* to the Scots. There is no mention in it of the Scottish mission, merely of the injustice suffered by the Scots in being deprived of their lawful possessions at a time when they were undergoing persecution and exile for their religion. Cardinal Francesco Barberini, nephew of Urban and his successor as protector of Scotland, also gave Mayne a letter, while the bishop of Vienna, Cardinal Klesl, then in Rome, wrote commending Mayne to his officials in Vienna.

62

Apart from the prominence of Mayne in the negotiations in Douai and Rome, there is very little reference to Würzburg as the source of the motive power behind these efforts. The three Scots abbeys and their communities are mentioned together as if of equal importance, although the abbot of Erfurt had no community and was living in Würzburg. As for Algeo, one can at least say in his favour that he co-operated in these constructive propositions and either dutifully signed or allowed his name to be used. Mayne was commissary of all three abbots in the negotiations over Vienna. With him, however, he had a third letter which indicates the real state of affairs: it was from the prince-bishop of Würzburg, also interceding for the Scots and commending the zeal and monastic observance of Ogilvie's community. Mayne went to Vienna in June or July and delivered the three letters with his own appeal to the emperor. The appeal is interesting, for after giving the usual version of the history of the *Scoti* on the Continent, it outlines the situation and plans of the Scots. Their monasteries are inadequate to house the number of excellent young men from the Scots seminaries who ardently desire to embrace the most exact form of Benedictine observance and to work for the conversion of their countrymen in Scotland and Poland; therefore the Scots want to have the Vienna abbey restored to them in whole or in part in order to introduce reformed observance there and help the Scottish mission. The appeal was signed by Mayne in the name of the three Scottish abbots, as well as by the protector of the Scots monks, the Count von Althan, leader of a German military order.

The emperor, on 1st August, referred the petition to his counsellor for such affairs, who on 3rd September delivered his judgment that the Scots had no valid claim. Ferdinand ratified the judgment and ordered Mayne and the nuncio to be informed of the decision.[3] Ecclesiastical politics in Vienna afford some help in understanding the background of the affair but lie outside the scope of this narrative. It is clear, however, that the key to the Scots' motives lies in the influx of novices into Würzburg and the mission scheme. In fact, had the Viennese monks understood the background in Ratisbon and Würzburg, they would have realised that their monastery was in danger whenever the Scots had constructive proposals for some counter-reformation project. It had been the case when Lesley and Winzet were re-establishing Scottish monks in Germany; it was certainly the case now; and a further attempt was to be made fifty years later when the abbot of Ratisbon planned to set up a seminary for boys from Scotland.

Mayne's mention of Poland in his petition is most interesting, because if he was responsible for drawing up the appeal it is the first sign known to us of the flaw of character which ruined his plans: a refusal to make-do with the means at hand, and a stretching out for the two birds in the bush. Propaganda were soon to discover this for themselves. The nuncio in Vienna had been instructed to obtain information about the Scots monks, as a result of which it was decided to set up a mission unit of seven monks under the direction of Mayne. Accordingly, in April 1625 a bull granting him various powers was despatched to Würzburg. Mayne, however, did not set out for Scotland and almost two years later he made further requests to Propaganda, some of which were granted. In the summer of 1628 Propaganda reassured the bishop of Würzburg that Mayne was still subject to his ordinary superiors; Mayne himself they ordered to go to Scotland at once. A year later, in August 1629, as he had not yet set off, his commission was revoked and Abbot Ogilvie was appointed mission superior in his place. Mayne did not, as far as we know, now go to Scotland as a simple missionary but attached himself to Erfurt and in December 1630 was transacting business armed with a commendatory letter from Abbot Wallace.[4] That same year he was making detailed proposals for the reform of the Scots in Germany, probably for the introduction of the stricter observance of the Lorraine Congregation.[5]

Two accounts belonging to a later date indicate that the Scots did not give up their efforts in Vienna when the emperor decided against them. One of these relates that the nuncio reacted vigorously against the decision and succeeded in obtaining an offer to have six Scots educated in Vienna or the equivalent in cash. Mayne, however, would not accept the offer as he still hoped to gain possession of the abbey and thought this in any case too small a cut of the abbey's revenues.[6] In 1630, according to the other account, the Scots were again, or still, trying hard in Vienna with the backing of Urban VIII. Interested parties, however, persuaded the emperor to make a compromise settlement, and the Scots were offered a lump sum of 3000 florins, which they appear to have refused. Then the wars put an end to the negotiations.[7]

Probably these negotiations should not be viewed in isolation from similar disputes over church property going on in Germany on a massive scale between Catholics and Protestants as well as among Catholics. On 6th March 1629 the famous Edict of Restitution was promulgated, the result of the ascendancy of the Catholic imperial electors and the emperor's religious advisers. Among other things the Edict declared Catholics justified in demanding the restoration of church property misappropriated since 1552, and the execution of the Edict was entrusted to imperial commissioners, exclusively Catholic. Not unnaturally the Catholic gains from the Edict were considerable. It also happened that in the years after 1626 Jesuits

PLATE 4.   Rebuilding after 1945

PLATE 5. St. James's and the Marienberg after 1945

and Benedictines in south Germany were engaged in a struggle for the possession of monastic property. This will be considered later as it is important for the development of the congregation movement among German Benedictines; here it is sufficient to say that Catholic reformers responded eagerly to the Edict, and although the commissioners had been instructed to restore confiscated religious houses to the order which had founded them, the counter-reformation orders and their supporters endeavoured to secure these when they considered the old orders incapable of administering them satisfactorily.[8]

That undoubtedly is the background to the attempt of the Würzburg Scots to secure the old Irish abbey of St Egidius (or Giles) in Nuremberg. This was the Scotic abbey which had become German in 1418 and been handed over to the town senate in 1525, and which Lesley and Winzet had made fruitless efforts to regain. We know of the attempt only through the correspondence between Francesco Barberini and the nuncio in Vienna, Pallotta.[9] On 9th June 1629 Barberini wrote to Pallotta saying that the Scots were about to apply for the restitution of their former monasteries, in particular that in Nuremberg, and asking Pallotta to further their requests with the emperor when asked to do so by the Würzburg abbot. The nuncio replied at the end of the month that he would. On 8th December William Ogilvie's prior arrived in Vienna bearing a letter from Barberini, to be kindly received by Pallotta and promised all help. One of Barberini's letters had a passage telling the nuncio that the Jesuits were competitors for the Nuremberg abbey.

The reader cannot but be impressed by the exceptional warmth of Barberini's language in favour of the Scots and by Pallotta's eagerness to help in a matter which touched the protector of Scotland so deeply. For all that, the affair came to nothing. Perhaps the commissioners discovered that the loss of the abbey had taken place before 1552, in which case the request for its restoration would be automatically turned down, and there was no appeal from their decision. In any case the invasion of south Germany by the Swedish army in 1631 put an end to the working of the Edict. As far as we know, the episode had no lasting effect; its only significance is to demonstrate the genuine good-will of Barberini towards the Scottish monks and the vitality of the Würzburg community at this time.

These same years had seen the prestige of William Ogilvie and his abbey grow. In November 1627 the bishop of Würzburg ordered a visitation to be conducted in the ancient and important abbey of Schwarzach, not far from Würzburg, as a result of which he released from office both the ailing abbot and the aged prior and appointed Ogilvie to be administrator. Ogilvie held this post until the following year and on St Benedict's day, 21st March, received the vows of a novice there. In June 1628, however, the German abbot died; an election was held and Ogilvie departed from the scene, to the undisguised delight of the Schwarzach chronicler. His short administration was not uneventful, for the accusation was made against him to the bishop that he had used Schwarzach assets to build up his own abbey.[10] Whatever the truth of this unlikely charge, Ogilvie must have stood high in the regard of the prince-bishop to have been entrusted with these duties in preference to native German prelates. Another office he had was that of judge in the special court for the degradation (that is, demoting from the clerical state) of clerics accused of witchcraft.[11]

At this time too, Alexander Baillie (who had quickly tired of being cellarer under Algeo at Ratisbon) produced a book of religious polemic, printed in English at Würzburg. The dedicatory epistle, dated January 1628, is to William Ogilvie who, having discharged his abbatial office and served the bishop notably well, had been 'chosen as most worthy of al the Prelates in the diocesse to be made Lord & Administrator of that noble and potent Abbacie of Swartzach, not without the immortal honour of al our Scottish Abbacies here in Germanie, & of our whole nation elsewhere'. Baillie speaks in the book of the relics of Macarius and the miracles attributed to the saint, as a result of which the abbey church was frequented by the people of Franconia.[12] Macarius was also slowly but steadily finding a place in the printed literature of Europe as a growing number of writers included him in their compilations.

In May of the same year a preliminary enquiry for the beatification of the martyred John Ogilvie was held in Würzburg since two of the chief witnesses to his ministry and sufferings were Frs Silvanus Mayne and James Hegate, monks of St James's. Both were summoned and examined, and their connection and friendship with the martyr made public; the part played by Mayne in particular, and his steadfastness under sentence of death, must have gained him renown in this Catholic province. Incidentally, when giving evidence, Mayne described himself as being in the act of setting off for Scotland to strengthen the Catholics in their faith and win back heretics.[13]

Ogilvie's monks had also begun to play their part in the university life of Würzburg. Four young Scots matriculated in 1624-25, and in 1626 the first place among the graduates was gained by Richard Tod, one of the recent arrivals from Douai.[14] In November 1628 Abbot Ogilvie was elected Rector Magnificus of the university; the original matriculation roll has a picture of his coat-of-arms and his motto, 'Non est mortale quod opto', to be translated roughly as 'What I choose is undying'. During his year of office Ogilvie's prior, Robert Forbes, and the poet-monk Thomas Duff also matriculated. In fact, in these years the Scottish abbey of St James occupied a more important position, and enjoyed a greater prestige, than perhaps at any other point during its occupation by the Scots. The bishop praised its observance; materially, too, it was flourishing. Ogilvie built a three-storey dwelling place for the monks, as well as setting up an outside gate and building beside it a guest-house,[15] on which one can still see his coat-of-arms and the date 1627. Clearly he aimed at removing the occasions of monks associating with externs.

Most of Ogilvie's achievements, however, were soon to be wrecked when the wars of religion reached south Germany. The imperial army came to Erfurt in June 1631, to be followed by the Protestant army of Gustavus Adolphus three months later. We are fortunate in having an eye-witness account of much of the campaign by a Scottish officer in the Protestant army, Colonel Robert Monro.[16] Erfurt was captured without bloodshed on 22nd September but eight thousand men were quartered on the town and its religious houses. The Scots monastery, however, seems to have escaped lightly.[17] A short time later the Swedish army advanced on Würzburg, occasioning one of the most striking incidents in William Ogilvie's whole career. As the Swedes closed in on the town in mid-October, the bishop and many of the notables fled.[18] Ogilvie played a prominent part in the deliberations of those who remained, was chosen as their delegate and, in the words of Monro, capitulated to the King on behalf of the Burgers, who were granted the same terms as Erfurt. A modern writer draws a verbal picture of Ogilvie meeting the king with the keys of the city in his hands, presenting them to him in the name of the bishop and the terrified citizens and succeeding by his pleading in assuaging the king's anger.[19]

On 14th October Ogilvie and a town official left the city to spend the night as hostages in the Swedish camp, and the next morning the gates of Würzburg were opened to the Swedes. Even if the townspeople thought a Scot more likely to gain favour with the Swedish king than a native Franconian, it is still a remarkable tribute to the position Ogilvie had made for himself in Würzburg. Colonel Monro records the incident and adds his comment: 'Here also we see that of old our Nation was much esteemed of abroad, especially the Clergie, who . . . had their Cloisters as here and at Erfurt, and he was a Scots man that brought the Christian Religion first into Franconia but was evill rewarded, being afterwards murthered.' Even a Protestant soldier of fortune claimed St Kilian for the Scots.

67

A tax of 80,000 imperials was laid upon the town; as Monro had said of Erfurt, 'the people were not troubled except in their means.' Then, on the 16th, the newly installed officials took an oath of loyalty to their captors. The town of Würzburg had surrendered, but the bridge over the Main was destroyed and the Marienberg, the fortress on the steep ground on the west of the river, held out. As Monro points out, whoever held Würzburg commanded the Main and hence all Franconia, so the Swedes set out to reduce the Marienberg. A vivid picture is painted of the attack on the fortress. 'Situated on a rock, and one arch of the bridge over the river being broken, it almost seemed impregnable. Moreover the guns of the fortress swept every approach . . . Only a single plank stretched from arch to arch fifty feet above the rapid stream, and yet the Scots, under Sir James Ramsay and Sir John Hamilton, succeeded, partly in boats, partly filing across the bridge in swift succession, to carry the out-works, after which the success of the final attack by the Swedes was assured'.[20] This was on 18th October. The next day, having installed a strong garrison, the Swedish army departed for Frankfurt.

The Scots abbey lay beside the fortress and in fact was on the fringe of the network of fortifications. The community was scattered. Two monks, Robert Forbes and a cleric not yet ordained priest, James Brown, found refuge in the ancient abbey of St Gallen across the Swiss border.[21] There were only three monks in the abbey in October 1633.[22] The Swedish forces remained in occupation for three years and the hostile soldiery quartered in the town and its religious houses was not averse to looting. It was also the systematic policy of the Swedes to plunder the libraries and send the booty back to Sweden; Uppsala university library owes a large part of its treasures to this enlightened barbarity. The library of the Jesuit university was transported there, and a small but valuable collection of manuscripts from it found its way into the hands of Archbishop Laud and thence into the Bodleian Library at Oxford.[23] The Scots abbey, however, was spared,[24] no doubt owing to the continued presence of Abbot Ogilvie. Probably his presence also saved the abbey church from the desecration suffered by other churches. He was in fact one of the four clerics appointed by the occupying authorities to deal with church affairs.[25]

The recapture of Würzburg by the imperial forces was as dramatic as its occupation by the Swedes, with once again Abbot Ogilvie playing an important part. On 18th October 1634, the third anniversary of the capture of the Marienberg, a prearranged plan was put into effect. It was agreed that as many of the garrison as possible should be pleasantly occupied that evening by their involuntary hosts. Accordingly, when the imperial soldiers forced

68

an entry, they had little difficulty in capturing the town. Ogilvie himself was entertaining the highest-ranking officers from the garrison at table in his monastery, which stood so near the citadel, when the attackers rushed in and overpowered them.[26]

The town had suffered cruelly. Since the bishop was still absent, four *Inspectores* were appointed to administer church affairs; Ogilvie was the first-named among them.[27] The citadel still held out but surrendered three months later, in January 1635. The following September Ogilvie died, and with him in the monastery were only two other monks. His epitaph in the abbey church described him as dying in old age having been a good financial administrator and having deserved well of Franconia.[28]

Some assessment of William Ogilvie's character should at least be attempted, even though we know remarkably little of the man himself. That he got on well with the prince-bishop and nobles in Franconia, as Abbot Whyte had said when presenting him as abbot of Erfurt, is really self-evident, for he could not otherwise have been so successful. Two most derogatory judgements on him have survived but in each case one can suppose evident bias. The Schwarzach chronicler in 1628 said that Ogilvie already regarded himself as abbot and administered the abbey to his own advantage. It is a plain fact that monks do not like having administrators from other abbeys imposed on them, and evidently Ogilvie did not succeed in overcoming this disadvantage. In 1632 the bishop of Ratisbon asked that Ogilvie should not be brought in to look after the abbey there as he was probably tarred with the same brush as Abbot Algeo.[29] As a judgement this is surely extraordinarily wide of the mark, because a greater contrast could hardly be imagined than between Ogilvie and Algeo. Probably the bishop knew that Ogilvie would be a most uncompromising opponent of his own designs to control the Ratisbon abbey.

Undoubtedly Ogilvie did not suffer fools gladly. His treatment of Francis Hamilton over the Erfurt abbacy, and his refusal to accept Whyte at Würzburg after the latter's final resignation hint more at ruthlessness than at a spirit of forgiveness. But we cannot really judge; perhaps Ogilvie saw the issues too clearly to allow himself to be swayed by feelings. He appears as a man of decision and incisive character, with the initiative, for instance, to live away from Erfurt when he saw that the revenues needed a chance to recover. The alleged illicit pact with Hamilton, followed by intrigue to prevent his accomplice from getting his share of the spoils, namely the Erfurt abbacy, does not square with what we know of him. That Ogilvie could command loyalty is shown by Hugh Wallace remaining at Würzburg as his lieutenant after 1615 instead of going to Erfurt. And finally, when a man is successful in a spiritual office

69

and shows no ambition in other directions, one can infer that he is not merely a good administrator but a spiritual man. Although we know nothing that touches William Ogilvie personally, he stands out as a leader of men and a great abbot.

In these years Ratisbon fared worse than Würzburg. Once again the documents are so numerous that only the briefest outline can be given.[30] In May 1627, having evidently fallen out with his former allies, Abbot Algeo fled. He was arrested in the territory of the duke of Bavaria and handed over to the bishop of Ratisbon, who imprisoned him in his castle at Werth and tried to make him sign a document of resignation. Algeo held out for fifty-one weeks before doing so. He was then committed to custody in the nearby abbey of Oberaltaich but escaped and made his way to Vienna, where he appealed to the nuncio, Pallotta. In November 1628 Pallotta asked for the documents of the case, which after some delaying tactics the bishop eventually produced. A legal process was begun and dragged on until in August 1630 the verdict was given in Algeo's favour. The point at issue was whether the bishop had the right to act as he had done with Algeo, who was subject directly to the holy see.

Although right in law, the decision was likely to prove disastrous for the monastery if it meant the return of Algeo. Francesco Barberini, the cardinal protector of Scotland, foreseeing the outcome of the process, therefore intervened and instructed Archbishop Rocci, the legate to the meeting of imperial electors in Ratisbon, to do nothing in Algeo's favour. Rocci accordingly, on hearing the verdict, did not put it into effect. Ogilvie and his monks at Würzburg, as well as the Ratisbon monks, had already stated their case against Algeo, for the affair had engaged the attention of the Würzburg Scots from the beginning. Almost two years before, in October 1628, one of them (no doubt Ogilvie) had written to Barberini to say he had heard the bishop was endeavouring to be appointed administrator of the abbey. The writer begged Barberini not to allow this, since it would spell ruin for the Scots, for not only had the bishop been trying for years to get the monks to accept his jurisdiction but he was responsible for the present calamity as he had put in Algeo as abbot.

Barberini was as good as his word. On 11th November 1630 Pallotta informed the Ratisbon prior, Alexander Armour, that Algeo had resigned but was to be compensated for the expenses he had incurred in Vienna and receive an annual pension as long as he remained away from his abbey. The Scots had other difficulties, too. That same week they had been appealing against the reformed Franciscans (known as Observants), whose minister general was in Ratisbon and wanted to obtain St James's for his order.

70

Armour, the prior, had been acting as administrator of the Ratisbon abbey since Algeo's arrest. By this time Hugh Wallace had left Würzburg for his own prelacy at Erfurt and had even collected some subjects, among them Silvanus Mayne. On 27th March 1631 Wallace and his monk John wrote to Barberini from Gorizia, on the present Italian-Yugoslav border. They had been forbidden by the holy see to proceed to Rome but were the delegates of the Ratisbon community, who wanted Wallace as their abbot and promised to introduce the reformed observance of the Lorraine congregation, already being followed by the Erfurt Scots. Barberini replied a fortnight later allowing the Scots to have an election.

His action was premature and no election took place. Armour continued to administer the abbey during the difficult days of 1632 when the movements of the armies brought hardship to the town. In June troops had been quartered in the monastery and on 1st July Armour died, so the nuncio suspended the obligation of paying Algeo's pension and made a temporary arrangement whereby the senior monk acted as superior. By January 1633 Abbot Wallace had left Erfurt and come to Ratisbon, where the community again wanted him as superior, while Alexander Baillie was once more cellarer there, having fled from Würzburg when the Swedes advanced on Franconia. In June the nuncio appointed Wallace administrator after telling the monks that no election could be held until Algeo sent his resignation directly to the holy see. This was the situation when the war came to Ratisbon.

We have an excellent account of the events from Baillie.[31] The Swedes captured the town in November 1633, imprisoned the bishop and forced all the religious houses to pay for his ransom. Wallace was imprisoned, the other monks fled. When the town was re-captured in July 1634 Wallace was released but died of the plague a few weeks later. The first Scots to return were Baillie and Brother Kilian Oswald, who had apparently been a novice at Würzburg.[32] Baillie wrote to the scattered monks to get them to return and in December was appointed administrator at their request by Barberini.[33] His qualities showed themselves at this juncture as he set out to restore order and solvency from the ruins. The methodical accounts of his administration during 1634-35 are still extant.[34]

What brought Baillie's administration of Ratisbon to an end was the death of his own abbot, William Ogilvie, in Würzburg on 17th September 1635.[35] The next day a Würzburg diocesan official drew up a list of the community present and absent, which agrees with the account written by Baillie. Only Edward Maxwell, who was prior, and Thomas Duff were in residence. There were two priests on the Scottish mission, William Gordon and Audomarus Asloan; Silvanus Mayne, Robert Forbes and James Brown (the latter still not ordained) were in Rome; Alexander Baillie was in Ratisbon; and a ninth man, William Maxwell, had been sent to Ireland for his health. In October 1635 Edward Maxwell died, leaving Duff the poet the only monk present. At the end of November the auxiliary bishop wrote to Baillie in Ratisbon asking him to summon all Würzburg monks to their abbey. Baillie agreed, promised to come himself, and also wrote to Rome. Then, in early February 1636 he set off for Würzburg, and Silvanus Mayne was appointed administrator of Ratisbon in his place by Barberini.[36] Mayne had taken Abbot Wallace's place at Erfurt; then, being himself expelled by the town authorities, who had been given possession of all religious houses by the Swedes, he found refuge in Rome.[37]

When Baillie arrived in Würzburg he found that a German administrator had been put in. By 3rd May, however, half a dozen monks had assembled, and on 10th June 1636 they elected Robert Forbes abbot. Of Forbes we know little except that he had entered Würzburg not long before 1614, had held successively the offices of cellarer and prior under Ogilvie, and after the Swedish invasion had taken refuge in St Gallen. He had gone to Rome at the end of 1634 as the agent of the Swabian congregation of Benedictines in order to get approbation of their privileges. The parties opposed to this, however, proved too strong and he was replaced in April 1636, after more than a year of fruitless endeavour, by the English Benedictine procurator in Rome, Fr Wilfrid Selby, who incidentally was no more successful than Forbes had been.[38]

Hopes ran high that Ogilvie's former cellarer and prior would follow in his distinguished abbot's footsteps. Only Erfurt still lacked a superior, and on 26th September Mayne wrote from Ratisbon to the chancellor there explaining that they were awaiting the arrival of monks from Scotland and Switzerland before holding an election.[39] Then, on 13th November 1636, Baillie, who had returned from Würzburg, was elected abbot of Erfurt by the Ratisbon chapter, consisting of four monks who had survived Algeo and the Swedes.[40] All three Scottish abbeys now had superiors, and before them lay the task of repairing the ravages of war and rebuilding from the remnants. It is worthy of note that both Ratisbon and Erfurt now had superiors who were Würzburg monks professed by William Ogilvie.

Notes

1 Copialbuch, f. 153r.

2 Mission plans and work will be dealt with fully in later chapters.

3 Hübl, 19-21. Documents in the archives of the Vienna Schottenabtei, Scr. 102, nos. 24-24e; Baillie, f. 28v-31r; VA, Epist. ad Principes, vol. 38, f. 94; printed in Camerarius, *De Scotorum Fortitudine* (Paris, 1631), 219-20.

4 Reg. BOA, Sch., Urk. 90.

5 Wieland, 94.

6 SCA, ML, Fleming, 18.5.1678.

7 Chronologia, 94; Indiculus, f. 45r.

8 *Cambridge Modern History*, IV, 109-14; Pastor, *History of the Popes*, XXVIII (London, 1938), 172-92.

9 VL, Barb. Lat. 6223, f. 154; 6219, f. 49, 104; *Nuntiaturberichte*, IV, 2, p. 202, 237, 411.

10 Fel. Red., 276-78.

11 Merzbacher, 66; *AU*, xxviii, 210.

12 P. 75-76.

13 Brown, 285ff.

14 Gropp, II, 170.

15 Ser. Abb.

16 *Expedition with the Scots Regiment* (London, 1637), Part II, 76-82.

17 J. H. von Falckenstein, *Historie von Erffurth* (Erfurt, 1739-40), 704; Scholle, 40.

18 For the Swedish occupation, see Gropp, II, 149-62; III, 424ff.

19 Fischer, 80, 160.

20 Fischer, 81.

21 Indiculus, f. 51r.

22 *AU*, viii, pt. 2, p. 72.

23 O. Walde, *Storhetstidens Litterära Krigsbyten*, I (Uppsala, 1916), 122-23; W. D. Macray, *Annals of the Bodleian Library, Oxford* (2nd edn. 1890), 83, 450.

24 Gropp, III, 451. This is also shown by Walde's silence on St James's library.

25 *AU*, viii, pt. 2, p. 37.

26 Gropp, III, 481; *Taschenbuch* (1795), 201-03.

27 *AU*, xiii, 285.

28 Wz. UB, M.ch.f.260, fo 101v; Wieland, 40.

29 VA, NVPC, 43, 24.9.1632.

30 Unless otherwise stated, the documentation is from VA, NVPC, 43; Reg. BOA, St. Jakob, Fasz. 33; VL, Barb. Lat. 6219; 6223, f. 229; 8627, f. 44-45; SCA, Rat. C 8, 4, 6; C 9, 9-12; *Nuntiaturberichte*, IV, 2, p. 332.

31 Baillie, f. 34v, 37rv, 40r.

32 "Necrologies", 197.

33 SCA, Rat. C 9, 13.

34 Mun. HSA, KLSJR, 12.

35 For 1635-36 see Reid, f. 112r; Wieland, 128-29; Baillie, f. 40r.

[36] SCA, Rat. C 9, 14.
[37] Brockie, *ad* Ratisbon.
[38] Molitor, II, 321-27; Weldon, 37.
[39] Erf. DA, GG VIe, f. 101r.
[40] Reg. BOA, Sch., Urk. 91, 92; Wz. SA, MRA, Stift 2613/K. 735, p. 141-44.

CHAPTER 7

Double crisis at Ratisbon

1637—41

The work of reconstruction did not go smoothly. Abbot Baillie's first task at Erfurt was to regain possession of his abbey from the town senate. This he did, but almost two years later he was not yet in peaceful possession, having been compelled to go to Würzburg because of the enemy garrison in Erfurt.[1] In Ratisbon Silvanus Mayne continued as administrator and not as abbot, presumably because the ex-abbot Algeo had not yet given his resignation directly to the holy see. Würzburg, too, suffered a major setback at the end of 1637 when the new abbot, Robert Forbes, died on 4th December without having yet received the abbatial blessing.[2]

Once again preparations were made to elect a new abbot, and absent monks were summoned to Würzburg. The community had dwindled sadly since the days when Ogilvie saw that his dozen monks each had a breviary. A number had died since 1630, including, it would seem, all four who came from Douai in 1623. Of the monks of Würzburg who survived, two were superiors, of Ratisbon and Erfurt respectively, at least one of the two missionaries remained in Britain, and the deacon who had gone to Ireland for his health does not re-appear in the records. The resident community under Abbot Forbes must have been very small, and now Forbes himself had died.

One of the two missionaries was Audomarus (or Omer) Asloan. On receiving the summons from Würzburg he left his mission and wrote to the bishop of Würzburg from London on 16th February 1638. Apparently he was coming to Würzburg to take care of the abbey, and it is quite possible that he was the only responsible person available for the task. Asloan waited for over a month in London, hoping, as he wrote to the bishop of Würzburg in March, to get a commendatory letter from King Charles. At this time, of course, the king had considerably more to occupy him than the requests of a Scottish missionary priest; in fact, never had the religious affairs of Scotland gone worse for Charles. It was seven months since the occasion on which Jenny Geddes is supposed to have thrown her stool at the head of the officiant reading from the new Prayer Book in St Giles's. The National Covenant was being drawn up and signed during these same weeks that Asloan spent in London. Charles, who had been absent from the capital, was back in London by mid-March, but evidently he did not grant Asloan an audience, for the latter says nothing of the king's return.

Towards the end of March Asloan got tired of waiting, commissioned a noble friend to deal with the letter, and set off for Germany. At Gravesend he was delayed by contrary winds, so that he did not reach Germany until late April. From Hamburg on 30th April, old style (a reminder that Germany had the new calendar whereas England and Scotland had not), he sent a third letter to the bishop, explaining the reasons for his delay and saying that even now he had been told he could not proceed to Würzburg without a safe-conduct. His purpose in writing, he said, was to assure the bishop that there was nothing half-hearted in his efforts to reach Würzburg and help his monastery of profession. He made his way across war-torn Europe, passing through France, and eventually arrived at Würzburg.[3]

It certainly seems clear that Asloan had not been summoned merely to record his vote in the election, and it comes as no surprise that he was elected abbot on 20th July 1638 and blessed, together with Alexander Baillie, in November.[4] The new abbot was a man of about forty-four, who had left Scotland in his fourteenth year. The first record we have is of his matriculation at Würzburg university in 1624, when already a professed monk; he would thus appear to be one of Abbot Ogilvie's recruits when the Würzburg community was doubling its size. For almost ten years before his election he was a missionary in Britain. His brother, George, ordained a secular priest in 1619, also worked on the mission and later became a monk at Würzburg during Audomarus Asloan's abbacy. It is reasonably certain that they were sons of the laird of Garroch, about a mile and a half west of Dumfries, a property which had belonged to Asloans since at least the mid-fifteenth century. The surname is the one nowadays written Sloan. One would normally assume that a name like Audomarus was a religious name, and thus John would be his forename; in monastic documents Audomarus alone would then be expected. The abbot, however, invariably used both and in fact usually put Audomarus first.[5]

A year after Asloan began his long period of office as abbot, the Scots abbey in Ratisbon was again plunged into serious crisis. On 26th October 1639 Silvanus Mayne died, leaving in the Ratisbon monastery only one young monk. The cause of the alarm was not merely the lack of monks but the attempt being made by some parties to take the monastery away from them. We have two contemporary descriptions of Mayne. One of them, supposedly by Fr George Wedderburn, a monk of Ratisbon, is preserved in Brockie's *Monasticon*[6] and must therefore be treated with the extreme caution requisite for all unauthenticated material handed on to posterity by that fertile author. Much of it is in fact highly suspect, although Wedderburn is said to have spent fourteen months in Rome with Mayne when both were refugees from Germany; also, it is couched in the language of hagiography. For instance, it is hardly credible that, as the account claims, Mayne in his noviciate kept the rule in its primitive rigour and not as later custom had tempered it. This would be quite contrary to the practice of any noviciate, which aims at making the aspirant fit in and not stand out. We can note that Mayne is said to have continued with these ascetical practices and that Wedderburn regarded him highly for them. The same esteem is apparent in the other account of Mayne, by Alexander Baillie, but Baillie also relates his imprudence as administrator of Ratisbon. Being zealous for discipline and reform, Mayne began at great expense to pull down part of the monks' living quarters and rebuild it. He had only two monks, and Baillie remarks that it was quite the wrong time for such operations.[7]

The work was still incomplete when Mayne died. We can recognise the same man as failed to lead the missionaries to Scotland because he planned something better, and who refused the compensation in Vienna because he hoped for more. As administrator of Ratisbon he appealed for help to the earl of Arundel, Charles I's ambassador to the emperor,[8] and a letter from Barberini to the duke of Bavaria commending the Scots may be the result of another such appeal.[9] It may also have been a sign of the approaching storm. No doubt Mayne's imprudence was at least a partial cause of the attempt made to seize the abbey.

On 26th November 1639, precisely one month after Mayne's death, the bishop of Würzburg, Francis von Hatzfeld und Gleichen, wrote to his fellow bishop in Ratisbon requesting him earnestly to protect the Scots as certain religious and clerics in Ratisbon wished to give their abbey to a different nation and religious order. Asloan travelled to Ratisbon with two of his monks and delivered the letter in person. The Ratisbon monks now, at some point before mid-December, postulated him as their abbot. This is the technical term used when the person elected is not eligible for election according to the letter of the law, as Asloan was not, being already abbot of Würzburg. Presumably they held an election because they knew of Algeo's death in an Austrian monastery in May 1639.[10] Since the postulation was invalid unless confirmed by the holy see, they then asked the nuncio to appoint Asloan administrator until confirmation came. In the event, though there was some delay, the pope rejected the postulation but appointed Asloan abbot *jure devoluto* (that is, the right had fallen to higher authority since the electors had not exercised their right properly and in good time). It was, in effect, confirmation.

Asloan's position was now one of considerable difficulty owing to the conflicting claims of his two abbeys. On 2nd January 1640 he sent one of his monks, Boniface Strachan, back to Würzburg to receive holy orders, and at the same time wrote to the Würzburg auxiliary bishop telling him of his troubles in Ratisbon, caused chiefly by the burden of debt. While he was trying to save the Ratisbon abbey for the Scots he wanted his own poor and humble monastery (he used the expressive word *pauperculus*) to be spared all important business, and himself to be given good warning if any matters did need to be dealt with. A fortnight later Asloan wrote to Bishop Francis himself, outlining his dilemma more clearly. He explained his difficulties at Ratisbon, then asked the bishop for his opinion and advice. The Scots monks wanted him to take over the Ratisbon abbey and they felt that this would help the Würzburg monastery too, as the latter could only with difficulty support an abbot. Personally he would rather give up the Würzburg abbacy than continue with a double burden. What was he to do? Asloan also begged to have the date for giving his annual account at Würzburg postponed until after Easter, since the ecclesiastical officials in Würzburg had designated 18th January for this as usual, in spite of his being absent. Bishop Francis's response was to commend him on 1st February as abbot postulate to the bishop of Ratisbon, presumably to ease the difficulties of Asloan's new charge.

This account of Asloan's doings in Ratisbon is derived from his letters to the bishop and his auxiliary at Würzburg and from letters to the Ratisbon bishop and his officials.[11] It is clear from the letters that the Ratisbon diocesan officials were trying to gain control of the Scots abbey. They asked the Scots by what authority they had elected Asloan as their abbot. Asloan too was summoned at one point to the bishop's chancery in Ratisbon, where a certain dean, after accusing him of slandering the Ratisbon clergy to the bishop of Würzburg, inveighed against the Ratisbon monks' interpretation of their privileges, their poor observance, the scandalous behaviour of Algeo, and so on. Asloan's comment was that he was right about Algeo but the privileges and exemption from the bishop's jurisdiction still held good.

Asloan's dilemma was resolved by his returning to Würzburg. Bishop Francis wanted him to appoint an administrator in Würzburg if he was going to remain any length of time in

Ratisbon.[12] Baillie, however, who apparently had no scruples about calling a spade a spade where churchmen outside Ratisbon were concerned, recounts that the hopes they had entertained of the bishop of Würzburg lending them money to pay their debts were dashed, and that Asloan, being compelled by threatening letters from the Würzburg officials either to return or resign, chose the former and set off for Würzburg on 1st February. This was the very day when Francis addressed his letter commending Asloan to the Ratisbon bishop. If Baillie's account is accurate here, one can hardly avoid the conclusion that Francis and his Würzburg officials did not know what each other was doing, which is very possible as Francis was bishop of Bamberg as well as of Würzburg and of necessity delegated much of the Würzburg administration. Baillie now took on the administration of Ratisbon while still remaining abbot of Erfurt.[13] At this time there was real unity between the Scots of Ratisbon and Würzburg, the effect of war and of threat from without, and the three houses were still being administered by monks of Würzburg. Ogilvie's work lived on.

Alexander Baillie gives a coherent account of these events but a seriously deficient one. There seems to have been a conspiracy of silence about certain matters, for not only does Baillie pass over them but documents which should be in the Ratisbon monastic archives are not there. Baillie narrates that the only monk left in the monastery at Mayne's death was Macarius Chambers, professed the previous year. A second monk, George Wedderburn, on hearing the news, returned to Ratisbon and together they wrote to Baillie asking him to come and take charge. Baillie dutifully set off, making a detour to call at Würzburg, and he and Asloan then travelled to Ratisbon together. He says nothing about the attempt to give the Ratisbon abbey to other religious, and nothing of Asloan's being elected abbot of Ratisbon; one is therefore forced to consider the trustworthiness of his narrative. After a careful reading of Baillie's account of the events from 1633 on, one sees clearly that it is very autobiographical. He was undoubtedly a good and careful administrator, and there seems to be no reason to doubt the general veracity of his well-documented narrative, but it does tend to show Baillie himself in a very favourable light. His account of the two to three months spent by Asloan in Ratisbon in the winter of 1639-40 is a mere statement of his own part in getting Asloan to take on the administration of Ratisbon, and then of his own assumption of the administration when Asloan was compelled to return to Würzburg. One suspects, too, that the appeal for help was sent to Asloan and not to Baillie. Asloan brought two Würzburg monks with him to Ratisbon whereas Baillie had none to bring. Most cogent of all, it was Asloan and not Baillie who was postulated abbot by the monks, and unanimously too. When Asloan returned to Würzburg, Baillie was merely the delegate left behind by Asloan, who was the abbot elect of Ratisbon and soon to be confirmed in that office by the holy see.

The various letters quoted in detail show the evidence for what is omitted or misrepresented by Baillie. But even if the evidence already cited were not conclusive, we would know the true state of affairs from a letter written by Baillie himself to the archbishop of Mainz in May 1640.[14] In it he describes himself as taking the place in Ratisbon of the abbot of Würzburg, who is also abbot of Ratisbon but residing in Würzburg. The account he gives of his call to Ratisbon is much more humble than the one in his narrative; he says he was summoned by the Ratisbon monks and the abbot of Würzburg to the election of a new abbot of Ratisbon, and one reason for his now staying there is that it will help to pay the debts of his Erfurt abbey. Baillie was in no mood to aggrandise himself as he does in the narrative he wrote later. The Scots had been discussing ways and means of paying the Ratisbon debts, and Baillie had heard that some of them wanted to sell the Erfurt abbey. Nobody had said this openly to him but he suspected that they would obtain Cardinal Barberini's consent and send it to the archbishop of Mainz. Baillie was warning the latter and begging him not to agree. A month later the archbishop reassured Baillie over the matter and instructed his officials in Erfurt not to permit any such thing to take place. Baillie wrote triumphantly on the letter that this prevented and disappointed the presumptuous designs and plots of Boniface Strachan and others at Würzburg.[15]

A second drawback of Baillie's narrative is his mealy-mouthedness where Ratisbon ecclesiastics are concerned. He says nothing about the hostility they showed after Mayne's death, and he actually speaks of himself taking on the administration of the Ratisbon abbey, helped by a letter of recommendation from the excellent bishop Albert. This was the same Albrecht von Törring who had been responsible for Abbot Algeo's appointment and had tried repeatedly to gain control of the abbey. Baillie had had dealings with Ratisbon since 1623 and could not have been ignorant of all this. Not only that, but the same bishop was about to instigate, or at least to further, a second attempt to get rid of the Scots from Ratisbon altogether. The episode concerns the Würzburg abbey intimately, not only because Asloan was abbot of both Würzburg and Ratisbon but also because Würzburg figured largely in the scheme.

The new emperor Ferdinand III held a Diet in Ratisbon which began in July 1640 and lasted over a year, and while he was in Ratisbon he tried to replace the Scots with Spanish Discalced

Carmelites. These may have been the same religious in whose favour efforts had been made when Silvanus Mayne died. Ferdinand wrote to Urban VIII, asking for the Ratisbon community to be merged into that at Würzburg, so that the Carmelites could then be given the Ratisbon buildings. The pope replied courteously on 24th November and said that his nuncio would give a definite answer.[16]

The bishop of Ratisbon next addressed a long letter to Urban on 2nd December; it is extremely tedious to read but tells us most of what we know about the whole affair. The Discalced Carmelites had been in Ratisbon for five years, during which time vain efforts had been made to find a site for them, but none was available nor would the Lutheran magistrates allow any ground to be sold. The emperor wanted the personnel and revenues of St James's to be transferred to Würzburg, which would give the Carmelites a place in Ratisbon, and the bishop agreed with him. For one thing, there were only three Scots monks in Ratisbon, not enough for choir and other commitments, while there was a similar shortage in Würzburg and Erfurt; in fact the three abbeys together contained barely enough monks for one community. It would also be better for the Scots themselves to have one flourishing monastery. The monks do not know German and so cannot help their neighbours or look after their own property; their financial position is bad, their buildings are in disrepair; nor can other monasteries help them, being in a bad way themselves. The bishop does not like Benedictine abbeys, for they scorn episcopal admonitions and prefer the treacherous help afforded by Lutheran civil authorities. All this and a great deal of praise of the Carmelites fill the letter.[17] Baillie's narrative, however, mentions the emperor alone as responsible for the episode. Albert von Törring has been described as the great counter-reformation bishop of Ratisbon, under whose rule most of the lost territory in the diocese was regained,[18] and perhaps he judged that German Carmelites would further the counter-reformation more effectively than Scottish Benedictines. Nevertheless Baillie, whether from prudence or some other motive, concealed the bishop's part in the affair.

The Scots knew of the petitions addressed to Rome by the emperor and his ladies and the bishop, and on 11th December they sent a counter-appeal to the cardinal protector.[19] Asloan also addressed two letters to Ferdinand, the second of them, a most eloquent appeal, on 22nd December.[20] After nine months of effort and correspondence, with Urban and Barberini standing firm in support of the Scots, the emperor finally gave way.[21] The difficulty over finding a site at Ratisbon was evidently overcome, for at some point in 1641 Ferdinand laid a foundation stone for the Carmelite house.[22] The date 1641 is still to be seen over the outside door of the church.

The letters written by the Scots prove that Asloan was still abbot of Ratisbon. The letter to Barberini was signed Abbot and Community, without any individual names, which shows they had an abbot, who could only have been Asloan. Much more convincing is the record of the two letters from Asloan to the emperor, formerly preserved in the Würzburg diocesan archives and now destroyed. There is no mention of Würzburg from beginning to end, and the second letter is signed Abbot and Community of Ratisbon, again with no individual names. The Scot who copied it in 1877, Alexander Reid, described it as written by Asloan, and it was in the Würzburg diocesan archives; yet it was all about Ratisbon and was signed by the abbot of Ratisbon. The conclusion is inescapable that Audomarus Asloan was still abbot of Ratisbon.

The documents concerning Asloan's election and appointment at Ratisbon are conspicuous by their absence from the Ratisbon monastic archives, just as mention of the matter is absent from Baillie's narrative. It is possible, though hardly likely, that it was agreed between Asloan and Baillie to be discreet about the real situation and let it be thought that Baillie was just one more administrator like Hugh Wallace eight years before, who also was simultaneously abbot of Erfurt and administrator of Ratisbon. In this case we must not accuse Baillie of deliberately minimising Asloan's role in the struggle to save Ratisbon. But Baillie was not like Wallace. The nuncio in Vienna appointed Wallace because an election could not be held, and we have the document saying so. But in 1640 Asloan had just been appointed abbot by Rome, there is no record of his resignation, and no record of Baillie's appointment as administrator. Baillie was in fact, as he himself wrote to the archbishop of Mainz, Asloan's vicegerent or delegate.

Deliberately or not, Baillie was responsible for misleading the historians of the Ratisbon abbey. They used his narrative and accepted its veracity, and any documents concerning Asloan's election and appointment were not in the abbey archives and could not be used to correct his version. Audomarus John Asloan, abbot of Würzburg, was also abbot of Ratisbon, the only time this happened in the history of the two houses. He himself played it down; we do not find him at any time drawing attention to the fact. The Würzburg chronicler, however, copying from his tombstone, reveals the facts to some extent and speaks of Asloan snatching the Scottish abbeys from the jaws of the invaders, both at Würzburg and elsewhere. The invaders were not the Swedes but the Catholic emperor, the bishop of Ratisbon, the Discalced Carmelites; and perhaps, as we shall soon see, Continental and Irish Benedictines were included in the description.

Notes

[1] Cat. Abb; Brockie, *ad* Erfurt; Scholle, 40; Wz. SA, MRA, Stift 2613/K. 735, p. 139-40.

[2] Chronicon; Reid, f. 112r.

[3] Reid, f. 112r-113r; Wieland, 129.

[4] Haim, A 7r;Gropp, II, 302; Wz. SA, MRA, Stift 2613/K. 735, p. 139-40.

[5] For Audomarus and George Asloan, see *IR,* xxii, 47-50.

[6] Brockie, *ad* Ratisbon, 1639.

[7] His account of these years is in Baillie, f. 40r-42r.

[8] BM, MS 15,970, f. 45-46.

[9] SCA, Rat. C 9, 15.

[10] *Mon. Germ. Hist. Necrologia,* IV, 340.

[11] Reid, f. 113r-116r; Reg. BOA, St. Jakob, Fasz. 31.

[12] Wieland, 130.

[13] Erf. Tent.

[14] Wz. SA, MRA, Lade 626, H. 1775, no. 1.

[15] ibid., nos. 2, 3; Reg. BOA, Sch., Akten, 41.

[16] VA, Epist. ad Principes, vol. 52, no. 268; Schedario Garampi, vol. 74, f. 191v.

[17] VA, Pio 213, f. 127r-132v.

[18] J. Staber, *Kirchengeschichte des Bistums Regensburg* (1966), 130 ff.

[19] Blair, f. 144r-145r.

[20] Reid, f. 116rv.

[21] Baillie, f. 42r.

[22] Gumpelzhaimer, 1274.

CHAPTER 8

The aftermath of war
1642—59

The cost of the Thirty Years War in Germany in terms of devastation and human misery was almost incalculable. Würzburg suffered less than many other places, yet the three years' occupation was sufficient to wreck most of what Abbot Ogilvie had built up. Steady income from possessions or investments has always been a necessity for any religious community not earning its keep by salaries, honoraria, school fees, or other such ways. All three Scottish abbeys were in this position and suffered chronically from shortage of means; this directly affected the number of their personnel, with the result that there was usually a direct relationship between the administrative ability of the abbot in the temporal sphere and the quality of the monastic observance. In time of war or other calamities the income of a monastery could be so reduced as to make the upkeep of a community impossible. The number of monks in Franconian monasteries was reduced drastically by the wars, and both the number and quality of novices offering themselves for admission was far below normal. Some indication of the state of affairs is given by the fact that it was not until 1642 that a common table, always considered one of the first essentials of monastic life, was restored at the abbey of St Stephen's, while the great abbey of Schwarzach had only seven monks in 1646.[1]

We have a description of the miserable state of the three Scots monasteries at this time, from the pen of Fr Boniface Strachan. Writing from Vienna on 20th November 1641, he gave an account of the Scotic monasteries in Germany, including the three the Scots still had.[2] He described graphically the difficulties at Ratisbon and the attempt of the emperor to dislodge the monks during the recent Diet, and said its revenues could support only one or two monks. The income at Erfurt could hardly support even one monk, while at Würzburg the revenues were very small, being diminished by the continuous wars. The history of the Scottish abbeys in the following years should be seen against this background of severe financial hardships.

There are indications of what Strachan was doing in Vienna. The Scots, we know, made a further attempt to recover the Vienna abbey in 1641 when its abbot died.[3] The date of his death was 27th November,[4] just one week after Strachan wrote his account; if Strachan used the old-style date because he was writing to Scotland, the abbot had died three days before. There can be no doubt that Strachan was trying to recover the monastery and he wrote that the Scots could gain possession easily but had not the means to support enough monks for their own needs, let alone train more to man other monasteries.

One cannot help being struck by the insecurity of so many religious houses in the German lands in the seventeenth century. Quite apart from the disputes between Catholics and Protestants as well as between Jesuits and Benedictines for the possession of old monasteries, there were attempts by other new religious orders to obtain religious houses for themselves (for example, the efforts to oust the Scots in Ratisbon) and attempts by Benedictines to gain or regain possession of other Benedictine monasteries. The Scots periodically tried to recover the Vienna abbey, which was Benedictine, and the Ratisbon Scots were shortly to have other Benedictines making such an attempt against them. Basically the reason was economic and caused by differences of opinion on the best way to wage the counter-reformation with the means at the Catholics' disposal. The insecurity of tenure may have been healthy in so much as it stimulated religious orders to safeguard themselves by keeping up numbers, but it is very unlike the cut and dried, legally defined situation in more modern times.

Throughout the seventeenth century in Germany the monasteries were making attempts to form themselves into groups professing the same observance, known as congregations, or to extend their congregation to include neighbouring monasteries that were not yet committed. Such, for instance, was the Bavarian Congregation, formed after a century of intermittent effort in 1684. Where the bishop retained a tight hold on all the monasteries in his diocese, imposed common constitutions on them and so on, the result was something approaching a diocesan congregation, though it was never so entitled; this was the case in Würzburg and some other dioceses. There was also the Bursfeld Union, a revival of the congregation that raised the level of German monasticism in the late fifteenth century. It was unique in that it aimed to cover the whole of Germany. It had remarkable success but failed in its ultimate object because of the refusal of the strong bishops to relinquish control of monasteries in their own diocese.

This bare outline is essential for the understanding of the negotiations in which Asloan was involved.[5] In April 1642, when the abbot who was president of the Bursfeld Congregation died, the abbots of Würzburg and Bamberg dioceses were cited to attend the chapter which would elect his successor.[6] The abbot of St Stephen's replied that the invitation could not be accepted as they were no longer in the Bursfeld Union, though he personally would like to be. The bishop was then requested to give his abbots leave to attend, but he ignored the letter. The person who first wrote on behalf of the Bursfeld Congregation was Leonard Colchon,[7] abbot of Seligenstadt on the Main not far upstream from Frankfurt. He was now elected as the new president in May 1642, a recognition of his zeal and labours for the Congregation, and at once he took up the matter of the Franconian abbeys with vigour.

On 10th June he wrote a pressing appeal to the bishop to allow the Bursfeld Congregation to exact chapter attendance, obedience, submission to visitations, and the rest, from the abbots in his two dioceses in the same way as former bishops had done. With the letter he enclosed a copy of the 1514 document which united St James's in Würzburg in its brief German monastic period to the Bursfeld Congregation. This was the basis of Colchon's appeal: that the Franconian monasteries had once been joined to the Bursfeld Congregation and therefore still belonged to it by right. He was continuing his successor's policy of recovering monasteries formerly in the congregation and making good the losses it had suffered. A week later he sent a monk to Würzburg to conduct negotiations, but the only result was a letter from the ecclesiastical counsellors of Würzburg saying that the matter needed careful consideration.

Colchon's emissary to Würzburg had been kindly received by Abbot Asloan, and to the latter Colchon now turned for help in furthering his plans. Asloan was certainly a good man to use as an intermediary and advocate, for he seems to have inspired the confidence of the bishops of Würzburg with whom he had dealings. He could not do as requested at once, since the unexpected arrival of Alexander Baillie from Ratisbon compelled him to make some business trip, but on his return to Würzburg towards the end of July he spoke with the bishop. The latter gave his consent to Colchon's petition and promised to persuade his counsellors to agree.

A few days later, on 30th July 1642, Bishop Francis died, to be succeeded by John Philip von Schönborn on 16th August. Within a fortnight Colchon had addressed an appeal to John Philip to ratify his predecessor's decision and had sent it to Asloan to deliver in person. Asloan waited until 18th September for a suitable opportunity to approach the new bishop, who a few days later sent a very encouraging reply to Colchon, saying that he would put the matter to his chapter and expected them to agree. No further progress was made, however, and the following April the Bursfeld chapter appealed once more to the bishop. Once again Asloan was asked to help. This produced no results, and yet another appeal was made in May 1644. Here, as far as we know, the matter ended. Perhaps the new bishop was more firmly in the saddle and was not prepared to relinquish control of the abbeys in his diocese, or the diocesan chapter may not have proved as co-operative as the bishop had expected.

Unfortunately we have only Asloan's side of the correspondence for the autumn of 1642. From the beginning Colchon had made flattering or diplomatic references to the Scottish abbot's zeal for the Bursfeld Union and the fact that St James's belonged to it by right. Asloan, when telling Colchon of his successful interview with the new bishop, informed him that St James's had in the meantime been united to the Scottish Congregation by the holy see, which would surely strengthen the union among the Scots rather than permit it to be weakened. It seems a fairly plain hint that he would appeal to Rome against any attempt to incorporate the Scots abbey into the Bursfeld Congregation. Rather tactlessly and inconsistently he added that Colchon could show his presidency by giving the poor Scots some financial help. The evidently angry rejoinder from Colchon was met with a respectful and friendly assurance of Asloan's high esteem for the Bursfeld Union, for which he had conducted negotiations so successfully. Nevertheless Asloan again made his point clear: he could not enter the Bursfeld Congregation without infringing the rights of the Scottish Congregation and the privileges granted to it by Rome.

Colchon was not to be deflected from his viewpoint. His appeal of April 1643 to the bishop mentioned St James's by name, and four years later, when sending word to the abbot of Schwarzach of spiritual favours received from the holy see, he asked him to pass on the information to other houses of the Bursfeld Union, including St James's. The Scots, however, were less likely to be won over than at almost any other period of their history. After the election of Asloan to the Ratisbon abbacy they were in exceptionally close union, and it was about this time that they decided to form, or re-form, a Scottish Congregation. The only evidence for this consists of a draft petition made out to Urban VIII and mentioning the encouragement to unite given to the Scots monks by his nephew, Francesco Barberini.[8] The date is almost certainly after 1640, when the Ratisbon abbey was under sustained attack, and must be before July 1644, when Urban died. But whatever the exact date, Asloan's references to a Scottish Congregation in his letters to Colchon show what was in his mind at the time.

We do not know what happened to these appeals. All we do know is that no Scottish Congregation was formed, which is not surprising when we consider that there were almost certainly not a dozen Scots monks in all. A number of recruits came from the Rome and Douai colleges during these years but not many stayed long; some were clearly unsettled in their clerical career. A better subject was Maurus Dixon, who was professed at Würzburg about 1639 and matriculated two years later. At some point, too, George Asloan entered the monastery. Lack of monks does not seem to have been a cause of anxiety at this period, but lack of income must have limited the size of the resident community quite as effectively as any lack of applicants. This presumably is why Abbot Asloan was able to spare men to work elsewhere. At any rate, Boniface Strachan obtained leave from Rome to assist the Spanish ambassador in Venice from 1644 to 1646;[9] there is no record that he ever returned to Würzburg. The abbey of Schwarzach was desperately in need of men, as is clear from the correspondence of its abbots with Colchon. Fr Benedict, a Würzburg Scot, is said to have been induced by Colchon to go to Schwarzach at some date before 1646;[10] although we do not know who this was, and it seems unlikely to have been Abbot Asloan's brother, it is not impossible. When a new abbot came to Schwarzach in 1646, Fr James Brown became his subprior for three years.[11] This is partial corroboration of the Scottish chronicler's ambiguous statement that Brown held the offices of prior and novice-master in the monasteries of Fulda, Schwarzach and St Stephen's.

The war was still going on, and the armies were still moving up and down the land, commandeering and plundering as they went. Baillie notes how this affected the security and income of the Ratisbon abbey, as well as how the finances steadily improved under his own administration. By 1646, he says, it was clear that the abbey could be preserved, and he himself was postulated abbot on 18th January of that year.[12] There is of course no mention of Asloan, but we can presume that the latter had sent his resignation of the Ratisbon abbacy direct to the holy see. Macarius Chambers, the Ratisbon prior, was then elected abbot of Erfurt on 12th March.[13] Before Chambers' election was confirmed, Asloan and Baillie agreed on joint action to find novices. Chambers and Fr Maurus Dixon were sent to Paris in mid-June and returned in September with two young Scots, David Keith and John Abercromby. Unfortunately for Baillie, the composite warring armies were in Bavaria, and the Ratisbon clergy were sorely harassed; Chambers and the two youngsters had to go to Würzburg, where Keith and Abercromby took the habit.[14]

It was probably when Chambers passed through Würzburg on

his way to Paris that Bishop John Philip supplied him with a commendatory letter to his new ordinary, the archbishop of Mainz, evidently at Asloan's request.[15] The following year, incidentally, John Philip was himself to become archbishop and elector of Mainz while retaining the see of Würzburg. He was thus one of the most important men in the Empire. Asloan, who had his confidence, was a man of some standing in Würzburg and in 1646 was elected rector of the university.[16] It was no doubt because of Asloan that a few years later, when the elector Palatine was visiting John Philip at Würzburg, the two electors came down from the fortress to St James's, where they stayed for several hours taking wine and conversing with the Scots. The visitor graciously said that he was a Scot as his mother was a daughter of James VI.[17] The monks might not have been so pleased had they known that this union was to lead to the Hanoverian succession in Britain, for the elector's sister's son was George I.

The year 1646 saw the three Scots abbeys reverting to normal government. Asloan, Baillie and Chambers were abbots of Würzburg, Ratisbon and Erfurt respectively, elected by the usual electoral bodies and each residing in his monastery. The year 1648 saw peace restored to an exhausted Germany. But although things were returning to normal, references to matters other than routine administration of finance and property at Würzburg in the dozen years after 1646 are scarce in the extreme. Baillie's narrative hardly mentions Würzburg. Abbot Colchon, president of the Bursfeld Congregation, entrusted Chambers at Erfurt with some business and arranged for an unsettled German monk to stay with the Scots at Ratisbon, but had no further dealings with Asloan until March 1651 when Fr James Brown and Bro Placid Keith spent a few days at Seligenstadt and discussed some matter with Colchon, who advised them that they were unlikely to obtain what they were seeking in the Bursfeld Congregation. They then proceeded on their way towards the monasteries of the Lorraine Congregation. The only clue to the nature of their business is that Colchon qualified it with the word *pius* and wished them well in the furtherance of the Benedictine order, which he said Brown evidently had at heart.[18] At this time, too, Asloan wanted Rome to renew the mission faculties granted to Abbot Ogilvie twenty years before, for he had monks suited for missionary work. The previous summer he had asked the prince-bishop to act as mediator in order to obtain the renewal more quickly.[19]

In Ratisbon meanwhile the Scots were about to be involved in one of the strangest and perhaps most dangerous episodes in their whole history. Intimately connected with it was a man who must surely rank as one of the most extraordinary characters of the century. Juan Caramuel y Lobkowitz, usually known as Caramuel, was born at Madrid in 1606 of international parentage. As a boy he was phenomenally precocious, taking a doctorate in philosophy at the age of fifteen. He became a Cistercian monk in Spain, and in 1634 the general chapter of his order, hoping because of Charles I's milder policy towards Catholics to restore the ancient monasteries, made him abbot of Melrose and vicar-general for England, Scotland and Ireland. Almost certainly he did not cross the Channel. Instead he went to the Netherlands, where he had a meteoric career in practically every profession except that of monk. In 1645 he became the Spanish envoy to the emperor's court, and three years later defended Prague against the Swedes, putting himself at the head of a corps of voluntaries and being subsequently decorated for bravery. He held various ecclesiastical offices at this period: abbot of the Benedictine monastery of Emaus in Prague (known also as Montserrat after the famous Catalonian abbey, since the emperor had refounded it with Spanish monks), superior general of the Benedictines in Vienna, vicar-general of the archbishop of Prague. He was called to Rome in 1655, became bishop of Campagna and then of Vigevano, where he died in 1682.

Intellectually he combined unparalleled brilliance and superficiality. He knew twenty-four languages and produced inventions in quite unrelated crafts and disciplines. The most conservative estimate of his works puts them at more than seventy; he even instituted a printing press to publish them. They are on all subjects and mixtures of subjects, for instance on solving moral questions by mathematical rules. Unfortunately almost everything he wrote is useless. Ironically, he is known to posterity, and to theologians in particular, because of the notoriety his accommodating views on moral questions gained for him: his contemporary, Pascal, likewise a precocious genius but of more solid achievements, attacked him, and with reason, in his *Lettres Provinciales*, while St Alphonsus Liguori, who is accepted as one of the greatest of moral theologians, called him *princeps laxistarum*. The character of this extraordinary man, who held such diverse ecclesiastical and secular offices in so many countries, and whose mind wandered over all fields of human knowledge, was probably the root cause of the trouble involving him and the Ratisbon Scots.

Caramuel was in Vienna and Prague from 1645 to 1655, and for most of this time he had dealings with Abbot Baillie in Ratisbon. Baillie, as his finances improved, became anxious to obtain the monks whom he could now support. We have seen how his effort to find novices in Paris helped Würzburg and not his own abbey. His anxiety to have more monks may not have been the initial cause of his relations with Caramuel but it was certainly the reason for their continuance. In November 1647 Caramuel told Baillie that he could not spare his prior in Vienna, an Irishman called Fr Columbanus Duffy, unless the move entailed promotion to a higher dignity than that of prior. Two months later he was offering to send Duffy to Ratisbon on condition that he was made Baillie's coadjutor as abbot. In early 1649 he sent him to Ratisbon for a holiday, then wrote to Baillie telling him to keep Duffy as prior and offering to send another Irishman to be a novice; he also warned Baillie of the dangers of having insufficient monks, as the Spanish Carmelites and the Servites wanted to have the Scots' buildings. This was in March 1649; the following August there had evidently been trouble of some sort over Duffy sending two novices to Vienna, and since Baillie had still said nothing about making him his coadjutor, Caramuel asked for his return.

There the matter rested for two or three years. Asloan at Würzburg was speaking in 1650 of monks being available for mission work in Scotland, and in the following year two Würzburg monks were touring monasteries of the Bursfeld and Lorraine congregations. Certainly Würzburg did not seem short of Scottish monks. In 1651 Baillie approached the English Congregation for help. The president was Fr Placid Gascoigne, who that year was also elected abbot of Lamspring near Hanover. This was an ancient Benedictine nunnery, handed over by the Bursfeld Congregation to the English monks in 1643, and was unique among English monasteries in having, like the Scots, abbots elected for life instead of priors for a period of four years as the English constitutions laid down. It was the only English monastery in Germany and in its system of government it resembled the Scots monasteries in Germany rather than the other English houses. Baillie wanted some form of union with the English, his chief motive being to get a few of their monks and novices. Gascoigne replied favourably, promising to put the matter to his congregation and send someone to Ratisbon to obtain further information. Nothing more was done, however, so Baillie then had to try some other means.[20]

In March 1652 we get one of the rare glimpses of the internal affairs of the Würzburg abbey, with Baillie at Ratisbon also coming into the picture. Abbot Asloan sent a most troubled letter to Cardinal Barberini in Rome appealing to the holy see and asking for a fair hearing.[21] It had been his aim since becoming abbot, he said, to preserve monastic observance and help the mission in Britain; and accordingly he had doubled the number of monks and also brought young men to Würzburg to enter the house. But the aspirants had left, and certain malevolent monks had been stirring up trouble against him. Having obtained no satisfaction from the bishop, these were now trying to put their case in Rome, while

Abbot Baillie was encouraging them and claiming that as abbot of Ratisbon he had the right of visitation in the other Scots monasteries. Asloan pointed out that this right had long since been taken over by the bishops of Würzburg, and in fact it had not been used by the Ratisbon abbot since the refounding of the abbey in 1595. We know precisely nothing about what the complaints, real or invented, of his dissatisfied monks actually were, and almost certainly the matter did not go much further, for it figures neither in Barberini's correspondence nor in Baillie's narrative. A few months later Cardinal Fabio Chigi, the secretary of state in Rome, was assuring Asloan of his good will and patronage.[22] He had known Asloan when he was nuncio in Cologne, and he was shortly to be Pope Alexander VII. Incidentally, it was he who summoned Caramuel to Rome on becoming pope, having known him too in his Cologne days.

At this very time Baillie in Ratisbon was at last giving way under the strain and falling in with Caramuel's designs. On 2nd June 1652 he wrote to Duffy, now prior in Prague, outlining his difficulties. He had only three priests and one laybrother; Abbot Chambers had been tried as a possible coadjutor and found wanting, so Baillie had sent him back to Erfurt. Baillie himself had been very ill and this was his grand climacteric, that is, he was in his sixty-third year (a particularly critical time, it was formerly believed, of a man's life). Wishing to have things settled before he died, Baillie promised to appoint the Irishman coadjutor at once, but nobody was to know except Caramuel and the nuncio. There is no mention of what was later declared to be Baillie's main reason for appointing Duffy, namely, the summoning of an imperial Diet to be held in Ratisbon.

The story of what ensued can be put together from Baillie's narrative and the *Informatio Juris et Facti* compiled during the resulting legal process.[23] When it became known that the Diet was to meet in Ratisbon, the bishop ordered that each religious house should have sufficient men in residence to meet the extra needs. Baillie, who was by now keeping his chronicle partly in English, wrote that, foreseeing 'a great concurss of people in our Kirk in tyme of parlament', he was compelled to ask Caramuel for the loan of some Irish fathers. He had wanted to get his extra men from Würzburg but had been frustrated 'be them of Wurtzburg disagreaing amang themselves at such an importune tyme'. With belated tact he crossed this out (or perhaps someone else did) but left it quite legible. This may be a reference to the trouble which had made Asloan write to Barberini, or it may even be the reason why Asloan complained of Baillie. The *Informatio* merely says that Baillie knew the abbot of Würzburg could only with difficulty spare any men.

Caramuel, having already some years before tried to get Fr Columbanus Duffy made Baillie's coadjutor, and having in vain suggested some form of union with the three Scottish abbeys, now sent Duffy and another Irishman on the understanding that Duffy was to be nominated coadjutor abbot. On 18th November 1652 Baillie appointed Duffy his coadjutor for the grave reasons, as he put it, which Caramuel had explained to the emperor. The pact was to be kept secret; even Baillie's community did not know of it. It was of course quite invalid, and Baillie knew it was. Scottish abbots were elected, as the *Informatio* said, from and by the monks of the three Scots abbeys. Duffy and Caramuel did not keep the secret, and naturally there was an outcry when the news leaked out. Baillie, who by this time was expecting some Scottish monks from Würzburg, wished to send the two Irishmen away, whereupon Caramuel arrived and created the trouble that only a man of his gifts and vitality could. The bishop now became interested as he himself claimed to have authority where abbatial elections were concerned.

The matter was apparently not yet public on 3rd February 1653, when Asloan sent a most cordial letter to Abbot Chambers in Erfurt, promising him some good Franconian wine but not mentioning Ratisbon affairs.[24] On 3rd April, however, Baillie wrote to the bishop admitting he had agreed to Caramuel's plan, and on the 27th he underwent a judicial interrogation. From this the interesting fact emerges that Baillie's own election and confirmation in 1646 had been carried through by the bishop's authority in spite of the abbey's exempt status. The bishop thus had a vested interest in proving the pact with Caramuel and Duffy to be invalid. With bishop and abbot united, if for different reasons, in opposing the Irishman's coadjutorship, the struggle was gradually won. The emperor and the nuncio decided not to support the Irishman, and the Roman authorities then came to the same decision. One cannot help feeling that Baillie was extremely lucky to be supported by the bishop and to be described in his report to Rome as a gifted but simple man deluded by the wily Caramuel and better fitted to rule his abbey himself than Duffy would ever be. In fact, when one considers that Baillie offered Duffy the coadjutorship in June 1652, a full year before the Diet actually opened, the suspicion remains that the Diet merely provided a handy excuse for his impulsive action.

The Scots had won the first round but now, as Baillie put it, 'the Irish left not off but begann to seek to be taken on among us as Scottsmen'. In other words, the Irish monks were claiming that they were the rightful owners, since the *Scoti* who founded the abbey were Irish. This time the proceedings were not extraordinary but consisted of an Irish appeal to Rome and the Scots' rebuttal of their claim; probably Duffy would have gone about things in this way before if Caramuel had not directed the course of events. In fact, approach to higher authority to regain former possessions characterised Irish Benedictine activity at this time, and the Ratisbon episode cannot be viewed in isolation. In 1646 the general of the Benedictines in Spain wrote to the nuncio in Ireland asking that six Irish Benedictines, including Columbanus Duffy, should be allowed to recover former monasteries in Ireland and become abbots.[25] Two years later an appointment was made to the priory of Roscarbery, which (incredible as it may seem) was referred to as a dependency of St James's in Würzburg.[26]

The text of the Irish supplication and the Scottish reply to it have survived in a small volume written by a later Ratisbon abbot, Placid Fleming.[27] The Irish said there were only ten monks in all, including the aged and infirm, in the three Scots abbeys; they wanted half the number of places, so that Scots and Irish would be equally represented. Their appeal concerned all the Scotic monasteries, and Ratisbon in particular; the Scottish reply is by Asloan, the Würzburg abbot, who answered the sixteen questions framed by the Irish and then asked nine in return. In some way or other the Irish monks had had access to the cartulary kept in the Würzburg abbey, for they cited documents from it with the correct folio.[28]

Danger also threatened from the bishop of Ratisbon. Baillie wrote just before Christmas 1653 to Barberini about the bishop's plan to have a seminary for religious in the Scots abbey and saying that the abbots of Würzburg and Erfurt joined with him in begging Barberini to prevent it. The bishop flatly denied that there was any truth in the story and promised to protect the Scots. The Irish claim had been referred from Rome to him, and in May 1654 he instituted an enquiry. Chambers in Erfurt was asked to attend but excused himself; perhaps Asloan was asked too, for he supplied information to support the Scots' case and also communicated with the nuncio. The English monks played some part on the fringe of the affair. Abbot Gascoigne of Lamspring, no longer president of the English Congregation, journeyed from Ratisbon to Würzburg and delivered a letter from the bishop to Asloan. This association of the two abbots is most significant in view of the union between the Scots of Würzburg and the English Benedictine Congregation which was to be effected a few years later.

Columbanus Duffy was calling himself prior of St John's in Waterford; he was not the only Irishman at this period who held the title, for there is recorded a papal bull conferring it on another Irish Benedictine.[29] The Scots wanted to know who had appointed Duffy as that house was subject to the Benedictines of Bath Cathedral, which as a point of mediaeval history seems to be factually accurate. Duffy claimed too that the Irish monks were expelled from the *Schottenklöster* under Elizabeth, a claim which Baillie's monks found easy to refute. But doubtless it was not because of their historical accuracy that the Scots won their case, but through the support of the bishop and Barberini.

The status of the three Scots abbeys changed again in 1655. Alexander Baillie, the Würzburg monk who more than anyone had controlled the destinies of the Ratisbon abbey since the Swedish invasion, died on 7th April 1655. Chambers, a monk of Ratisbon, was elected as his successor but retained the Erfurt abbacy by dispensation of the archbishop of Mainz.[30] Erfurt was never again to have an abbot of its own; for a time the Ratisbon abbots were simultaneously abbots of Erfurt, but eventually Erfurt lost its abbatial status and merely had priors appointed by its superior, the Ratisbon abbot. Chambers had not pleased Baillie when the latter had considered him as a possible coadjutor; he was not satisfactory as Baillie's successor either.

For most of the decade 1650-60 there is an almost complete dearth of information about the Würzburg abbey. There are a few references to individual monks: Maurus Dixon, prior in 1653,[31] Placid Keith matriculating in 1654, Fr Benedict Asloan dying in 1656. When the curtain lifts again in 1660-61 we find that the union with the English Congregation had just been ratified and that, of the six resident monks, two were very recently professed and two belonged to English monasteries. In other words, shortly before Asloan's death his community had apparently dwindled down to almost nothing.

The monastic chronicler, writing about thirty years after Asloan's death, praises him unreservedly. Asloan, he says, was a kind man, patient and easy to get on with, loved by all and in particular by Bishop John Philip, elector of Mainz. He built a guest-house, had two altars put in the church and made out new account books. His tombstone says that after ruling for twenty-three years he left his abbey in a flourishing state. There is only one reason for doubting the objectivity of the praise bestowed on him, and that is the small size of the community he left behind him. We can ignore the comment of the chronicler, who adverted to this and blamed Cromwell's persecution. Quite apart from the fact that persecution would drive recusants overseas rather than keep them at home, the numbers of students at the Scots colleges do not seem to have fallen off. The drop in numbers at Würzburg makes one wonder what significance is to be attributed to hints of trouble in the monastery or to references to Würzburg monks engaged outside their

95

monastery. Was there some serious flaw in Asloan's government?

What little evidence there is points in the abbot's favour. When a community numbers half a dozen, the death of two members makes a difference: Fr Benedict Asloan died in 1656, and Fr James Brown in March 1658.[32] The drastic shortage in numbers, as far as one can judge, was a quite recent development, since Asloan had been applying for mission faculties in 1650 and had lent monks to Ratisbon during the Diet four years later. In the autumn of 1658 there occurred a most illuminating incident. Two young men, William Baillie and a former Presbyterian minister, Alexander Gordon, arrived from Rome to enter the novitiate at Würzburg. Asloan accepted Baillie willingly but, as he was expecting four youths who had already arrived at Amsterdam on their way from Scotland, he directed Gordon to Ratisbon. There Abbot Chambers consoled the slighted Gordon and gave him the monastic habit. Asloan had the last laugh, however. Gordon soon left and thereafter admitted freely that his only purpose had been to spy on Catholic institutions.[33] The episode not only shows that Asloan's judgement was far sounder than Chambers' but also that Asloan took steps to remedy the lack of monks. He had sent Maurus Dixon to Scotland for the purpose,[34] the first instance we have of such a commission. He also took positive action in his last year of office to stabilise the condition of his monastery and provide a successor for himself, as we shall see on consideration of the union with the English monks.

A portrait of Abbot Asloan, painted when he was in his forties, has survived.[35] The subject has a head and hands large in proportion to his body. His moustache and little tuft of a beard are black although his hair is receding. He is certainly not handsome. He has a long nose, thick lips and a large jowl but the wide-open eyes have a calm and intelligent expression. Unless the painter was lacking in the basic skills, the abbot's body was inclined to be dwarf-like but he was a person to be reckoned with. This rather ugly little man, who could win the affection of his monks and of the patrician prince-bishop, had preserved a testimonial from his fellow missioners to his good work while on the mission.[36] His letters and his actions, little though we know of either, give the impression of competence. Colchon, the president of the Bursfeld Union, said he would have been pleased if Asloan, who was so good at carrying burdens, had been elected in his place.[37] Allowing for the amenities of letter-writing, for this was in a letter to Asloan himself, it is not likely to be too far-fetched. After all, Colchon had chosen the Scot as his agent in a most important negotiation, and the event showed his choice to have been wise.

The only evidence in his disfavour is the trouble with his monks in 1652, and this is far outweighed by the testimonies in his favour. The Schwarzach chronicle records the great help rendered by Asloan to their abbot,[38] while a Scots Jesuit who visited Würzburg in 1652 wrote that Abbot Asloan was 'ane brave man and mickle esteemed'.[39] Michael Haim, a Würzburg cleric who wrote a book on Macarius, praised Asloan highly in the dedicatory epistle. On balance we must conclude that Audomarus John Asloan filled the office of abbot very competently in exceptionally troubled times.

Notes

[1] Gropp, II, 168, 175; Wolff, 304.

[2] NLS, Adv. 17.1.9, f. 225-28.

[3] Indiculus, f. 45rv; Chronologia, 94-95.

[4] Lindner, 15.

[5] Darm. SA, V.B.3, Konv. 101, Fasz. 6, f. 1-18; Colchon, f. 64v, 67v, 69r, 74v, 98r, 100v, 34v, 107v, 301r.

[6] Text in Gropp, II, 168-69 n.

[7] For him see *Neue Deutsche Biographie*, III (Berlin, 1956), 318; Volk, 367.

[8] Blair, f. 131r-142r.

[9] Giblin, 55.

[10] Volk, 381.

[11] Fel. Red., 300, 304.

[12] Baillie, f. 40r; Cat. Abb.

[13] Baillie, f. 56; Wz. SA, MRA, Stift 2613/K.735, p. 141-48.

[14] Baillie, f. 57r.

[15] Wz. SA, MRA, Stift 2613/K.735, p. 149-52.

[16] See Appendix B.

[17] Indiculus, f. 25rv.

[18] Colchon, f. 321r, 329r, 368r, 367r, 612r.

[19] KJP, nr. 517/1.

[20] Reg. BOA, St. Jakob, Fasz. 32.

[21] VL, Barb. Lat. 8627, f. 48.

[22] KJP, nr. 2569.

[23] Baillie, f. 74v-79v; SCA, Rat. C 9, 16; Reg. BOA, St. Jakob, Fasz. 32.

[24] Reg. BOA, Sch., Akten, 43.

[25] *Commentarius Rinuccinianus* (Dublin, 1932-49), II, 487.

[26] *Collectanea Hibernica*, ii (1959), 49.

[27] NLS, Adv. 29.7.1; additional documentation in VL, Barb. Lat. 8627, f. 49, 56; Reg. BOA, St. Jakob, Fasz. 32; SCA, Rat. C 9, 18; Baillie, f. 79v-80r; APF, SOCG, 297, f. 245, 298, 300, 396.

[28] NLS, Adv. 29.7.1, f. 20r, 21v.

[29] *Archivium Hibernicum*, xv (1950), 5-8.

[30] Ratisbon, Library of St. James's, Wassenberg's Ratisbona Religiosa, f. 109v.

[31] SCA, Rat. C 9, 16.

[32] VL, MS Vat. Lat. 10,100, f. 7v.

[33] *Colleges*, 116; *Blairs Papers*, 90-91.

[34] Haim, A 7v.

[35] Reproduced in T. A. Fischer, *The Scots in Eastern and Western Prussia* (Edinburgh, 1903), opp. p. 234.

[36] KJP, nr. 517/1.

[37] Colchon, f. 74v.

[38] Fel. Red., 333.

[39] *Blairs Papers*, 151.

CHAPTER 9

Restoration at Würzburg
1660—79

The year 1660 forms a natural division in the history of both the Roman Catholic mission to Scotland and of the Scots abbey in Würzburg. In the case of the former the reason is the Restoration of Charles II, an event which had little direct influence on the Würzburg Scots. What gives the year its significance in their history is the combination of several factors. Before his long rule came to an end, Abbot Asloan made an agreement with the English monks to provide the Scots with help, should it be needed, and also an outlet for their missionary zeal. The help was not needed for long; the community began to grow and aspirants continued to enter the monastery. From this date extracts from the visitation records have been preserved, so that we have a reasonably accurate picture of the community from now on. Even if the agreement with the English Congregation was not of sufficient importance in itself to make the year an outstanding one, 1660 nevertheless marks the beginning of a new period as regards our knowledge of the Würzburg abbey.

The documents of the agreement between the Scots of Würzburg and the English Benedictine Congregation[1] consist of twelve Articles of Union signed by the Scots and followed by approbations signed by various English officials. The Articles themselves are written in the first person, and one paragraph concerns a purely Scottish affair. Evidently the Scottish monks drew up the Articles; an approbation was then added and signed by Abbot Gascoigne at Lamspring on 7th September 1660; then they were taken to Würzburg and signed on 15th October, five weeks later, by Asloan and two of his monks. Gascoigne signed in his capacity of Procurator General of his congregation in Germany, appointed with full powers by the general chapter of 1653. It seems clear that the chapter had deputed him, the only abbot in the congregation and the superior of the only English house in Germany, to undertake negotiations with the Scots. The request emanating from Ratisbon in 1651 for some form of union had thus not been forgotten, as Abbot Baillie thought, but had been referred to the next general chapter; or perhaps Abbot Asloan of Würzburg had also requested something similar. Certainly it gives added significance to Gascoigne's visit to Würzburg in 1654. A year after the two parties to the agreement signed, the Articles were referred for confirmation to the English general chapter held at Douai. Six monks deputed by chapter to consider the matter declared themselves in favour of it on 1st September 1661. Two days later, when the Articles had been read in a plenary session of the chapter and formally approved, the president general and the secretary of chapter signed an official declaration to this effect and added the great seal of the congregation.

There is a marked difference between these Articles of Union and the agreement made by Scottish and English monks in 1623. Both agreements have the same mission arrangement: any Scot sent by his abbot to the mission will have those privileges and faculties which English monks have, and will be subject to English authority for the duration of his missionary work. But here the likeness ends, for whereas the earlier agreement contained merely a general affirmation of confraternity and spiritual union, the new pact was a thorough-going and comprehensive affair providing for 'union and incorporation' and dealt with fundamental points. Some of the Articles legislate for what is to happen when monks live in a monastery of the other nation: payment of travelling expenses is to be arranged between the superiors of the respective houses; monks are to wear the habit and follow the customs of the monastery where they are residing at the time; they have the same voting rights as other monks in the monastery where they reside.

There is an important limitation, however, to the free exercise of voting rights: only a Scot is to be abbot of Würzburg, and only an English monk is to be superior in an English monastery. To this article some copies of the Articles add a clause declaring one of the signatories, Fr Maurus Dixon, to be elected coadjutor abbot to Asloan with right of succession. The insistence on a Scot 'always and infallibly' being abbot of Würzburg is considerably weakened by the limiting clause 'provided he is suitable' found in some copies, and the infallibility is further called in question by an article requiring any English monk appointed abbot of Würzburg to see that Scottish novices are brought into the house.

Other articles deal with the facilities and organisation of the English Congregation that were lacking to the Scots. The latter are to be free to attend the English general chapter or not. The financial levies laid from time to time on the English houses are not to be obligatory for the Scots, who will instead use their discretion as to whether they contribute or not. If the English procurator in Rome or elsewhere transacts business for the Scots, he is to have expenses refunded as well as receiving a fee for his services.

The jurisdiction and rights of the bishop of Würzburg are mentioned several times, and the subjection of the Scots to his authority stands out clearly. His approval, as well as that of the holy see, has been necessary for the union; he has power to remove abbots for grave canonical reasons; the election of Maurus Dixon needs his consent. In fact this subjection to the bishop prevents any more thorough assimilation of the Scots to the English Congregation; because of it they are not to be bound by the English statutes in the same way as the English monasteries are. The Scots are, however, willing to accept an unofficial visitation by the English president general once every four years (his term of office), but at the expense of the English with possibly some financial contribution of their own.

We can now turn to a consideration of the motives for the union and the immediate consequences of it. Fr Maurus Dixon later declared that the English monks wanted to have help from the Scots in the staffing of their northern missions[2] but, although one cannot rule this out, the Scots were the immediate beneficiaries. There are revealing references in the agreement to the lack of men and means at Würzburg. The final article arranges for English monks to help, should they be required, with the instruction of novices at Würzburg and in any other pressing need which might arise later. A clause making this a reciprocal agreement is added at the end, but it will be seen that English monks were at once required at Würzburg and at least one was already there.

Why did only Würzburg monks enter into the agreement when it was the Ratisbon abbot who had first suggested it? The answer to this would seem to be, not that the situation in Ratisbon had improved, but that the ineffectual Abbot Chambers was unlikely to enter on anything so constructive. One can also ask why there was a lapse of seven years between Abbot Gascoigne's commission in 1653 and the signing of the Articles. The year 1660 suggests that the Restoration had something to do with the pact. Cromwell had made Scotland subject to English enactments and stimulated the desire in Scotland for union with England. Both countries welcomed Charles II back in the early summer of 1660; no doubt Scots and English recusants abroad were even more pleased than their Protestant compatriots at home. Both Scottish and English monks would naturally look forward to the new opportunities given them to help their homeland, and they had perhaps never before been so united in aims and sentiment. Abbot Gascoigne's approbation expresses the hope that the union will provide solace for 'our common fatherland Great Britain', and the president general also speaks of 'our fatherland Great Britain'. But the Scots, who drew up the Articles, do not mention this aspect.

There is, however, one concrete reason for the monks of Würzburg wanting to use the resources of their more affluent English brethren in 1660. The key is provided by a list of the resident community in Würzburg at the time of the episcopal visitation made on 4th February 1661. Asloan had died on 24th January, three months after signing the Articles, and the only Scots priests left in residence were Maurus Dixon and Placid Baillie, the two who had signed the Articles with him; there were also two Scots novices and two English monks. The six resident monks in February 1661 were Maurus Dixon, aged 43, and Placid Baillie, aged 28; Anselm Touchet of St Gregory's, Douai, and Placid Shaftoe of Lamspring; Macarius Brown, aged 22, and William Dunn, aged 17, both professed on 1st November 1660. The last two are explicitly described as Scots.[3]

There may have been two other monks of Würzburg not in residence. Boniface Strachan is listed in the Ratisbon necrology as dying in 1664, though nothing is known of him after his period in Venice. Placid Keith, who is found in no necrology, is said to have been in Poland in 1662.[4] The Würzburg necrology for this period is too imperfect for any firm conclusion to be drawn that the omission of Strachan and Keith means they severed their connection with the abbey at some point before their death.

It is reasonable to suppose that the young monks Brown and Dunn were two of the four youths who had travelled from Scotland in the autumn of 1658. The most likely explanation of the agreement with the English monks is that Asloan wished not only to bring in recruits but to see to their training. The list of February 1661 states that Shaftoe had been in Würzburg for two years and says nothing about how long Touchet had been there. It would certainly seem that one of them was novice-master, for Dixon was cellarer during these years[5] and Baillie had himself entered the monastery very shortly before. The final article calling for help with the training of novices is thus easily explained. When he signed the Articles, Asloan, who had been ill for some time[6] and had only three months to live, seems to have been trying to provide for the future. Hence the election of Dixon as coadjutor with right of succession, although this was not ratified until after Asloan's death, and hence the insistence that Würzburg was to be preserved for the Scots even if an English abbot was elected through lack of Scots.

Audomarus Asloan died in the night of 24th-25th January 1661 and was given a place in various German monastic necrologies. Dixon administered the monastery, as probably he had been doing during Asloan's illness, and arranged for an election, which took place on 25th February, three weeks after the visitation.[7] It was no doubt a foregone conclusion that Dixon should be elected. The new abbot, although he used the English spelling of his surname, was a Scot, possibly from Berwick or the Lothians, where there were Catholic Dicksons at the time.[8] He had studied philosophy and theology at Würzburg university,[9] had been prior and cellarer, and had successfully accomplished missions to Paris and Scotland to bring back recruits. Dixon was perhaps the only choice, but he seemed qualified for the office of abbot.

In the light of what he said later about the English monks and their missions, one suspects that Dixon did not altogether approve of the union. It does not seem to have had any important consequences except in missionary work, and as soon as Dixon was elected he turned to other sources for help. The abbot of Schwarzach had reason to be grateful to the Scots for the help given to his monastery by Asloan. He was present at Dixon's election and granted his request for the loan of one of his monks, Fr Maurus Boudetius, who now went to live with the Scots and was cellarer for almost two years.

The next year the German abbey helped still more. Alan Chisholm, who had been a soldier, entered the monastery at the age of nineteen and was sent to Schwarzach for his year of novitiate, while a German laybrother, Bro. Joseph Beussel, lived in St James's for a time. Another German monk, Fr Bernard Zinck, taught philosophy in the Scots abbey from 1663 to 1666, and his *Theses* in logic, which he printed, were defended (presumably at a public disputation) by Brown and Dunn.[10] One is led to suppose that the two English monks left Würzburg fairly soon after Dixon's election. Even if the loan of a German monk as cellarer can be explained by the fact that one was urgently needed to replace Dixon, sending the next novice to Schwarzach and borrowing a German professor of philosophy suggests strongly that the article concerning the training of novices was no longer operative.

Dixon was blessed as abbot and took the oath of fidelity to the bishop on 20th August 1662.[11] In the following years two more young Scots, Bernard Maxwell and Ninian Graham, joined the community. At a visitation in December 1665 there were present the abbot and four Scots aged from 21 to 26, namely Dunn, Chisholm, Maxwell and Graham. Baillie and Brown had departed for the mission, and the two English monks are not mentioned. Almost exactly three years later, at a visitation, the same persons were present, with the addition of James Blair and Columbanus Fraser. At the next visitation, in January 1672, yet another two had entered, Marianus Irvine and Christian Abercrombie, while William Dunn had gone to the mission.[12] Abbot Dixon now had seven young men, three of them priests, with him in the abbey and three of his monks were working as missionaries. None of the novices since Placid Baillie in 1658 had come from the Scots colleges in Douai or Rome; their numbers suggest that they were the fruit of recruiting errands to Scotland. This was to be the pattern for the rest of the century.

Meanwhile, as had happened so often in the previous half century, the Ratisbon abbey was once more in a dangerous state of crisis. In the ten years since his election Abbot Chambers had succeeded in squandering what his predecessor had built up, and at the beginning of 1666 he simply departed, leaving debts behind him. He went first to Vienna, then to Bologna, where he found a place in the archbishop's household.[13] In July 1666 the bishop of Ratisbon forced a visitation on the monks who remained; they protested to the nuncio at Vienna and Cardinal Francesco Barberini that the bishop (who, incidentally, died within a month) had threatened to drive the Scots out of their abbey and was ignoring their privilege of exemption from his jurisdiction.[14] The only known result of the unfortunate proceedings is that Abbot Dixon of Würzburg at some point between January and June 1667 was appointed administrator of Ratisbon,[15] and since Erfurt had no abbot but merely a monk put in charge by Chambers, Dixon was superior of Erfurt also. Apart from Chambers himself, monks of Würzburg had been superiors of Ratisbon and Erfurt since 1634, and now the abbot of Würzburg had charge of all three Scottish houses.

In the course of his duties as superior at Ratisbon, Dixon on 21st November 1669 received the vows of Bro. Placid Fleming, aged twenty-seven.[16] One wonders, did Dixon at the time have any idea of the significance of the event? It was to be the salvation of the Ratisbon abbey. Thomas Fleming, a descendant of the earls of Wigtown, was born at Kirkoswald in Ayrshire in October 1642. After receiving his education in Edinburgh he was a naval officer, and it was apparently in Dublin about the age of twenty-three that he became a Catholic. Not long afterwards he was captured by Moorish pirates and spent some time in captivity before being recaptured and freed by the Spanish. In 1667 he entered the Scots college in Paris, but went to Ratisbon the following year and took the habit. A year and some months after Dixon received his profession, that is, in the spring of 1671, he was ordained priest.[17]

In the summer of 1672 the Vienna nuncio was concerning himself once more with the Ratisbon Scots. If the abbot of Würzburg, he wrote to them, was unable to administer their monastery effectively because of his advancing years (he was fifty-four) and its distance from his own abbey, then a new superior was needed; and if they would send him full information about Chambers, he would see what could be done. Exactly eight days later Chambers, in the presence of the cardinal archbishop of Bologna and other

104

dignitaries, resigned his abbacy. In October the nuncio accepted the resignation and gave leave for an abbatial election.[18] Dixon's administration does not seem to have been very successful. Finding himself unable to visit Ratisbon more than twice a year or to stay long when he did visit it, he had appointed Fr Athanasius Chambers, a cousin of the abbot, as cellarer there. It was not a fortunate choice, the situation was deteriorating rather than improving, and Dixon himself realised it.[19]

It was inevitable that Fleming, this gifted, energetic, determined man, should rise to the top. He was elected abbot on 5th December 1672 and at once confirmed by the bishop of Ratisbon acting on his authority as the delegate of the holy see.[20] This was merely a matter of words: the bishop was confirming the election on his own authority and inserting the phrase as a concession to the abbey's traditional privilege of exemption. But already Fleming had given proof of the sort of man he was: he was just turned thirty, had been in Ratisbon only four years and a priest less than two years, yet he declared that he only accepted his election in accordance with the abbey's ancient privilege of exemption granted by the holy see. The suffragan bishop accepted this, then proceeded to confirm the election on behalf of the bishop. Since this was a matter in which the rights of the holy see were involved, the case went to the nuncio and the Congregation of the Consistory in Rome. Dixon, who had been present at the election, was called on to testify to what had taken place. Eventually the election was quashed, Fleming renounced his confirmation by the bishop, and he was then provided to the abbacy by the holy see.[21] It was, however, not until about twenty years later that he received the abbatial blessing.

Placid Fleming was abbot in Ratisbon for the next forty-seven years, until January 1720. All this time he worked tirelessly to build up his community, improve its economic position, and safeguard its position and its right.[22] He founded a seminary to ensure a supply of novices for his monastery and thus of missionary priests for Scotland; he restored the Erfurt house and secured professorial posts for his monks in the university there. His correspondence was voluminous, his activities many and varied, his appeals for aid to his abbey unceasing. He is the greatest man produced by the Scottish monasteries in Germany in the course of their existence. Had he been in a more favoured position he would certainly have made his mark in history, but he chose to join himself for life to a poor and struggling institution which was threatened on all sides by powerful interests. His life's work was successful, with the result that his abbey continued to flourish after his death until the Napoleonic era when the secularisation laws extinguished monastic life in most of western Europe.

During Abbot Fleming's period of rule there were five abbatial elections at Würzburg; in other words, as five abbots succeeded each other at Würzburg, the same effective abbot at Ratisbon was going from strength to strength. The position of the two Scots abbeys relatively to each other was gradually and permanently transformed. Both monasteries had had their ups and downs since Würzburg was refounded in 1595, and on the whole the downs had been more prolonged and more serious at Ratisbon. Several times the Würzburg monks had had to come to its rescue in its dire need. Fleming was elected abbot at a time when its fortunes were at an extremely low ebb.[23] As his vigorous rule began to take effect, his abbey gradually climbed into a position of parity with St James's in Würzburg, then continued to expand in numbers and importance until it was undoubtedly the senior partner in the combination. The days when Würzburg monks could be called to the rescue of their countrymen in Ratisbon were over.

Abbot Dixon, accompanied by Fr Alan Chisholm, had gone to Ratisbon for the abbatial election in December 1672. That same month Fr Bernard Maxwell, the subprior at Würzburg — there does not seem to have been a prior — wrote to Fleming to offer the congratulations of the Würzburg Scots. It is, incidentally, typical of Fleming that he should have preserved his correspondence and so provided an important source for the history of the Würzburg Scots. Since Maxwell was Dixon's second-in-command and was to succeed him as abbot, there is added importance in his words to Fleming. His election was, says Maxwell, 'most acceptable and gratefull news unto all and every one of us' and the community felt it their duty to congratulate him 'by reason of the former acquaintance and friendship contracted between you and us when you was here with us'. They would support Fleming in his efforts to help his monastery and their 'poor country' and hoped for the 'continuing of correspondence and friendship betwixt the houses as formerly' and also 'increasseing and augmenting of it'.[24]

This letter to a certain extent sets the tone for the succeeding years, although Fleming was too strong a character for relations to be merely pleasant without entailing some measure of commitment to his activities. Alan Chisholm remained at Ratisbon until October 1673, and when his conduct was not entirely satisfactory, Fleming seems to have dealt firmly with the offender and informed Dixon of it. From Dixon's letter to Fleming we learn something of the difficulties of life in Franconia at this time. It was a period of complicated political and military move and counter-move in Louis XIV's war against the Dutch. The country round Würzburg was clear of the French but still had three imperial regiments in it. The clergy and religious houses were greatly burdened; the Scots had for the last five weeks been compelled to maintain four horses with provender, while their property in the country had been destroyed and their provisions consumed by the soldiers.[25]

The interests of the Ratisbon and Würzburg abbeys coincided, and at times conflicted, with each other in two main spheres: the finding of recruits for their novitiates and the sending of priests to the mission field. The two spheres were closely connected, for not only did the arrival of new recruits enable men to be spared for mission work but it was very often the missionaries in Scotland who found the recruits and even accompanied them on the long and difficult journey to Germany. In this matter, of course, Dixon had a start of eleven years on Fleming, and we have seen that at the time of the latter's election he had three monks on the mission and four young men studying for the priesthood.

If the immediate effect of the rapprochement between Würzburg and the English Benedictines was the help given to the Scots in training their novices, another effect, perhaps equally immediate, was the help given by the Scots in the staffing of the English missions. The two monks who were novices in 1660 worked and died in England, so that clearly the advantages of the agreement were not one-sided. Dixon, whose view of the English was disenchanted, asked Rome in 1669 for powers to send his own monks to the mission as he saw fit, but his request met with no response. The question of credentials and powers (or faculties, as they are called) for missionaries will be dealt with elsewhere, but it is necessary to understand that Roman Catholic missionary priests need faculties to hear confessions, absolve from excommunication, and so on; these faculties can only be given by a superior who has received the power to grant them. For most of his period of rule after 1669 Dixon was engaged in efforts to have a Scottish Benedictine missionary unit set up, with power vested in its head to grant faculties to missioners sent to Scotland.

Lists of resident monks survive from 1661. From 1676 on, we also have the correspondence between Bernard Maxwell and Abbot Fleming, and between the two Scots abbots and Rome. In each case only one side of the correspondence has survived, the letters received at Ratisbon and Rome, but these provide documentation of the community life and missionary plans which was entirely lacking before. In May 1676 Abbot Dixon was giving an account of his abbey.[26] The buildings were in good condition, and there were nine monks in residence as well as missionaries. The resident monks were persons of piety and learning, able to teach and conduct activities in public. Bernard Maxwell had gone to Scotland the previous year and returned with some promising youths. The abbey was in a better state than at any time since its restoration. In point

107

of fact Dixon was probably right in this, if one excepts the half dozen years before the Swedish invasion, even though his purpose in writing was to show that the monastery was worthy to be given mission faculties for its own members.

While the Würzburg abbot tried to have an organised Benedictine mission established, Fleming at Ratisbon was engaged in begging and planning to promote much bigger schemes. Quite soon after his election he was trying to regain the Vienna abbey or at least obtain substantial compensation for its loss;[27] later he wanted a share of some revenues in Oberpfalz that were earmarked for religious purposes, since, as he pointed out, the Scots monasteries in Germany were too poor to be of much assistance to their fatherland.[28] It was Fleming's plan to have never less than four boys from Scotland studying at Ratisbon.[29] At Würzburg Dixon pursued his own plans and activities in an effective if less ambitious and far-sighted way. Bernard Maxwell set off for Scotland in the late summer of 1676 and offered to do any commissions for Fleming and find him recruits. He returned to Würzburg at the end of October the following year without having done anything for Fleming as he had not heard from him but with two young men for his own monastery.[30] Other Würzburg monks likewise travelled between Germany and Scotland.

It is apparent that the union with the English had broken down almost completely. No English monk is mentioned at the visitations of 1665, 1668, and 1672 (which means that none appeared before the visitators and leads one to suppose that none was present), although Fr Bernard Sanderson, an English monk of Lamspring, died in Würzburg in June 1669.[31] Dixon, nevertheless, was still obliged to obtain faculties for his monks from the English Congregation, even though the arrangement became increasingly difficult in practice. James Blair had faculties made out to him in January 1678 by the English president.

In this year, 1678, we have another account of the Würzburg community. Abbot Fleming had invited Maxwell to visit Ratisbon but Abbot Dixon had refused him leave, saying that numbers were too small to permit this. There would soon be only three priests in residence besides the abbot, as Fr Christian Abercrombie was about to go to Scotland for his health. At the moment the community consisted of the abbot, four priests and four student monks, but Mass obligations were not onerous and did not demand the presence of many priests.

At this very time Fleming rubbed Dixon the wrong way by suggesting that the two young men brought recently from Scotland to Würzburg should join the Ratisbon community, presumably because Ratisbon had more need of recruits. Dixon was very put out at the suggestion. Bernard Maxwell, who was in constant correspondence with Fleming, strongly urged him to come to Würzburg and confer with Dixon. It was necessary, he said, for the growth and well-being of the Scottish abbeys that the two abbots should understand each other and remove all misunderstanding, and he makes it clear that he is not referring to the minor matter which occasioned his letter but to other 'such mistakes as are apparent between you'. He added that Dixon would be willing to take trouble to achieve this end but was prevented by age and infirmity from going to Ratisbon, so it was up to Fleming to make the journey to Würzburg. The suggestion was accepted, and Maxwell wrote again three months later to say how glad he was that Fleming was coming.[32]

An outline of the comings and goings between Scotland and Würzburg, and of Dixon's efforts to obtain faculties and help, has been given in order to show the activity and vitality of both abbot and community at this period. Journeys to and from Scotland were a regular occurrence; so was the arrival of fresh recruits. The abbot died on 16th March 1679, aged sixty-one, a considerable age for those days, and less than a year before his death he was still planning and working for the mission. The community at his death numbered a dozen in addition to himself; there were three priests in residence (Alan Chisholm, Bernard Maxwell and Marianus Irvine) and five priests on the mission (Placid Baillie, Macarius Brown, Ninian Graham, James Blair and Christian Abercrombie). Four monks were studying for the priesthood in the abbey: Gregory Seaton and Kilian Herries, who had probably come with Maxwell in the winter of 1675-6, and Augustine Bruce and Boniface Mackie, who had arrived with him in the autumn of 1677.[33] William Dunn had died on the English mission in 1675,[34] and Columbanus Fraser at Würzburg two years later.

This is the largest number of monks recorded since William Ogilvie bought the extra breviaries in 1625. To have taken up office with a permanent resident community of one priest and two novices and to have so built it up in eighteen years seems an outstanding achievement. Strangely enough, the monk who compiled the chronicle not long after Dixon's death merely wrote that he had ruled quite well considering his ability and had repaired a hall on the eastern side of the monastery. This faint praise certainly seems the product of bias or failure to grasp what Dixon had achieved. Undoubtedly he had his human weaknesses and limitations. His letters, for instance, show a tendency to take, as far as one can judge, a harsh view of the English monks, and he took offence at Abbot Fleming's sincere if tactless request. Possibly a psychologist would find something significant in his handwriting, which with its small letters and enormous tails and loops makes his correspondence look like the gambols of eccentric spiders and is very trying to anyone who has to read it.

Bernard Maxwell, however, in his letter to Fleming on the occasion mentioned, gives what is clearly a sound judgement on his abbot: he is 'a man of his owne humour yet . . . condescending to thinges which concerne the publike good'.[35] The later chronicler, writing eleven years after Dixon died, had much more than his predecessor to say in his praise, calling him a man of great frugality, zealous for the public worship of God and monastic discipline, a lover of study; he bought vestments and chalices and repaired the church roof, bought books and gave encouragement to study, rebuilt the hall, increased the number of monks, and was administrator of Ratisbon and Erfurt for some years. This is surely a more fitting summary of his long period of rule.

Notes

[1] Edited in full in "Scots and EBC".

[2] SCA, ML, Dixon, 24.5.1676.

[3] Reid, f. 119rv.

[4] Wieland, 108.

[5] Haim, A 7v; "Scots and EBC", 57.

[6] Haim, A 8v.

[7] Fel. Red., 333; Wieland, 130.

[8] *Blairs Papers*, 256, 257.

[9] BRB, MS 8979-82, f. 29r.

[10] Fel. Red., 333-35; A. Kaspar, "Studiengeschichte der Abtei Münsterschwarzach vom dreissigjährigen Krieg bis zur Säkularisation", in *Abtei Münster-Schwarzach. Eine Festschrift* (1938).

[11] Conjectural amendment of 1622 in Reid, f. 117r.

[12] Reid, f. 119v.

[13] APF, SOCG, 308, f. 269r; Cat. Abb.

[14] SCA, Rat. C 9, 19-21; ML, C (Propaganda), 14.9.1666.

[15] APF, Acta, 36, f. 2, 30-31; Reg. BOA, Sch., Urk. 546.

[16] Reg. BOA, Sch., Akten, 15.

[17] Hammermayer, "Restauration", 41-42.

[18] SCA, Rat. C 9, 24, 23, 26.

[19] Cat. Abb; Brockie.

[20] SCA, Rat. C 9, 26.

[21] SCA, Rat. C 8, 15; VA, Acta C. Consist. 1673, f. 531-53; 1674, tom. 2, f. 501-10; ibid., Resolutiones 1671-75, f. 325r; ibid., Decreta 1627-84, f. 400r; NVPC, 184.

[22] Hammermayer, "Restauration", 43 ff.

23 For a description see FA, Rat. 14, *ad* Fleming.

24 Maxwell, 14.12.1672.

25 Reg. BOA, Sch., Akten, 319, 22.10.1673.

26 SCA, ML, Dixon, 24.5.1676.

27 Hübl, 21-23; Renz, xvi, 82-83.

28 SCA, ML, Fleming, 3.8.1677.

29 SCA, ML, Fleming, 15.12.1676, 18.5.1678.

30 Maxwell, 25.8.1676, 1.12. 1677.

31 Birt, 48.

32 Maxwell, 5.3.1678, 30.3.1678, 22.6.1678.

33 Reid, f. 117v; Maxwell, 30.3.1678, 21.5.1679; SCA, ML, Dixon, 24.5.1676.

34 "Three Scots", 239.

35 Maxwell, 30.3.1678.

CHAPTER 10

Abbot Maxwell's Rule

1679—85

Abbot Dixon died on 16th March 1679 and a fortnight later Bernard Maxwell sent word to Ratisbon that the prince-bishop of Würzburg had fixed the date of the abbatial election for 7th August.[1] On 1st April he received a letter from Brussels containing news from England, and one from the Cardinal of Norfolk about mission work. He sent both on to Ratisbon and suggested that Fleming should reply to the cardinal. Norfolk's letter had no doubt been addressed to Dixon, and its being sent to Fleming by the Würzburg prior indicates the position that the dynamic abbot of Ratisbon had now assumed among the Scottish Benedictines. It is not clear what the constitutional arrangement was at Würzburg for the interregnum between the death of an abbot and the election of his successor. Maxwell, who was already Dixon's lieutenant, evidently retained his position and continued to administer, and this is a common and widespread arrangement; but it also appears that the senior monk, in this case Alan Chisholm, had some say, perhaps even joint control.

It is laid down in St Benedict's rule that monks do not send or receive letters except through the hands of the abbot. In a primitive form of monastic life this is a natural arrangement but it is less natural when letter-writing is an accepted activity of an educated man, and it begins to offer difficulty when a monk is ordained priest and exercises an apostolate in any way or when he has dealings with persons of standing outside the monastery. Conditions of modern life have therefore brought about a modification of the original rule in most monasteries, and even so there are occasions when monks deem it better all round if certain correspondence is not conducted through the usual monastic channels. They are not going behind their superior's back but safeguarding the success of their negotiations or the rights of other parties concerned.

When Maxwell tried to restore understanding between the two Scots abbots in 1678 the letters between him and Fleming were evidently not subject to Dixon's inspection, and Maxwell arranged

PLATE 6.   Early 20th century view of the east end of the church

PLATE 7. The east end of church after the destruction of 1945

for Fleming to send his reply to an address outside the monastery. Fleming's address-book at a rather later date has four such covering addresses for Würzburg monks.[2] Maxwell now, although temporary superior, did much the same thing again. He said that Chisholm knew nothing of the letters he was enclosing, and the following month he asked Fleming to write anything he did not want Chisholm to know on a separate sheet. All was well, he said, but Chisholm was curious about letters. It is easy to deduce that Chisholm was not in favour with either of the correspondents, and Maxwell ironically calls him Seigneur instead of Senior.

The abbey at Würzburg presents the usual spectacle of a monastery during an interregnum. Life goes on as usual as far as is possible but arrangements for the coming election assume the greatest importance. Maxwell wrote to Fleming in May and June. In the first letter he mentioned the expected arrival of two aspirants, a painter in Amsterdam and a person still in Scotland, and in the second he told Fleming that the young monks had begun their course of philosophy the previous week. If all the absent monks came for the election there were not going to be enough cells for all. There was little hope of a reply from Placid Baillie owing to the troubled times. Frs Ninian, James and Christian were, however, expected; the last-named had written and Maxwell had left it to him to inform the others of the abbot's death. All this is very typical although an intelligent system of voting by proxy or by affidavit *in absentia* could have greatly simplified the arrangements.

There is, incidentally, an intriguing postscript to the first letter: the suffragan bishop had given Maxwell a prophecy made by one Bartholomaeus regarding 'the Conversion of our Countrie', and it was enclosed for Fleming's edification. This is evidently Bartholomaeus Holzhauser (1613-58), founder of an institute of secular priests living in common, known as Bartholomites, to whom the Würzburg seminary was entrusted in 1654. But he is perhaps better known for his visionary and prophetical writings, among which was a prediction (produced in 1646) of the execution of Charles I and the ruin of the Roman Catholic church in Britain for 120 years. It was no doubt this that Maxwell received, for these prophecies circulated in manuscript and did not begin to be printed until the end of the eighteenth century.

When he wrote the second time Maxwell had received no further news from 'Admirall Christian with his squadron', in other words the missionary monks. This letter is chiefly filled with the matter of Fleming's vote. Alan Chisholm had been saying that Fleming could not have a vote in the forthcoming election if he acted as scrutator, that is, one of the officials who counted the votes. A book on canon law had been consulted, which said that it was permissible provided the scrutator cast his vote before he began the count. Marianus Irvine, the scholar of the community, had told Chisholm this but in vain. Maxwell's advice to Fleming was to ignore the objection, because all the other monks wanted him to come and to have a vote; therefore he should come and act as scrutator, and if any difficulty was raised over his vote he could give it to a Würzburg monk or one of his own monks to cast.

It would appear from the election documents[3] that Fleming and his monks were summoned to the election. One must always remember that in Würzburg it was the diocesan officials who made the arrangements for occasions that are, at least nowadays, usually within the competence of the monastery itself or the congregation to which it belongs. All the same, it seems unlikely that summoning the Ratisbon abbot was regular practice or that, even on this one occasion, each monk of Ratisbon was intended to have equal voting rights with the Würzburg monks. On the other hand one must not presume that procedure was cut and dried as it is now; voting was probably less secret, with election by compromise or compromissaries always a possibility. In the event only seven monks signed the election document, the three priests already in residence and the four students. Maxwell was elected abbot. It seems a natural and a wise choice, for he had been prior for a number of years, even if technically called subprior, and had administered the monastery after Dixon's death. His letters too give an impression of maturity and breadth of vision.

Of his background we know nothing, but the surname is one of those most frequently met with in the records of the Scots colleges. Probably he came from the south-west, where Catholic Maxwells continued to play a notable part in the life of their church until recent times. He had a cousin, John Brown, in the papal guard,[4] and one wonders if this was the Douai student of that name from Galloway who had Maxwell connections on his mother's side and had tried his vocation at Würzburg. The new abbot had entered Würzburg in 1663 at the age of twenty-two and was thus thirty-eight, with sixteen years' experience of monastic life, when elected. Twice at least since his ordination to the priesthood he had gone to Scotland and returned with recruits for the monastery. When he was refused leave to visit Ratisbon by his abbot, he was very disappointed and considered the reasons given inadequate. Nevertheless he wrote that he was happy at Würzburg and confident that he had the love of his superior and brethren. In spite of his disappointment he could write that the matter of his visit to Ratisbon was a trifle; certainly he did not suffer from the small-mindedness which is the occupational risk of those living a non-active — one avoids the word 'contemplative' — religious life.

He considered the co-operation of the two Scots **abbots** necessary for the continued growth of the monasteries and their apostolate, and urged Fleming to visit Würzburg to smooth away misunderstandings. Clearly he shared with Fleming the view that growth and expansion were possible and should be aimed at. His judgement on his own abbot, that he had his peculiarities but was zealous for the common good, strikes one as shrewd yet kindly. Thus Würzburg now had an abbot whose qualities commanded respect and who yet had the vigour of youth, being not yet forty. Perhaps even more important, Maxwell was a personal friend of the formidable Fleming and shared his ideas, at least to some extent.

The two abbots were the same age, though Maxwell had entered monastic life five years before Fleming. Nevertheless, Fleming's seven years' experience as abbot gave him the leading role in the partnership and he had also the stronger personality. Maxwell appointed as his prior Fr Marianus Irvine, who had sent his greetings to Fleming in all three letters written by Maxwell before his election. One can deduce that the new prior and Fleming were likewise on terms of sympathy and friendship. The reign of the new abbot began in an atmosphere of cordiality towards his confrere in Ratisbon. Fleming had sent greetings for Maxwell's name-day, St Bernard's, 20th August; now Maxwell reciprocated the good wishes for St Placid's day, 5th October. He apologised for not replying sooner but had been waiting for his confirmation in the abbacy by the bishop, who was frequently absent, being also bishop of Bamberg. He declared, too, that he accepted Fleming's advice to write not oftener than once a month, just as he would accept his advice in other matters too. The letter is signed 'Your most Reverend Paternities most affectionat and sincere Brother and humble servant'. Only one side of the correspondence has survived but probably Fleming signed in much the same way; 'humble servant' had no more significance than 'yours sincerely' nowadays.

Much of the correspondence between Würzburg and Scotland was conducted through a Scot, Mr Kennedy, in Brussels. Having heard from him that Fr Ninian Graham was in Holland, Maxwell summoned Graham to Würzburg and also recalled Abercrombie from Scotland, reminding the latter of Fleming's 'New fleete', that is, the recruits for Ratisbon. All this Maxwell retailed to his fellow abbot as well as his hopes to have the new choir, now completed except for the carpenter's work, in use before Christmas. In reply Fleming told him of the repairs and rebuilding he himself was doing at Ratisbon. When Maxwell next wrote a fortnight later — he wrote four times in October 1679 in spite of his resolution — a wandering monk of Ratisbon, Anthony Gray, had arrived at Würzburg. Maxwell would like to have kept him until his own men came from Scotland, but he sent him on to Ratisbon so as not to run any risk of interfering with Fleming's plans. Anxiety not to stand in Fleming's way or be misunderstood by him is almost painfully apparent in Maxwell's letters. For instance, he had got Kennedy in Brussels to advance money for the journey to Würzburg to the painter coming to enter the noviciate, but he was clearly afraid of offending Fleming who might want him instead.

That same month Fleming offered to send one of his monks to Würzburg, which may have been altruistic but was in keeping with a policy to get rid of unsatisfactory survivors from the bad old days before he became abbot. He told Maxwell that Fr Benedict Hay, a Würzburg monk who had gone to live at Ratisbon some time previously and had had a rather chequered career, was absent without leave. If neither Hay nor his own monks from Scotland came, and so far he had not heard from them, Maxwell was willing to accept Abbot Fleming's offer. He also wanted a decision to be reached on the voting rights of monks not in major orders at abbatial elections in both Scots abbeys, and uniform practice introduced for allotting places in choir and refectory to each other's monks. His own suggestion was that one visiting monk should be given precedence over the resident monks, with other visitors going by seniority with the rest.

Würzburg lies on the direct route from Ratisbon to the Channel. From Würzburg one then goes to Frankfurt, thence up the Rhine to Cologne, and so either to Brussels and the Flemish ports or in a more northerly direction to Antwerp, Rotterdam and so on. It is therefore only to be expected that travellers between Ratisbon and Scotland should pass through Würzburg. Two brothers of Fr Erhard Dunbar, a monk of Ratisbon, thus arrived towards the end of November at St James's, where one of them fell ill, so that it was two or three weeks before they continued their journey to Ratisbon. The painter, one Alexander from Aberdeen, likewise arrived on St Andrew's day and asked to be accepted into the Würzburg community. Maxwell wrote to Fleming to apologise for depriving him of a possible recruit, explaining that it was Alexander's own choice which he himself had suggested when they left Scotland together two years before. But he was determined, he said, not to offend Fleming or be 'emulous' for his own monastery. This, incidentally, is the first time that Maxwell mentions what was to become a recurring theme with him: that the Würzburg monastery could not take any more recruits until its revenues were increased.

It is also at this time that James, duke of York and brother of Charles II, is first mentioned. Maxwell wrote: 'I thought he (Mr Kennedy) had beene gon to Scotland with the Duke of York, by reason I have not heard from him this long time by past . . . We

116

hope to heare good news from Scotland shortely since (His) Higheness the Duke of York is gon thither and was receaved so gallantly there. If he and our King his Brother understand another weele which I hope they doe, he will I hope with our Scots Lads suppress whatsoever the(y) begin in England'. The abbot of Würzburg thus knew that James had retired to the Low Countries after the Popish Plot and that there had been differences between James and Charles. At Würzburg there was still no sign of the missionary monks returning, but the two abbots were on the best of terms. Maxwell had concluded some business over breviaries for Fleming, and Fleming had concurred in Alexander's receiving the habit at Würzburg. The year 1679 and Maxwell's first months as abbot ended with high hopes for Catholics in Scotland even if in England the outlook was still grim; that at least was how Maxwell, and no doubt many other expatriate Scots, saw it.

In 1680 Abbot Maxwell wrote twenty-one letters to Placid Fleming in Ratisbon. Though they are practically the only extant source, they make 1680 perhaps the best documented year of the seventeenth century as regards the affairs of St James's and give one the opportunity to see a typical year of its life. Maxwell may have visited Ratisbon in January, since he speaks of a letter of his sent from Ratisbon to a cousin in France, but possibly it had been merely sent there for forwarding through the French ambassador, who resided in Fleming's monastery. News reached Würzburg at the end of that month that Macarius Brown, still on the mission in England, had been imprisoned. Even though the panic reaction to the Popish Plot was abating, Maxwell feared that he might be executed. There was bad news of two other absent monks. Ninian Graham died at some point before March, five days after returning to Scotland; he had set out for Würzburg to take part in the abbatial election but had got no further than Holland. Placid Baillie died at some point before 23rd June, when printed notices of his death were sent to Ratisbon for distribution to Bavarian monasteries.[5]

No new recruits came to Würzburg this year but there were four young men pursuing their divinity studies and the painter doing his year of noviciate. One of the students, Gregory Seaton, had bad health and showed a disinclination to study, while the prior was seriously ill in June. The death of two priests in Scotland or England made no difference to the finances of the monastery. In early 1680 Maxwell made out the annual accounts for the bishop's officials and found that, for the third successive year at least, ends did not meet; he knew because he had performed that task for Abbot Dixon. At the end of the year he and his community would not accept Fleming's offer of some young men as it would be difficult to maintain those already in residence and more could not be taken without financial help, and this was unlikely to materialise while the threat of war with the French lasted.

Because of the poverty of the Scots monastery the bishop of Würzburg told his officials not to take any money when he conferred the abbatial blessing on Maxwell. Fleming, after almost eight years, had not yet been blessed, being determined to obtain apostolic authority for the blessing yet equally unwilling to pay the official or unofficial fees. Accordingly, when Maxwell asked him to receive his blessing at Würzburg with him, the Ratisbon abbot declined the offer. Maxwell then invited Fleming to be present, but in the event he received his abbatial blessing on 15th July at less than forty-eight hours' notice. Perhaps nothing shows the subject status of monasteries in Würzburg more clearly than this, when one thinks of what is taken for granted nowadays. Two neighbouring abbots were summoned, at similar notice and without Maxwell's knowledge, to act as assistants, and the ceremony took place in the chapel of the bishop's fortress residence.[6] Probably the date was chosen to fit in with the bishop's journeys between Würzburg and his other diocese of Bamberg. The newly blessed abbot's comment was on the graciousness of the bishop in waiving all fees, inviting some neighbours and speaking in kindly fashion of the Scots. He would, so Maxwell hoped, be a good friend to St James's.

Had Maxwell been incensed with Fleming at the time of his blessing, it would have been only natural. Some words had been spoken or written — we do not know by whom but they evidently emanated from Würzburg — which gave offence to the Ratisbon abbot and his monks. Fleming seems to have expressed his displeasure to his fellow-abbot, who replied in homiletic vein, speaking of the virtues of patience and charity and quoting from the epistles of St Paul. One's impression is that Maxwell was a genuinely spiritual man who read his Scriptures assiduously in Latin and quoted from them with facility in the same language.

Later that month, April, he welcomed the news that Christian Abercrombie, a Würzburg monk, was bringing recruits from Scotland for Fleming. When Abercrombie sent a letter ahead from Frankfurt to announce his arrival, Maxwell forwarded it to Ratisbon, apparently without opening it, to prove to Fleming that he was dealing in a completely straightforward way with him and would make no attempt to keep any of the young men for his own abbey. On 20th June Abercrombie, his four companions and a Würzburg student-monk set off by coach to travel the eighty miles to Ratisbon. Of the recruits Maxwell wrote: 'They are very pretty youths as you desired them, and excellent wits and capacitie for studyes, and which is the chiefest of all they are already weelle

118

advanced in their studyes haveing ended their Gramar all of them'. A little later he made the remark that the Scots were now able to be discriminating about applicants, whereas formerly they had of necessity received some 'of smal qualifications'.

Maxwell asked Fleming not to keep the two Würzburg monks more than a fortnight, then wrote a week later to ask for their immediate return because of the prior's dangerous illness. Twice again he wrote, and on 14th July a further letter contained his regret, very mildly expressed, that Fleming had seen fit to keep Abercrombie yet another week, for he would thus not be present at his abbatial blessing. On the 24th Abercrombie was back at Würzburg and took up important duties as cellarer. Had the boot been on the other leg, and a Ratisbon monk been detained after doing the Würzburg abbot a signal favour, Fleming would not have hesitated to point out the enormity of the offence. Maxwell had sent gifts brought by Abercrombie from abroad, including a pair of stockings; he apologised for them not being black but Abercrombie himself would confirm that he had brought no black ones with him from Scotland. Though only one side of the correspondence is available, it is hard to avoid the judgement that Fleming was somewhat cavalier and Maxwell over-anxious to please.

Permission was given in the summer of 1680 for the Scots to celebrate the feast of Macarius, their founder, with a solemn Mass and sermon, and some literary work was done on Macarius by the Scottish monks at this time. The matter has special significance since devotion to Macarius was to assume importance far beyond the bounds of Würzburg that same decade. Maxwell had also inherited the problem of how Benedictines were to conduct their apostolate in Scotland. Propaganda in 1679 had decreed that they were to receive faculties from the Prefect of the secular clergy there and might succeed to pensions when the present recipients retired or died. It was an arrangement calling for a great deal of goodwill in its administration to make it acceptable and helpful to the monks. Alexander Leslie, a secular priest who was returning to Rome after making a visitation of the Scottish mission, was about to pass through Ratisbon, so Maxwell asked Fleming to put the monks' case to him. He also wanted Leslie's backing, extraordinary as it may seem, for the recovery of the pre-reformation Benedictine monasteries in Scotland.

Maxwell's letters contain a great deal of miscellaneous information, much of it of more than passing interest, about local Würzburg matters as well as Scots at home and abroad. The plague was nearing Franconia in October 1680 and a service was held in Würzburg cathedral to stay its course. We know that there were bans on the admission of strangers for this reason during these years.[7] A Capuchin friar noted for his miracles visited the town that same month; Maxwell spoke with him and obtained an interview for his young monk, Gregory Seaton, whose health gave cause for anxiety. A learned ecclesiastic in Würzburg, Francis Fabritius, was writing a work on noble families and had borrowed a book of genealogies from the English envoy to Ratisbon through the good offices of Abbot Fleming. Lord Middleton, a Scot who was the English ambassador in Vienna and was later to be one of James II's secretaries of state, spoke with Maxwell when he passed through Würzburg on his way to Ratisbon and Vienna in July, and two months later Maxwell hoped to meet Bevil Skelton, the former English ambassador to Vienna and a friend of Fleming.

There were numerous contacts with Scotsmen. General Count Leslie owed the monks money, and two influential namesakes of his were to be asked to press him for payment. Two brothers named Bruce were coming from Rome to enter the Scots abbeys and were thought by Augustine Bruce of Würzburg to be his cousins from Fife. Erhard Dunbar of Ratisbon passed through Würzburg on his way westwards and again on the return journey, this time with three more recruits for his abbey. A certain Mr Fraser, having decided not to enter the Würzburg noviciate, stayed on several weeks there before setting out for Ratisbon. Christian Abercrombie wrote to Scotland and passed on messages from Ratisbon, just as earlier in the year he had sent news from Scotland, including the deaths of Maxwell's mother and Lady Irvine of Drum. There were also contacts with the English monks of Lamspring: Maxwell wrote to them on behalf of Fleming and received obituary notices of monks which he sent on to Ratisbon. This is a year which there is no reason to consider untypical, one in fact in which there was, if anything, less missionary activity than was usual.

On New Year's day 1681 the Würzburg abbot wrote to Fleming about 'a Comet star with a tayle wonderfully long' (also recorded in a contemporary work on astronomy)[8] which had been seen over Franconia and was supposed by the populace to herald war with the French. He wanted Fleming to get some document from the French ambassador, who was living in the Ratisbon abbey, so that the Würzburg Scots would be spared by any French invaders. In the autumn, shortly after the Imperial Diet had threatened Louis with war when he occupied Strasburg, the request was repeated more earnestly. Other troubles beset the abbot of Würzburg that year. Alan Chisholm had become unsettled and in July tried to obtain admission to a neighbouring monastery. The Scottish monks were willing to let him depart but insisted that he must go right away and join the Maurist or Bursfeld congregation, which Chisholm did not want to do. He and his abbot then compromised on Ratisbon, and Maxwell wrote to put the matter to Fleming. A month earlier he had told Fleming that Christian Abercrombie was going back to Scotland and would see to any commissions for him. Fleming's reply was to accuse his fellow-abbot of acting secretively in keeping the news of Abercrombie's departure and Chisholm's decision from him until the last moment.

Maxwell now explained that the decision to send someone to Scotland had been made only recently and that Chisholm had kept his own intentions secret until they were discovered. Again it is a letter full of declarations about the need for fraternal charity and his own determination to preserve it. The correspondence continued but with some diminution of smoothness. The requested document for the French ambassador still did not come, while the scholar Fabritius was complaining that Fleming must be offended with him as there was no sign or even promise of the books he had been requesting for almost a year. At the end of December Fleming seems to have said that he would do nothing for the Würzburg monks until he saw what Abercrombie in Scotland would do for him; this, said Maxwell, showed a lack of trust whereas he himself would do anything for Fleming.

Finance was a recurrent worry for Abbot Maxwell. He would have liked to accept more young men for training as monks and hence as missionaries, and was being pressed to do so, but felt unable to take in any more until the abbey's income increased. Both the Cardinal of Norfolk and Will Leslie (who was the agent of the Scottish clergy in Rome and brother of the Alexander Leslie already mentioned) were given an account of the state of the monastery and its difficulties.[9] There were nine monks in residence; the annual revenues did not exceed 600 guilders, a large slice of which had to be given to the prince-bishop's government in tax, the so-called *subsidium charitativum*. There were three monks on the mission but no other priest could be spared until the young monks completed their studies, and it was impossible to provide any means of support for the two already in Scotland. Maxwell assured Will Leslie that he would never fail to help in any way he could though for the present he was unable to do more.

As regards sending another priest this was undoubtedly true, for there were only Marianus Irvine, who was teaching the students, and Alan Chisholm, who was not considered suitable for mission work. The latter, incidentally, changed his mind about going to Ratisbon and was content to remain in Würzburg. The number of young monks had risen to six by the clothing of a very promising recruit, Ambrose Cook, in July. There were twice this number in Ratisbon, as its abbot told Leslie, but Fleming was making prodigious efforts to get support and help; probably what he

121

regarded as Maxwell's timidity was one reason for his irritation with him. Leslie wanted the two Scots abbots to plan mission work together. Maxwell was only too willing to do this, as also to work in complete harmony with the secular clergy in Scotland and have faculties given to his monks by the secular Prefect instead of by the English Congregation. Nevertheless, nothing positive resulted; nor, when Maxwell tried to have a separate Benedictine mission established, did Fleming encourage him in the least.

The monastery had only nine cells, all of which were filled except one kept vacant for Abercrombie, so that James Blair, who was contemplating returning from the mission, would have to accept makeshift quarters if he came. It is perhaps at this time, 1682, that one sees Maxwell's rule at its best. The prior considered the young monks to be good students, from whom some future professors of philosophy and theology might be obtained. Two received the diaconate this year, so the abbey would soon have two more priests. They had talent in other directions too. Maxwell wrote:

> 'Our young men who now are studying their physicks have this time bygon applyed their spare houres in learneing of figurall and Chorall Cant, and also in the Violl, wherein they have now made such progress that they practise the same now and then in our Church, and after this must doe more frequently, and for their greater incouragement I have made them a New Organ, which is now so far advanced that we have severall times already used it, and I hope before St Benedicts day it shall be compleated.'

Erhard Dunbar at Ratisbon was asked to provide extra pieces of music to add to their repertoire. The rebuilding of the choir in the church had also been completed. Though there was no room for the recruits who desired admission, Maxwell had a plan to build half a dozen cells for monks and a few guestrooms. The cost, a thousand dollars, was far beyond his means but he had presented a petition to the prince-bishop for help.

Not that everything was perfect. The bishop was absent on St James's day and so did not visit the monastery; his present of 'wine, bread and severall sortes of fishes' was a poor substitute for the favourable answer they hoped for when he came. The painter, Bro John Alexander, ill and confined to bed since the previous December, died on 25th May. There was also a disagreement with Fleming. General Count Leslie of Balquhain,[10] a distinguished soldier in the imperial army, owed the Scots monks some money on account of Fr Benedict Hay, the monk who had tired of Würzburg and Ratisbon in turn. Fleming wrote for it without success; so in the winter of 1679-80 did Maxwell. Now, when the bishop sent the fish instead of the hoped-for thousand dollars for St James's day, Maxwell asked his fellow-abbot for what was owing to him on Hay's account. The result was an ominous silence, correctly interpreted by the sensitive Maxwell. On 5th November 1682 he wrote to Fleming that this was his fourth letter yet he had received none in return; if the latter was offended by his request for the money on Hay's account he ought not to be, for it was a contract confirmed between Fleming and Abbot Dixon before Maxwell became abbot. Fleming finally broke his silence in December and gave his reasons for not paying, to which Maxwell answered that he did not accept the reasons but considered the preservation of charity more important and so would drop the matter till they met.

There was a visitation at the beginning of December, merely the routine procedure, and the bishop's officials who conducted it declared themselves satisfied. The list of the community drawn up on the occasion[11] shows no change, for nobody had replaced Alexander the painter. Later in the month Boniface Mackie was ordained priest although he still had part of his course of studies to complete. In the spring of 1683 the little community was struck by illness.

'Bro Kilian, whose deathe hath not a litle troubled us all here, he being so very young and of very greate expectation as any he hath left behinde him in the Monasterie . . . his infirmitie was a hott fever or a bastard pleurisie as our Doctor called it, with a stitch in his right syde . . . but before he dyed it cam to his left side'.

Both abbot and prior fell ill 'of the same infirmitie' and it was only with difficulty that the convalescent Maxwell was able to attend the bishop's funeral after the body, according to immemorial custom, had lain in St James's for the night. Thomas Ogilvie arrived in August to be a laybrother; he could cook and had the qualification, most useful in south Germany, of being able to brew beer. Two months later Augustine Bruce had been ordained priest, and James Blair had returned from Scotland with a fourteen-year-old boy, William Stewart.

When only one priest besides the abbot and prior was in residence, the monastic offices had of necessity to be shared out among the theological students. At the visitation of December 1682 Gregory Seaton was cellarer, and Bruce sacristan. The composition of the community changed considerably, however, in the following twelve months. With the ordination of two priests and the return of one from Scotland, there were now six priests in residence; after two deaths and two promotions through ordination, there were only two divinity students; and the tally was completed by the

123

laybrother aspirant and the boy of fourteen. There were soon further changes. James Blair obtained leave to join the English Dominicans in Rome, whereupon his abbot warned Placid Fleming, about Easter 1684, not to give too much credence to him if he called in at Ratisbon on the way. By August, however, Blair had already been to Italy and departed for yet further pastures new. Blair's departure left nine in residence, but Maxwell complained that only six were of use in choir, because Gregory Seaton through laziness and infirmity was of little help, while the recently clothed Ogilvie, now Bro. Joseph, was a laybrother and the boy Stewart could not be expected to help. (One wonders why Maxwell accepted him and not some 'prety youth' who had 'ended his Grammar' like the recruits for Ratisbon).

In February 1684 Fr Benedict Raith of Ratisbon died in the Würzburg monastery.[12] He had been in charge at Erfurt until July 1679, just a month before Maxwell's election, when he abandoned his post and went to Würzburg. There he made his peace with Fleming.[13] He is mentioned in none of Maxwell's letters and was certainly not in the Würzburg monastery in the years which intervened until his death. The prior was again very ill in May of 'a hot fever' and in August caught the *Rotflecke* (some infectious disease with red spots) from a young monk. It was at this time that Maxwell decided to send Seaton to Ratisbon in the hope that he would study better there; Seaton went and at Ratisbon he died on 12th February 1685, aged twenty-seven.[14]

Maxwell himself died a month later, on 17th March. No letters of his to Fleming have been preserved since the previous August, so we have no means of telling whether his death was sudden or followed a gradual decline in health. He did, however, sign a document on 8th February.[15] Similarly, there is no precise information on the community he left behind him, but one can presume that it was much the same. The boy Stewart did not persevere, Abercrombie had apparently settled down happily in Scotland, and James Blair had not severed his connection with Würzburg. In fact he spent part of 1685 very profitably from the historian's point of view, copying out English Benedictine documents for Placid Fleming,[16] probably in Ratisbon, where he was in September of that year.[17]

Europe continued to be troubled. The armies of Louis XIV disturbed the peace in the west, while in July 1683 the Turks besieged Vienna. Maxwell had remarked at the time on the troops passing through Franconia. The troubled times had affected Maxwell and his monastery indirectly. The prince-bishop whom he had petitioned for financial help died in 1683. His successor was sympathetic and told the Scots abbot he would like to help, but his exchequer officials were not eager to make any grant until the general outlook improved. When the bishop and his court attended the High Mass in the Scots abbey on St James's day 1684 and afterwards dined with the monks, they promised help, and indeed this had twice been recommended in diocesan chapter meetings, but they also told Maxwell he must have patience and wait for better times. The abbot had had a like disappointment the previous September when a German general died and was buried in the Scots' church, for although there was talk of the large legacy he had left them, he had in fact died suddenly and intestate.

Abbot Maxwell's rule leaves one with the impression that he found the difficulties and problems confronting him rather more than he could manage. He began his period of rule with the annual accounts failing to balance and he ended it with capital debts. Lack of revenue and accommodation prevented him from accepting the young men who offered themselves, or the boys whom he was asked to train for the religious life. His only solution to the impasse, financial help from the prince-bishop, was impeded by external circumstances. Whereas the more determined Fleming bombarded Rome and Munich for help in circumstances which had originally been even less favourable than at Würzburg, Maxwell accepted his position and failed to break out of the ring of difficulties which beset him. In spite of his ideas for the expansion of the Scots abbeys, his own monastery was, if anything, in a rather less favourable position at the end of his period of rule than at the beginning. And though he tried conscientiously to co-operate with Fleming, he must have found dealings with his tougher and more successful partner very trying. Is it far-fetched to suggest that the difficulties with which he was faced contributed to his death at the early age of forty-four?

The judgement of the historian trying to trace the progress of the monastery need not coincide with that of the monks who lived under Maxwell's rule. In this case the assessments do not conflict although they have comparatively little in common. The chronicler, who wrote a few years later, considered that Maxwell was rendered suitable for his office by kindness allied to humility and tireless zeal for the monastery's well-being. That he encouraged study, as the chronicle says, is borne out by the constant references in his letters to the progress of his young monks in their divinity and to the scholars who asked him for books or information. It is clear from the same source that he consulted his monks about affairs pertaining to the common good and did not try to rule autocratically. The letters show touches of humour, and we have a very pleasing picture of him fostering the musical talent of his young men and even providing a new organ to encourage them.

125

After various illnesses and trials patiently borne, so the chronicler concludes, he died peacefully in the Lord on 17th March 1685 and was buried in the church in front of the entrance to the choir. Of all the seventeenth-century monks of Würzburg he is the one whose personality stands most clearly revealed in the seventy letters of his that have been preserved, and anyone who reads them will find much to corroborate, and nothing to contradict, the favourable judgement on Abbot Bernard Maxwell made by one of his monks.

Notes

[1] Unless otherwise stated, the source used for the present chapter is Maxwell's correspondence with Fleming.

[2] FA, Rat. 8, f. 14v, 15v, 16r, 29v.

[3] Reid, f. 117v.

[4] SCA, ML, Maxwell, 30.8.1681, 22.10.1681.

[5] Dates of death in "Necrologies", 199 need correction.

[6] All details are corroborated by Chronicon and Gropp, II, 513.

[7] Gropp, IV, 797-98.

[8] Gottfried Kirch, *Neue Himmels-Zeitung . . . von den zweyen neuen grossen im 1680 erschienenen Cometen* (Nuremberg, 1681).

[9] SCA, ML, Maxwell, 22.10.1681.

[10] For him see Col. Leslie, *Historical Records of the Family of Leslie* (Edinburgh, 1869) III, 112-13.

[11] Reid, f. 119v.

[12] *Colleges*, 263.

[13] Reg. BOA, Sch., Akten, 43.

[14] Pfarrbuch (funerals).

[15] Wz. SA, Würzburg Stadt R.A. 86, f. 431v.

[16] This is Blair (see Bibliography).

[17] Pfarrbuch (baptisms).

CHAPTER 11

Under a Catholic king and after
1685—96

About five weeks before Abbot Maxwell's death Charles II died in London. Four days later, on 10th February 1685, his brother, the duke of York, was proclaimed King James VII at the Mercat Cross in Edinburgh. He was to reign for rather less than four years and in that time was to make strenuous efforts to restore the Roman Catholic faith in Scotland. However much or little one may sympathise with his aims, there can be no doubt at all about his sincerity, and none about the imprudence with which he tried to achieve them. By the end of December 1688 he had departed from the shores of Britain for good, leaving behind him both in Scotland and England an overwhelming majority determined that no Catholic sovereign should ever again rule over them. At Würzburg and Ratisbon the Scottish monks had shared the high hopes of what the rule of a Catholic king would mean for their church in Scotland. They were drawn into the plans and activities of James as he pursued his purpose, and they shared the disaster of the Revolution. Marianus Irvine governed the abbey at Würzburg for a period almost co-terminous with James's reign: Maxwell died a month after James came to the throne, and Irvine died a month before James fled to the continent. The history of Irvine's abbacy can hardly be separated from the rise and decline of the king in Scotland. It also happens that information on the internal affairs of the abbey at this time is sparse in the extreme. No letters of Irvine as abbot have been preserved, so that there is no detailed account of monastic affairs such as came from Abbot Maxwell's pen. The effect is to throw the progress of events in Scotland into even greater prominence.

The first news of the monastery comes from a letter of Irvine on 1st July 1685.[1] He had not yet been elected abbot but, in his capacity of prior appointed by Maxwell, was administering the monastery. Irvine wrote to tell Fleming in Ratisbon of the arrangements for the abbatial election. The prince-bishop had fixed it for 23rd July but the monks wanted it brought forward a week so

127

as not to hinder preparations for the feast of St James on the 25th. Christian Abercrombie had written from Scotland, and the change of date would presumably make no difference to him or other monks on the mission. Irvine therefore had got the suffragan to ask the prince-bishop, at the time in Bamberg, to agree to the earlier date. There was the further question of Fleming's vote in the election, and it was doubtful if the bishop would allow it, but Irvine wanted Fleming and his community to remember the Würzburg monks in their prayers. The abbey had met with a piece of good fortune such as the unfortunate Maxwell never had: the provost of the cathedral chapter had left the monastery a legacy of 500 florins in return for weekly Masses, and Irvine was going to clear off capital debts with it within a week or so.

At the election, which took place on the date originally fixed, 23rd July, and which Fleming did not attend,[2] Marianus Irvine was unanimously elected. A few days later he matriculated at the university. As with his predecessor, Maxwell, the new abbot bore a name commonly met with among priests at the time; he was, it seems, also related to at least one of them. He had a cousin of that name, possibly a priest, known in Rome in 1674 and was related to the priest John Irvine called 'Belty'. The Irvines of Belty, near Kincardine, were Catholics and closely related to the Irvines of Drum.[3]

He entered Würzburg at some point in the years 1669-71. When Maxwell was elected abbot in 1679, Irvine became his prior and also taught the young monks philosophy and theology throughout Maxwell's rule. Fleming, who likewise thought highly of him, wanted to have him as professor for his own students at Ratisbon but Maxwell naturally could not spare him and Irvine's own students declared they would go with him if he left Würzburg.[4] So once more St James's had a new abbot who was respected for his qualities and stood high in Fleming's estimation. There was one serious drawback, however, and that was Irvine's health: he had been dangerously ill in the summer of 1680, ill again in May 1683 and yet again twelve months later. He died just over three years after his election, and the only time he is mentioned in a source outside Würzburg it is because he was ill.

The election was confirmed by the prince-bishop on 13th September but it was not until June 1687 that the new abbot received the abbatial blessing and mitre, together with four German prelates, at the hands of the bishop.[5] Unlike his predecessor he was not beset with financial worries. The timely legacy had cleared off capital debts, and the Catholic king of Scotland was to give a helping hand. There is a record of 'fees and pensions to officers of State and others signed at Whitehall the 31 Oct 1685, with

PLATE 8.   The east end of church after rebuilding

PLATE 9.   Aerial view from south-east

additional pensions since'. These are payments to Scots, and among the allowances made to churchmen is £100 'to the Abbey of St James in Würzberg'.[6] It was not charity pure and simple, however; the abbey was expected to help in James's plans for the propagation of the Roman Catholic faith in Scotland.

References to the internal affairs of the monastery are, as has been said, extremely scanty. In January 1687 Irvine is recorded in a letter of Fleming's as being sick of a hot fever,[7] a phrase which Maxwell too had several times used of his prior. In 1688 Irvine built two bathrooms and two chambers above the wine press for the use of the sick brethren and guests. At least, one presumes that 'bathrooms' is what is meant by *hypocausta*, the sweating-rooms of Roman baths. That same year a plenary indulgence for visiting the abbey church on St James's day was obtained through Fleming but apparently the document got no further than Ratisbon.[8]

Two monks who had come from Ratisbon were in the Würzburg abbey in these years. Augustine Gordon was a student at the university and in 1688 received major orders at Würzburg.[9] The other was an aspirant, Alexander Falconer, who petitioned twice at Ratisbon for the monastic habit but was not considered suitable. He then went to Würzburg and was clothed as Bro. Bernard by Abbot Irvine.[10] He did not persevere. These few references are the sum of what we know of the abbey itself until on 22nd November, 1688 Marianus Irvine died after only three days' illness. The chronicle records that he died with christian resignation and deserved on account of his profound learning in philosophy and theology to enjoy a longer life and more peaceful times.

The chief interest during these years is centred less in the monastery itself than in what has been called the triangle of forces: Scotland, Germany, Rome.[11] Fleming had tried unsuccessfully to get himself appointed king James's resident in Ratisbon but he had considerable influence over Sir George Etherege, better known (and indeed better qualified) as a dramatist than as a diplomatist, who succeeded to the position. He was also friendly with the French envoy, who actually lived in his abbey. It was almost certainly Fleming who obtained from James a pension for both Ratisbon and Würzburg and for the Benedictine monks in Scotland. He was intimately concerned in two projects which affected the Scottish mission and the Scots abbeys very much. The first was the appointment of a bishop in Scotland: Fleming threw his influence on the side of a secular priest, Lewis Innes. The second project was the sending of Benedictine missionaries — and more than that, the setting up of a Benedictine house — in Scotland.

Both matters require fuller treatment elsewhere but one must at least ask how much Irvine was concerned in them. It was Fleming who lobbied and wrote indefatigably; Irvine was silent, though Fleming declared that they would have pressed Innes's candidature together if Irvine had not been ill. Over the mission to Scotland Fleming wrote and appealed for travelling expenses, but it was Irvine who supplied more than half the priests even though the Ratisbon community was now larger than his own. It would certainly seem that Fleming's plans included Würzburg monks as well as Ratisbon ones, and it can only be presumed that Irvine was content to let Fleming make the arrangements.

Christian Abercrombie was already on the mission in Scotland, Macarius Brown in England, and four other Würzburg monks went to Scotland in 1687-88. Alan Chisholm was thus the only priest left in the monastery with Abbot Irvine, and an attempt was made to take the abbey away from the Scots.[12] One of the missioners, however, Boniface Mackie, being unwell in Scotland was back in Würzburg by November 1688, so that when Irvine died there were six persons in the monastery: Chisholm and Mackie, two novices and two others.[13] A fragment of almost contemporary chronicle comments: 'Happy is he who learns from the troubles of others! Let future abbots take care that there are never less than six monks in residence, three of them priests and three clerics'. The context is obviously the distress caused when James fled and Lord Chancellor Perth was imprisoned, and most of the Würzburg priests were unable to leave Scotland.[14]

James fell into error after error in dealing with his subjects in his two kingdoms. It is probably fair to say that what preserved him for so long was the not yet forgotten episode of the interregnum under Cromwell, and it is probably equally true that what finally decided his subjects to get rid of him was the birth of his son. At least this is true of England, and 'the Revolution was made in England and imported to Scotland'.[15] The birth of a son meant that rule by a Catholic king was not going to be a temporary interlude which could be borne but a regime which would now be continued for unknown generations. It was at this point that the Scottish monastery in Würzburg played a central part in the events that were to decide the history of Scotland and England for the next century and are not entirely without relevance even today.

James had married Mary of Modena in 1673 and three children had been born to them between 1676 and 1682. Christian Abercrombie writing from Scotland in May 1682, for instance, had given the news of Mary's lying-in at Stirling.[16] But no child had survived and it was six years since the birth of the last; James was expected to die childless, in which case the heirs to the throne were his Protestant daughters, the offspring of his first marriage. Then, on 10th June 1688, a son was born to Mary and baptised the next

130

day. The event was doubly unexpected since the queen's doctors had miscalculated the date by a month.[17] There was an outcry, and the story was spread that the child was not the son of James and Mary. Various circumstantial explanations were given: it was the child of some other woman, it was smuggled into the palace in a warming-pan, and so on.

On 22nd October the king summoned a large gathering of notables and of persons in his household in order to prove that the infant was indeed the son of himself and Mary.[18] Three days later the solemn ceremonies omitted at the child's baptism were performed in the chapel of St James's palace, where the king had installed a community of English Benedictine monks.[19] The next month the duke of Orange, husband of James's Protestant daughter, landed in England and James left for the continent, having sent his wife and baby son on before him. One curious sequel to the episode is that in 1693 the pope, at James's petition, fixed the feast of St Margaret of Scotland on 10th June, the birthday of this child. The celebration of the feast in Scotland was transferred in 1903 to 16th November, the anniversary of the saint's death, but the rest of the Roman church still keeps it on 10th June.[20]

The story of the birth of the Prince of Wales and the subsequent Revolution is very well known in its general outline. One important aspect, however, has escaped the attention of historians, and that is the poor health of the child. The infant suffered from epilepsy or convulsions like Mary's previous children, and nearly succumbed to them. The doctors did their best, prescribing a concoction made from black cherries, which was supposed to be good for the ailment, in place of the nurse's milk. Not surprisingly the remedy was unsuccessful and the child was expected to die. The queen, however, had heard about St Macarius and his miracles. Human remedies having failed, divine ones must be tried. Abbot Irvine was asked by Mary to send relics of Macarius at once to London, and on 27th August Bro Joseph Ogilvie set off with them. One piece was placed in the bandages wrapped round the royal infant's head, and never again did he suffer from convulsions or show any sign of the disease. At this distance of time it is impossible to make any firm judgement on the nature of the cure. Nevertheless the salient facts remain: the child was dangerously ill and not expected to live, yet he survived and the Glorious Revolution took place. And the cure was attributed to the merits of Macarius of Würzburg.

There are several extant accounts of the episode. That of Joseph Ogilvie himself adds a second remarkable happening. A Protestant woman who hid some particles of the relics in her clothing to escape detection was at once converted to Catholicism and could not rest until she and her family had abjured their heresy.[21] Another account dates from the beginning of 1695 when the earl of Perth passed through Würzburg on his way to Rome. It was printed in 1741 and said that the Old Pretender (for he was the infant) still carried a relic of Macarius on his person.[22] Yet another account, written about 1706 when the child was now eighteen and had had no recurrence of the illness, adds that the papal nuncio in London, d'Adda, ordered the remaining particles of the relic (that is, those not placed in the child's bandages) to be publicly exposed for veneration in the royal chapel. The source of this too was the earl of Perth, who at the queen's request told one of the Würzburg missionaries to write an account of what had happened. And, adds the writer, many were the promises made to the Würzburg abbey in honour of St Macarius and in gratitude for the benefit he conferred, but the rebellion against James prevented them from being kept.[23]

At the beginning of 1689 James was in exile, Perth in prison. The Würzburg monastery had no abbot and only two priests in residence. The senior by profession, Alan Chisholm, being left in charge, wrote to Rome for the grant of an indulgence on the coming feast of St James and told Will Leslie how few monks were in the monastery. The election of a new abbot did not take place until July 1689, fully eight months after Irvine's death. The delay was plainly occasioned by the lack of news from Scotland. By 7th July no letters had come, while only Ambrose Cook had managed to escape to the continent.[24] One of the two novices, Bro Isidore Ogilvie, made his profession to the abbot of St Stephen's on 25th July, the feast of St James, and the election was held the following day. It seems clear that the profession and the election were timed so that one more resident monk would have voting rights. The suffragan bishop presided, the abbots of St Stephen's and Neustadt were present together with the noble dean of the cathedral chapter and the bishop's treasurer. In fact the dignitaries present outnumbered the electors, because the missioners although canonically summoned had not appeared. With all due formalities Alan Chisholm the senior, Boniface Mackie the cellarer and Isidore Ogilvie the newly professed elected the fourth monk present, Ambrose Cook. On 9th August his election was confirmed and the following day he received the abbatial blessing in the neighbouring monastery of Oberzell, whose abbot was likewise awaiting his blessing.

John Cook was born in 1660 at Preston in Scotland, presumably either the village near Prestonpans in East Lothian or that near Duns in Berwickshire. Having graduated at a university, almost certainly Edinburgh,[25] he became a soldier in the French army and served a year in Rome, then entered the Würzburg abbey in July

1681, taking the name of Brother Ambrose. Probably he became a Catholic at some point after his graduation. Abbot Maxwell considered him the most promising of his young monks, for he called him 'a youthe of good expectation' and wrote: 'Our young Master of Arts, now Br. Ambrose, give(s) sufficient satisfaction as yet to all, and studies so weele that he will be best of all the others'.[26] When James VII came to the throne, Cook was nearing the end of his theological studies. Having been ordained priest he was sent in 1687 to Scotland, where he was chaplain to the earl of Perth and gained his esteem. When James's reign came to its sudden end, Cook managed to leave Scotland, stayed with the Maurists on his way through France and was in Würzburg by July 1689. When he was elected abbot he was only twenty-nine years old, had been only seven years out of the novitiate and a priest for only four of these.[27]

Superficially the situation bears certain resemblances to that at Ratisbon in 1672, when an abbot not yet thirty was elected to lead a community consisting of a mere handful of monks. The cause of the low numbers at Würzburg, however, was not the misrule of the previous abbot but the too generous response of Abbot Irvine to the request for missionaries. Three of his priests were imprisoned in Scotland. One of them, Augustine Bruce, released after five or six months in prison, arrived back at Würzburg in July 1690 and was at some point, certainly before April 1696, appointed prior.[28] On the way from Scotland he had spent nine months with the Maurists at St. Denis. There were two newcomers when Cook was elected: Isidore Ogilvie and (probably) Placid Crichton. Three others entered the house very shortly after, Gregory Cheyne, Anselm Gordon and Maurus Strachan,[29] while a further aspirant, Bernard Douglas, made his profession within the next few years. In 1695 most of the resident monks were young and studying theology at the public schools.[30] Würzburg was thus not suffering from lack of new blood, nor was there any load of debt when Cook took charge of the monastery. With the election of a talented young man to the abbacy, in circumstances which were bound to improve as the situation in Scotland returned to normal, one might have expected notable progress at Würzburg; and indeed things did go well for a time.

One of the most interesting features of Benedictine history arises from the looseness of the organisation in what, although it has no central governing body, is termed the Benedictine order. There is no general chapter with power to legislate for the various regions and congregations. In other centralised orders, ideas and reforms might arise in one province but their spread to other provinces is most likely to be the result of their adoption by the general chapter or its equivalent. With Benedictines, however, the spread of ideas could only come about through the zeal of monks seeking to propagate them, or through their voluntary adoption by others who were favourably impressed. We have already seen something of the zeal of the Bursfeld monks for propagating their reformed observance; now the ideals of the Maurist Congregation in France were making their impression. The celebrated Mabillon had visited Ratisbon in 1683 and been kindly received by Abbot Fleming,[31] and even before this at Würzburg Abbot Maxwell had referred to the possibility of French (i.e., Maurist) observance being introduced into German monasteries.[32]

Towards the end of 1688 Fleming had begun negotiations to have one of his monks accepted for a final year of theology by the Maurists.[33] The monk in question, the newly ordained Augustine Gordon, arrived at Würzburg the following year on his way to France, and Cook took the opportunity to write to Mabillon.[34] After returning thanks for the hospitality he had received from the Maurists, he told Mabillon of his election and how little it agreed with his aspirations for a solitary life. The only solace he had was that perhaps God wished to use his unworthy person as a means for restoring monastic discipline in Würzburg. Cook also wanted the great Benedictine scholar to write to him about the fruits of the Mass and the practice of accepting stipends and legacies for saying Masses, so that, as he put it, nothing contrary to God's honour would be done. The letter concludes with respects and greetings to the Abbot General, the prior of St Denis and Doms Germain and Thierry, and an assurance that never would he forget the kindness he had received. Maurist influence was important in two ways at Würzburg: it led the Scots to do historical work, and Cook's reference to restoring monastic discipline meant in fact introducing Maurist observance.

Cook set about material improvements, the concomitant of reforms in observance. They are recorded in detail in the chronicle. In the year of his election he had the hall under the dormitory made into a refectory. The next year he bought two large psalters for use in choir, as well as French and Latin books at the Frankfurt fairs. The monastery garden was redesigned, the dormitory was whitewashed and little openings made in the doors of each cell after the manner of the Maurist congregation. Those who are not acquainted with monasteries from the inside should perhaps be told that the so-called dormitory is really a corridor of small rooms or cells where the monks live and sleep, and that some present-day monasteries drawing their inspiration from the Maurists still have these apertures in the cell doors, so that technically the monk can never be said to be in a private room of his own. Compartments were also made in the library for each monk, and wooden lattices put into the cloister; at least one presumes that library and cloisters are what the chronicler meant by his Greco-Latin *musaeum* and *perestylium*. Similar improvements were made in 1691.

One of the last things mentioned in the 1690 version of the chronicle was the scheme for union between the Scots abbeys in Germany, which the writer piously hoped might be brought into effect without delay. In a letter to Abbot Fleming, dated 12th July 1690, Cook declared himself resolved to co-operate in the project but dared not let the Würzburg officials know of his intentions. Even if a degree of union such as existed in other congregations was not possible, he wanted some sort of union in Germany and complete union in the mission field and would place no obstacle in the way. Eighteen months later Fleming penned an eloquent appeal to the auxiliary bishop at Würzburg.[35] To summarise it briefly and passing over the inevitable references to the Scottish apostles of Germany, it proposed that Ratisbon, Erfurt and Würzburg should unite to educate missionaries for Scotland, help each other in case of need and promote good and uniform observance. The auxiliary was to tell his prince-bishop that nothing beyond this was in the Scots' minds, certainly not any infringement of the bishop's rights and jurisdiction, which would be expressly safeguarded.

Nothing came of the scheme, and twenty-five years later Fleming stated that the Würzburg monks refused his offer of union and asked their bishop to protect them from his advances.[36] It is unlikely that he was speaking of some different project or occasion, but Fleming's accusation does not agree with the willingness expressed in Abbot Cook's letter. The obvious inference is therefore that the Würzburg Scots changed their mind. Perhaps Fleming showed himself too masterful and frightened them off, or this may be another illustration of the change that became apparent in Cook himself. Someone, possibly Gregory Cheyne, writing about 1725, described the ups and downs of Cook's career.[37] For the first two years Cook held out a strict rule of life for himself and others, then he lost his fervour, began to seek worldly company and allowed monastic discipline to relax as he indulged in feasting and drinking. The tone of Cheyne's account is moderate and in fact glosses over some of Cook's later excesses; it can therefore be considered as objective and it provides a key to much that would otherwise be extremely puzzling. Cook was a man pulled in two directions, an almost classic example of the conflict between good and evil, and the testimonies to his character and abilities vary enormously.

The first accounts we have are favourable. Besides Cook's own letters to Fleming and Mabillon, which testify to his zeal at the time, a rather shadowy character who frequented Würzburg praised him highly. This was Francis Sergeant, an English secular priest.[38]

Sergeant stayed in the Scots monastery from November 1688 until the following May, seems to have been some sort of chaplain to German troops in Württemberg, then went to London in 1691 and was writing from Edinburgh four years later. He was on the best of terms with the Scots in Rome and corresponded frequently with them as well as with Würzburg. At Christmas 1690 he wrote that Abbot Cook was 'a very worthy, compleat and generous Prelate', and again eight months later used much the same language.[39] The prince-bishop, Johann Gottfried von Guttenberg, also thought highly of the new abbot. On St Joseph's day (19th March) 1691 Cook celebrated the pontifical Mass *coram episcopo* in the church of the Discalced Carmelites, was invited to dinner afterwards with the bishop, and sat at table in the place of honour, taking precedence over the abbot of Schwarzach. This may sound trivial but the bishop was a ruling prince, Cook was only thirty-one, and Schwarzach far exceeded in importance the little Scots abbey. At any rate each copyist of the chronicle thought it significant enough to be included in his narrative.

Ample proof that Cook's first fervour did not last is provided by the visitation acts of August 1693.[40] The preamble mentions difficulties which had arisen in both temporal administration and regular discipline, and some of the enactments suggest strongly that Cook was living in too grand a style. Not more than three men and a boy were to be employed, no guest was to reside if he could not pay for his keep, only benefactors were to be invited to meals, the abbot was to give up costly correspondence (whatever that might mean). Bro Joseph, who had been staying in England and was now in France with letters of exchange, was not to be allowed to impose on the monastery under pretext of expecting a legacy in Scotland. Cook's own life had declined in fervour, for he was told to attend monastic duties more regularly, say Mass more often, and not bring women into the premises but conduct necessary business with them in the porch (where no doubt there was a parlour).

The acts urged the abbot to consult his senior monks and chapter before making important decisions, such as buying and selling. This illustrates two trends of his rule: the unsound administration of temporalities and the lack of consideration for his monks. Three enactments told Cook to appoint two confessors and allow the brethren to make use of either, not to impose penitential practices on the monks, and to grant two walk-days each week with an extra drink. This last refers to the practice of going for a long walk together for exercise, and anyone who has done this in a monastic habit will appreciate the point of having something to quench one's thirst on return to the monastery. In addition Isidore Ogilvie was to embark on higher theological studies, and the abbot had to see that the monastery doors were locked at night and keep the keys.

These comprehensive directions were for the abbot's instruction; there were others for the community. One has to discriminate between phrases or exhorations which are mere matters of form, being found in the Rule or elsewhere, and those which are framed to meet a specific situation. Telling the prior to show good example is most probably a stereotyped phrase, but he was also to observe the pauses in choir recitation (a direction which has no doubt occurred in countless acts of visitations through the centuries) and to proceed with discretion and charity in correcting the brethren. Probably this prior was Augustine Bruce, the man who knew Maurist monasteries at first hand.

The regulations for the brethren in general concern choir office, food and recreation. The portions to be sung at Matins and Lauds are listed; all else was to be merely recited. The monks were to have meat three times a week at dinner and supper, and soup at supper on monastic feast-days. A period of recreation for every day except Friday was laid down. It seems plain that the regulations were made in the brethren's favour, but they were warned not to abuse the opportunity for recreation by grumbling or strife. When government is bad, monks quickly become discontented.

The two Scots abbeys remained in close contact with each other. Augustine Bruce was two weeks at Ratisbon after leaving the Maurists in 1690, the year in which the two abbots were of one mind on union between their monasteries. Two monks of Ratisbon, Columba MacLennan and Joseph Falconer, matriculated at Würzburg; the former took his doctorate in 1695 and was still in Würzburg a year later. The chronicle[41] records visits of Ratisbon monks to Würzburg and vice versa. The earl of Perth, whose chaplain Cook had been in Scotland, visited both abbeys. Having been released from imprisonment in Scotland, Perth made his way by stages to Rome, where he arrived in May 1695.[42] At the end of the previous November he was in Nijmegen and writing: 'I would fain pass Christmass with Abbot Cook, who lived with me at Stobhall, but I fear I shall not reach his monastrie'. His party did, however, reach Würzburg by January, where 'my lord and (by dispense) my lady lodged at a convent of Scots Benedictine Monks, of which father Cook, once my lord's chaplaine, is lord abbot'. The bishop too received Perth kindly, then the party moved on to Ratisbon, a town with 'another Scots convent of the same order, where we lodged and were well entertained'.[43] Abbot Fleming noted that Perth promised his help to the monastery.[44]

Perth was in Rome at the same time as a very strange character, Joseph Ogilvie, the Würzburg laybrother who had taken the relics of Macarius to London. Perhaps the most remarkable thing about him is the influence he seemed to exercise over his superiors. He is probably the 'brother who has been often to and fro and knows all the conveniences', whom Cook promised to send with Francis Sergeant to England in 1691. Two years later, as we have seen, Ogilvie had been living in England, then in France, at the monastery's expense. In 1695 he was in Rome with Will Leslie, the Scottish clergy agent. Alan Chisholm asked Ogilvie to obtain a favour from Leslie and to greet Lord and Lady Perth for him. On one occasion Perth wrote to Leslie: 'Bro Joseph tells me you take care of my Catt'. Since Ogilvie was on friendly terms with the influential Leslie and the noble ex-chancellor, it comes as less of a surprise that the Roman authorities instructed him to take holy orders. At least that was how Ogilvie put it — it was no doubt his own desire — and the Würzburg monastic chapter in February 1696 accepted him as a clerical member of the house. For a further fifteen months, however, he remained in Rome acting as Leslie's secretary. His stay there finally came to an ignominious end when Fleming proved that he had been tampering with his letters and had sent some of them to Abbot Cook.[45] Ogilvie returned to Würzburg in May 1697 and was rewarded by receiving the tonsure from his abbot.

In September 1697 Fr Macarius Brown died after thirty-four years of work as a missionary in England and left a legacy to his monastery. The following January Abbot Cook and Joseph Ogilvie set out to Scotland to collect it.[46] The story of Cook's delay in returning to Würzburg goes beyond the limits of this narrative but the fact that he went to collect the money in person suggests strongly that the windfall was most welcome, and the monastery was in fact heavily in debt. Cook's administration of temporalities has therefore to be considered, and it cannot be dissociated from his spiritual administration. There are three main sources for the story of the decline: the writings of Alan Chisholm, the letters of Abbot Fleming and the visitation acts of 1693 already described. Chisholm's evidence must be taken with caution, for Perth in 1699 blamed him for much of the opposition to Cook in his own community, adding that he was 'an old dozed body' led astray by James Blair.[47] On the other hand, much of what he says finds corroboration elsewhere.

According to Chisholm, Cook started off debt free but 'being young elected Abbot he began many things (against the consent of his Conventuals) which he now finds will not succeed'. Much of the blame is laid on Joseph Ogilvie, whose advice Cook followed and who pushed him to contract debts to finance his own journeys to Scotland, England, France and Italy. By 1699 the debts amounted to 3000 crowns. One can often accept the concrete facts given by

Chisholm while rejecting his comments such as that Cook never intended to repay the debts or that the monastery was 'as hell' to Ogilvie. Fleming corroborates the facts by saying that Cook by his extravagance had ruined what his careful predecessors had built up and in eight years contracted debts of 4000 dollars. The times, however, had not been easy. There had been armies in Franconia in 1689 and 1691, while in 1695 Chisholm wrote that the monastery had more monks than it could support in time of war and some would have to be sent away. He also said, mildly for him, that the abbot's economy was not as acceptable to the bishop and his visitators as that of previous abbots. It can be noted that in 1693-94 an embargo had been laid on goods going into the town of Ratisbon, with the result that Fleming actually had to send half his monks away.[48]

There was a harsh strain in Abbot Cook's character which now began to assert itself. The 1693 visitation gave evidence of his imprudent severity towards his monks. A few years later the bishop appointed Cook to carry out visitations in the abbeys of Schwarzach and Neustadt, the latter apparently in February 1696. Alan Chisholm declares that Cook's severity made the name of Scot hated, as he tried to force Maurist observance on the abbeys he visited, and that he was hard and unmerciful to the monks of his own and other monasteries while being indulgent to himself. His testimony is backed to some extent by Fleming, who wrote that the bishop persecuted religious and used 'a good freind of myne (clearly Cook) to execute his wrath'. Fleming also has a distressing story about Cook's harshness at Schwarzach.[49] The story of Cook's trying to enforce Maurist observance has most probably some foundation, for there are indications of something of the sort in his own monastery (the apertures in the cell doors if nothing else), and both Cook and his prior knew Maurist monasteries at first hand.

There are signs, too, that Cook's rule in his own monastery was harsh, at least towards the younger monks. Of the older monks, Chisholm and Augustine Bruce continued to reside, Boniface Mackie went to the mission about 1694 while Christian Abercrombie seems never to have left it, and James Blair and Joseph Ogilvie lived only intermittently at Würzburg. Among the younger brethren, Gregory Cheyne and Maurus Strachan each took a doctorate in Arts in 1695 and appear to have remained at Würzburg during the following years. The others were less settled, as we know from two main sources: the chronicle recording their comings and goings, and a letter of Abbot Fleming in April 1697.[50] Isidore Ogilvie may have attended university after the visitation of 1693 but he spent some time at Ratisbon in 1695, and Fleming refers to his having been used like a galley slave. In autumn 1696 he began to teach philosophy in the abbey of Neustadt but departed suddenly five months later.[51] Placid Crichton fled in 1695, was captured and sent to Ratisbon for two months, and a year later went to the abbey of Seligenstadt; Fleming's letter suggests that he had run away for the second time. Anselm Gordon had disappeared without trace when Fleming wrote, while Bernard Douglas had been in Ratisbon for ten months and was resolved not to return to Würzburg as long as Cook's rule lasted — which cannot be long, added Fleming. The Ratisbon abbot's source for much of his information is prejudiced — he admitted it was Douglas — but the Würzburg abbey was clearly in a troubled state.

For all that, Cook cannot be written off as a person entirely lacking in merit and good intentions. The bishop, in spite of the visitation acts of 1693 which he personally signed, continued to think highly of him. Not only did he use Cook to carry out visitations, but he delegated him in November 1696 to perform the blessing of the new abbot of Neustadt. There are many testimonies during Cook's absence in 1698-99 to the favour in which he was held by the bishop and others.[52] His prior, Augustine Bruce, thought him the fittest among the Scots to deal with the bishop. Fleming, who wrote that he was in the bishop's favour, was willing to concede that the bishop was a good man even if he was a lawyer and litigious and made use of Cook to persecute other religious. Alan Chisholm gives much the same testimony by saying that the ecclesiastical officials in Würzburg did not like Cook because he sided with the bishop against them. The earl of Perth likewise retained a good opinion of the Würzburg abbot. He considered that much of the trouble at Würzburg arose from the rebellious spirit of the monks, instigated by James Blair in particular, and he tried to offer justifications for Cook's long absence to the bishop. Fleming spoke of Perth's continued regard for the absent abbot, adding on his own account that Cook 'wants not witt'. The university authorities evidently thought so too, for he had the rare distinction of being elected Rector Magnificus for three successive academic years, 1694-97.

The terminal point of this narrative is the departure for Scotland of its first post-reformation Roman Catholic bishop in the autumn of 1696. This was Thomas Nicolson, who was consecrated in February 1695 but was obliged by circumstances to remain on the Continent. He was in Cologne when, on 20th June 1696, Abbot Cook visiting the town was directed by the nuncio to his lodgings. Cook and Nicolson travelled together to Würzburg, where the new bishop stayed with the monks for two and a half months. During his stay in Germany both he and Abbot Fleming were in touch with Will Leslie, the Roman agent for the Scottish clergy, and it was at this point of time that the prince-bishop of Würzburg made Leslie his own agent in Rome.[53] The significance of Nicolson's visit to Würzburg is that Abbot Cook agreed whole-heartedly with the changes which the appointment of a bishop in Scotland would entail for his monks on the mission; it also showed that Cook was still capable, in spite of the defects of his government, of pursuing an enlightened policy, acting with decision and commending himself to influential persons.

While staying at Würzburg Nicolson was invited by Fleming to visit Ratisbon. He could not accept but arranged to meet Fleming at Nuremberg, half-way between the two Scots abbeys. He went there with Bruce, the Würzburg prior (the abbot being unwell at the time), on 9th August, only to find that Fleming did not keep the appointment as the letter telling him of the arrangement had been delayed. Accordingly Fleming travelled to Würzburg, where the two Scots abbots and the new bishop spent three days together. The fruit of the meeting is to be seen in a report to Propaganda of 13th November 1697. The two abbots would send to Scotland any monks on whose services Nicolson called; they had told their monks to take Nicolson as their sole superior while in Scotland; and Nicolson had full powers over monks in Scotland and could even send them back to their abbeys if they proved unsatisfactory. This, says the report, is most encouraging, especially if other religious follow the Benedictines' example. The Scots monasteries are described as being in flourishing condition in regard to observance and studies, and the two abbots as being meritorious and esteemed by all. The student of Würzburg history can hardly accept this as unconditionally true of Cook and his abbey but it relieves the dark picture considerably. Leslie wanted letters of thanks to be sent to the two abbots, and further letters and even papal briefs to be sent to their patrons, including the prince-bishop of Würzburg. And not without reason, for after the meeting at Würzburg the mission work of religious orders in Scotland would be carried out on a different basis. A new era in the history of the Roman Catholic church in Scotland had begun, and the two Scots abbots had helped greatly to give it a fair start.

Notes

[1] Reg. BOA, Sch., Akten, 320.

[2] For Fleming's visits to Würzburg, see Reg. BOA, Sch., Akten, 320, 15.1.1692.

[3] SCA, ML, Chambers, 11.7.1674; *Blairs Papers*, 257.

[4] SCA, ML, Maxwell, 5.11.1681; Reg. BOA, Maxwell, 23.8.1682.

[5] Ser. Abb., confirmed by Gropp, II, 541 and Weiss, 56.

[6] *Cal. State Papers Domestic*, 1689-90, 382-83.

[7] SCA, ML, Fleming, 21.1.1687.

[8] Reg. BOA, Sch., Urk. 683; SCA, ML, Fleming, July 1688.

[9] *SM*, xxiv, 763.

[10] Reg. BOA, Sch., Akten, 15.

[11] Hammermayer, "Restauration", 43. This paper is the source for Fleming's activities unless otherwise stated.

[12] Dennistoun, f. 138rv.

[13] SCA, ML, Chisholm, 20.5.1689.

[14] Dennistoun, f. 333r.

[15] Cit. G. Donaldson, *Scotland: James V to James VII* (1965), 383.

[16] Maxwell, 7.6.1682.

[17] J. P. Kenyon, *The Stuarts* (1958), 174-75.

[18] Hay, *Genealogie,* 58-59.

[19] Weldon, 231.

[20] D. McRoberts, "Scotland's sole canonized saint", in *Claves Regni,* xix (1949), 33.

[21] Dennistoun, f. 138rv.

[22] Gropp, I, 694.

[23] CRS, xxv (1925), 106-07.

[24] Reid, f. 118r.

[25] *A catalogue of the Graduates . . . of the University of Edinburgh* (1858), 113.

[26] Maxwell, 23.7.1681, 11.1.1682, 15.3.1682.

[27] Reid, f. 120r.

[28] Reg. BOA, Sch., Akten 320, 12.7.1690; Wz. SA, Würzburg Stadt R.A. 86, f. 433.

[29] Reid, f. 120r.

[30] SCA, ML, Chisholm, 29.7.1695.

[31] BN, fr. 19,652, f. 339-40.

[32] Maxwell, 18.8.1680.

[33] BN, fr. 19,656, f. 101-04.

[34] BN, fr. 19,650, f. 71.

[35] Reg. BOA, Sch., Akten, 320.

[36] SCA, ML, Fleming, 17.12.1716.

[37] Continuation of Ser. Abb. (o.23).

[38] CRS, xl (1943), 90. Mistakenly called a monk of Würzburg (Hay, *Failure,* 76, 56).

[39] SCA, ML, Sergeant, 1689-91, 1695.

[40] Wz. SA, Urk. 50.24.

[41] See Dennistoun, f. 333r-335r for this period. Reference to it will not be repeated.

[42] A. Joly, *Un converti de Bossuet, James Drummond, duc de Perth* (Lille, 1933), 270.

[43] W. Jerdan (ed.), *Letters from James Earl of Perth* (Camden Society, 1845), 50,91.

44 SCA, ML, Fleming, 22.2.1695, 19.4.1695.

4P SCA, ML, Sergeant, 19.8.1691; Chisholm, 29.7.1695; Perth, 16.11.1695; E, 1696, 34; Cook, Fleming, Ogilvie, 1697.

46 "Three Scots", 242-43.

47 SCA, ML, Perth, 13.6.1699.

48 SCA, ML, Chisholm, 10.3.1698, 13.6.1699, 8.9.1699, 29.7.1695; Fleming, 24.11.1699, 22.12.1693, 19.10.1694.

49 Continuation of Ser. Abb. (q. 56); SCA, ML, Fleming, 11.3.1698.

50 SCA, ML, Fleming, 2.4.1697.

51 Weiss, 65.

52 SCA, ML, Bruce, 25.6.1698, 19.4.1699; Fleming, 14.1.1698, 11.3.1698, 24.11.1699; Chisholm, 13.6.1699; Perth, 13.6.1699.

53 Scots College, Rome, MS 3/20.

143

CHAPTER 12

The Benedictine background

It goes without saying that, like all human institutions, Benedictine monasteries and groups of monasteries have developed constitutionally since their early days. From the sixth century, when St Benedict composed the (on the whole) very general provisions of his Rule, to the twentieth century, when all Benedictine monks are listed in the same directory and their abbots attend regular congresses in Rome, there has been constant development and, in the second half of the period at least, a constant movement towards unification. But even now Benedictines do not constitute a religious order, for they have no central superior or governing body; the most that can be said is that the individual national groups or congregations, though differing widely from each other, resemble religious orders in their general organisation. Within most of these, moreover, the local abbots possess a considerable degree of autonomy. For all practical purposes, most abbeys are independent of each other and of any superior except the holy see. They are also, except in certain minor matters, exempt from the jurisdiction of the bishop of the diocese in which they are situated.

To understand the position of the Scottish monks of Würzburg in the seventeenth century, one must not imagine that Benedictines were organised as they are today, and in particular one must abandon the notion of Benedictines as such being exempt from the authority of the local bishop. Exemption was a privilege granted only to the more important abbeys. St James's in Ratisbon was exempt, was in fact a consistorial abbey, whose abbot had to be proclaimed as duly elected in a papal consistory.[1] St James's in Würzburg had no such privilege.

The status of the Würzburg *Schottenkloster* before the Reformation was determined by two main factors. The first was the establishing of the Congregation of the Scots. When the Lateran Council in 1215 decreed that Benedictine houses were to unite into congregations on a regional basis and hold general chapters every

144

three years, a special arrangement was made for the Scotic monasteries, grouping them according to nationality and not locality. The head of the congregation, the Ratisbon abbot, had considerable disciplinary powers. The Scotic congregation held together until the fifteenth century, and even when it began to break up after 1400 the Würzburg abbot continued to attend chapters at Ratisbon. In the late fifteenth century, when the chapter of 1479 re-affirmed the unity of the congregation, the Würzburg abbots were Irish monks of Ratisbon elected by the general chapter.

The other factor was the very real power of the prince-bishop of Würzburg. In the later Irish period it was he, and not the Ratisbon abbot, who carried out visitations; the abbots elected by the Ratisbon chapter took an oath of obedience to him on the occasion of their confirmation;[2] it was he who brought about what he called the reform of the monastery by bringing in German monks in 1497 and who later permitted, or perhaps even arranged for, its temporary union with the Bursfeld Congregation. St James's was thus subject both to the bishop and to the Ratisbon abbot who was head of the Scotic Congregation. One must be careful, however, not to interpret the word 'congregation' in its modern sense. The Scotic Congregation was a capitular union, that is, its abbots met in chapter, and it was also something much more, because the Ratisbon abbey was the mother-house of the others. Both these types of group, the capitular union and the mother-house surrounded by its offspring, were to disappear with the Reformation.[3]

After the upheaval of the Reformation the Ratisbon abbot continued to look on St James's in Würzburg as a daughter-house and therefore subject in some way to his authority. The seventeenth century was also characterised, particularly in Germany, by the constant efforts among Benedictines to group together for mutual support. The tensions among the Würzburg Scots over their status can only be understood in relation to the traditional role of the Ratisbon abbot, the authoritarian rule of the prince-bishop of Würzburg, and the advances made by the various German Benedictine congregations. To these must be added the desire to share in the good fortune of the English monks, who had established a national congregation on the Continent with ample faculties and privileges for missionary work in their homeland.

The relations of the Würzburg Scots with the Ratisbon abbey and their own bishop during the seventeenth century have been mentioned time and again in the preceding chapters, for they are central to the history of the monastery. The background to it, however, the movement towards congregations, also needs consideration. The final session of the Council of Trent in

December 1563 had legislated for the regular orders and given them an impetus to reform. One decree in particular had ordered the exempt monasteries to arrange for chapter meetings and visitations among themselves; in other words, the equivalent of diocesan synods and parish visitations was considered salutary for monasteries also. The decree did not envisage congregations with uniform observance in each monastery but merely the capitular union already prescribed in 1215. Nevertheless it did lead to the formation of closely-knit congregations, which the holy see encouraged as being more susceptible to influence from Rome. The new congregations were real corporate entities, with common statutes for each house and some form of permanent central control. There were basically two kinds, the federal and the centralised. In the former the monk took his vows for his own monastery, which thus became his family, and the monastery had its own abbot elected for life. In the latter the congregation and not the individual monastery was the family of the monk, and each monastery surrendered much of its individuality to the central governing body. Only the Hungarian Congregation is today organised on this basis. The federal type, the one taken up by seventeenth-century German Benedictines, is the form of congregation that has almost universally prevailed.

Attempts by popes and their emissaries to form centralised congregations among Benedictines in German-speaking lands were made in the late sixteenth century but came to naught. In the early seventeenth century, however, alarmed by the fate which was liable to overtake and did overtake monasteries without an adequate community, the German abbots themselves pressed for union. Congregations were formed in Switzerland, Swabia, Austria and the dioceses of Salzburg and Strasburg. For the most part these were not exempt; indeed the motive of a bishop in erecting a congregation in his diocese was usually to ensure that monasteries did not join a congregation outwith his control or gain exemption. The history of German Benedictines in the seventeenth century is largely a story of conflicts between bishops and monasteries, and among the most uncompromising bishops are to be counted the prince-bishops of Würzburg.

If the German abbots were opposed by the diocesan bishops in their efforts to form unions, they were impelled to make these efforts by the dangers which threatened. They had suffered great losses of property at the Reformation and were liable to suffer more through the demands made by and for the energetic, apostolic Jesuits. Some time shortly after 1626 three Jesuit provincials and about thirty priests met at Ratisbon, with the intention of gaining support among the temporal rulers for their plan to obtain German

Benedictine monasteries and revenues for their own use.[4] Some, perhaps the extremists among them, declared that Germany would never prosper until the Benedictines were extinct like the Templars. Already in 1625 a union of all German monasteries had been proposed and had been taken up by the Bursfeld Congregation. Originally the Bursfeld Congregation was due to a reforming movement which had done much to raise the level of German monasticism before the Reformation. Though it had suffered severe losses during the Reformation period it still comprised about forty monasteries, chiefly in Westphalia and the dioceses of Cologne and Trier, whose abbots attended its general chapter. In 1627 the Bursfeld president sought authority from Rome for the uniting of all German Benedictine monasteries into one congregation. This won the approval of the nuncio Carafa, and in October 1630 an invitation was sent to the various abbeys and groups to meet at Ratisbon the following January. In spite of the strong objections of bishops and temporal rulers the meeting took place and approved of the plan for union. All were to join the Bursfeld Union, which had the privilege of uniting monasteries to itself even when the bishop refused consent. A further meeting was fixed for July 1631 but was never held, and Rome, under pressure from the bishops and imperial electors, declared the proposed union null and void.

The situation had been complicated by the imperial Edict of Restitution in 1629 restoring all property formerly owned by religious bodies and taken away from them since 1552. Naturally the Benedictines tried to regain what was once Benedictine property; as we have seen, the Würzburg Scots tried to regain the old Scotic abbey in Nuremberg. The Jesuits, too, made efforts to get former monastic property for what they considered (and probably with reason) more useful purposes. The scramble came to a sudden end when the Protestant armies overran south Germany in 1631. There followed, nevertheless, an energetic battle in print between Jesuits and Benedictines, the chief protagonist of the monks being a Fr Romanus Hay (whose name despite its appearance is German and not Scots).[5] The matter was finally settled by the peace of Westphalia in 1648 by which whoever had church property on 1st January 1624 kept it. Besides the devastation caused by the war, much German Benedictine property was thus once and for all settled under Protestant ownership. But the idea of an extension of the Bursfeld Union had taken hold, and there were to be intermittent efforts among the German congregations to unite.

What was the position of the Würzburg Scots in this constitutional struggle? The language found in the various documents can cause confusion, since we find the Scots asserting

147

the existence of a Scottish Congregation and at the same time exerting themselves to form one. The congregation in existence was the union formed in 1215 and of little practical moment in the seventeenth century, while the union they hoped to form was a congregation of the post-Tridentine sort. The best way of answering the question is therefore to observe what actually happened and to note in particular what general chapters the Scots abbots attended and who carried out visitations of the abbey. In both cases the answer is decisive. By and large the Scots abbots attended no general chapters, and it was invariably the Würzburg diocesan officials appointed by the prince-bishops who carried out visitations of the Scots abbey. The conclusion, therefore, is inescapable: St James's, Würzburg, belonged to no Benedictine congregation.

It is possible, nevertheless, to distinguish temporary modifications of this basic position. The re-foundation of the monastery in 1595 was done entirely on the terms of the bishop, who laid down the horarium and imposed stringent conditions for the abbey's continued existence. In spite of this, Bishop Echter allowed the Würzburg monks to have both active and passive voice in the Ratisbon chapter (most clearly seen, perhaps, in the affair of Algeo's coadjutorship) and was willing to let Abbot Whyte behave as an abbot general with jurisdiction over the Würzburg abbey. The first two abbots seem to have been elected at Ratisbon. It was Whyte who administered the monastery when its first abbot resigned, who released Abbot Hamilton from his monastic obligations in 1606, who then lived at Würzburg without being its abbot and tried to control the Ratisbon abbey from a distance. It is possible, of course, that this was because the Würzburg authorities insisted on some sort of abbot being in residence. All the same, at this time Whyte behaved like the president of a congregation and he used the language of one, calling himself Visitor General with power to remove other abbots from office. In April 1615 he actually said that the three Scots abbeys formed one congregation and acted together for its well-being.

Even at this time, of course, the Würzburg abbey was not exempt, that is, it was subject to the bishop. But monasteries could still be members of a congregation and take part in its general chapters without being exempt. This might have happened with St James's if Whyte had been a successful superior. Instead, as we have seen, Julius Echter issued an ultimatum at the end of 1614, as a result of which the Würzburg monks held an abbatial election in Würzburg, probably the first time this happened.

Echter's successor, a reforming bishop like himself, had already gained experience in ruling the diocese of Bamberg. One of his first acts in Würzburg was to convoke a synod of Benedictines, and he told them, after the solemn opening ceremonies, that he had summoned them for the furtherance of regular discipline and uniformity among the various monasteries. The monks then accepted, rather than themselves decided upon, proposals for reform and common observance. The text that was drawn up states now and again that the prince-bishop wanted such and such to be done. The enactments included a very detailed horarium for choir office, meals and study, detailed regulations for food, clothing and recreation, and much else besides. The same liturgical books were to be used, the same ceremonial observed. Little of importance was overlooked, and there were sections on enclosure, silence, the vow of poverty, the noviciate, the sick. The Scots abbot and prior agreed to all this and signed like the rest. St James's now formed part of what was, in fact if not in name, a German diocesan congregation but one without power to arrange its own general chapters and visitations.

The appointment of William Ogilvie, after a visitation in 1627, to administer the abbey of Schwarzach is an example of what submission to the bishop and his officials could mean. Schwarzach had belonged to the Bursfeld Union like St James's and seems to have considered itself as still belonging, but was unable to carry out what this entailed in practice.[6] An attempt by the Bursfeld Union in 1630 to return to Franconia was unsuccessful.[7] Thus, when the war came to Franconia, the abbeys in Würzburg diocese, St James's included, formed a centrally controlled group on their own. The pact with the English Congregation in 1623 was merely a spiritual union together with an arrangement for mission faculties.

After the Swedish occupation the monasteries of Franconia and Bavaria were in a sorry state, nor was recovery possible while the threat of hostilities lasted. The very destitution of Ratisbon obliged the Würzburg Scots to go to its help, so that for a time the superiors of all three Scottish monasteries were monks of Würzburg. This of course did not affect the status of the Würzburg abbey, but the attempts to expel the Scots from Ratisbon gave a further impetus to unity. Abbot Asloan of Würzburg had been appointed abbot of Ratisbon by the holy see, following on his election by the Ratisbon community. The Würzburg officials had then told him to return to Würzburg if he wished to remain abbot of his own monastery. He did so, leaving Ratisbon in the hands of an administrator, and so was in the strange position of being abbot of two monasteries simultaneously. The third Scots abbey, Erfurt, although not exempt, was recognised by the archbishop of Mainz to be dependent on Ratisbon. Thus Asloan was legally in control of all three abbeys.

To this must be added the attempts made by the emperor and bishop in 1639-41 to confiscate the Ratisbon abbey and oblige the Scots monks to go to Würzburg. As the legal superior, Asloan was directly involved. There was also the stimulus given by the final success of the English Congregation. English monks who had entered Italian and Spanish monasteries had begun to do mission work in England, then had founded houses of their own, and after much controversy had established a congregation in 1619. It was at first subject to the Valladolid Congregation but the bull *Plantata* in 1633 recognised its coming of age and granted complete exemption and permanent mission facilities. The bull was first promulgated to the English community at Douai in 1634, then promulgated to the whole Congregation at the next general chapter in 1639.

Not long after this the story was current among the Scots that in the years 1606-09 the abbot of St Vaast in Arras had offered property and revenues if students at the Scots College in Douai would take the habit, and that on the Scots' refusal the English monks received his help instead. The Scots also believed that the English monastery at Dieulouard in Lorraine had belonged to them of old. They felt that the good fortune of the English monks should really have been their own.[8] It is in fact possible that the continuity with pre-reformation monasticism in Scotland achieved at Ratisbon acted as a stimulus to the English monks to effect something similar.

The desire of the Scots at this time to form a congregation of the new type can be explained by Asloan's position as superior of all three houses like the president of a centralised congregation, the need to unite in order to withstand attack, and the stimulus given by the success of the English monks. Until the chronology is established more precisely, one cannot say whether the attempt of the Bursfeld president to re-unite St James's to his congregation was an additional persuasive to form a Scottish Congregation or whether it ran counter to the already explicit plans of the Scots. As we have seen, Asloan in 1642 was perfectly willing to help the Bursfeld Union to establish itself once more in Würzburg but not to have the Scots included in it, though St James's had been joined to it in its German period. He told Colchon that St James's had been re-united to the Scottish Congregation and that the rights and privileges of the Scottish Congregation prevented it from joining the Bursfeld Union. This was unacceptable to Colchon, because the Bursfeld Congregation considered the separation of any member null and void, since monasteries belonging to it had received privileges and had taken an oath binding for all time.

Asloan's language has misled the chief historian of the Bursfeld Congregation into thinking that the Scottish Congregation resisted

Colchon's proposals.[9] But no Scottish Congregation had yet been formed and the petition to form one was not granted, if indeed it was ever presented. Its suggestions are therefore of little practical importance. In brief, however, the Scots wanted a congregation with all the privileges granted to the old Scotic Congregation or to modern congregations since, and so have the same favour shown them as was recently shown to the English. The Ratisbon abbot would be president for life and have all competent jurisdiction but could be deposed if necessary; he would also be prefect of their mission to Scotland. There would be a general chapter every five years, which would appoint persons to carry out the annual visitation of the monasteries. The Scots also wanted comprehensive privileges and favours, and the return of all alienated property both in Scotland and on the continent. One of the most significant features of the petition is the desire for exemption of the president, the congregation and the individual abbots from the jurisdiction of the diocesan bishops.[10]

Both the Bursfeld Union and Würzburg ecclesiastics were making efforts to restore monastic life after the upheaval of the Swedish invasion. Franconian monasteries in general took over new constitutions adapted from a *Caeremoniale Benedictinum* printed in south Germany in 1641. The bishop delegated abbots to join with his officials in carrying out visitations; thus, after the Scots had received a visitation of this sort, Abbot Asloan joined in doing the same in the neighbouring abbey of St Stephen's. This was in 1643, when the Bursfeld Union was trying to get the Würzburg abbots to attend their chapters and accept their visitations. In this year the Bursfeld authorities put in one of their monks as abbot of a monastery in Würzburg diocese, and he refused to accept the visitators sent by the bishop.[11]

The Bursfeld Union, however, was fighting against odds that were too great and does not seem to have tried again to enter Würzburg diocese. In 1651 two Würzburg Scots were received by the Bursfeld president, then went on to the monasteries of the Congregation of Lorraine. It is more than likely that they hoped to inaugurate some sort of union in observance if not in organisation. One of the two was James Brown, in whose historical work written shortly after occurs the significant remark that the monks of the Lorraine Congregation would surely help the Scots by training their young men if they were united, *si essent uniti*. This apparently means the introduction of their reformed observance, which in 1631 was followed by the Scots at Erfurt and perhaps also at Ratisbon. One should note, too, that Brown was at Rome and later at Ratisbon with Silvanus Mayne, who influenced him considerably and had himself been acquainted with the Lorraine abbeys.[12] The

Lorraine Congregation, however, was one of the centralised type in which the family unit was the congregation as a whole and the local superiors were appointed for a term of years by the general chapter. It is difficult to imagine that the Scots wanted to lose their identity in such a body, or that it had the faintest chance of establishing itself in the diocese of Würzburg. But the Würzburg Scots felt its influence, no doubt in much the same way as they were influenced by Maurist observance and ideals at the end of the century.

The Union with the English Congregation in 1660 has been described in detail, in its provisions and in its effects. There seems little point in looking for analogies or similar unions, for quite possibly it is unique in monastic annals. Perhaps if an abbot more sympathetic to it than Dixon had ruled Würzburg after 1661 the significance of the union would have been greater. The jurisdiction of the prince-bishop was expressly safeguarded, and it provided for such things as a friendly visitation by the English president every so often in addition to the bishop's visitations. There is no record that an English visitation ever took place or that a Würzburg abbot ever attended an English general chapter. Really the Union provided for English help and opened the door to English influence but scarcely affected the constitutional status of the abbey. Its importance lies in the missionary sphere. Undoubtedly, however, it increased the Scots' awareness of what the English Congregation was and did, and a considerable number of English Congregation documents were transcribed and preserved by the Scots.

In 1652 the Ratisbon abbot had been saying that he had the right to hold visitations in Würzburg. The chances of his doing so after a lapse of almost four centuries, especially in that prince-bishopric, were of course negligible, but it showed that the traditional position of the abbot of Ratisbon regarding the other Scots monasteries had not been forgotten. Abbot Asloan of Würzburg summed up the real position more accurately two years later in his answers to the Irish monks' questionnaire when they were trying to gain admission into the Scots abbeys. Replying to a question on monastic property and revenues, he said that the bishop and his councillors knew about them, because it was their concern alone. Regarding the abbey's status, he replied that at the present time it was not exempt but it was united to the other Scots monasteries insofar as they were members of the same nation and order, and when they were attacked from without they combined to help each other.[13] It is clear that the Würzburg diocesan authorities did not mind how much coming and going there was between the Scots in Würzburg and Ratisbon, nor how much they co-operated in missionary work, provided it did not affect the status or the observance of St James's. In 1691, only three years after the monastery had sent almost all its priests to Scotland, the bishop in a report to Rome said that Scots monks went as missionaries by his leave.[14]

When, after a century or more of intermittent effort, the Bavarian Congregation was founded in 1684, pressure was put on Abbot Fleming of Ratisbon to join it. This was a matter in which his exempt status was largely irrelevant, because it was usually the exempt abbots who, not being subject to the bishop, took the lead in forming these regional congregations. Fleming resisted, basing his stand on the abbot of Ratisbon being head of the old Scottish Congregation.[15] It was no doubt the formation of the Bavarian Congregation that stimulated Fleming to think once more about a Scottish Congregation. In 1685 James Blair transcribed for Fleming the petition for a Scottish Congregation made in 1640-44 and a summary of it. The originals from which he copied have been preserved. However, his transcript also contained a second summary very like the first but with one great difference: the rights of the bishops were to be preserved. The president's jurisdiction was not to infringe these, abbatial elections were to be confirmed by the bishop, and the congregation was not to be exempt.[16] Since the original of this has not, as far as we know, been preserved, it may well be that it is Fleming's adaptation of the 1640 petition, made to improve his chances with the bishop of Würzburg. Politics, after all, is the art of the possible. On the other hand, there is no mention in his correspondence at this time of any plan to found a Scottish Congregation.

The first sign of such a project belongs to the year 1690. We have seen how Abbot Cook in that year agreed to Fleming's plan, adding, however, 'I durst not lett it be known at our court I had such a thought', and how Fleming in January 1692 sought to enlist the support of the Würzburg suffragan and promised that there would be no diminution of the bishop's authority. The matter was open enough for the monastic chroniclers to record it and express their hope, in writing for Mabillon's collections, that it would soon be accomplished.[17] Writers on the Scots monasteries commonly assert that a Scottish Congregation was formed in 1692. It would seem that the origin of the assertion can be traced back to a writer in 1895, who gives some of the terms of the agreement from a document in the Ratisbon monastic archives. According to this, the three abbots with the approval of their superiors (the holy see, the archbishop of Mainz and the bishop of Würzburg, respectively) formed a congregation. Abbot Fleming of Ratisbon was elected president for life, and thereafter a president was to be chosen every six years by the three abbots and a delegate from each monastery. Provision was also made for the death or resignation of a president in office. Because of the antiquity of the monastery and the privileges granted to it by pope and emperor, the abbot of Ratisbon was to take first place, then came the abbot of Würzburg, and lastly the abbot of Erfurt; and their priors were ranged in the same order.[18]

The evidence is overwhelming, however, that no congregation was formed. The document, which is not to be found, was no doubt merely the draft of an agreement that was never signed. We have Fleming's own testimony that the Würzburg Scots drew back; there is no reference to it in any Würzburg document or writer; the chroniclers of the monastery say nothing of it, neither does Brockie in his *Monasticon*. When references occur to a Scottish Congregation as actually existing, the word must be interpeted to mean the union brought about by the Lateran Council and not a juridically constituted body. When Ratisbon abbots continued to describe themselves in terms such as *Matricularius et Visitator* of all Scots monasteries in Germany,[19] the title must be taken as merely traditional, in the same way as modern British coins bear the title 'Defender of the Faith', bestowed on Henry VIII by the pope. Thus, in a compilation sent to Mabillon, probably by Fleming, the Ratisbon abbot is described as formerly having jurisdiction *de facto* over all Scottish monasteries and still having it *de jure*.[20] Of course, an abbot like Fleming was always willing to make his jurisdiction actual once again.

A summary of the Würzburg monastery's status in the seventeenth century, given by Fleming but with less than his usual objectivity, is worth quoting. According to this, John James Whyte, abbot of Ratisbon, recovered the Würzburg monastery at great expense and put in some of his monks. It was not long before these severed all connection with Ratisbon, but finding they could not exist alone they united themselves to the English Congregation. After a time the English realised that they reaped no advantage from their union with Würzburg, so they had it rescinded by Cardinal Norfolk's authority. Fleming therefore invited the Würzburg Scots to join with Ratisbon on the same terms as for the union with the English Congregation, but they absolutely refused and invoked the bishop's protection against all overtures from Ratisbon.[21] The main stages of the monastery's progress are fairly accurately described, even if the picture is distorted. In particular the proposed union of 1692 remains a mystery; the Würzburg monks were in favour of it, yet its subsequent rejection by them or the bishop is not mentioned in the correspondence with Rome that has survived.

It is clear that no Ratisbon abbot after Whyte interfered in the running of the Würzburg monastery. The very real power of the Würzburg officials, on the other hand, is everywhere apparent.

154

They conducted the visitations and arranged the abbatial elections. In 1640 and 1699[22] they summoned the absent abbot to return. In 1640 we find them exacting annual accounts from the abbot, and it was they who knew the state of the monastic property in 1654. Abbots of Würzburg explicitly called themselves subjects of the prince-bishop. Even the holy see did not interfere in Würzburg affairs, though one finds nuncios and the cardinal protector of Scotland making decisions on Ratisbon, which was exempt from the bishop and thus subject directly to the holy see. Twice Propaganda ordered visitations of the three Scots abbeys in Germany, in 1627 and 1668, in each case at a time when the affairs of Ratisbon were at a very low ebb. Since all three abbeys are mentioned without any distinction, not much value can be attached to remarks in 1668 about their being directly subject to the holy see although the local bishops claimed jurisdiction over them.[23] The remarks fit quite well the situation in Ratisbon at the time but do not fit that in Würzburg. We can be fairly sure that no visitation was carried out by an apostolic visitor in Würzburg, for not only did the bishop have jurisdiction over the Scots abbey; he was also the temporal ruler.

Notes

[1] For this see *The Apostolic Camera and Scottish Benefices 1418-88*, ed. A. I. Cameron (Oxford, 1934), xx-xxiii.

[2] Copialbuch, f. 105v, 108r.

[3] For post-reformation Benedictine unions see Molitor, I, 312-73.

[4] P. Volk, "Ein Säkularisationsplan sämtlicher deutscher Benediktinerklöster zu Anfang des 17. Jahrhunderts", in *SM*, xlvii, 146-56.

[5] P. Lindner, "Verzeichnis aller Aebte und . . . verstorbenen Mönche der Reichsabtei Ochsenhausen", in *Diöcesanarchiv von Schwaben*, xvii, 119.

[6] Wolff, 306.

[7] *WDGB*, vi, 135.

[8] Indiculus, f. 26v, 51r.

[9] Volk, 381.

[10] Mun. HSA, KUSJR, Fasz. 9; copy in Blair, f. 131r-142r.

[11] Gropp, II, 168-69.

[12] Indiculus, f. 27v-28r, 51v.

[13] NLS, Adv. 29.7.1, f. 5rv, 39v-40r.

[14] *AU*, iv, pt. 3, p. 14.

[15] FA, Rat. 16a.

[16] Blair, f. 142r-144r.

[17] BN, lat. 12,675, f. 218r.

[18] Renz, xvi, 83.

[19] FA, Rat. 7, f. 5v.

[20] BN, lat. 12,675, f. 221v.

[21] SCA, ML, Fleming, 17.12.1716.

[22] SCA, ML, Bruce, 15.3.1699; Chisholm, 13.6.1699.

[23] Giblin, 46-47, 75-76.

CHAPTER 13

Mission work
before the Restoration

There were many colleges and religious houses of Scottish, English and Irish Catholics on the continent, all of which differed from the Scottish Benedictine monasteries in one important particular: they had been founded as a consequence of the success of the Reformation in Britain and had of their nature a missionary ethos, whereas the *Schottenklöster* had been founded in the twelfth century, had come into the possession of Scottish monks (at least in principle) before the Reformation and were part of the traditional church life of Germany. Missionary activity was a temporary addition to the claustral life of the Scots monks. The other institutions were counter-reformation centres of their very nature, the Scots abbeys only by force of circumstances. In spite of this the Scots Benedictines made a contribution, not very large but by no means negligible, to the missionary effort during the seventeenth century.

It is not easy to determine the extent to which missionary activity entered into the plans of John Lesley and Ninian Winzet in their refounding of the Scots abbeys. While in Rome, they could not have been ignorant of the counter-reformation efforts of the English Catholics there, nor of the interest of Gregory XIII in recovering their homeland for Catholicism. In his memorial to the pope, among his reasons why the German abbeys should be handed over to the Scots, Lesley listed the education of young Scots who would help to restore the Catholic religion in Scotland, and he added that if the handing over was not possible immediately, at least part of their income could be used to educate missionaries for Scotland. Lesley's intention, as far as one can make out from the rather vague language, was not that the Scots monks should be missionaries but that they should reside in their monasteries and educate missionaries.

This was the language used in addressing Gregory XIII; the petitions to the German dignitaries for help made less mention of the advantages to Scotland. For instance, of Winzet's eleven reasons why the Vienna abbey should be restored to the Scots, not one mentioned the benefit to Catholicism in Scotland.[1] This may of course have been merely politic. Lesley did try to obtain free places for one or two Scots students in Eichstätt seminary; he and Winzet quite possibly did stress their apostolic aims when they approached Bishop Echter in Würzburg; and there may well have been some potential Scots missionaries educated by Winzet in Ratisbon. Nevertheless, whatever the aims of Lesley and Winzet were, we know of no positive contribution made to the Scottish mission by the Ratisbon abbey during Winzet's period of rule. The entries in the Ratisbon necrology concerning monks working on the Scottish mission at this time must be disregarded; they are fabrications of the early eighteenth century.[2]

In 1594 Clement VIII's brief to Bishop Echter linked the projected restoration of the Würzburg abbey with benefit to Scotland. There is no conclusive evidence, however, that the Scots monks themselves looked on the restoration of the abbey as a means of helping Catholicism in Scotland, nor, if one can judge from the conditions laid down by Echter, that he did either. It is likely, all the same, that Echter and the monks had something of the sort in mind even if it was not put explicitly into writing. The papal brief may have been echoing Echter's prior communication in its reference to helping Scotland. Less than a year after the refounding of the Würzburg abbey the monks and the bishop were conferring on a plan to do exactly this. David Anderson, the Presbyterian minister, reported that the priest Adam Simpson had been sent from Ratisbon to Rome by the Scots abbots to obtain leave for some of the monks to return to Scotland to 'traffic there with the papists' and bring back boys to Germany. This Adam Simpson is perhaps to be identified with one Adam MacCall who makes his first appearance at Ratisbon in 1597. The identification is tempting. Both had the forename Adam and were from Edinburgh; for what it is worth, too, the priest Simpson was in Galloway in 1594-5[3] and the priest MacCall was to be found there many years later.

Anderson also reported a meeting which took place at Würzburg on 19th April 1596, at the instance of the nuncio in Germany, between Scottish papists and Julius Echter. It is not clear who took part, but presumably the Benedictines are meant since the setting is wholly German. The purpose was to plan the project that Simpson had gone to Rome to get permission for, namely, the sending of some priest to Scotland who would spy out the land and consult with the Catholics there; he would also bring back boys between the ages of twelve and eighteen, some of whom would become monks in the abbeys the Scots already had or hoped to obtain, while others would be trained as missionaries by the Jesuits. Echter, said

Anderson, had agreed to maintain sixty such youths, the bishop of Salzburg forty, and the bishop of Ratisbon twenty. Anderson thought that either Abbot Irvine or his prior Hamilton would be sent to Scotland that summer, 1596, to carry out the project.

It is more difficult to judge of the accuracy of this information than of the details Anderson gives concerning the monks themselves, for it is corroborated by no known source. That Simpson went to Rome and that the meeting in Würzburg took place seems most likely, since Anderson's factual accuracy is considerable. The list of monasteries to be acquired for the Scots included Vienna but also some with no Irish connections whatsoever. The figures of the students to be given board, lodging and education by the German bishops are fantastically high and cannot be taken seriously. One feels that Anderson laboured under the handicap of spies who have to rely on rumour or on reports which have not lost in the telling.

Whether anything at all came of these plans is difficult to say. Given the tiny size of the Würzburg community at the time, three men in all, it is unlikely that Irvine or Hamilton could leave for Scotland until some new men arrived — Hamilton, we know, stayed and took a theological degree — while the unsatisfactory progress of the new foundation could not have been conducive to constructive plans. The statements found in print about missionary work done by the monks in the years before and after 1600 are very general and give no source.[4] They are apparently based on a passage of George Conn[5] saying that, around the 1580s, men of various religious orders, including Benedictines, went to Scotland to remedy the lack of priests there. Conn supplies no names and gives no authority for his statement. There is no record of any monk of Ratisbon or Würzburg going to Scotland, and probably no monk spent a long continuous period in Scotland.

The first certain reference to a Scottish Benedictine in Scotland comes from an almost frivolous source. The monk Thomas Duff was an inveterate rhymer whose poems occasionally got him into trouble. Like a schoolboy who has suffered the confiscation and return of his diary, he wrote in Latin in a crude cipher on the cover of his manuscript volume of poems: 'In 1621 Fr Alexander, the prior, took this book from my cell, and the abbot gave it back to me on 5th April 1622 when he was going to Scotland'. As one can see, the note leaves it in doubt which of the two is meant by 'he', but we can presume it was Alexander Baillie, both because one can hardly imagine the visit of a mitred prelate to Scotland going unrecorded in either Scottish or Franconian sources, and because Baillie, in his book written not long after, showed signs of knowing contemporary Scotland at first hand.

159

Now, 1622 is one of the important dates in the history of the Catholic church in Scotland, for in that year was founded the *Congregatio de Propaganda Fide*, commonly known under the familiar title of Propaganda, a word which has unfortunately developed unpleasant connotations in modern times. Very briefly, Propaganda has charge of all missionary lands, and when the Catholic church becomes sufficiently strong to stand on its own feet in any territory, Propaganda relinquishes control of it. The opinion has been expressed that 'the modern Catholic Church in Scotland owes everything to this Congregation',[6] although its help to Scotland in the seventeenth century has also been summarised as 'too little and too late'.[7] But beyond any doubt Propaganda is of supreme importance in the history of the post-reformation Catholic church in Scotland.

It is unlikely to be a coincidence that the Würzburg Scots took active steps towards doing systematic missionary work at the same time as Propaganda set about its gigantic task. It is of course possible, though not at all likely, that the Scots monks had already made efforts, which have gone unrecorded. Nevertheless the series of events which began in Würzburg in 1622 cannot be understood without allowing for Propaganda, as a catalyst if not an active agent.

It needs to be realised that normally Catholic missionaries cannot be free-lances. The Roman Catholic church is a hierarchic one, the ultimate superior being the pope, and priests do not usually exercise the powers received at ordination except by licence of a superior. Certain acts, such as granting absolution in confession, lifting a sentence of excommunication or dispensing from a law of the church, are considered to require also jurisdiction on the part of the priest. It follows, then, that he requires to be given licence by lawful authority to exercise his ministry and that his powers are restricted by the terms of the licence. These powers or licence are called his faculties. Just as the priest cannot exercise his ministry without faculties, so the faculties themselves cannot be granted except by a superior who has received power to grant them, and ultimately the authority comes from the pope himself.

There is nothing very surprising about this when one considers the legal restrictions that are taken for granted by most people: nobody, for instance, may drive a car without a licence or practise medicine without a recognised qualification, ownership of property depends on possession of title-deeds, and so on. What is surprising is the contrast in seventeenth-century Scotland between the necessity of having faculties and the very unsystematic way in which they were granted. Propaganda could give faculties for the countries under its control, but its coming into existence in 1622 did not deprive other bodies of powers they already possessed. Jesuits continued to receive faculties for Scotland from their own superiors, presumably because the General of the Jesuits possessed powers received directly from the pope to grant faculties for all mission countries. Hence the bitter struggle between Propaganda and the Jesuits. The superiors of the English Benedictine Congregation evidently had power to give faculties to any Benedictine monk for the whole of the British Isles. In England and Scotland the efforts of the various bodies giving faculties for mission work were not co-ordinated. Tension, and at times strife, naturally resulted, particularly in England in the early seventeenth century.

No adequate study of the Scottish mission has yet been written, and thus the background against which the missionary efforts of the monks must be seen is in many ways obscure. It should be realised that in the first decades of the seventeenth century there were never more than seventeen or eighteen priests in the whole of Scotland. In 1623 there were fifteen, belonging to five religious orders; not one was a secular priest, although there had been some seculars on the mission.[8] The secular clergy were much handicapped by the lack of any organisation, and one way out of their difficulties was to enter a religious order.[9] There was no co-ordinated mission, and no general superior or bishop in Scotland. The first two English Vicars-Apostolic, when they were appointed, were nominally ordinaries of Scotland too, an arrangement that was virtually a dead letter from the start. The Irish Franciscan mission to the Gaelic-speaking half of Scotland was, to begin with, controlled from Flanders. This, evidently, was the pattern of missionary work in Scotland at the time: small groups of religious, working independently of each other, each subject to superiors on the Continent.

We can now consider the missionary efforts of the Scottish monks. In January 1623, eight months after the Würzburg prior set off for Scotland, Fr Silvanus Mayne was the bearer of letters concerning mission work from the English Benedictines in Douai to the Scots abbots.[10] The English president urged the Scots to set up a mission to their homeland, a project which he said was feasible since there were students in the Scots college at Douai who wanted to become monks and so could replace the priests who went to Scotland. The English Congregation had faculties for the whole of Great Britain and would grant them to the Scots. The same facilities and privileges would be given to the Scots as were available to English monks who belonged to some congregation other than the English (e.g., the Cassinese) but desired to work on the English mission. They would be provided with the necessary faculties to carry out their mission work and given whatever help

161

they needed. While on the mission they would be subject to the rules and superiors of the English congregation but this would not prevent them from transacting any business entrusted to them by their abbots or from being recalled to their own monasteries. They would be eligible for appointment to offices in the English Congregation, attendance at its chapter, and so on. No burden would be placed on the Scottish monasteries, and no share in the rights of the Scots would be asked, except perhaps occasional hospitality for an English monk who was travelling in South Germany.

The three Scots abbots sent a grateful acceptance of the English proposal. They promised that, as soon as replacements could be found, suitable men would be sent to Scotland who would be subject to the laws and superiors of the English Congregation, with the reservation that their abbots could use them for any special business if necessary. This letter was signed at Würzburg at the end of July 1623. The following spring the Scots monks were working to establish a mission of their own.

The gist of their petition, sent to Cardinal Francesco Barberini, was as follows: The monks of Ratisbon, Würzburg and Erfurt, seeing the successful results produced by two of their men who had been sent to Scotland a few years previously, and having at present other men who could be sent, want a mission to be set up, with the customary faculties and under the direction of Silvanus Mayne, a man of exemplary life who had been imprisoned and exiled for his religion. The petition was drafted into the form of a request to the pope for a mission to Scotland like that of the other religious orders, with the same favours, faculties and privileges, and was put on the agenda of the monthly meeting of Propaganda held on 17th April 1624. The reaction was favourable. The pope gave instructions that the nuncio in Vienna should make enquiries as to which monks were suitable and in particular find out what he could about Mayne.[11]

We can follow the ensuing correspondence. Barberini wrote three days later telling the nuncio to find out the number of monks available, their education and way of life, then choose the most suitable among them and send their names to Rome. In particular he was to inform himself about Mayne since it was most important that the superior should outstrip the others in learning and virtue. On 11th May the nuncio replied that he would obey instructions and send a precise report.[12] What he did was to pass the request on to the bishop of Würzburg, Philip Adolf von Ehrenberg. Nothing more was heard until six months later, when the bishop replied to say that in Würzburg there were four Scottish monks suitable and ready for mission work, while others were studying philosophy and theology in order to prepare themselves for the mission. He told the nuncio of Mayne's imprisonment and sentence in Scotland ten years before, then went on to speak of the other Scottish monasteries. In these, he said, were three suitable priests, of whom two had been working successfully during the past years in Scotland; and in the Scots seminaries were students who wanted to become monks in the German abbeys.

The bishop wrote on 3rd November. The nuncio sent the letter on to Barberini on the 16th, explaining that the fault for the delay was not his, and it was produced at the next meeting of Propaganda on 17th December. One can still see the notes made on the backs of the letters, together with the final minute. It was decided to set up a mission with these seven monks under the direction of Mayne, who had suffered so much for the faith. Four days later fresh instructions were sent to the nuncio, to the effect that since there was such a shortage of priests in Scotland it was important for Mayne and his companions to be sent there at once and for the young Scots aspirants to take the habit as soon as possible. The pope being most anxious about this, he was to write to the bishop of Würzburg telling him to see about the missionaries and send their names, and he was to entrust the bishop with the task of seeing that the young monks were encouraged to fit themselves for serving God and their country. The nuncio was told to exercise more than ordinary diligence and to say where the necessary documents and faculties for the monks could be sent in order to avoid delay.[13]

On 11th January the nuncio replied that he had written to the bishop and that, to save time, the documents should be sent direct to Würzburg through the bishop's agent. The officials of Propaganda received the letter on 4th February and set about asking the Holy Office for faculties for Mayne and his seven companions.[14] Two months later a formal document was drawn up in the name of nine cardinals of the Congregation of the Inquisition (or Holy Office) and on 24th May 1625 it was despatched to the bishop of Würzburg for delivery to Mayne. It gave various faculties to him and eight fellow monks, who were to be good and suitable men, assigned to the task by Mayne himself but with the consent of the abbot-general or provincial. What strikes one on reading the document is that the cardinals were more concerned with preserving the integrity of the Catholic faith and shielding it from all possible dangers than with helping the monks to carry out their mission. The monks were authorised to read condemned books for the purpose of refuting heresy and to absolve their penitents from the ecclesiastical penalties incurred for heresy or schism, reading condemned books or even possessing them. But the faculties were hedged around with clauses which deprived them of much of their value. Heretical books were treated like dangerous radio-active material: for instance, the monks had to tell the ordinary which ones they had so that, if anyone died suddenly, he could see that they were burnt.[15]

The letters and minutes have been described in detail to show how the affair of the Scottish Benedictine mission was managed. One cannot help being impressed by the anxiety of the Barberini pope and his nephew to help Scotland and by the efficiency and despatch with which Propaganda conducted its business. The correspondence and notes (written apparently by officials who were perfectly bilingual in Latin and Italian) throw much light on how Propaganda worked, at least in its early stages. At no point did it communicate directly with the Scots abbots or Mayne. It issued instructions to the nuncio in Vienna, who in turn communicated with the bishop of Würzburg.   It decided to set up a mission of the men chosen by the bishop and it was to him that the bull for Mayne was despatched. If there was consultation between the bishop and the Scots abbots, this apparently did not interest Propaganda, though the bull did in the event provide for Mayne assigning the missionaries himself. Propaganda was working through the diplomatic channels already in existence, and of necessity it handled a German prince-bishop very cautiously. Perhaps it was deliberately cutting out the religious superiors. The event, too, was to show that Propaganda, like other mortals, had to learn from experience.

This is a convenient point to consider some questions that suggest themselves. What missionary work were the Scots monks already doing before the bull was issued to Mayne? Why did the English monks make their offer, and why did the Scots accept it and then at once turn to something else? As regards mission work before the end of 1624, the references are plentiful enough but fail to paint any coherent picture. The Würzburg prior went to Scotland in April 1622. The petition to Propaganda in 1623 spoke of two priests sent there some years before, and the bishop of Würzburg reported that two monks, not of Würzburg, had been there during the previous years. A report on the Scots college in Rome prepared about 1624 said that it was customary to send some monks of Würzburg to Scotland.[16] Another report, sent by two Scots friars to Propaganda in June 1623, said there was one Benedictine in Scotland, the only one from Ratisbon or Würzburg who had gone there, and that Adam MacCall was in Northumberland and ought to be in Scotland.[17] All one can say for certain is that two monks were on the mission and one of them was MacCall, but this must be taken as a minimum. On his way to Scotland MacCall had stayed with the English monks in Douai, and at their request a letter extending his leave of absence was sent to them.[18] He had gone to the mission at some point after 1619, when he was cellarer at Ratisbon, probably about the end of 1620, for he had been twenty years on the mission at the time of his supposed death in 1640.[19] It would certainly seem that he at least had faculties from the English congregation.

Mayne likewise received hospitality from the Douai monks on his way to Scotland but, as far as one can judge, never reached his destination. Instead, he returned to Würzburg with the three Scots seminarists and the English letters. One might suggest that Mayne, sent to Scotland, got as far as Douai and then, struck by the possibilities opened up by English help and an influx of novices, returned to Würzburg instead. Then, as the Scots reflected further on the possibilities, especially after the recent establishment of Propaganda, and perhaps also offended by the appointment in 1623 of an English secular priest as ordinary for the whole of Britain, they decided that they could run a mission by themselves. That, at least, is a working hypothesis.

The whole tone of the 1623 correspondence suggests that the initiative came from the English side. One is entitled to ask why. The Douai prior wrote that the English monks desired ardently to be united with the Scots in a mission covering the whole of Britain. Was this purely apostolic zeal, or was it also an attempt to strengthen their own position vis-à-vis either the new Propaganda or the new ordinary or other English missionary bodies? The English president told the Scots that members of religious orders experienced difficulty in obtaining faculties at Rome because of opposition both open and secret, a fairly clear reference to the internal strife among missionaries to Britain. In the event, as we have seen, the new pope, Urban VIII, and his nephew, Francesco Barberini, who was protector of Scotland and a member of Propaganda, showed themselves very favourably disposed to the Scots monks. The reply of the Scots referred to the difficulties met with by Mayne at Douai, difficulties which it hinted were caused by the envy of certain parties. It is highly probable that these were the Jesuit superiors of the seminary, who would not have been pleased to see five useful young men going off to be monks, because at this period it was the Jesuits and not the secular clergy who benefited most from the Scots colleges. In fact the relevant entries in the Douai register complain of the disrespectful way in which two of the students, Maxwell and Maclean, demanded their release.

One finds very often that missionary effort was made by the Ratisbon and Würzburg monks in common; Erfurt can be ignored as it hardly ever had a community. The bishop of Würzburg was presumably accurate in saying that the two men already on the mission were not monks of Würzburg. The condition of Ratisbon under Abbot Algeo was hardly conducive to preparation for a difficult apostolate, although one student at a Scottish seminary, George Wedderburn, did enter the abbey the following year. To what extent was the state of affairs there responsible for two men from Ratisbon being on the mission already? The charge was to be levelled from time to time against the Scots abbots that they sent difficult subjects to the mission, and it is a fact, then as now, that dissatisfaction with the monastic life leads monks to seek work outside. One can agree that a monk sent out because he is unsatisfactory at home is unlikely to be satisfactory in the mission field, but by no means all monks seeking mission work themselves are likely to be unsatisfactory. If it is instability which drives them to seek fresh work, admittedly the prospects of success are not good. But there is need of some realism here. One is reminded of the character in Ian Hay's book who said there ought to be a statue to 'The girl who married someone else', since the disappointed young man then departed to some outpost of empire where he performed deeds of valour. In a somewhat similar way one can attribute a fair amount of missionary work done by monks to disagreement with their superior. The point being made is by no means a frivolous one. The fact that a monk goes on the mission because of a disagreement with his superior does not necessarily prejudice his value as a missionary, any more than a young man's enlisting in the army because of a disappointment in love necessarily prejudices his value as a soldier.

While Propaganda was making its enquiries prior to setting up the Benedictine mission, Mayne had been conducting negotiations, backed by the pope and his cardinal-nephew, for the recovery of the Vienna abbey. The project was linked with the missionary plans, and Mayne's appeal to the emperor made mention of the influx of seminarians and the scheme to help the Scottish mission. The petition was refused, however, before the bull setting up the mission was issued. There must naturally have been many practical difficulties to overcome before some or all of the nine monks with faculties could set off for Scotland. Nothing was achieved for over eighteen months, and then it became clear that the difficulties were largely of Mayne's own making. Instead of doing the work entrusted to him within the terms of reference, he was trying to organise something bigger and better. In early 1627 he approached Propaganda with several requests.[20]

On 30th January the congregation turned down two of them: he was not to add another three monks to his group destined for Scotland, since the arrival there of so large a number in time of persecution would be dangerous; neither was he to send other monks to work among expatriate Scots in Poland, Prussia and Germany, since those lands were so far from Scotland, where he was supposed to be going. Mayne's appeal to the emperor had likewise mentioned mission work in Poland as well as Scotland. In answer to a third request, for a visitation of the three Scottish monasteries, in which he said observance had completely collapsed, the nuncios in Vienna and Cologne were instructed to appoint a visitor from the reformed Lorraine Congregation of Benedictines. That Ratisbon under Algeo was in a sad state is beyond doubt, but Erfurt was not really a monastery and Würzburg was in a flourishing condition. A fourth request was favourably considered: it was for the removal of the clause requiring the consent of the ordinary for the exercise of the faculties, since the said ordinary was the English Vicar-Apostolic, who was in hiding, and in fact English missionaries were making the same request.[21] The cardinals exerted themselves to find some solution which would safeguard the Vicar-Apostolic's authority, and on 22nd February they substituted the consent of the nuncio in France. At this meeting Mayne's application for a subsidy to defray the expenses of the journey to Scotland was granted, and a week later the amount was fixed as twenty crowns to be paid at once, with a further hundred to follow as soon as the monks set off. The Benedictine mission to Scotland was now under the superintendence of the nuncio in Paris.

Still Mayne did not go. A further fifteen months passed, and in June 1628 Propaganda was dealing with representations made to them by the bishop of Würzburg that Mayne was claiming as prefect of the mission to be exempt from obedience to his regular superiors. Abbot Ogilvie and the bishop were told that they could exercise their authority over him, because mission work did not exempt religious from ordinary obedience; it merely meant that they could not be removed from office without Propaganda's consent. Mayne also was informed of this and was ordered to set out at once with the companions chosen not by himself but by his superiors.[22]

Twelve months later he had still not yet set out. Barberini told Propaganda on 22nd June 1629 that Mayne's mission was of no use whatever, both because Mayne had no authority in the Scottish monasteries and for what the minute cryptically terms other reasons. His prefectship and faculties were withdrawn, and Abbot Ogilvie was appointed in his place.[23] A papal brief was despatched that same day to Ogilvie setting up a mission consisting of him and eight other monks and giving them faculties to be exercised with the consent of the nuncio in France. A meeting of the Holy Office on 2nd August then approved the faculties and granted them for seven years.[24] Both the documents and the faculties themselves are much more workmanlike than those sent to Mayne four years before; Rome was learning fast. It is hard not to feel a certain sympathy for Mayne, for the arrangement made by Propaganda was unworkable, but it also seems evident that he was not the right man for the undertaking.

The terms of the papal brief, as well as the whole history of the episode, make it clear beyond shadow of doubt that Ogilvie was prefect of the Benedictines only and not of the Scottish mission as a whole. The word 'mission' was used in Propaganda documents to denote a mission-field (as in modern speech) but also a missionary unit. Thus one finds the standard phrase, 'the Scottish mission', used beside such expressions as 'the Benedictine mission to Scotland'. When Mayne and Ogilvie were termed 'prefect of the mission', the meaning is that each was prefect of the Benedictine missionary unit. It is perhaps misunderstanding of the phrase which has led to the statement found in print that Abbot Ogilvie was prefect of the Scottish mission.

In the years that followed there were at least three monks working as missionaries, while the Swedish invasions were ravaging their monasteries in South Germany. Ogilvie died in 1635, the faculties granted by Propaganda expired the following summer. The faculties were not renewed, and we know that in these years the flourishing Würzburg community dwindled. We can agree with the later abbot of Würzburg who wrote that the Swedish wars ruined the missionary plans of the monks.[25] The bull of 1629 gave faculties for England as well as Scotland, and, as we have seen, the English Congregation claimed to give faculties for both countries to any Benedictine. It was therefore possible to work in either country with faculties from either source, nor was there anything, at least in theory, to prevent a Scots monk having faculties from both sources simultaneously. The expiry of the Propaganda faculties in 1636 thus did not put an end to missionary work by Scottish monks.

A report made at the English general chapter of 1633 stated that two Scots monks had been subjected by their own superiors to the English Congregation superiors for the duration of their stay in mission territory.[26] When Abbot Ogilvie died two years later, two monks of Würzburg, William Gordon and Audomarus Asloan, were listed as being on the Scottish mission. We also know that Adam MacCall from Ratisbon was on the mission throughout this period, for this was explicitly stated in a report in 1632.[27] It is possible that other Scots monks worked as missionaries for a time, but if so the fact is not recorded. It is therefore most probable that it was two of these three who were referred to by the English general chapter. It is also most probable that one of these two was William Gordon, since he died in the English monastery at Paris in 1638 and is included in the English Benedictine necrology.[28] Gordon, incidentally, was the brother of the first Marquess of Huntly, whose religious vicissitudes had enlivened the Scottish scene for half a century.

The other Würzburg monk, Asloan, went to the mission in 1628-9, for he had been over nine and almost ten years[29] there when he left for Würzburg in the spring of 1638 at the summons of the bishop. From Newcastle, having received the summons, he went to London. The agent of the Holy See at the court of Henrietta Maria was the Aberdeenshire secular priest, George Conn, whose despatches to Rome at this date shed interesting but not altogether edifying light on the Catholic missionaries. It appears, for instance, that Conn himself gave mission faculties. Catholic religious walked openly through the streets of London, so that Conn feared an incident and complained that they caused scandal as they frequented taverns and were addicted to tobacco. The Benedictines had frequent internal disputes, in which Conn himself was called on to intervene. In particular there was a controversy between the monks of the English and Spanish congregations over a legacy of a hundred crowns. In his despatch of 27th April (o.s.) 1638 Conn described a puzzling incident. There were, he said, great divisions among the Benedictines because those from Scotland did not want to belong to the English Congregation, and the same was true of the Cassinese. The other day he was with the provincial of the English Congregation when the man claiming to be superior of Scotland arrived, with some priests of both parties. Conn let them argue as long as they spoke civilly, but as soon as they began abusing each other he imposed silence and told them that if they had anything to say which would make for peace and concord they could arrange a day and he would gladly listen to them.[30]

One might presume that this Scottish superior in London at the time was Asloan, except that the latter had arrived in London in mid-February and left for Gravesend and Hamburg towards the end of March. Was it then William Gordon, who died later that year at Paris, or the third Scot, Adam MacCall? The subject of the dispute is not known, and it is quite unexpected to find more than one Scots monk in London and disputing with English Benedictines.

Carlo Rosetti, Conn's successor as agent of the Holy See in London, likewise sent regular despatches to Rome. On 12th October 1640 he reported what an informant had told him the day before about the terrible happenings in Scotland. Maxwell, earl of Nithsdale, had alone in Scotland remained loyal to Charles I and had retired to his castles. The Scots, after besieging them for some months, had taken them and had killed forty gentlemen of the name

169

of Maxwell and two priests, a Benedictine and a Franciscan, though Nithsdale and his wife had been spared.[31] Some of this information is undeniably accurate. Nithsdale was besieged for thirteen weeks in his castles of Caerlaverock and Threave and then sent word to Charles that he could hold out no longer. Charles told him to capitulate on the best terms he could. Accordingly on 26th September 1640 Nithsdale surrendered, both garrisons being allowed to march out with all the honours of war. Later the two castles were dismantled as Nithsdale continued to take an active part against the Covenant.[32] The story told to Rosetti reads like a rumour based on a substratum of truth. The monks at Ratisbon, however, accepted the story and identified the monk as Adam MacCall; they told the emperor in December 1640 that MacCall after twenty years of work in Scotland converting heretics had been cruelly done to death by them some weeks previously.[33] Perhaps we can accept the episode as evidence that Adam MacCall was living in the south-west in 1640 even if he did not meet a violent death there.

MacCall worked in S.W. Scotland, but previous references had been to Northumberland as his and Asloan's field of activity, while Asloan was described as having worked in Scotland and England. The political frontier between Scotland and England was not the most natural boundary, and there was a natural and easy route along the Solway-Tyne valley from Galloway to Newcastle. Probably the three Scots monks worked on both sides of the border, as we know was done by George Asloan, who was a secular priest and later became a monk. He was on the Scottish mission, if not precisely domiciled in Scotland, in 1623-24, and in 1628 he was living on the frontier and applied to Propaganda for the renewal of his faculties in both kingdoms.[34] At this time Scotland and England had quite separate civil administrations although Charles I was king of both countries. Nevertheless, the factors making for unity in sentiment had been growing, and the religious and political divisions tended to split the island according to ideology rather than region. English and Scottish Catholics thus tended to have increasingly more in common.

No other names of Scots monks working as missionaries at this time have been recorded. Ironically enough, the only two names which have found their way into print are those of Frs Silvanus and Leander,[35] but Silvanus Mayne seems never actually to have worked as a missionary in Scotland, while the other is the Welshman Leander Jones, who was twice president of the English Congregation. With Adam MacCall, as far as we know, the missionary activity of the Scots Benedictines came to an end, and the handful of monks in Germany fighting for survival were in no position to continue it.

There is evidence, however, that the missionary ideal continued to animate the Scots in Würzburg. The will was there even if the execution was beyond their powers. In the draft petition for a Scottish congregation drawn up shortly after 1640 they wanted the president of the proposed congregation to be the prefect of their mission to Scotland. The monks would get their faculties from him and from him alone, and would take an oath to serve the mission until their faculties were revoked.[36] In the years after 1648 James Brown wrote a series of works on the Scots and their monasteries in Germany, from which it is clear that he was vitally interested in the expansion of Scottish monasticism with a missionary ethos.[37] He recounted that, when a refugee at St Gallen during the Swedish invasion, he turned down the abbot's offer to accept him as a monk as he would not be able to help Scotland if he entered the Swiss abbey.

We can discount his story of the offer made by St Gallen about 1580 to educate two young monks for work in Scotland, since we know the Swiss abbot was so angry when a similar demand was made only fourteen years later. Brown, however, insisted that this offer would still be open. He also reported that the president of the Lorraine congregation and the Maurist *visitator* of Normandy were willing to educate young monks to be missionaries; he wanted various monasteries, including that in Vienna, to be given to the Scots to supply helpers for the Scottish mission; he commended the mission work of the English monks. It is clear, too, that he reverenced the memory of Silvanus Mayne, so it is perhaps to Mayne, in spite of everything, that one should attribute some of the abiding missionary spirit at Würzburg. And certainly the Würzburg monks stimulated interest in the Scottish mission among influential German dignitaries.

In 1650 Abbot Asloan had missionary plans and wrote to the prince-bishop to solicit his help. He had some monks suitable for mission work, so he wanted a renewal of the faculties granted to Ogilvie for the British mission twenty years before. Since it would be a nuisance, he wrote, both to the monks and the holy see to have to send in repeated applications, the Scots were petitioning to have faculties without restriction of time or number of persons, just as other congregations had; and they wanted the prince-bishop to act as mediator to get the petition granted more speedily. They also wanted the faculty to consecrate chalices and altars as there were no bishops (who would ordinarily do this) in Scotland or England.

Two years later, when appealing to Cardinal Barberini against malcontents, Asloan again insisted that one of his major aims since becoming abbot had been to further the mission begun in Great Britain by the Scots monks and that he had in fact helped this mission and brought young men to Würzburg for the purpose, but his plans had been thwarted. The letter of 1650, with its reference to other congregations, gives the impression that the Scots were going to petition for a mission of Scots Benedictines, irrespective of which abbey they belonged to and presumably with Asloan as prefect. Perhaps the petition was never sent to Rome; certainly it was not considered at a monthly meeting of Propaganda as the 1624 petition was, and certainly it was never granted. The plain fact is that the Scots abbeys were not geared to systematic mission work. Any joint action was made difficult by the existence of two abbots independent of each other and with no common superior or governing body, such as a general chapter, to direct policy.

Asloan spoke as if he had given concrete help to what he twice called not the Scottish but the British mission. Perhaps he did send men to work on the Anglo-Scottish border with faculties provided by the English Congregation, though a report on Scotland in 1655 listed other religious there but no monk.[38] At this period there is a dearth of any sort of information about the Würzburg abbey, and one must be more than ordinarily cautious about arguing from silence. On the other hand, the references to mission work at this date in the Ratisbon necrology are almost certainly fabrications. So too, probably, is Brockie's description of Benedict Raith, a Ratisbon monk, as a missionary during the Cromwellian period.[39] All we do know for certain is that the number of monks at Würzburg was reduced but Asloan acted to remedy the shortage. In 1658 he accepted a student from Rome as well as four young men brought from Scotland by Fr Maurus Dixon, whom he had sent on a recruiting errand. For the monks, mission work and recruiting activity can hardly be separated.

An important development took place in 1653 when the mission of secular priests in Scotland was set up under the leadership of a prefect. Surprising though it seems, secular priests until then had no superior in Scotland. Propaganda was informed in 1657 that the Scottish mission had been more effectively served by secular priests than by regulars and that the remnant of Catholicism in Scotland had been preserved by the labours of the seculars.[40] This may have become true after 1657, but it had hardly been so before then. It is surely a case of the myth being created and influencing the subsequent course of events. The historical scholar Thomas Innes (1662-1744) could write that around 1600 religious 'were brought in to the clergy's assistance and by their procurement', which seems to be either a misreading or a deliberate adaptation of the passage from George Conn already quoted.[41] But, whatever the truth of it, conditions for mission work in Scotland by monks were going to be different, once the body of secular priests was organised.

172

Notes

1 Hewison, I, cxviii-cxx; "First Mission", 63-64.

2 "First Mission", 64-65.

3 Hammermayer, "Reformation", 250.

4 Gordon, v; *IR*, vii, 119, 121; Bellesheim, III, 391-92.

5 Conn, 143-44.

6 W. J. Anderson, "Narratives of the Scottish Reformation, II", in *IR*, vii, 114.

7 M. V. Hay, "Too little and too late", in *IR*, vi, 19-21.

8 APF, SOCG, 312, f. 60v; VL, Barb. Lat. 8628, f. 84; C. Giblin, *Irish Franciscan Mission to Scotland, 1619-1646* (Dublin, 1964), viii.

9 cf. *IR*, xii, 16, 24.

10 Full text in "First Mission".

11 APF, SOCG, 384, f. 267-71; Acta, 3, f. 100r.

12 APF, Lettere, 3, f. 86r; SOCG, 330, f. 364r.

13 APF, SOCG, 330, f. 515-18; Acta, 3, f. 172r; Lettere, 3, f. 209v-210r.

14 APF, SOCG, 312, f. 141r, 144v.

15 Copialbuch, f. 151v-152v.

16 VL, Barb. Lat. 8629, f. 26r.

17 APF, SOCG, 312, f. 60v-61r; VL, Barb. Lat. 8628, f. 84v-85r.

18 "First Mission", 160, 167.

19 See note 33 below.

20 APF, Acta, 4, f. 177v, 189v, 192v; Istruzioni, 1, f. 110v.

21 P. Hughes, *Rome and the Counter-Reformation in England* (1942), 341-42. See also a recent article by M. Lunn, "Benedictine opposition to Bishop Richard Smith (1625-1629)" in *Recusant History,* xi (1971), 1-20.

22 APF, Acta, 6, f. 76r.

23 ibid., f. 298rv.

24 KJP, 517/1; Reg. BOA, Sch., Urk. 682; SCA, ML, Dixon, 11.11.1676.

25 SCA, ML, Dixon, 11.11.1676.

26 CRS, xxxiii (1933), 264.

27 VA, NVPC, 43, 4.9.1632.

28 For him see "Three Scots", 233-38; "Scots and EBC", 60.

29 Haim, A 6v; KJP, 517/1.

30 VL, Barb. Lat. 8642, f. 114r, 133r, 145r, 90r, 194rv.

31 VL, Barb. Lat. 8648, pt. 1, f. 241v-242r; APF, SOCG, 84, f. 109r, 115v.

32 H. Maxwell, *A history of Dumfries and Galloway* (1896), 249-50.

33 Reid, f. 116rv.

34 For Asloan see *IR,* xxii, 47-50.

35 Apparently following Bellesheim, IV, 81.

36 Blair, f. 137rv. 143v.

37 Chronologia, 99-100; Indiculus, f. 28v, 51r, 63r; "Trilogy", 130-32.

38 APF, SOCG, 297, f. 324-31.

39 SCA, Brockie's Monasticon, Tom. III, Carmelites, Bervie/Inverbervie.
40 APF, SC Scozia, I, f. 11r; Giblin, 57.
41 *IR*, vii, 119.

CHAPTER 14

Mission work
encouraged and thwarted
1661—79

Abbot Asloan's rule, which lasted from 1638 to 1661, links together two comparatively well documented periods in the history of the Würzburg abbey and its missionary work, and spans the almost undocumented gap of twenty years between them. His monastic career also links two flourishing periods in the abbey's history: he was at Würzburg under Abbot Ogilvie before the Swedish invasion, and the community expanded steadily after his own death. Though numbers were very low at the end of his rule, it was Asloan himself who began the period of growth by having young men brought from Scotland in 1658 and then by signing the articles of union with the English Benedictine Congregation shortly before his death.

By these articles[1] the missionary agreement of 1623 was re-affirmed if not re-established: any Scot sent to the mission was to have the same faculties and privileges as the English monks and was to be subject to the rules and superiors of the English Congregation for the duration of his stay on the mission. He would now, however, have the English faculties by right, as a member of the united Scoto-English body. As we have seen, the union had no very lasting effects in Würzburg except in the matter of mission work. Asloan seems to have been, if not exactly an Anglophile, at least one who welcomed union of English and Scots. He had worked in the border lands, was in the habit of referring to the 'British' mission, and inaugurated the union with the English monks before he died. Whether his successor, Maurus Dixon, thought this way is more than doubtful. Nevertheless Asloan's policy, even if it was not to be continued, had done much to keep alive the missionary spirit at Würzburg, and his foresight enabled Dixon to put missionary plans into effect.

A report on Scotland about 1660 lists various secular and religious priests working there but no Benedictine.[2] The monk Placid Keith was absent in Poland in 1662 and was perhaps working among Scottish expatriates. It is, however, in the year after this that reliable information about Würzburg missionary effort begins. Macarius Brown, who was one of the novices when the agreement with the English monks was signed, went to the mission in 1663 and stayed there until his death in 1697, a period of thirty-four years. Every indication is that he served on English Benedictine stations during the whole of the period.[3] Placid Baillie left Würzburg at some time before the end of 1665 and is said to have worked in Scotland and England.[4] The second novice at the time of the union, William Dunn, left for England at some point after November 1668; he died in Northumberland in 1675 and, like Brown, was aggregated to the English Congregation and found a place in its necrology.[5]

Thus by the end of 1655 two monks had departed for the mission. A further two had gone by the end of 1670, as we learn from a letter of Dixon's. The names of only three have been recorded, but these figures are so surprising, considering there were only two able-bodied priests in the community in 1660, that one is impelled to seek a reason. Two of the four worked and died on English Benedictine mission stations; Baillie also at this time would certainly have English Congregation faculties and almost certainly worked in England. A report on the Scottish mission in 1668 includes various religious among the priests working there, but still no Benedictine.[6] The fourth man no doubt likewise had English faculties, but may have been only a short time in Britain, perhaps to bring news and recruits from Scotland.

Why did at least three monks depart to do mission work in England so soon after the union of Scottish and English monks? The English offer of faculties can be viewed under two aspects: as an outlet for Scottish missionary zeal, which was of benefit to the Scots, or as a means of obtaining extra Benedictine priests for their own missions. The question must be asked whether some unwritten agreement was made between Scots and English, something like: You help us by providing a novice-master and another priest at once, and we will provide men as soon as possible for your mission stations. Certainly this happened in practice, and Maurus Dixon, who became abbot a few months after the articles of union were signed, was later to say that the English solicited the union in order to get priests to supply their mission stations.

We know nothing about work done on the Scottish side of the border by any of these monks. Abbot Dixon evidently did not like the situation, though we do not know precisely why not, and about the middle of 1669 he sought powers from Rome to send monks to the mission as he himself should think fit. Obviously this entailed having the power to grant them faculties. But days had changed in Rome. The person Dixon wrote to was Will Leslie, agent of the Scottish secular clergy in Rome. The letter is lost; all we know is that Leslie did not reply.

PLATE 10.   Schottenanger before 1945

PLATE 11

PLATE 12

Portal and tower, south side of church, before 1945

The setting up of a mission of secular clergy to Scotland was intimately connected with the appointing of Will Leslie to be their agent in Rome. From about 1650 Leslie performed this function, remaining in the post for over fifty years. As he was a man of intelligence and determination, his influence grew with the years. He was appointed the first permanent archivist of Propaganda and was thus at the centre of the affairs of the Scottish mission. There is no doubt that his life's work was successful. By the end of his career Scotland had a bishop taken from the ranks of the secular clergy, who was in control of all mission work in Scotland; by then, too, the secular priests were the largest and most influential body of missionaries. It is worth emphasising that this was very far from being the case when the secular priests were first organised in 1653.

No adequate biography or assessment of Will Leslie has yet been written.[7] We can reject the picture of him as the cunning old spider sitting in the centre of his web in Rome and scheming the downfall of the Jesuits and all their works.[8] All the same, in Scottish affairs at least, he was a determined opponent of the Jesuits since they were the most powerful body not subject to Propaganda or to the prefect of the secular clergy. It does not seem likely that Leslie would favour the setting up of a Benedictine mission to Scotland when his main object was to make the secular mission supreme. In general, letters sent to Leslie have been preserved, but not letters from him apart from those addressed to Paris; there is thus no record of his answers to Germany except for what can be gleaned from the ensuing letters of his correspondents. He himself filed away letters received but did not note if he replied. One therefore has to judge as best one can whether the Scots abbots were appealing to a man who was in fact hostile to their plans.

In 1670 an emissary from the Highlands was in Italy seeking help for his Catholic fellow-countrymen, and Propaganda decided in November to make use of Fr Ephraim Reid, a native Gaelic speaker from Tain who had been a graduate schoolmaster and was now a monk of Ratisbon.[9] Letters were therefore sent both to the acting superior at Ratisbon and to Abbot Dixon, the administrator.[10] Some clerical error was made, for Dixon wrote in January 1671 to Cardinal Antonio Barberini, prefect of Propaganda, that there was no monk called Chrysostom and no native Highlander at Würzburg. He added that there was a Highlander named Ephraim at Ratisbon whose presence there was necessary, but he would see if he could be spared. Dixon took the opportunity to tell the cardinal about his own wishes and how he had written to Will Leslie asking him to get powers for him from the cardinal protector and Propaganda to send monks to work in the homeland; that was eighteen months ago and he had received no reply. At the moment there were three monks already on the mission, and one on his way back. If Propaganda, therefore, granted faculties and something to defray journey expenses, he would do all he could to help the mission.[11]

Neither party received satisfaction. Reid stayed where he was and Dixon was given no help. The following year he repeated his request, again to no avail. The next evidence shows an English Benedictine dignitary working in the same direction as Dixon, though perhaps for very different reasons. It is a letter dated 25th February 1675 from the aged Abbot Gascoigne of Lamspring,[12] who had negotiated the union with Würzburg on behalf of the English. Unfortunately it is damaged and one cannot be sure to whom it was addressed, but probably it was to Will Leslie. The relevant passage is worth quoting in full:

'Please also to (sp)eak with him [apparently Fr Augustine Latham, the English Congregation agent in Rome] about a Mission for the 2 Monasteries of Wirtzburg and Ratisbon, independent of our President and dependent of their owne Superiors, which busines I am persuaded you yourself alone can be able to effect: but if any assistance from his Eminence my Lord Cardinal of Norfolk you think to be necessary, I doubt not but Mr Latham wil prevail with him to effect what you propose to him and think fitting.

There is speech of an Immediate dependence of their Missionaryes to the Congregation de Propaganda fide, in which some difficulty is made. But if it is understood only of a general kind of care and supreme Inspection, requiring some times to be informed how they behave themselves in the Mission . . .'

Here the damaged letter becomes unintelligible, but the abbot seems to be saying that a loose supervision of the Scots monks by Propaganda should be acceptable. The important point is that English Benedictine authorities were advocating a Scottish Benedictine mission separate from their own.

Not long afterwards, in January 1676, three individual Scots monks were the subject of deliberations at a monthly meeting of Propaganda. Attempts to obtain Irish priests for the Highlands having failed, the procurator of the Scottish secular clergy (that is, Will Leslie) was asking for Ephraim Reid to be sent. John Irvine, a secular priest who had been on the mission for eight years, wanted to retire and become a monk in Germany; the prefect of the mission seconded his request, and Leslie suggested that Irvine's brother at Ratisbon should take his place in Scotland. Finally, Athanasius Chambers requested faculties for the border country of Scotland and England; he was the monk who had been appointed by Dixon

178

to manage Ratisbon affairs and he had departed for the monastery of Subiaco after the election of Placid Fleming. Propaganda agreed that Reid should be sent and that Irvine should be replaced by his Benedictine brother; the case of Chambers they remitted to Cardinal Barberini.[13] The interesting point is that nothing whatever resulted from the decisions. Chambers remained in Italy. Reid was actually voted his journey money at a subsequent meeting[14] but was still in Germany at the end of the year, when Abbot Fleming promised to send him to Scotland if a replacement for him arrived. John Irvine never, as far as we know, became a monk although he is said to have died in Germany not long after.[15] Propaganda seems to have been working with less than its usual efficiency at this time. Irvine's brother (more likely, his cousin) was presumably Marianus Irvine, who was a monk at Würzburg and not at Ratisbon, and he stayed in his monastery.

It seems that Propaganda — or perhaps, more accurately, Will Leslie — was quite willing to add useful individual monks to the secular clergy mission but was disinclined to set up an independent Benedictine mission. The two abbots in Germany, however, wanted some permanent mission arrangement, and Dixon in particular was growing impatient. In May 1676 he sent Leslie an urgent letter.[16] He had been writing, he said, for seven years but had received no reply, and he wondered if the letters had been intercepted. Certainly they have not survived. At Leslie's request he gave an account of Würzburg, which has been quoted in an earlier chapter, then went on to speak of the mission and faculties. The passage, although lengthy, is worth quoting in full.

'Our Missionars carryes themselfes very well to the great satisfaction of their paenitents, which causes noe little hatred by the English, as I am informed by one of our religious, whom I send the last year to Scotland about some bussines and who returned in Winter with some prettie youthes to be bred in pietie and discipline according to your former Counsell . . .

Be pleased for the zeale you carrie to gods glorie, and the great love to helpe your countrie . . . (to) procure our monasteries for both Kingdomes faculties, as I offtnen (sic) desyred, independent of the Englishe or any other, assuring you withall that noe persons shall be send that are not qualified mature and exemplar. It is true that wee had formerly and our Missioners hes for the present, faculties from the Englishe, being before some yeares inwyted and sollicitated by them to incorporate us amongst them and supply their residences in England, they wanting then persons for the Mission; but now fearing that wee will incroatch upon them by our increment and our peoples good

179

carriage, they seeme to retract the incorporation and dismember us, whereof, good sir, doubtles you have more information. Therefore once againe for gods cause wee unanimous intreate you earnestly, you will be pleased to concurre and procure us faculties according to the foresaid end, for which god almightie and the monkes in heaven will reward you, and wee as long as wee leave will never forget you . . .'

This was enclosed in a letter of Fleming's and sent to Rome. By mid-August Dixon had received no reply and wrote again to Leslie.[17] He asked what Propaganda intended to do about the Scots monks, as it was not pleased about the English giving them faculties. The monks were, he said,

'reiected from the Englishe and not accepted or maintained by the Congregation, which seemes not to be for gods glorie and conversion of our countrie. Therefore I intreat you good sir, be pleased to impart your mynd, whereby I may take course of our people, who with the assistance of god may prove good operarii in vinea Domini, and not obiect the day or the morrow that wee provyde noe persons for the monasteries and countrie, otherwayes wee must seek recourse and remedie where (we) can . . .'

In November Dixon wrote yet again.[18] Fleming had been told by Leslie that Dixon's two letters had arrived in Rome and that a reply had been sent to Würzburg. Accordingly Fleming asked Dixon to pass on this answer. But Dixon had not received it, and he therefore asked Leslie to 'reiterate his answer', promising yet again: 'according to your counsell and instruction wee will cooperate to our power'. With this letter he sent a copy of the faculties granted to William Ogilvie as prefect of the mission in 1629, which he said would have been continued but for the disastrous effect of the Swedish wars.

'Wherupon, good sir, you can (easi)ly see that it is noe noveltie for us to have faculties for the Mission; if it please you to renew or amplifie them it would be most gratefull to us and honourable to you . . .'

Fleming was not at all pleased about this. A month after Dixon, he too wrote to Leslie.[19]

'The Abbot of Würtzburg hath written to me that your Letters are not come to his hands and that he hath sent you ane Copie of some old faculties they formerly had, desireing you to renew them. Bot sir, I hope that you will procure faculties for both Monasteries, and in procureing of them have ane speciall

Consideratione of the praerogatives and priviledges of this Monasterie, both for its antiquitie, dependance upon the Apostolique See, and the jurisdictione it hath had these many hundred years over all the rest of the Scots Monasteries in Germanie as there Matricular, and the great expenss it hath bein at, not only in defending them bot even in Recovering againe to the Natione that Monasterie of Würtzburg which is only ane filiale of this, and tuyce planted by it.

Some tyme agoe, your Reverence did writt that we should choose ane prefect of our owne. Bot sir to shune many Inconveniences, I think it ane great deall better that our Religious in the Missione depend upon your prefect, the Superiours hier haveing power to send and recall them, according to the Necessities of there Monasteries. Bot the speciall poynt that I wold recomend to your Reverence is, that you obtaine the faculties for all our Kings Dominions . . . for it is ane matter of great Concernement to us, which I fear the English will endeavour to hinder als much as they can, if they know of it.'

It was in this letter that Fleming expressed his willingness to send the Gaelic-speaking Ephraim Reid to the Highlands if another monk returned to Ratisbon. He also outlined his scheme for educating four boys at a time in his abbey and sending some of them at the end of their humanities to the Scots college in Rome. Fleming was now embarking on his plans for founding a seminary for Scots boys in Ratisbon. He was to scheme and strive for this during the next decades but his progress and ultimate success are outwith the scope of the present narrative. It is already clear, however, that the two abbots did not see the proposed Benedictine mission in quite the same light. In reply to Leslie, Fleming wrote again in April 1677.[20]

'Now I return you Sir many thanks for the favorable expressiones in it and for the kynd promises you are pleased to make us of your Charitable assistance to thir Monasteries. And as to our Mission I fear it will be hard for us to obtaine faculties for England against there will, especially sieing the Cardinal is for them, and I think it not our prudence by urgeing it too much to ex(a)sperat them, bot rather to yeild to the tymes and take faculties for our owne Countrie, expecting ane more favorable occasione to have them extendit for England also. It is true it will be hard for us to begine ane Missione, yet the haveing of faculties will conduce very much to the good of thir monasteries, tho we should only send bot thrie or four from both, for besyds the good they will doe at home, it will keip ane good Correspondence betuixt our Countrie and thir Cloisters, and be

181

ane means to fournish us alwayes with Religious and youthes to studie, and it will lykwayes make the Religious apply themselves more diligently to vertue and learneing, sieing they can alwayes have the expectatione to be sent home and applyed to the Exercise of there Talent, when sufficiently qualefied, and it will obtaine us the favour of severall good patrons hier, when they sie us profitable at least in helpeing to propagate the faith againe in our owne Countrie, and many other good effects will follow from it. Bot tho the propaganda will grant us ane formal missione with our owne prefect, yet I am still of the mynd that it is not necessar for us to choyse on(e) for so small ane number as we will have in the begineing but thinks it a great deall (better that) they depend upon your prefect, and that will both make your prefect (and your) Missioners to have ane greater kyndnesse for them, sieing they will have there dependance of you, and be as it were on(e) Body, and if therefter any Inconvenience be found in this, the remedie of electing our owne prefect can alwayes be made use of.'

It is helpful to remember that at this time Fleming had sent no monk to the mission, with the possible exception of Anthony Gray, who entered Ratisbon about 1660 and seems to have spent most of his subsequent life wandering over Europe. He is said to have worked for eight years in Scotland,[21] and Fleming supplied him with a testimonial that he had worked as a missionary in Scotland and among Scots in Poland before 1687.[22] Since there is no record of his activities in any report to Propaganda, one can either conclude that he was not present when a report was being drawn up or that the compilers of reports tended to neglect, or be ignorant of, priests who had no particular status. One should bear this in mind when arguing from the silence about Benedictines in Propaganda sources after the secular mission was established in 1653.

Gray cannot be said to have formed part of the new community which Fleming was building up at Ratisbon and which in 1677 was still at a very early stage of development. Dixon, on the other hand, had been sending men to the mission for at least fourteen years and had been trying for eight years to get power to grant faculties to them himself. While Fleming was corresponding with Will Leslie, Dixon was complaining about Leslie's silence to a German dignitary at the Roman court.[23] The latter told him in February 1677 — this is to judge from Dixon's reply the following month — that the English monks had petitioned against the Scots. Dixon said he had always suspected this even though they tried to persuade him that Propaganda had reprimanded them for giving faculties to the Scots and had forbidden them to continue granting faculties for England. Strange behaviour, added Dixon, when the Scots are incorporated in their congregation and enjoy the same privileges and faculties as members of the same body.

As far as one can make out from Dixon's letter, the English monks gave two reasons for their action. As regards the first, said Dixon, the Scots supplied for the lack of English monks, especially in the north, where stipends were lower (which frightened the English) but the reward was very great (which pleased the Scots). The second reason seems to have been that Scots and English did not agree and English priests did not go to Scotland, so why should Scots priests go to England? English priests did not go to Scotland because the Scots were poor, said Dixon, and as for disagreement there were quarrels among the English themselves. He thought that if this were explained to Propaganda, undoubtedly it would allow access by Scots and English priests to each other's country, although the Scots, being poor, would not be able to provide for incoming priests unless Propaganda gave a pension to them as it did to the secular clergy. Dixon expressed willingness to work for this arrangement and added a postscript about Abbot Ogilvie's faculties, which were granted for the whole of the British Isles. The copy of them sent to Leslie could be seen, and it would be a good idea to show them to Cardinal Howard. We learn from the letter, too, that Leslie had still not yet replied to Dixon.

The desire of both abbots to have faculties for England as well as Scotland is rather puzzling, unless perhaps monks were assured of means of support in the north of England but not in the south of Scotland. One now finds the monks of Würzburg asking explicitly for an annual stipend from Propaganda. But before going further, we should consider Will Leslie's side of the correspondence about faculties. Dixon received no answer to his letters from 1669 on. Leslie then wrote in 1676 about something different. Dixon sent two more letters, to which he received no reply although told that one had been sent. He therefore wrote again to Leslie but still got no reply. As for Fleming, he received a letter from Leslie telling him that the reply he wanted had been sent to Würzburg. When he got a second letter saying that the English objected to the Scots being granted faculties for England, he wrote back but was complaining fourteen months later about receiving no answer.[24] Dixon's earlier letters to Leslie have been lost but those of 1676-77 reached Leslie and were filed away by him. The reader must judge whether, as seems likely, Leslie hedged and equivocated or whether he sent replies which were lost in transit.

Throughout this period the Würzburg abbot had been sending men to do missionary or recruiting work in Britain. Macarius Brown certainly, and Placid Baillie most probably, were in English mission stations all the time, while William Dunn was in one until his death in August 1675. Ninian Graham was in Scotland in the spring of 1678 and expected back that summer; he had left Würzburg some time after January 1672.[25] Bernard Maxwell had been in Scotland after 1672 and had returned to Würzburg, probably with two aspirants in the winter of 1675-76. He set off once more in the late summer of 1676 and returned at the end of the following year, again with two aspirants. Christian Abercrombie set off for Scotland at the end of March 1678, chiefly, we are told, for his health. James Blair, having returned to Würzburg not long before August 1678, set out again almost at once. The monk Chambers at Subiaco was able to write with some accuracy that Würzburg monks went freely to Scotland.[26] The information about comings and goings is found mainly in the letters of Bernard Maxwell at Würzburg to Abbot Fleming.[27] The story of Blair's second journey and his faculties is recorded in a quite different way.

In 1677 Alexander Leslie, brother of Will and like him a secular priest, was instructed by Propaganda to go to Scotland to make a visitation. It was really a fact-finding mission rather than a visitation, as he had no power to make decisions but was to report back to Propaganda. Among other things, he was to make every priest in Scotland show his credentials and faculties and to inform Propaganda of them. Accordingly Alexander Leslie reported on the secular prefect's faculties and explained that the Jesuit superior refused to show his and actually had the audacity to ask to see Leslie's own. There was, however, one Benedictine, Blair, who showed his credentials.

Abbot Dixon, in September 1676, gave James Blair (or Hepburn, as he was called in Scotland) letters of credence to say that he was going to do missionary work in Great Britain. Then, in January 1678 the English Benedictine president at Lamspring granted faculties to Blair; they were for Scotland only but could be used in England on his journey to and from Scotland provided he was not more than three months on the road. Blair behaved very correctly: the following July he showed the faculties to the secular prefect in Scotland, who signified his approval on the back of them. For good measure Blair also showed them to a Jesuit, Thomas Young, who wrote on them in Latin: 'I see no reason why anyone should object to these faculties.' In spite of this, Leslie reported that Blair's faculties caused a great stir among the Scots, who refuse to recognise English jurisdiction in any way. All this was copied by Alexander Leslie for Propaganda's information.[28]

Faculties constituted one need of monks going to Scotland; the other was means of support. The great advantage of sending a man to an English Benedictine station was that it solved both problems at once. When both English and Scots came to dislike the arrangement, the abbot of Würzburg had to look for other means of support for his missionaries. Will Leslie was not being very helpful, but Dixon did not give up. In February 1678 the prince-bishop of Würzburg wrote on his behalf to Propaganda.[29] Among the workers in the Lord's vineyard in Scotland, he said, the monks from the German monasteries held by no means the last place, but the Catholics in Scotland could not support them. The monks therefore wanted Propaganda to supply an annual stipend of fifty crowns as it did for secular priests.

When the secular mission to Scotland was set up, it was given an annual subsidy of five hundred crowns from Propaganda for the support of ten priests,[30] which explains the nature of the bishop's request. Almost three months after the bishop wrote, the secretary of Propaganda informed Will Leslie, who was out of Rome, of the bishop's letter and said there was no way of granting the request since Propaganda wished to subsidise only ten missionaries in the whole kingdom, so that when one died another deserving man would then succeed to his pension.[31] This was not merely obstructive tactics. A general meeting of Propaganda the year previously had decided that two priests could have faculties for Scotland but not a salary for precisely this reason.[32] When the next meeting of Propaganda considered the bishop's request, the secretary outlined the position; the cardinals decided to reply to the bishop that the Benedictines would come up for consideration in due course,[33] meaning presumably when some of the present ten died.

The Würzburg Scots were undoubtedly in a difficult situation. Their repeated petition for their own mission, such as William Ogilvie had once directed, received no answer, and indeed the Ratisbon abbot was opposing the appointment of a monk as prefect of it. The English Congregation was refusing to give them faculties for England. Whether Propaganda was behind this decision or not, the result for the Scots monks was the same. The English president remained willing to grant them faculties for Scotland, but this still left them without means of support in Scotland and (if we can trust Alexander Leslie's report) was unacceptable to the Scots. It seems clear that missionary work based on Würzburg was being stifled for want of outlet. Propaganda, or Will Leslie, seemed willing only to ask for or subsidise individual monks, such as Ephraim Reid and Marianus Irvine, whom it recognised as filling a particular need. Abbot Dixon regarded the prefecture and powers given to his predecessor in 1629 as an argument for the establishment of a similar missionary unit, but the situation had changed since then. Whether Propaganda was still setting up such units in other countries

185

in the 1670s or not, it was unlikely to favour doing so for Scotland. This was the position when Dixon died in March 1679. He had two monks (Brown and Baillie) on English Benedictine missions, one (Graham) somewhere on the road from Scotland to Germany, and two (Blair and Abercrombie) in Scotland on a temporary basis. That, at least, is the picture given by the letters of Bernard Maxwell, who was soon to be elected abbot.

Notes

1   Full text in "Scots and EBC".

2   *IR*, viii, 111.

3   For Brown see "Three Scots", 241-44; "Scots and EBC", 61.

4   Gordon, 582.

5   For Dunn see "Three Scots", 238-41; "Scots and EBC", 60-61.

6   APF, CP, 23, f. 178v; Giblin, 74; Gordon, 627.

7   For him see Gordon, 575-76.

8   As in Hay, *Failure*.

9   For him see "Highland Monks", 96-97.

10   APF, Acta, 39, f. 200r; SOCG, 424, f. 232-37.

11   APF, SC Scozia, I, f. 713-14.

12   SCA, ML, Gascoigne, 25.2.1675.

13   APF, Acta, 46, f. 9v-11v; SOCG, 457, f. 128-31, 135-38, 142v.

14   APF, Acta, 46, f. 59v.

15   Gordon, 566.

16   SCA, ML, Dixon, 24.5.1676.

17   SCA, ML, Dixon, 15.8.1676.

18   SCA, ML, Dixon, 11.11.1676.

19   SCA, ML, Fleming, 15.12.1676.

20   SCA, ML, Fleming, 27.4.1677.

21   "Necrologies", 187.

22   Reg. BOA, Sch., Akten, 186.

23   SCA, ML, Dixon, 6.3.1677.

24   SCA, ML, Fleming, 28.6.1678.

25   Reid, f. 119v.

26   SCA, ML, Chambers, 27.4.1677.

27   Maxwell, 14.12.1672, 25.8.1676, 1.12.1677, 5.3.1678, 30.3.1678.

28   SCA, Visitation *Ristretto*, f. 19v-20r.

29   APF, SOCG, 469, f. 100.

30   Bellesheim, IV, 44-45; Gordon, viii, xii.

31   SCA, ML, C (Propaganda 1653-94), 22.

32   APF, Acta, 47, f. 169v.

33   APF, Acta, 48, f. 114.

CHAPTER 15

Integration into the
Scottish mission obstructed
1679—85

About two weeks after Dixon's death a letter arrived at Würzburg addressed to him. Bernard Maxwell sent it on to Ratisbon, saying it contained 'not bad hopes from Cardinal Norfolke at Rome' and suggesting that Fleming should reply to it.[1] The cardinal was informing the abbots of a decree of Propaganda that monks going to the mission were to receive their faculties from the prefect of the secular clergy and could hope for one of the ten annual pensions in the same way as the secular priests. Maxwell himself was elected abbot a few months later. None of the five Würzburg monks on the mission came to the abbey for the election, but their number was reduced to two the following year.

Christian Abercrombie was recalled to Würzburg after Maxwell's election and arrived in the summer of 1680, bringing with him some recruits for the Ratisbon community. After escorting them to Ratisbon he returned to his own abbey and resumed his former occupation of cellarer. Ninian Graham died early in 1680. He had been half expected back in Würzburg as early as 1678, then expected for the abbatial election. Having left Scotland and travelled as far as Holland, he was told to continue his journey to Würzburg but had spent the journey money on drink. Maxwell remarked, too, that these were not 'the least of his extravagances and miscarriages'. Graham returned to Scotland and died on the fifth day after his arrival there. Placid Baillie died a few months later but no details of his death have been preserved. The only piece of information we have is that Maxwell's letter to him before the election in 1679 was sent to Lamspring and forwarded to Baillie from there. One would surmise from this that Baillie was on an English Benedictine mission station, but against this is the fact that he is not included in the English Congregation necrology.

The Würzburg monk in England, Macarius Brown, was imprisoned early in 1680. Maxwell, who had already commented in two letters on the serious difficulties facing English Catholics as a result of the Popish Plot, was afraid that Brown might be executed as so many others, including two Benedictines, had been. In fact, however, although a Benedictine laybrother, Thomas Pickering, had been executed the previous May, neither of the two men Maxwell mentions, Frs Maurus Corker and Cuthbert Wall *alias* March, was put to death. Both had been sentenced but were reprieved and remained in prison until 1685.[2]

Thus, of the five Würzburg missionaries, James Blair was the only one still on the mission and at liberty. Still no monk of Ratisbon had gone to the mission (always excepting Anthony Gray) but recruits were arriving in the abbey. Fr Erhard Dunbar, who came from Islay, a place with steady Catholic associations, was a monk at Ratisbon.[3] At the end of 1679 his two brothers passed through Würzburg on their way to join him, four more recruits arrived with Christian Abercrombie from Scotland, then Fr Erhard himself passed through Würzburg on his way north-westwards in September 1680 and returned over two months later with three more youths. In the new year Fleming wrote to Will Leslie in Rome outlining his plan for establishing a place of education for Catholic children, especially those from the Highlands. He had ten boys at Ratisbon studying their 'grammar'. Fleming wanted John Irvine, a secular priest then at Padua, to become a monk and teach at Ratisbon since he would thereby help the Scottish mission by educating future missionaries.[4]

While Fleming was engaged in laying foundations, Maxwell at Würzburg wanted a working arrangement to be made at once. Alexander Leslie had completed his visitation of Scotland and was expected to pass through Ratisbon on his way to Rome. The Würzburg abbot therefore wrote to Fleming:

> 'I would wish you also to be instant with Mr Lesly when he shall come concerning the obtaineing to us for the mission faculties and pensions for those that shall be sent thither from our houses, and I doubt not but that he may doe much for us at Roome if he retaine that kindeness for us that he seemed to have had when I was with him in Scotland, and the more easily he will obtaine it that the Cardinall of Norfolke did write to us the last yeare if you remember that the Congregation de propaganda fide had decreed that those that were sent from us to those places should have their faculties from Alexander Winster otherwise called Mr Dumbar, pensiones vero annuas tum maxime eis sperare licebit, cum aliquis ex senioribus defecerit, these are the Cardinals own words.'

Alexander Winster or Dunbar was the prefect of the secular clergy in Scotland, a position he was to hold almost to the end of the century.[5] There was, however, something else that Maxwell wanted:

'I could wish also that the pretensiones to our monasteries in Scotland were also indeavoured at Roome, and in my opinion now were the best time for agenting such a bussiness for if the times grow shortely better . . . we may come to have greater opposition.'

It seems extraordinary to find such hopes and plans in 1680, but we have seen that the Reformation continued to be viewed as a reversible process by these *émigrés*. No doubt, too, the acceptance of the Roman Catholic duke of York in Scotland as commissioner of Charles II had raised their hopes still further, and in fact the duke did establish religious houses when he succeeded to the throne a few years later. Maxwell was even willing to send a monk to Rome to push their claims if Leslie did not support them. He asked Fleming for his views but they must have been less sanguine than his own, for nothing more was heard of the plan. In the event Leslie turned south from Brussels to Paris and so did not visit the Scots abbeys.

By March 1681 Propaganda had considered Alexander Leslie's report and issued its decrees. Perhaps the most important was the allotting of districts to each priest, with the order that he must not exercise his ministry outside it. A great step forward in the organisation of the Scottish mission had been made. It is clear, however, that Maxwell had misjudged the help he could expect from Alexander Leslie. Leslie's bias is obvious. Everything he wrote was designed to strengthen the position of the secular prefect and weaken that of the religious. His fire is concentrated mainly on the Jesuits, but there was one section on Benedictines in his lengthy instruction: 'Is it expedient for monks to come to the Scottish mission? is there need of them? can they subsist, and if so, how?' Leslie replied that it was not expedient, for three reasons: first, they send difficult people, those not wanted in the monastery; then, there is no way to control them and they disturb everybody; lastly, they refused to send a Gaelic-speaking monk to the Highlands. Of course the last reason was not the result of on-the-spot investigation but of previous knowledge. Leslie added a suggestion which rather undermines his case against the monks: if their Eminences want to send Benedictines, it will be necessary either to appoint a superior general or to subject them to the prefect of the mission.

The report is enormously long and only a very few points can be mentioned.[6] The sole monk referred to is James Blair, and that was because of his faculties; no Benedictine is found among the list of priests serving the various places. Leslie also reported that there was no movement of priests between Scotland and England, nor should there be. Propaganda decided to send Leslie to Scotland to see that the decrees were implemented. He thereupon said that he needed to make various petitions and receive the answers before he set off. He wanted the faculties of both seculars and regulars to be the same, so that a cause of discord might be removed (since the Jesuits had wider powers than the seculars); the cardinals replied: 'No change just now'. He wanted all regulars to be obliged to show their faculties to the secular prefect on arrival in Scotland; the cardinals replied: 'Decision deferred'. In one major way, therefore, the disunity in the Scottish mission remained.

The Cardinal of Norfolk had succeeded Francesco Barberini as protector of Scotland. Since Alexander Leslie's report had stressed the shortage of priests in Scotland, Propaganda's first decree in March 1681 was that those Scottish priests outside Scotland, secular or regular, who in Norfolk's opinion were suitable for the task, should be sent to the mission. That same month Norfolk wrote to Abbot Fleming asking for Ephraim Reid to be sent. Fleming sent the letter on to Reid, who was in charge of the Erfurt house, and about the same time, whether in reply to the letter or not, told the cardinal of his efforts to make the Ratisbon abbey 'serviceable for the Conversione of our Countrie'.

Reid answered that he was fifty and unwell, had forgotten his Gaelic and felt unable to do mission work in the Highlands. His letter was sent to Will Leslie by Fleming, who added that he would 'dispose' Fr Ephraim to go but could hardly do so until some other help was available.[7] There the matter rested for a time; Fleming was making desperate efforts to get help for his seminary, and very little was forthcoming from Rome, even in the matter of letters of recommendation. One wonders if Leslie considered the sending of Ephraim Reid the touchstone of the Scots monks' sincerity; this was the third time in ten years that the request for his services was made without effect. Fleming continued writing to Rome for help and in April 1682 sent a strong letter to Leslie saying that he had written several times and received no answer.[8] Leslie finally replied in July pointing out the objections to allowing John Irvine, the secular priest at Padua, to take the habit at Ratisbon. This produced a statement from Fleming, who was still annoyed by Leslie's silence, of the measures he was prepared to take to make Ratisbon of service to the Scottish mission.[9] In the following year, however, Irvine went to Scotland;[10] one wonders if Leslie had been working for this all along.

Probably as an indirect result of Propaganda's decree about priests outside Scotland, Christian Abercrombie was sent once more to the mission. The manner of his going reveals much of how the Würzburg monks under Maxwell's rule looked on mission work. In or about early June 1681 Fr Alan Chisholm was 'deponeing upon his conscience' in chapter that someone should be sent 'and this did give the first occasion of thinking to send any thither so soone'. His abbot suspected that Chisholm was motivated by a hope of being sent himself, but, as Maxwell said,

> 'Our Fr Alan desired before a long time to goe for the Mission but it was denyed in nostro Capitulo by all by reason that he is not thought qualified for such a function.'

Was the Würzburg community always so conscientious about sending only suitable men? We have seen Alexander Leslie's allegations in this regard, and one must admit that they seem to have some foundation. When James Blair returned from Scotland some time later, he was given leave to enter the Dominican order 'upon the accompt that he could neither give satisfaction, nor receave satisfaction from our people since his comeing here'. Ninian Graham is another case in point. Maxwell's remarks upon his conduct have been quoted already. The Cardinal of Norfolk expressed fears (so apparently Will Leslie told Maxwell) that the common German vice, drinking, had crept in among the Würzburg monks. Maxwell asked Leslie to tell the cardinal that this was not so and that he would certainly not send any such person to the mission. He added, however, that the deceased Ninian Graham, who had been sent home some years before to visit friends, had the vice a little, having learned it among the German soldiers with whom he served before coming to Würzburg, and probably the cardinal's suspicion arose from this.[11] If Maxwell's statement is to be taken literally, Graham was not a missionary but was merely on leave of absence in Scotland.

As late as November 1680 Macarius Brown was still in prison in England and Maxwell feared for his life. By the following June, however, he was apparently at liberty, for Maxwell was expecting a letter from him about Abercrombie's journey. Abercrombie set off in August and by the end of the month had landed at Kirkcaldy and made his way to Edinburgh. From there he seems to have gone to the north-east, since he wrote several times about the Leslies of Pitcaple in Aberdeenshire and the four Highland youths that Fleming wanted to enter his new seminary. Alexander Leslie, who had returned to Scotland, was supposed to be helping to find them. In the autumn of 1682, according to Maxwell, both Abercrombie and James Blair were 'very weele provided with places and have now made many acquaintance and frends to our Order, which if they returne they feare all will be lost'.

The abbot added that Abercrombie did not enjoy good health in Germany and 'wee also neede at leaste one there to correspond with the house here and to agent our litle affaires there, all which make me to deliberat whither I shall call F. Christian backe, or let him

191

stay there'. Abercrombie did remain but Blair returned in the autumn of 1683. Unlike Abercrombie, he seems to have worked in the south, for he brought with him a boy, William Stewart, recommended by Lady Traquair and told Maxwell of his dealings with the Catholic Baillie Haliburton in Dundee. There were now only two Würzburg monks on the mission, Abercrombie in Scotland and Brown in England, and this was the case for the remainder of Maxwell's rule. Still Fleming did not send any monk to Scotland, but Abercrombie acted as agent and informant for him as well as for his own abbot.

Correspondence between Würzburg and Scotland was carried on through the intermediary of any suitable traveller and also through a Mr Kennedy in the Low Countries. This was the man who was later Sir James Kennedy and became Conservator of the Scottish Staple at Veere in January 1683. He was a Catholic and personally known to James VII;[12] he also supplied Maxwell with news and helped travellers to the Scots abbeys on their way. When Kennedy left Brussels for London in the summer of 1682, Maxwell wrote that correspondence was difficult in his absence. He repeated the remark when Kennedy took up his post at Veere, and four months later lamented that he had had no news from Scotland or England since Kennedy left Brussels. Kennedy's son was later a monk of Ratisbon for a time and then served as a secular priest in Scotland.[13]

With what faculties did Abercrombie go to Scotland? One would have expected, after Propaganda's decree of 1679, that he went to Scotland and there received faculties from the secular prefect which were not to be used outside the district assigned to him. Since he could not expect to receive one of the ten pensions, he would have to go to a district where the Catholics or some well-to-do person could support him. It is clear, however, that no such arrangement was made. When Abercrombie set off on 5th August 1681 he wrote to Alexander Leslie in Rome expressing his willingness to help and assuring him that the Würzburg monks desired to serve their country. His abbot enclosed the letter in one of his own;[14] both men had known Alexander Leslie in Scotland. Maxwell wanted to know what financial support his men on the mission could really expect as a result of the decree of 1679 that monks could succeed to one of the ten pensions. He also wanted the help of Alexander and his brother as 'two most concerned in that affaire':

'Which decree if it . . . have its due effect which I hope it will, it depending altogether in your kindeness to us, and your recommending of us to the foresaid Coledge of Cardinals de propaganda fide, which I doubt not but you will doe: it will prove with time very profitable for our Countrie, for if I could

PLATE 13

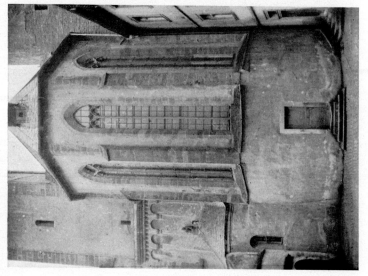

PLATE 14

Apse and 'Scots dwarf', east end of church, before 1945

PLATE 15. Church interior, looking east, before 1945

see any way of our peoples subsisteing there, it should be my greatest indeavour to receave and breede young men for the assistance of the same, and you cannot but sufficiently know how difficill it is to subsist there without any such assistance.'

On 27th September, before this letter reached Rome, Will Leslie wrote to Maxwell on behalf of the Cardinal of Norfolk. The correspondence between Maxwell and Rome in the autumn of 1681 is difficult to follow since, of the five letters written, two pairs crossed in the post. Naturally the writers did not get to grips with each other and since their viewpoints were quite diverse the results of the correspondence were inconclusive. We know roughly, from the abbot's reply some time in October,[15] why Will Leslie wrote. Having expressed delight at making Will's acquaintance, even if only by letter, Maxwell told him that as regards help to Scotland, 'You shall finde me as willing to concurre thereuntill as any man liveing', and he promised: 'I . . . would with all my hearte assiste and doe for it to my abilitie.' This was a prelude to explaining that he could not do as the cardinal wished (clearly, to educate missionaries) because of the abbey's limited revenue, and suggesting that the pope might ask the bishop and chapter of Würzburg to help the monastery and thus Scotland.

It is a badly written letter, wandering back and forth from one subject to another, and it is also a begging letter in answer to a begging letter:

'Moreover I hope his Eminence and your Reverence will also obtaine from his holyness and the Congregation de propaganda fide some assistance for those two that are actually in the Scots mission, and those also who shall be sent after this.'

He wanted Leslie to press for the execution of the 1679 decree and promised on his side: 'For concurring and agreeing with the Abbot of Ratisbon for furthering such good and pious ends I shall never be wanting.'

In the meantime Will Leslie had received the letter sent by Maxwell to his brother and had replied to it (4th October) since Alexander was by now in Scotland. He thus wrote two letters to Abbot Maxwell in a week, the only two he ever sent him. We know what Will Leslie wrote in the second letter, both from Maxwell's reply and from his description of it to Fleming. To the latter Maxwell wrote:

'Not long since I receaved two letters from Roome from Don Gulielm Leslie, the first from him selfe, and the last an answere to a letter I did write to his Brother Mr Alexander Leslie whom I thought to have beene at Rome . . . In these letters he informes

193

me of severall things concerning our Mission in Scotland, and first that the Pope and Cardinalls de propaganda fide hath ordered that all Religiouse there should have their faculties from the superior of the secular priests there untill we increase so there that we can have a body and a superiour of our owne there: my minde he desires to know concerning this, and for my parte I am very weele pleased thereat and for the present I cannot sie how it can be otherwise; your minde and opinion I desire to know with the soonest.'

Leslie had also told the Würzburg abbot that missionaries now had to stay in their own districts and that Propaganda gave a subsidy for the priest in places with the 'fewest Catholiques, for where the Catholiques are numerouse they offer to maintaine their owne priest.' This is a description of what another decree resulting from Alexander Leslie's visitation meant in practice. The decree itself said that the subsidy was to be distributed by the prefect according to need,[16] a more flexible and sensible arrangement than allotting it irrespective of circumstances to ten priests chosen once and for all.

Abbot Maxwell's reply to Will Leslie's second letter is very long and repeats a good deal of what he had already written to Leslie and to Abbot Fleming, but it deserves to be quoted at some length as it throws considerable light on the position of the Würzburg abbey as regards mission work for the remainder of Maxwell's rule.[17] After expressions of friendliness to Alexander Leslie, who hardly deserved them after his visitation report, the abbot said:

'As to the distribution of the Priests in the Mission by the Order and command of the Pope and Cardinalls, and of there being all subject to one superiour ad interim, a secular Priest, I for my parte make no difficultie therein, but rests very weele contented therewith: so that with time as you say in your letter, crescente numero Religiosorum they may have a superiour of their owne, if God Almightie of his infinit mercie shall grant that the Catholique faithe shall have a footeing there, and that you may see my willingness the more, and also see that we shall not seeke our owne privat interests, I shall with the next write to mine there to rest satisfied with the distribution of places your superiour there shall make, and also be obedient to him in every thing lawfull, as they would and ought to be to me, and that they also lay aside all emulation and idle Iarres (jars) about priviledges and such.'

Maxwell was willing to accept a role subsidiary to that of the secular clergy and produced a strange version of history to justify it:

'In former times we have beene so successfully assisteing to the secular Clergie to the gloriouse conversion of so many Nations.'

The different way of distributing the annual subsidy from Propaganda still left unsolved the problem of supporting monks on the mission. The abbot therefore wanted Leslie and the Cardinal 'to give Orders to yours in the Mission that mine there may have some assistance from them in that kinde . . . that is if they shall be assigned to such places and persons from whom they cannot expect their full maintenance.' He could send no more monks for the time being and could support no more persons at Würzburg, but was willing to help when it should become possible. He wrote:

'Nevertheless to satisfie your desire it shall be my indeavour to procure and receave some highlanders as soone as I shall see a way to maintaine them here.'

Once again he promised to co-operate with Fleming:

'I shall never be wanting, and ever to my power be most willing to any thing that can concerne either the good of our Countrie, or his seminarie.'

The other problem, that of faculties, was also reviewed by Maxwell.

'We have had this time bygon some union with the Inglish Muncks of our Order and have hitherto alwayes had our Faculties for the mission from them who have faculties for all of our Order, for all our kings Dominions. This union is also almost now decayed, only as yet we have our faculties from them ever untill we can have them elsewhere, and if this proiect succeede betwixt you and us, which I hope shall, we will from hence take our faculties from you.'

Thus Propaganda's decree for the monks had still not been put into practice two and a half years after it was issued. Evidently Abercrombie had gone to Scotland with English Benedictine faculties, as had the other monk there, James Blair. Nor did any new arrangement come into force. Will Leslie never replied to either of the letters Maxwell wrote him. The cardinal and Leslie had wanted the two Scots abbeys to help at once by supplying missionaries, especially Gaelic speakers, and by educating students, especially Highlanders. Both abbots explained the difficulty they had in meeting the requests and themselves appealed for help, which was hardly to Leslie's liking. Probably we can attribute his silence to this. We can also with some justification be sceptical of the sincerity of the promise to give the monks a prefect of their own when their numbers warranted it, for it does not harmonise with the schemes of the Leslie brothers to make the seculars supreme.

Maxwell had been very expansive, not to say enthusiastic, in his last letter to Leslie. One can see the same man as was so eager, having been elected abbot, to co-operate with and please his fellow abbot in Ratisbon. Naturally he was hurt and disappointed by Leslie's silence. It was about this time that Leslie was treating Fleming in similar fashion over the request for the services of the secular priest at Padua, and we have seen that Fleming dealt firmly with him. Maxwell, a less strong character, complained instead to his fellow abbot:

'I have not heard from Mr Leslie at Roome this halfe yeare past notwithstanding that my last to him required also an answere, what he is doeing or whether he be deade or hiding I know not; and as for the seculare Clergie their kindeness to ours in Scotland I heare not much thereof, and although Mr Alexander Leslie in his letter to me promises all kindeness to this place and those of ours there, yet our F. Christian signifies to me that he finds more in words than effect, which I can easily beleeve, for the Clergie now every where are sett to mortifie the Regulars, and if they could subsist without the helpe of Regulars not onely in Scotland but every where now a dayes they would willingly sett them aside (sed haec inter nos).'

That was in June 1682. Maxwell was prepared to take practical steps to remedy the situation, as he told his fellow abbot the next month:

'You may easily see and perceive, that if it were not for the promoteing of Gods glorie, and for the good of our houses, we have but smal incouragemente to receave or accept of any upon their, I mean the secular Clergies, desire or recommendation, since they are and begin to be so particular to us, and if with time we ever intend to send any to our Countrie it seemes we must indeavour to obtaine priviledges and faculties for our owne there immediatly from Roome independenter of the Clergie, but I feare they have put a stop thereto by comeing before us, and for to try what can be done in the same, it is long since I have had thoughts of sending our P. Prior to Roome to see what can or may be effectuated therein.'

Maxwell's proposal was that the prior, Marianus Irvine, should act on behalf of both Scots abbeys, which would share the expenses involved. He explained, however, that Irvine could not be spared that year. The Ratisbon abbot was evidently not enthusiastic about the proposal, and six weeks later Maxwell wrote again:

'As for our uniteing our selfes with the secular clergie in

196

Scotland, it is certaine they will never make us equall with them, therefor it will be necessare for us to obtaine faculties and priviledges for our selfes, if it be possible to obtaine them, and I see no reason they should denye us, since the English monkes have the like. It is true as you specifie in your letter that we were united with the English Congregation, at least this house was, as the contract betwixt us and them show which I have by me, but it seemes bef(ore) severall years they are tyred of us, and desire our companie n(o longer) for they make difficultie to give us faculties any m(ore).'

At this time, however, Fleming stopped replying to Maxwell for a while, and it was not until August 1683 that the latter broached the subject again:

'Moreover F. Christian is pressing that we should indeavour to procure from Roome faculties for our owne people our selves, and as undoubtedly you know, we have written severall times to Rome anent the affaire but never could effect any thing therein, and I beleeve never will untill we send one to Roome for that purpose to agent therein.'

Fleming promptly and actively discouraged the proposal. Only a fortnight later Maxwell was accepting his arguments about the difficulties of the journey and agreeing to defer the plan. No more was heard of it, and Maxwell's rule and Charles II's reign came to an end almost simultaneously with no arrangement for mission work made. Würzburg monks could hardly take up mission work unless they were sure of means of support beforehand. There may have been very few, if any, available for such work but Will Leslie's silence effectively blocked the avenue to it.

Notes

[1] The chief source for this period is Maxwell's letters to Fleming. References to them will not be given.

[2] Birt, 68, 76; Weldon, 219, 223.

[3] For him see "Highland Monks", 97-98.

[4] SCA, ML, Fleming, 7.1.1681.

[5] For him see Gordon, 625; Bellesheim, IV, 115 ff.

[6] SCA, Visitation *Ristretto*, f. 2v, 3r-5v, 18r; Bellesheim, IV, 131.

[7] SCA, ML, Fleming, 1.4.1681, 29.7.1681; ML, Reid, 8.6.1681.

[8] SCA, ML, Fleming, 14.4.1682.

[9] SCA, ML, Fleming, undated (endorsed: c. August 1682).

[10] Gordon, 628, 566. This is John Irvine, *Cuttlebrae*.

[11] SCA, ML, Maxwell, 5.11.1681.

[12] J. Davidson and A. Gray, *The Scottish Staple at Veere* (London, 1909), 229-32, 304.

[13] Reg. BOA, Sch., Akten, 320, 12.7.1690; SCA, ML, Norfolk, 24.2.1693; *Colleges*, 122.

[14] SCA, ML, Abercrombie, 5.8.1681 (date altered to 15th August; cf. also Maxwell, 6.8.1681); ML, Maxwell, 30.8.1681.

[15] SCA, ML, Maxwell, endorsed 22.10.1681.

[16] SCA, Visitation *Ristretto*, f. 2v; Bellesheim, IV, 131.

[17] SCA, ML, Maxwell, 5.11.1681.

CHAPTER 16

Integration into the Scottish mission achieved
1685—97

When the Catholic James VII ascended the throne and the chancellor, the earl of Perth, became a Catholic, conditions for the Catholic missionaries changed completely even if not all at once. For the monks, support of their missionaries in Scotland ceased to be a problem, since a pension was paid to each abbey in Germany and the monks in Scotland were also awarded a pension of £200.[1] The other, less pressing matter, that of faculties, was likewise solved: one cannot imagine there being any difficulty when James was summoning priests to Scotland and the chancellor was actively helping them. This at least was the situation in the second half of James's reign; there is remarkably little evidence of Benedictine missionary activity in the first two years.

The moving spirit, certainly the person most actively engaged, in promoting work by Benedictines in Scotland was Abbot Fleming. Maxwell's successor at Würzburg, Marianus Irvine, either agreed with Fleming's views or fell in with them. On several occasions, too, Fleming said he was acting on behalf of all the Scots monks in Germany, and he seems to have made arrangements for Würzburg monks as well as his own. Placid Fleming was probably the most outstanding and capable man among the Scots Catholic émigrés at the time, but he had made a deliberate choice of joining his fortunes to those of the poor Ratisbon abbey,[2] and he never went back on it. He was nevertheless intensely interested in all matters concerning his church and country. When a Catholic king succeeded in Scotland, Fleming began at once to make his influence felt in the weightiest matters.[3]

He made two, possibly three, journeys to London, and before the first he obtained faculties from Norfolk. No doubt a cardinal protector always had power to grant them. Fleming's were made out to him at Rome on 2nd June 1685 and were valid for England and Scotland, but not Ireland, and for as long as he remained there unless Norfolk revoked them.[4] Thus, far from Fleming having powers to grant faculties to his monks, he had to obtain them for himself. The situation over faculties and pensions was unchanged in those early days of James's reign. Athanasius Chambers, the Scots monk at Subiaco, was told by Norfolk:[5]

'As to the Scottish Mission all I can doe is to give you faculteys, as I will when you desire to goe theather, but I fear the Propaganda will not give a Viaticum, nor a maintenance theare, since that which they give is complained to be to little for those to whome it's appleyed.'

It is in a letter of Chambers at this time that one finds a reference, perhaps the earliest, to the refounding of a Catholic religious house in Holyrood. James had already fitted up one of the rooms in Holyrood as a Catholic chapel.[6] Now Chambers wrote: 'If the queenes chapel in Edenburgh suld be in the hands of the benedictanes as that of Londone is he (Norfolk) could provyde me ther.'[7] English Benedictine monks had been serving the queen's chapel at Somerset House in London since 1662, and James founded a Benedictine monastery in St. James's palace when he succeeded to the throne. The general chapter of the English Congregation was actually held there in 1685. It was here three years later that an English Benedictine received episcopal consecration and the baptismal solemnities of the infant Prince of Wales were held.[8] Erecting a religious house in a Scottish royal palace was thus not quite so strange and singular as it appears at first sight. It can only be considered here insofar as it involved the Benedictines.

Richard Augustine Hay[9] was a Scot who went to France as a boy and became an Augustinian canon, the order which had held the abbey of Holyrood before the Reformation. In September 1686, having received a commission from his superior to refound the order in England and Scotland, he set off for his native land. The preparations for opening the chapel in the former council chamber at Holyrood were well advanced. The secular prefect, Alexander Dunbar, performed the opening ceremony on St Andrew's day, and on Christmas day, 1686 there were solemn services at which Christian Abercrombie was present. Hay recorded that 'Mr Abercrombie, of the Order of St Benedict, a man not mutch skill'd in singing, did officiat' and also presided at an evening service consisting of a psalm, a hymn and a litany. In a letter Hay was even less complimentary, saying that Abercrombie 'is an honest man enough, but as nature has not favoured him with a good vocal organ, and he has been long away from his monastery (where I imagine there is not much in the way of singing), the poor Father acquitted himself very ill of his office',[10]

The opening of the chapel was merely the first step. The old abbey church was still being used as the Protestant parish kirk, so the congregation was given notice to quit the following July, as the church was to be fitted out for Catholic worship and handed over to a religious order. At first it was intended for the Benedictines. In February 1687 the French ambassador in Ratisbon asked his king to give a donation to Fleming, who intended to send nine persons, including six priests, at Easter to Scotland, where the chancellor had prepared a church and small monastery adjoining the royal palace of Edinburgh. Louis XIV duly made a grant towards the cost of the journey. A month later Fleming himself described the group as eight priests, with a laybrother and an organist, sent at Perth's request to make the first public Catholic foundation in Scotland.[11] Hay himself remarked that 'his Majestie was inform'd the Church of Holyroodhouse belong'd of old to the Benedictins'.

The project soon broke down. Fleming wrote to Charles Whiteford, procurator of the Scots college in Paris, at the same time as the Protestant congregation was being ejected:[12]

'I hear that your Canon Regular, the Lady Roslins son (i.e., Hay), has hindered us from getting our Church and Residence, and is lykwayes Disappoynted himselfe, tho he made great offers that the French of his order would not only provyde the place, but even make all the buildings and reparations on there owne expensses; which is more then we are able to performe.'

To Lewis Innes, the principal of the Paris college, he wrote:[13]

'As to the Abbey Church I am no wayes anxious nor sollicitous, and Doe with a perfyt resignation submitte my selfe to his Majesties Gracious Determination, And it would be no lesse acceptable to me if the King would be pleased to Doe something for the Monasteries we have as yet abroad.'

No religious order was, in the event, settled in Holyrood, and Fleming summed up the situation for Will Leslie in 1688:[14]

'As for the Abbey Church, it being founded for the Canon Regulars, and they makeing great offers, I soon past from our pretension to it, and so much the more easily that the Jesuits had informed the Court that we were not able to Discharge the Duetie; And now they are as much against the Canon Regulars, alledgeing them to be Jansenists.'

The church was nearly ready for consecration when the mob sacked it in December 1688. Meanwhile the Canongate Kirk had been built for the ejected Protestants and remains the parish church until the present day.

In the matter of the appointment of a bishop, Fleming also acted

201

with great energy. A Vicar-Apostolic had been given to England in 1685, which encouraged the Scots to press for the same in Scotland. The Jesuits, however, naturally opposed any candidate hostile to them, while the parties pressing for an appointment were on the whole opposed to anyone who favoured the Jesuits in the slightest. Fleming flung himself unequivocally on to the side of the secular priests who wanted a bishop and one firmly opposed to the Jesuits.[15] It is this, rather than the vicissitudes of the negotiations and the personalities of the candidates, including Fleming himself, which is important for the history of the Benedictine mission and indeed of the Scottish mission in general.

Fleming, when he arrived back in Ratisbon from London towards the end of 1686, had already very firmly renounced his own candidature and applied himself to support that of Lewis Innes, a secular priest who was the principal of the Scots college in Paris. He told Whiteford that he himself was not the new bishop but had procured a more deserving one, adding that Innes knew 'the Benedictins were alwayes the best freinds to the Clergie, and there truest *Copiae auxiliares* in there Necessitie.'[16] The Ratisbon abbot was confident of the agreement of his colleague at Würzburg, for when describing his own efforts on Innes's behalf he said:[17]

'To the Cardinal I was somewhat more pressing, and to give it more authoritie, Did writ as Representative of the Regular Clergie hier in Germanie, and had joynd the Abbot of Wurtzburg with me, if he had not been sick of ane hott feaver; however as soon as he recovers, his letters shall follow myne.'

Even when Christian Abercrombie in Scotland defaulted from the party line, Fleming did not waver. In the spring of 1688 he informed Whiteford:[18]

'Pater Abercrombie has joyned himselfe to the Padres (i.e., the Jesuits); This will make a schisme among us, for I am resolved to stand and fall with the Clergie; and sieing Abercrombie has acted in severall things very Deceitfully, and even against mr Innes, he deserves not your Correspondence, or that you should in any wayes Countenance him.'

James eventually nominated two bishops, Lewis Innes and another secular priest, Thomas Nicolson, but the Revolution, coming before the appointments took effect, put an end to the matter for the time being.

Clearly, during his stay in London in 1686, Fleming's efforts concerned the appointment of a bishop and the establishing of a monastery in Holyrood. The sending of monks as missionaries to Scotland must also have been discussed, because immediately on

202

his return he set about getting faculties for them. He asked the Cardinal of Norfolk, as the latter wrote to Athanasius Chambers at Subiaco:[19]

'F. Placide Fleming Abbott in Ratisbone is returned some time since from London wheare (h)is presence required a shorte voiage, and now he writes of his desire to send F. Ephrem Reed Priour of S. James in Erford, F. Augustin Bruce, and F. James Bruce to Scotland, giving them very good characters for that mission, and desiring I would give them faculteys, as I (releying and charging strictly his conscience) have done for one yeare, with reserve of recaling them without any other reason, but *beneplacito*; whearefore I desire to have (inter nos) the trewest character you can give me of them, only for to governe my selfe best by. The Abbott desireth a Viaticum for them from Propaganda fide, but heare is nothing to be gotten, since all it giveth annually was long since determined and distri(b)uted on the nominated persons.'

The request for Chambers's opinion is extraordinary, especially since he had left Germany in 1673 before either of the Bruces had entered religion. The interesting point, however, is that Augustine Bruce was a monk of Würzburg. Monks of the two houses were, it would seem, acting together, and Fleming was making the arrangements. This is also the first certain case of any Ratisbon monk taking up mission work in Scotland for almost fifty years.

The figures given for the group to be sent to Scotland by Fleming at Easter 1687 vary slightly; we can, however, take Fleming's own figures, not only because they come from him but because they are the most detailed. Thus eight priests with a laybrother and an organist were going to Scotland. The question one wants to ask is twofold: Did the number include men already in Scotland, and did it include monks of Würzburg? It is an academic question because the Holyrood project fell through, but eight priests could hardly have left Ratisbon at once and no laybrother, as far as is known, belonged to the Ratisbon community, whereas Würzburg did have Bro. Joseph Ogilvie.

The figures given of monks actually sent by Fleming to Scotland likewise vary, even in his own statements. For instance, he was later to tell the Ratisbon chancery that he had sent four priests to Scotland in 1687, but shortly afterwards he was saying to the abbot of St Gallen that he had sent six. Fleming apparently included Würzburg monks in his figures or not, as it suited him. He would presumably have to confine himself to Ratisbon monks when addressing Ratisbon authorities but could include monks of Würzburg when writing further afield. The date 1687 is the one usually found for the departure of the monks, though one can note that at the end of 1686 Fleming told the duke of Bavaria he had sent four priests to the mission the previous spring.[20] This too was a petition, however, and therefore Fleming was trying to awaken sympathy and obtain financial help; he could, for instance, without stretching the truth too far, include Christain Abercrombie, who was in Scotland already, or himself, since he spent part of 1686 in Britain.

We are on much firmer ground as regards monks who did pastoral or missionary work in Scotland in the last year of James's rule, irrespective of when they arrived. There were eight and we know their names. Three were from Ratisbon, the two given faculties by Norfolk and another Gaelic speaker, Erhard Dunbar. Incidentally, when the faculties given by Norfolk lapsed after a year, somebody would undoubtedly renew them; Ephraim Reid remained over a quarter of a century in Scotland. We know in some detail when the five Würzburg monks went to Scotland. Christian Abercrombie was there already. The Würzburg chronicle records that Augustine Bruce and Ambrose Cook were sent in April 1687 by order of James VII. James in that year summoned available priests from other places on the Continent.[21] If we take as strictly accurate the chronicler's statement that Abbot Irvine sent four priests to Scotland in 1687-88,[22] then it was at this time that James Blair and Boniface Mackie set off. To this should be added the continued work of Macarius Brown in England and the journey of Bro Joseph Ogilvie to London with the relic of Macarius in August 1688. The only persons who remained in the Würzburg monastery were the abbot, who was soon to die, Alan Chisholm, and some student monks not yet priests. This was a really remarkable self-sacrificing missionary effort, and one that put the monastery itself into jeopardy.

We can accept as substantially accurate the statement of a historian of the Scottish mission that the monks did not arrive to help the mission until the second half of 1687.[23] Perth wrote to Cardinal Norfolk in February 1688: 'Of late wee have got over 6 or 7 monks from Germany, some of them very good men and like to prove able missioners. They would fain be upon the same foot as the others.'[24] Fleming was able to tell Will Leslie: 'Our Monks Does pretty well in the Mission, and My Lord Chancellour Declares himselfe Content and Satisfied with them.'[25] Whatever the source of their faculties, Fleming had no wish for them to have a superior of their own but rather to be subject to the secular prefect. The arrangement did not work smoothly, however, because of the heat engendered over the question of a bishop. Fleming had already expressed fears that Dunbar 'will endeavor to revenge himselfe on the Religious we send home',[26] and he informed Whiteford as early as July 1687:[27]

'I must tell you in Confidence and sub rosa, that pater Abercrombie, in severall of his letters, has been alwayes informeing me against Mr Dunbar, and once or tuyce also against mr Burnet,[28] and I haveing ordained my Religious to goe and wait upon mr Dunbar at there arryvall and receave there Directory from him as Superior of the Clergie, he endeavored by all means to hinder them, and has been extreamely offended with on(e) of myne ever since upon that account.'

There was no longer need of any grant from the subsidy supplied annually by Propaganda, even if Fleming had had to beg for journey expenses. The pension of £200 from the king for missioner monks has been mentioned. At Martinmas 1688 a grant was paid to the Benedictine monks 'whom we ordered to be sent for from beyond the sea.'[29] James's reign and the public favouring of Catholicism came to an end simultaneously within weeks of the payment, but it can be noted that this was the largest number of monks in Scotland from the time when the pre-reformation communities died out after 1560 until a monastery was founded in the Highlands in the late nineteenth century.

We are fortunate in possessing an account of the missionaries in Scotland at the Revolution, drawn up by James Bruce at Ratisbon in 1690 for Will Leslie.[30] After explaining that he had not spent very much time on the mission, having made a journey back to Germany with some young men shortly after his arrival in Scotland, he gave a summary of the secular priests and Jesuits, and finally of the monks:

'Our Benedictine fathers were but few in respect of the rest. Father Abercromie who resided at Aberdone in a gentlemans hous of the name of Irvine has been a good tyme in the missione, and remains stil about the same place wher he was. Father Blaire who had also been in the mission befor some yeirs resided in a gentlemans house near Edinburgh called Coatts and the gentleman's name Byrrs. He remains also still about Edinburgh. Father Reid stayed some litle tyme about Edinburgh and afterwards went north and resided with the lard of Schivess wher he abyds still for anything wee know. Father Dunbar stayed also at Edinburgh and then went south into Galloway. There he stayed above a yeir at Dumfriess in Lieutenant Ratries house to whose troop he was also a chaplaine and went up with the forces into England but is now lurking in the Hylland hills with the kings party if there be any yett remaining. Father Cook stayed some tymes at Drumond and other tymes at Stobhall but is now come over, and so is Father Georg Bruce who stayed about Edinburgh but after the troubles went north with the Maister of Tarbot wher he was taken as I said befor and after his Imprisonement came over. Father Makie stayed not long in the mission for he was sick almost the whole tyme he was in Scotland having resided at Edinburgh, and I stayed some litle tyme at Edinburgh and then went into Galloway untill the troubles arose that I returned into Edinburgh againe untill I found a conveniency to come over.'

Boniface Mackie was in Würzburg before his abbot's death in November 1688, James Bruce was able to leave Scotland after the Revolution, and Ambrose Cook was at Würzburg in time to be elected abbot the following August. Bruce records that 'Father Cooke made a good successful mission in Drumond and Stobhall where he reseved severals, and found the people well Inclined'. Probably he owed his position in Perth's household to the fact that he was a graduate of a Scottish university, and certainly Perth always retained a respect for him. These were the only three to escape capture and imprisonment. George (that is, Fr Augustine) Bruce 'was taken neir Methil and brought to Dundie'; later he 'came from Scotland . . . after five or six monseths imprisonment in the tolboth of Dundie, having been sett at liberty by ane act of banishment, which (was) past upon him and procured by his own freinds.' He spent 'betwixt eight and nine monseths' at St Denis near Paris and was back at Würzburg in July 1690.

The remaining four were not so fortunate and spent longer periods in captivity. All save Dunbar were probably captured fairly soon, and thus a list of four monks in captivity including Augustine Bruce and excluding Dunbar[31] presumably refers to early 1689. Dunbar was with the troops loyal to James and may have remained with them until they disintegrated in 1690. In February 1689 his abbot, hearing he was safe, sent instructions for him to return to Germany,[32] but four years later Dunbar was still a prisoner. Abbot Fleming in early 1693 appealed to both the Ratisbon diocesan chancery and the prince-abbot of St Gallen for help, saying that two monks of Ratisbon and two of Würzburg, five Jesuits and six secular priests were imprisoned and destitute in Scotland, and he had had to send 300 florins to keep them alive, though the monastery had hardly enough bread for its own residents. Fleming added some details of his own two monks. Erhard Dunbar was in prison in Edinburgh; he had not only as a military chaplain converted many hundreds of soldiers but also whole villages to the Catholic faith. Ephraim Reid's imprisonment had been so rigorous that his health was ruined incurably.[33]

Before the end of 1693 Dunbar was back at Ratisbon and was appointed prior.[34] Reid never returned but (despite the ruined health!) remained in Scotland for twenty years more and lived to be over eighty. The two Würzburg monks were also released. James Blair was one of a number of exiled priests who in June 1693 sent a letter from Douai to the nuncio in Paris thanking him for the 'charity' he had sent them during their imprisonment.[35] He arrived back in Würzburg exactly a year later.[36] The last man, Christian Abercrombie, seems to have been the longest in prison. Thomas Nicolson reported in November 1694 that all priests in the hands of the government had been banished and 'Mr Abercrombie the Monk . . . has 6 weeks to clear affaires and then to be gone.'[37] As far as is known, however, he never left Scotland but, like Ephraim Reid, remained on the mission until his death twenty years later. Of the many hundreds whom he reconciled or converted to his church, one was his own dying father; another, in 1688, was a young man named Strachan, who travelled to Würzburg two years later and eventually became abbot.[38] This is an almost classic example of how an exiled community continued to propagate itself.

Mention of Thomas Nicolson leads to one of the decisive turning-points in the history of the Scottish mission, one in which the two Scots abbots played a notable part. Conditions in Scotland must have changed very quickly for the better, as far as Catholics were concerned, about 1694. Boniface Mackie was sent to the mission from Würzburg at this time, and a report to Propaganda stated that four of the forty priests in Scotland were monks but only the seculars received a pension from Propaganda.[39] Renewed efforts were being made to obtain a bishop for Scotland, and Thomas Nicolson was appointed vicar-apostolic in August 1694. At once Fleming wrote to Will Leslie to offer congratulations and to promise that if the new bishop cared to call on his monks as auxiliary troops, they would be subject to his jurisdiction as much as the secular clergy, and Nicolson could also dismiss them if he had the slightest complaint against them.[40] Nicolson was consecrated bishop at Paris in February 1695 and set off for Scotland, but there was a serious obstacle in his way. He had been exiled after the Revolution, his brother giving security of 3000 florins against his unlawful return; therefore, if he could not obtain a passport from the government in Britain or at least a cancellation of the security, his brother would be in grave danger of financial ruin. The new bishop was obliged to remain on the Continent while various influential persons tried to overcome the difficulty, and it was thus that at the end of June 1696 he arrived at Würzburg as Abbot Cook's guest.

Both Scottish abbots were in agreement over mission work. Nicolson wrote to Will Leslie that he had found Cook both very kind and of the same mind as himself regarding the Scottish mission, and so had been persuaded to stay with the monks. Fleming, too, a few weeks earlier had repeated his promises to Leslie and offered to send a Ratisbon monk, Columba MacLennan, to serve in the Highlands if he received journey money and a pension. It was a valuable offer, for MacLennan was a native of Lewis and had just taken a doctorate at Würzburg university. In August Fleming travelled to Würzburg, where the two Scottish abbots and the new bishop came to complete agreement over mission work by monks. Nicolson gladly accepted the offer of a Gaelic-speaking monk, and Fleming in his account of the meeting to Leslie again described the monks as merely the *copiae auxiliares* of the secular clergy.[41]

It is the voluntary assumption of this role, one most probably not acceptable to the Jesuits of the time,[42] and the promise of complete subjection of monks to the bishop while on the mission, which makes the activity of the two abbots at this time so important. Nicolson left Würzburg in mid-September, sailed to England that autumn and, after a period under arrest in London, reached Scotland the following summer. Columba MacLennan, having been granted his journey money and a pension by Propaganda, reached the north of Scotland about the same time as the bishop.[43] From there he wrote to Ratisbon asking to have his fellow Gael, Erhard Dunbar, to work with him in the Highlands. Fleming agreed and Propaganda again made a grant,[44] but Dunbar died in Germany not long after.

The significance of the abbots' agreement was seen in the next few years. James Blair had spent a year in Britain in 1696-97 but had returned to Würzburg,[45] while Macarius Brown died in England in 1697. Three Benedictines were missionaries in Scotland in 1696,[46] and thereafter there were four missioner monks permanently in Scotland: Boniface Mackie in Edinburgh, Christian Abercrombie in Aberdeen, Ephraim Reid at Fyvie (seat of the Countess of Dunfermline), and Columba MacLennan in Knoydart.[47] More important was the help given to the new bishop in his efforts to gain effective control of all mission work in Scotland. Nicolson was well aware of the difficulties he faced. In 1695 he petitioned Propaganda to prevent priests already on the mission from retaining faculties wider than those he could himself give. A little later he asked for powers to summon suitable religious to the mission, to examine the suitability of all priests, including religious, and assign them to districts as he saw fit, and to dismiss them if necessary. In his desire to control religious, he was following in the footsteps of the English vicars-apostolic, since Propaganda had decreed in October 1695 that all religious, even the

Jesuits and the privileged English Benedictine Congregation, were to be subject to the vicars-apostolic in everything which concerned the cure of souls. Nicolson petitioned for the decree to be extended to Scotland, where he was the sole vicar-apostolic, and on 27th August 1697 a general meeting of Propaganda granted his request.[48] The Scottish mission now had a single major superior, and the two Scots abbots had not only actively assisted him to gain this end but had voluntarily promised more than the decree laid down.

If Fleming had been the more active in promoting this settlement, it was no less the desire of the Würzburg abbot also. Cook wrote later of his intentions regarding the Scottish mission:[49]

'I am resolved to send none but whom our Worthie Bishop shall motu proprio desire, and of whose behaviour I am sure; and those that are upon the place, he has all power to send them back or retain them as he pleases, and it shall allwayes be my orders to them that they be the most obedient subjects he has.'

Will Leslie, seeing the success of almost half a century of effort, was not lacking in gratitude. In November 1697 he prepared an account for Propaganda of what the abbots had done and of their excellent relations with Nicolson and the secular clergy, all of which gave excellent hopes for the future (he said), especially if other religious followed the Benedictines' example.[50] Propaganda accepted the recommendations of the report the next month.[51] But perhaps nothing shows the improvement of relationships better than the elderly Will Leslie's request to Fleming that a Benedictine should succeed him as procurator of the Scottish mission in Rome. Fleming, hard-headed and quite devoid of worldly ambition, replied that it would be better to have a secular priest who knew Italian and had studied at Rome.[52] There could hardly be a greater contrast with the report of Leslie's brother in 1681 which said it was not expedient for monks to be sent to the mission.

The final act of the drama took place at Aberdeen a few years later. There was now a bishop in Scotland, one who had received powers to control all missionary work and to whom the Benedictines had freely and on their own initiative submitted. The Jesuits, the largest and most influential body of missionaries belonging to a religious order, also submitted, and on 7th February 1701 their superior in Scotland signed a formal acknowledgement that Jesuits were subject to the vicar-apostolic in whatever concerned their pastoral work. Christian Abercrombie, monk of Würzburg, was one of the witnesses.[53]

Notes

[1] *Cal. State Papers Domestic*, 1689-90, 382-83.

[2] SCA, ML, Fleming, August 1682.

[3] For Fleming's activity during James's reign see Hammermayer, "Restauration", 65 ff.

[4] SCA, Rat. A 1, II, 11.

[5] SCA, ML, Norfolk, 30.6.1685; printed in CRS, xxv, 81.

[6] See J. Harrison, *The history of . . . Holy-Rood* (1919), 216, 218-23; C. Rogers, *History of the Chapel Royal of Scotland* (Grampian Club, 1882), ccxviii-ccxxvii, ccxli-ccxlvi.

[7] SCA, ML, Chambers, 4.6.1685.

[8] Weldon, xxv-xxvi, 196, 226, 231.

[9] For him see *Dict. Nat. Biog.* and Hay, *Genealogie*, 48 ff.

[10] ibid., 55 ff; O. Hunter-Blair, "A Scotch canon in France", in *The Month*, lxviii (1890), 75.

[11] Hammermayer, "Restauration", 69, 87.

[12] SCA, ML, Fleming, 8.7.1687.

[13] SCA, ML, Fleming, 21.8.1687.

[14] SCA, ML, Fleming, 6.4.1688; printed in Hammermayer, "Restauration", 89.

[15] Fleming's part in the affair can be followed in Hay, *Failure*, 33-37, although the author's judgment on him can hardly be accepted.

[16] SCA, ML, Fleming, 8.1.1687.

[17] SCA, ML, Fleming, 21.1.1687.

[18] SCA, ML, Fleming, 23.3.1688.

[19] SCA, ML, Norfolk, 15.1.1687; printed in CRS, xxv, 82.

[20] Mun. GSA, K.s.3292, 23.12.1686.

[21] Gordon, 567.

[22] Dennistoun, f. 138rv.

[23] SCA, Thomson MS, chap. 1.

[24] *IR*, xi, 62.

[25] SCA, ML, Fleming, 6.4.1688; Hammermayer, "Restauration", 89.

[26] SCA, ML, Fleming, 29.4.1687.

[27] SCA, ML, Fleming, 8.7.1687.

[28] David Burnet, sub-prefect of the mission.

[29] Harrison, 222, citing Treasury Sederunt Book, December 1688.

[30] Edited by M. Dilworth, "The Scottish mission in 1688-1689", in *IR*, xx, 68-79.

[31] Hay, *Failure*, 71.

[32] SCA, ML, Fleming, 22.2.1689.

[33] SG, Bd. 321, f. 322; Reg. Regens.

[34] Reg. BOA, Sch., Urk. 27 (2.12.1693); Pfarrbuch (baptisms).

[35] SCA, ML, C (Propaganda 1653-94), 16.6.1693.

[36] SCA, ML, T, 6.7.1694 (unsigned but in Fleming's hand).

37 SCA, ML, Nicolson, 12.11.1694.

38 "Necrologies", 200.

39 APF, SC Scozia, I, f. 467-69 (in *IR*, vi, 19 wrongly attributed to 1688).

40 SCA, ML, Fleming, 19.10.1694.

41 Scots College, Rome, MS 3/19; SCA, ML, Fleming, 5.6.1696, 18.9.1696.

42 Cf. Hay, *Failure*, 29-30.

43 APF, Acta, 67, f. 32v-33r; SOCG, 526, f. 185-88; SCA, ML, Fleming, 7.5.1697; "Highland Monks", 100.

44 APF, Acta, 67, f. 442v-44v; SOCG, 528, f. 620-29; SC Scozia, I, f. 871-77; SCA, ML, Fleming, 24.9.1697, 14.1.1698.

45 Dennistoun, f. 334v; SCA, ML, Bruce, 23.5.1698.

46 Gordon, 629.

47 APF, SC Scozia, I, f. 886; "Necrologies", 186, 200.

48 SCA, ML, B (Propaganda 1694-1709); APF, Acta, 67, f. 318r-320v; SOCG, 528, f. 112-17; cf. Weldon, 227-28.

49 SCA, ML, Cook, 15.8.1700.

50 SCA, ML, T, 13.11.1697; APF, SOCG, 528, f. 624-25.

51 APF, Acta, 67, f. 443v-444r; ML, Fleming, 14.1.1698.

52 SCA, ML, Fleming, 24.9.1697.

53 SCA, ML, T, 7.2.1701.

CHAPTER 17

The 'Scottish Legend' and Macarius

Many aspects of the relations between the Scots and their neighbours in Würzburg have been touched on in the preceding chapters. It goes almost without saying that the position of the Scots in Würzburg was unique, but how did the Scots and others regard this position? The answer is to be found in the first place and in general in the works of the sixteenth-century Scottish historians. The fictitious early history of Scotland can be traced back as far as Fordun's *Scotichronicon* compiled towards the end of the fourteenth century. This remained in manuscript, however, until the early eighteenth century, and it is therefore principally to the printed histories that one looks for the circulation of the widely believed stories about the achievements of the Scots in Germany. The stories might have their origin in the *Scotichronicon* (or its sources), but they owed their circulation in Europe to the printed word.

In the fictional history Scotland was converted to Christianity in 203 A.D., and there was an unbroken line of kings from 330 B.C. down to the reigning Stuart dynasty. All that concerns us here, however, is the story of Christian Scots on the Continent. Fordun included an account of the Franco-Scottish alliance according to which Achaius, king of Scotland, made a pact with Charlemagne, and then Duke William, Achaius's brother, fought for Charlemagne in Europe. The *Scotichronicon* also told of the monastic foundations made by Sts Fursey and Foillan in Gaul and Belgium, the martyrdom of St Kilian at Würzburg, and the career of Marianus Scotus the Chronicler in Germany.[1] All were called simply Scots by Fordun, though nowadays we should call them Irish. The *Scotichronicon* was amplified about the middle of the fifteenth century by Walter Bower, and one of the additions stated that Duke William founded many famous Benedictine monasteries in Germany. Bower lists the places where these were. Ratisbon, Erfurt, Nuremberg and Vienna are included, while Würzburg appears twice, under its classical name *Herbipolis* as well as its German name.[2]

John Major's *History of Greater Britain* was printed in 1521. Major was comparatively cautious and moderate but even his work included the fictional account of the Franco-Scottish alliance and the foundations made by William. To this he added the details that there were fifteen of them, to be ruled by Scottish monks only.[3] Hector Boece's *History of the Scots*, published in 1527, was much less cautious. The alliance with Charlemagne was chronicled in circumstantial and fictitious detail, concluding with the foundation of monasteries in Germany and Italy in which none but Scots were to be monks or abbots. And, said Boece, there are yet sundry abbeys in Germany in which William's instructions have been followed unchanged.[4]

The king of Scotland accepted this view. In 1528-29 the Scots abbot of Ratisbon visited James V at Stirling, and as a result James sent several letters to dignitaries in the Empire asking for the monasteries founded by William to be restored to the Scots.[5] It has to be remembered that the Ratisbon abbey was made over to a Scottish abbot by a papal bull in 1515 on the grounds that the *monasteria Scotorum* belonged rightfully to Scots and had been wrongfully acquired by Irish monks. The Scots and the Roman authorities accepted this view; the Germans whom it concerned either accepted it or were obliged to conceal their disagreement. Perhaps one may repeat at this point that the *Scoti* on the continent in general had been Irish, as had been the Ratisbon group of monasteries from their foundation down to 1515.

In 1533 the German Catholic theologian Cochlaeus could speak of gratitude for the missionary work done by Scots in Germany,[6] and seven years later the Scottish Lutheran Alesius (Alexander Alane) said in an address to Frankfurt university that Germany had been evangelised by Scots.[7] This belief was given explicit expression in print by John Lesley in his *History*, which he published in 1578 in the midst of his partially successful exertions to have the Scotic monasteries restored to the Scots. Not only is the story of William's foundations repeated but the Scotic saints Columbanus, Gall, Kilian, Colman and even the Englishman Boniface, all of whom laboured in German lands, are explicitly called Scots.[8] With Lesley and his protégé, Ninian Winzet, the legend reached maturity as far as the monasteries were concerned. The documents concerning the restoration efforts in 1576-78 contain this version of history. The German dignitaries accepted that their country received Christianity through the apostolic labours of Scottish missionaries and that monasteries founded for the exclusive use of Scots had in the course of time been handed over to German monks or put to other uses. There was as yet, however, little discrimination between houses which had been German since Carolingian times and those

213

which had belonged to Irish monks comparatively recently. Thus the abbot of St. Gallen, the eighth-century monastery which was named after an Irish saint but had probably never been an Irish house, was importuned to give help to the Scottish exiles.

The handing over of the Würzburg abbey to the Scots in 1595 must be seen against this background. The event was considered to be a return of the monks who had held the monastery until a century before, as a restoration to the nation which had brought Christianity to Franconia. In this connection the acceptance of St Kilian as a Scot was of considerable significance, for he had preached the gospel in Franconia and been martyred there, his body lay in Würzburg cathedral and he was the patron of the diocese. Not only that, but the Scots monastery had been founded in honour of St Kilian and for his compatriots, its church contained an altar of St Kilian, and so on.[9] The name of Kilian, their patron saint, has never ceased to be held in honour by the people of Würzburg, while, in the seventeenth century at least, Kilian was a fairly common surname.[10] The view of the Scots monks and of the citizens of Würzburg was that the Scots had returned to an ancestral home. The inaugural oration delivered by Francis Hamilton did not fail to stress this point.

The beginning of the seventeenth century saw a great strengthening of this 'Scottish legend' through the power of the printed word. A type of literature came into being which was a natural development of Bishop Lesley's *History*, namely, the Scottish Catholic exiles' glorification of their country's Catholic past. They claimed thirteen and a half centuries of heresy-free Christian history before 1560, during which Scotland was a second Thebaid, a nursery of saints and scholars, who not only shed lustre on their homeland but took the light of the gospel to most of western Europe. The first work of this kind was George Thomson's *De antiquitate Christianae religionis apud Scotos,* a short treatise published in 1594 and given wide circulation by its inclusion in a well-known work in 1607.[11] The German lands figured particularly in it, and naturally a fairly prominent place was given to St Kilian; the fact that Scots monks still lived in their old monasteries in Germany was held up as both a remnant of ancient glories and a living proof that their claims were valid.

Thomson added little that was new and he wrote before the Würzburg abbey was given to the Scots. It was not long, however, before Dempster, George Conn and Camerarius produced less moderate works of this type. The latter two gave special mention to Würzburg, where, as they said, Kilian's compatriots had returned to their rightful inheritance in 1595.[12] Naturally the Irish reacted strongly against this wholesale appropriation of their saints, hence the bitter controversies between Scots and Irish during the first half of the seventeenth century. On the whole, the Scottish version held the field in seventeenth-century Germany, probably because the monks bore the name of Scot rather than through the power of their misapplied erudition in arguing their case. The effect of a name like Bonnie Prince Charlie or Bloody Mary is infinitely stronger than learned arguments. The more scholarly among the Germans were to scout some of the fantastic legends and try to distinguish between Scotland and Ireland, but by and large the Scottish version was accepted. Their German neighbours might be scornful of the poverty or shortcomings of the Scots, they might even at times consider that the Scots had outstayed their welcome, but never did they look on them as intruders who had no right to be there.

For penurious exiles this must have been of incalculable psychological benefit. There is no need to emphasise how the Scots remained entrenched in their belief and expressed it on all possible occasions. Its significance for their literary productions will be considered elsewhere. In the material sphere it was of use to them, since it emboldened them to make petitions as of right, while gratitude to the Scottish nation undoubtedly stimulated Germans to make benefactions to the monks. There was even a popular belief, of which the Scots made use, that the Empire and the Scots monasteries had been founded together and that one would not survive the other.[13]

The identity of the *Scoti* was no merely academic or sentimental matter. The Scots had obtained possession in Ratisbon on the grounds that it was a Scottish foundation, had pressed their claims in Würzburg on the same grounds and had them accepted by Bishop Echter. They continued to believe that the now German abbey in Vienna was theirs by right; the letter of Rudolf II in 1578 admitting their claims in principle was frequently mentioned in their writings and petitions. They lived in hopes, as their historical compilations show, of receiving help or compensation from monasteries with a Scotic history, real or fictitious. They even hoped that some of these might be restored to the Scots. The replacing of Scots monks by Germans was seen as a reversible process, as was the Reformation and the expulsion of the monks from their houses in Scotland. Certainly pre-reformation categories and relationships were considered as still valid. Though it may have been mere sentiment which led the great abbey of St Gallen to give help to Scottish monks, one finds Irishmen in 1648 describing Roscarbery Priory in Ireland as a dependency of Würzburg, which it had been in the fifteenth century. If the Scots could claim houses lost to their nation in the course of time, so could the Irish. It was

215

essential for the Scots that their version of history should be accepted.

The attempts of Irish monks to regain possession in Ratisbon in 1653-54 have been described in an earlier chapter. There seems to have been no such attempt made in Würzburg, perhaps because of the very different status of monasteries in the prince-bishopric. The prestige of the Scots in Würzburg must also be taken into consideration. That they enjoyed greater esteem than the Ratisbon Scots in the second quarter of the century is shown, if by nothing else, by their inclusion in the works of Conn and Camerarius, where Ratisbon is hardly mentioned. Their prestige as Scots was also greatly enhanced by the events and publications relating to their founder Macarius.

Macarius must have been quite well known at Würzburg, at least among the educated, in the first years of the seventeenth century. Two mediaeval accounts of his life circulated in manuscript, embodied in the *Vita Mariani* and the *Libellus* respectively. Three works of Trithemius containing the story of Macarius also circulated in print or manuscript, the *Compendium* of the history of St James's and the two versions of the Annals of Hirsau; he had written these works while abbot of St James's in its German period. Two influential printed books likewise mentioned Macarius. The celebrated but anti-clerical Bavarian historian, Aventinus, describing the foundation of the *Schottenklöster*, wrote that the bishop of Würzburg summoned the learned and abstemious Macarius to his town and built a church for him.[14] Shortly afterwards Eysengrein published his book on ecclesiastical writers, giving one for each year. Under the year 1139 he had St. Macarius with the story of the miracle from the forged foundation charter of St James's, taken apparently from Trithemius's *Compendium*, and to Macarius he attributed a work *de laude Martyrum*.[15]

Nobody should under-estimate the influence of either a manuscript or an early printed book. Eysengrein's paragraph on Macarius's surely apocryphal work was to be cited over the centuries, even in the article on Macarius in the *Dictionary of National Biography* in 1893. In 1595 was published a book listing Benedictine saints and notables, among them Macarius;[16] the source cited was Trithemius's first version of the Annals of Hirsau. That same year Francis Hamilton used the other version when he spoke of Macarius in his oration.

That Macarius was the first abbot of the Würzburg *Schottenkloster* and had changed wine into water was one of the things the educated, or at least the learned, South German was supposed to know, even before Trithemius's account of his life was printed. There now appeared in print, in 1601 and 1604, the historical and spiritual works of Trithemius. The former included the first version of his Chronicle of the ancient abbey of Hirsau, in which under the years 1139-40 were accounts of the founding of the Würzburg monastery for the compatriots of Kilian and the miracle worked by its first abbot, Macarius, when he turned wine into water. The spiritual works included his *Compendium* of the history of St James's from 1139 to the sixteenth century.[17] Presumably this was included among the spiritual works because of the prominence it gave to the life and miracles of Macarius. At some time, too, probably in that decade, Macarius was given a place in the collections of Possevinus, the learned Jesuit who reprinted George Thomson's little treatise. Macarius was now far better known than when the principal accounts of his career were in manuscript only.

In 1614-15 there took place in Würzburg a remarkable sequence of events: the finding of Macarius's tomb, the solemn translation of his body to a place of honour, and a series of miracles attributed to his merits. One wonders how far the finding of the tomb was due to Trithemius's drawing attention to it and its inscription, especially as a story of its miraculous discovery was later to gain wide currency. By dealing with the documents in chronological order one can trace the growth of the legend. The events of 1614-15 are vouched for by contemporary documents. The first is a diary entry recording the finding of the body on 26th February 1614. It states simply that the saintly first abbot of St James's was found on that date, that he had changed wine into water, had died in 1152 and lain hidden for 462 years.[18] Then on 1st February 1615 Julius Echter wrote an inscription in a book when he came to St James's for the exhumation[19] (though the inscription itself is not evidence for the exhumation).

The third testimony is the oration delivered by the suffragan bishop of Würzburg, Eucharius Sang, on 31st May 1615, on the occasion of the solemn translation of Macarius's remains from the old chapel where they had lain to the monastic church.[20] The bishop repeated the Scottish version of history (taken, apparently, from George Thomson)[21] in which the heresy-free Scots brought the gospel to other nations, witness Boniface, Colman and Kilian. The later Scottish monastic writers, incidentally, were to quote this passage of Sang frequently. To these three saints the bishop added a fourth, Macarius, and then proceeded to give his life at considerable length from Trithemius. The finding of the body, on the other hand, receives little space. Macarius, says the bishop, was buried in the place from which he has been taken today; for some years his name and memory were forgotten in this city, it was even forgotten in which part of the old chapel his body lay, but God did not wish it to remain longer in an obscure place. As to the fact that we do not venerate his relics by exposing them on altars or wearing them in lockets, as we do with other saints, the reason is that he has not yet been canonised by the holy see. When that happens, we will not fail to venerate him.

This is guarded language, especially in a flowery oration. The bishop says neither how the tomb was discovered nor why the body was moved; the remark 'God did not wish it to lie any longer in an obscure place' tells us nothing. One may well ask: would the bishop, who quotes Thomson and Trithemius with such fervour, have omitted all mention of supernatural intervention leading to the discovery, and of supernatural events taking place after the discovery, if he had known about them at the time?

The story of Macarius naturally found its way into the works of the Scots glorifying the Scottish Catholic past. Dempster's *Menology* in 1622 omitted him, but two of his other works published that year gave him mention.[22] In Dempster's *History* printed posthumously in 1627 Macarius was given considerable notice.[23] To the volume attributed to Macarius by Eysengrein Dempster added two more, and he informed the reader that Macarius's family was still in Argyll. For this sort of thing, of course, Dempster can be ignored. He cites Trithemius and Possevinus, for Macarius was now in the printed literature of Europe. Then comes the remark 'His body is said to have been translated to the middle of the church'. Dempster in Italy had heard something about the translation of 1615, but the story was still simple and devoid of details.

In 1628 George Conn's work spoke of the Blessed Macarius, famous for miracles,[24] and three years later Camerarius included Macarius in a calendar of Scottish saints with his feast on 19th December.[25] One can distinguish between writings containing only the biography of a saint (which are not merely academic as they are intended to edify) and those furthering devotion to him or at least describing the already existing devotion. The technical word for this devotion is *cultus*. There is no hard and fast distinction to be drawn between the two types of writings, but attributing a feast day to Macarius, as Camerarius did, implies that he had a cultus recognised as legitimate by the Church.

German hagiographers at once began to include Macarius in their collections. Matthew Raderus, a Jesuit, gave him a place in 1624 in a volume on Bavarian saints and cited the previous literature, both manuscript and printed.[26] One of his sources was the manuscript history of Jerome Grünewald, a Carthusian writing near Ratisbon about 1616,[27] who related what the Scots abbot of Ratisbon had told him about the recent discovery of the body. A dozen years later another writer on Bavarian history, Andrew

Brunner, described Macarius's career and the foundation of St James's, with a marginal heading: The Sanctity of Blessed Macarius the Scot.[28] Aventinus and Trithemius, incidentally, had called Macarius an Irishman, and therefore authors like Raderus did the same, but this would hardly affect the spread of his fame.

Macarius was also steadily acquiring greater significance among the Scots monks. A dozen years after the translation, as we know from Alexander Baillie's book, the Scots' church was frequented by the people of Franconia because of Macarius's relics. In the autumn of 1637 Gilbert Chambers, on receiving the monastic habit at Ratisbon, took the name of Brother Macarius, and one can be sure that he and later Scots who took the name were called after the Würzburg abbot and not some ancient saint from the Middle East. It is probably no coincidence that Chambers' superior at the time was Silvanus Mayne, a monk of Würzburg. When Abbot Asloan appealed to the emperor in December 1640 he quoted a prophecy of St Macarius that Germany would not defect from the Catholic faith as long as the Scots remained there.[29] The draft petition for the formation of a Scottish Congregation, belonging most probably to the early 1640s, also shows that the cultus of Macarius had developed greatly. The travesty of classical Latin in which the petition is written makes the exact sense difficult to determine, but the petitioners wanted a plenary indulgence to be granted, under the usual conditions, to those who visited their churches on certain days. An additional indulgence was requested for Würzburg, on 23rd January, when the relics of St Macarius exposed in the church are honoured by a great concourse of the people.[30]

Other documents date from this period. One of them has survived only in a late transcript but two references to the works of Trithemius as being composed a hundred and thirty years before show the date of the original to be about 1640.[31] A decree of Urban VIII had forbidden veneration of saints unless certain conditions held good, such as cultus going back over a century, inclusion in the writings of the Fathers, or longstanding approval by pope or ordinary. The Würzburg document sets out to show that in Macarius's case these conditions are fulfilled.[32] The evidence is chiefly from documents: the foundation charter of St James's, a calendar and a necrology from the Scots abbey in Ratisbon, both three centuries old, and some of the printed works mentioned already.

Until it is known what sources were used by Trithemius, the principal author cited, the cautious historian will not willingly attribute a date earlier than Trithemius's day to much of it. Here, however, the point is not the reliability of Trithemius's history but his place in the chain of testimonies to the cultus of Macarius. The foundation charter mentions the miracle of the wine and water and Macarius's reputation for holiness. The fact that this document, still extant, is a forgery does not invalidate it as testimony; it merely means that we must attribute the testimony to the date of fabrication, that is, about 1170-80, and not to the supposed date of foundation. There would seem to be no reason for rejecting the Ratisbon calendars, and thus we have evidence for the fourteenth century too. Other evidence for the period before 1595 is produced: Trithemius's account book, still extant, in which he mentioned expenses for work done on the tomb of Macarius,[33] a mid-sixteenth-century German administrator seeing to the repainting of Macarius's picture on a pillar in the church with the word Saint prefixed, and a group of three stone statues in the church representing the Madonna, St Benedict and St Macarius. The latter has a hand upraised in blessing, denoting (says a later writer) the miracle of the wine and water.[34]

All this may not amount to very much but it shows that there had been a tradition of veneration paid to Macarius. It is easily understandable that Macarius and his tomb had fallen into oblivion in the sixteenth century when Würzburg was on the brink of becoming Lutheran and St James's lay in ruins. Whatever one concludes about the seventeenth-century development of the cultus, veneration of Macarius was not itself an invention of the Scots. And about 1640 the monks, for some reason, did a certain amount of research to produce evidence for this and to prove that the cultus was lawful according to the norms laid down by the holy see.

Seventeenth-century hagiography can hardly be discussed without mention of the Belgian Jesuits, called Bollandists after the most celebrated among them, who formed the massive project of publishing the *Acta Sanctorum*, or critical editions of the Lives of saints. The work was to follow the calendar and deal with each saint under the date of his feast. The two volumes of the *Acta Sanctorum* for January were published in 1643, the intention being to cover the remaining eleven months systematically and as soon as possible. This no doubt accounts for documents of these years relating to Macarius in the Bollandist archives. The first, sent in 1645 by Peter Reichard, a Jesuit professor at Würzburg university, is in the hand of Maurus Dixon and consists of the Life of Macarius taken from Trithemius and Bishop Sang, with a list of miracles worked at his tomb since the translation in 1615.[35] There were four miracles in 1615, seven in 1617, one in 1618, one in 1619 and two in 1622, a total of fifteen in the years following the translation. A final miracle belonging to 1643 is added, and a note explains that there is popular devotion to Macarius and that numerous other miracles were worked, the record of which was lost through the wars and the deaths of the monks; some of the monks of the time are still alive but they think it best to confine themselves to the miracles committed to writing rather than risk inserting any unauthentic ones.

It is beyond the scope of this study to pass judgement on the sanctity of Macarius or the authenticity of the miracles. The acceptance of these, however, and the growth of the cultus concern the history of the Scots intimately. The impression is given that someone recorded the miracles up to 1622, then nothing further was noted until the list was asked for over twenty years later, when a final recent miracle was added to the list. Two miracles concern noble families connected with bishops· of Würzburg, while important officials are cited as witnesses, some of them still alive at the time of writing. Many of the characteristics of saints' shrines are in evidence: petitioners ask to speak to the monks or beg their prayers, sometimes at their request the tomb is opened and a silver reliquary containing Macarius's head is brought out, the grateful recipients of favours return and make *ex-voto* offerings. Whatever one's conclusion as to the genuineness of the cures claimed, they could hardly have been the invention of the monks. The Scots accepted the miracles and made the most of them, but they did not invent them.

In the following year, Reichard had been in touch with Abbot Asloan, who told him that Macarius was reputed a saint and had his tomb in a place of honour in the church but that no Life and Miracles existed (meaning, obviously, no ancient *Vita*). The date of this, July 1646, is confirmed by the Jesuit's remark that a former student of his had recently been sent from Würzburg to Paris to look for recruits.[36] We know that Maurus Dixon, who had studied at Würzburg university, set off on this mission in June 1646.

Three important publications were produced not long after, in the space of half a dozen years. In 1655 the well-known Benedictine writer, Bucelinus, published his *Menology*, which remained the classic work down to modern times. Under 24th January he gave an account of Macarius, citing as sources Trithemius and Abbot Robert Forbes, who supplied much information both in writing and by word of mouth;[37] Forbes had died in 1637. The three volumes of the *Acta Sanctorum* covering February appeared in 1658. The *Vita Mariani* was printed in full with a commentary under the 9th, the feast of Marianus Scotus of Ratisbon, and thus the most important mediaeval source for Macarius was now in print. Then, in 1661 appeared the most influential of the three books since it was devoted entirely to Macarius, the only one of its kind in the seventeenth century.

In July 1660 Bolland's fellow-workers set out on a literary

journey through Germany and Italy, in the course of which they visited Würzburg. This is perhaps what stimulated Michael Haim, doctor of theology and parish priest of St Burkard's in the vicinity of the Scots abbey,[38] to publish a Life of Macarius in German. The work is extremely rare and there is no copy traceable outside Würzburg. One might wonder how it was possible to fill almost two hundred printed pages, even small ones, when so little is known about Macarius. But the book is frankly didactic. A chapter on, for instance, one of Macarius's virtues consists of a sermon on the virtue coupled with the remark that Macarius was an example of it. Episodes are invented, such as Macarius attending to the spiritual welfare of the ship's crew when he sailed from Scotland to Germany. Haim tells us that Macarius as a boy did not spend Sunday on the streets picking up bad language, which will surely make anyone smile when he reflects that the saint's boyhood was passed in twelfth-century Ireland.

The only useful part is at the end, where Haim considers the seventeenth-century events. He gives the story of the finding of the body in detail. Gabriel Wallace, a Scots monk of great holiness, was in the habit of sleeping for only three hours and spending the rest of the night in prayer and watching. He led a most penitential life and wore an iron chain, which became half embedded in his flesh and was preserved after his death. Often, while praying at night, he heard angelic music and song in the place where Macarius lay buried, and came to the conclusion that it must mean something. He told his superior, who thought Macarius might perhaps be buried there and commanded him to investigate. He did so, began to lift the stones and found the grave and the body, with various inscriptions or writings showing that it was Macarius, who had turned wine into water. The discovery caused a great stir in Würzburg.

Haim goes on to tell of the present suffragan bishop in Würzburg, named Söllner, who in 1614 was studying the humanities and often recreated with the Scots student monks in their monastery, sometimes in the very chapel, ruinous and used as a wood store, where Macarius lay. Hearing of the discovery, he went to see for himself; he saw the skeleton, was filled with feelings of awe, and a beautiful odour came forth from the grave and inspired in him great devotion to Macarius. His Lordship, says Haim, is willing to testify to this under oath. For these and similar reasons Bishop Echter had the body taken with all solemnity to the choir of the church.

Gabriel Wallace was in fact a monk of St James's in 1614, and men were still living in 1661 who remembered the finding of the body. One of them, the suffragan bishop, was willing to testify, if not to the finding itself, at least to the impression made by the event. Haim could hardly have printed this had it not been true. Could he have printed the story of the miraculous finding if it was a later invention? Or, to put the question differently, could a later invention have so gained credence as to be printed while persons who had lived through the events of 1614 were still alive?

The question here is not whether Gabriel Wallace in fact wore an iron chain, spent most of the night in prayer and heard angelic music where Macarius's body lay. It is rather whether he and everybody else believed the story of the finding at the time or whether it came into currency later. If it was current at the time, the amount of truth in it is a subject for investigation; if it came into currency later, it can be dismissed as an invention. In favour of its early currency is the undoubted fact that something must have induced Bishop Echter to make the solemn translation. To this must be added Haim's citing the living suffragan bishop as witness to the stir caused by the finding, and his juxtaposition of the whole story of the miraculous finding. Clearly the bishop and others who had lived through the events accepted the story in 1661.

Against this is the complete lack of reference in the 1615 oration to anything out of the ordinary about the finding. The translation could have been due to nothing more than finding the epitaph described by Trithemius about 1510: 'Here lies Macarius, first abbot of this church, through whom God changed wine into water.' Dempster had heard before 1625 (when he died) of the translation but apparently not of any miraculous events. Camerarius in 1631 was in exactly the same position. In 1645 Dixon made out a list of the miracles following the translation but said nothing about any events before it. Quite apart from the nature of the events (which sound like stereotyped hagiography, in the bad sense of the word), is it likely, or even possible, that they were known in Würzburg in 1615 yet Dempster and Camerarius had not heard of them fifteen years later, while Bishop Sang and, later, Maurus Dixon in Würzburg did not consider them worthy of mention? The more one reflects on this, the less likely it seems. Far more likely is that in the forty-seven years between the finding and Haim's book, even while elderly people in Würzburg could remember the translation, the legend came into being. James Brown, in a work which he completed in 1655, unconsciously gives a hint that this was the case, for he says that the body was found by the agency or rather, *as the Würzburg citizens relate*, by the merits of Gabriel Wallace, a man of great austerity and holiness. This would also indicate that the legend grew outwith the monastery. Brown incidentally adds the interesting detail that an unsuccessful search was made after 1615 for the bodies of Macarius's three successors as abbot, who likewise had a reputation for sanctity.[39]

Haim's book contained a list of miracles, the same as the list made out by Dixon but omitting the first, and based probably, as we have seen, on some list compiled by 1622. He also relates that relics of Macarius were sent by Abbot Asloan to Cardinal Francesco Barberini and were venerated by the Jesuit professor, Reichard.[40] The Macarius story had reached maturity. The liturgical celebration of his feast, however, still had a long way to go. In the year 1679-80 this was advanced a decisive step forward.

On 22nd December 1679 the abbot and monks of St James's petitioned the bishop's councillors for permission to celebrate Macarius's feast with a solemn sung Mass and panegyric and to announce it from the pulpit beforehand.[41] The reply is not clear, because the surviving document breaks off abruptly in the middle of a sentence, but evidently the outcome was satisfactory. A little later the Scots addressed themselves to the bishop. He had given them leave a few months before to celebrate the feast of St Macarius, so they, not wishing to go wrong, were asking what rite and solemnity they could use and in particular whether they could announce it to the people and give a panegyric. One should interpret the language of these requests and replies in the light of legislation strictly controlling all authorisation for public veneration of saints. This is doubtless why the Scots mentioned the public panegyric and public announcement in particular. The reply came on 2nd October 1680. They could continue the cultus of the Blessed Father Macarius in their church and celebrate his feast on his day of death, 23rd January, with public solemnity and a festive sermon if there was a concourse of the people.[42] This is a legal Latin document, almost certainly drawn up by canon lawyers, and as such must be carefully interpreted. Leave is given to continue the cultus, not to inaugurate anything, and it is confined to this one church. We shall perhaps never know if the Scots had already been keeping the feast liturgically.

It cannot be a coincidence that the Scots produced their version of the Life of Macarius in the same year as they petitioned for his feast to be solemnly kept. At least three extant MS copies contain the 1679 version. It is probably no coincidence either that Abbot Maxwell assumed office that year. The Life is the same as its forerunners, namely, an account of the saint's life taken from Trithemius, the miraculous finding by Gabriel Wallace, the translation, and the miracles worked at the new tomb. There are one or two curious features about the list of miracles. An early miracle has been inserted. On the tenth day after the translation, that is, in June 1615, a large bone was seen in Macarius's old tomb although the contents of it had been thoroughly sifted at the time of the translation and many visitors had inspected the tomb without seeing it. It was duly taken to the new tomb. Now, even the most ardent believer in miracles prefers them to have some purpose. The Scots in 1679 would surely not have invented so pointless a story, but where did they get it from after sixty-four years? Perhaps it was in the original list and was omitted by Dixon and Haim, who saw no point in recording it. A second curious feature is the omission of the 1643 miracle mentioned in the earlier lists, as well as of one miracle attributed to 1661.[43] The list thus jumps from 1622 to 1674, which has one miracle, then there are two in 1679, the year of writing, and a concluding paragraph to the effect that cures and thanksgiving for cures are an almost daily occurrence. But this list of miracles, with its gap of half a century in the middle, was copied and recopied by the Scots.

In 1679, too, the Benedictine Bucelinus published a chronicle of his order, in which, under the years 1614-15, he quoted Haim on the finding of Macarius's body and the subsequent miracles.[44] This was the third Benedictine publication in a dozen years to feature Macarius. The other two were illustrated menologies taking only one saint for each day.[45] In each Macarius was promoted to being the principal Benedictine saint on 24th January and was portrayed sitting at table with the pope and seeing in a vision the collapse of his church tower in Würzburg. This was a story in Trithemius's *Compendium*. The second of the two productions is hagiography of the worst type, with the lushest of language and a wealth of fictitious incidents and conversation pieces, the pious equivalent of a romantic historical novel.

Bernard Maxwell wrote to his fellow Scots abbot in Ratisbon telling him of the permission to keep Macarius's feast with solemnity. Presumably January 1681 was the first time it was done. Nothing is said about this occasion in Maxwell's surviving letters, but he describes how in January 1682 there was a large gathering and a sermon preached by a Jesuit. A year later he told Fleming that the congregation was reduced because of bad weather but was still good.[46] The keeping of the feast of Blessed Macarius by the Scots on 23rd January had become an annual feature of Würzburg life.

Two other miracles are recorded for the early 1680s and two for 1688, one of the latter being the cure of the infant Prince of Wales.[47] The cures listed from the beginning mention epilepsy and diseases of the head more frequently than other afflictions, which is probably why King James and his queen sent for a relic of Macarius. The request shows that the cultus was widespread; the subsequent cure helped to spread it still further. Before the end of the century the Scots were observing two feasts of Macarius, the feast itself on 23rd January and the translation on 31st May, for which Abbot Maxwell had been seeking Roman permission through Will Leslie as early as 1681.[48]

This concludes the story of Macarius as far as the scope of the present work is concerned. One might say more about the various days ascribed to his feast, might even show that this example of the growth of a cultus was not unique but had its parallels in that century and that part of Germany, but it would take one too far from the history of the Scots. In spite of the many gaps in the documents and chain of evidence, what has survived is enough to show the growth of Macarius's cultus from nothing to a widely popular, officially approved veneration, with public liturgical solemnity though confined to one particular church. The significance of it is its effect on the status of the Scots in Würzburg. One can imagine the sermons that were preached: about the Scot Kilian bringing the gospel to Franconia, the Scots abbey being founded in Kilian's honour, and its first abbot, the Scot Macarius, still working wonders by divine favour in Würzburg. They, the Scots monks, were following in the footsteps of Kilian and Macarius, they were heirs to a long and noble tradition.

A few words should be said on the subsequent story of Macarius. He became known among Scottish Protestants, if not for quite the same reasons, and was given a place in George Mackenzie's *Writers of the Scots Nation* in 1708 and eventually in the *Dictionary of National Biography*. His cultus also developed further in Würzburg.[49] In 1731 a confraternity of St Macarius was formed and received grants of indulgences from Rome. His remains were taken from their tomb in 1771 and set on an altar dedicated to him, then in 1818, when St James's was no longer a monastery, solemnly translated to the Marienkapelle in the market square. There were special ceremonies and veneration during the octave of his feast, and he was regarded as one of the patron saints of Würzburg. Devotion to St Macarius lasted into the twentieth century, and he still has a place in the diocesan calendar. In 1945 the remains were damaged in the air-raids, taken to a place of safety and somehow lost. Thus ended the story of Macarius, but in the Marienkapelle is still to be seen the stone tombstone made in 1615, with an effigy of Macarius bearing in one hand a crozier and in the other a wine beaker (see Plate 1).

Perhaps the last word should rest with the Bollandists. In the reprint of the February volumes in 1735, their commentary added a note to the relevant passage in the *Vita Mariani*: 'We shall deal more fully with him under 19th December, which is the day of death of Bl. Macarius.'[50] The Bollandists were accepting Macarius as a saint, even if not a technically canonised one, and thus as worthy of inclusion in their scientific production. On the other hand, the documents on Macarius from their archives were placed under the heading of 19th December together with some other lesser-known saints, and the names were followed by the significant word *Omissi*.[51] The volumes of the *Acta Sanctorum* for December have not yet appeared, but when the one dealing with 19th December is published, it is unlikely that Bl. Macarius, Abbot and Confessor, will have a place in it.

Notes

[1] Lib. III, cap. 37, 44, 48; Lib. IV, cap. 47.

[2] Ed. W. Goodall (Edinburgh, 1759), Lib. III, cap. 57.

[3] Lib. II, cap. 13.

[4] Lib. X, fol. CXCV r.

[5] *IR*, xvi, 192; *The Letters of James V*. 157-58.

[5] ibid., 241.

[7] *IR*, i, 53.

[8] Lib. IV, 47, 54, 60, 61; Lib. V, 65.

[9] Wieland, 42-43.

[10] G. Meyer-Erlach, "Der Name Kilian", in *Die Mainlande*, iv, 43; Merkle, *passim*.

[11] A. Possevinus, *Bibliotheca Selecta* (Cologne, 1607), II, 394-98. Imperfect translation in Scottish Hist. Soc. *Miscellany* II (1904), 117-32.

[12] Camerarius, *De Scotorum Fortitudine*, 163, 218-19; Conn, 40-41, 45.

[13] Indiculus, f. 17v.

[14] *Annalium Boiorum Libri Septem* (Ingolstadt, 1554), VI, 4, p. 631.

[15] Guilielmus Eysengrein, *Catalogus Testium Veritatis* (Dillingen, 1565), 95v.

[16] A Wion, *Lignum Vitae* (Venice, 1595), III, p. 420.

[17] *Opera Historica* (Frankfurt, 1601), II, 128. *Opera Pia et Spiritualia* (Mainz, 1604), 3-16.

[18] Dr Kerler, "Unter Fürstbischof Julius. Kalendereinträge des Tuchscherers Jakob Röder", in *AU*, xli, 53.

[19] Schott, 103-04.

[20] Reprint in Gropp, I, 686-90.

[21] Scottish Hist. Soc. *Miscellany* II, 126-27.

[22] *Apparatus ad Historiam Scoticam*, 13; *Scotorum Scriptorum Nomenclatura*, 14.

[23] Dempster, 446-47.

[24] Conn, 61.

[25] *De Scotorum Fortitudine*, 202-03.

[26] *Bavaria Sancta*, II (Munich, 1624), 254-57.

[27] A. M. Kobolt, *Ergänzungen und Berichtungen zum baierischen Gelehrten-Lexikon* (Landshut, 1824), 117.

[28] *Annalium Boiorum . . . Pars III* (Munich, 1637), 345-46.

[29] Reid, f. 116r.

[30] Blair, f. 135v.

[31] Reid, f. 105v-106v.

[32] Wieland, 118 wrongly lists the decree itself as an argument for Macarius's fame as a saint.

[33] Wz. UB, M.ch.f.340, fo 13v.

[34] Wieland, 35-36.

[35] BRB, MS 8979-82, f. 31-32.

[36] ibid., f. 29.

[37] G. Bucelinus, *Menologium Benedictinum* (Veldkirchen, 1655), 67-68; Wz. UB, M.ch.f.260, fo 104r.

[38] 1656-64 (Stamminger, 9).

[39] Indiculus, f. 35rv.

[40] Haim, 153-54.

[41] Reid, f. 105r.

[42] Reid, f. 188r; Copialbuch, f. 175r.

[43] Found in Gropp, I, 693; IV, 231.

[44] G. Bucelinus, *Benedictus Redivivus* (Veldkirchen, 1679), 177, 182.

[45] *Annus Mariano-Benedictinus* (Salzburg, 1668), *ad* 24. Jan. Ae. Ranbeck, *Calendarium Annale Benedictinum* (Augsburg, 1675), I, 163-71.

[46] Maxwell, 13.10.1680, 22.2.1682, 27.1.1683.

[47] Dennistoun, f. 342r; Gropp, I, 694; II, 231-32.

[48] Dennistoun, f. 336r; SCA, ML, Maxwell, 5.11.1681.

[49] For the later period see Reid, f. 105r, 107-08; Gropp, II, 123-27; H. Dünninger, "Processio Peregrinationis", in *WDGB,* xxiii, 105-06; *Verehrung des heiligen Makarius* (Würzburg, 1907), 28-47.

[50] *Vita Mar.*, 371, note d.

[51] BRB, MS 8979-82, f.1r.

CHAPTER 18

Scholarship and literary work

From the point of view of study and scholarship, the Würzburg abbey was given a very fair start indeed. The Ratisbon abbot who set it on its course was John James Whyte, a man with a considerable reputation for theological learning. Its first Scots abbot, Richard Irvine, was a graduate of St Andrews. The first prior, soon to be elected abbot, was Francis Hamilton, who quickly gained a reputation for scholarship. His Latin oration containing lengthy passages from pagan and Christian authors as well as Greek quotations was printed and later included in an eighteenth-century collection of Würzburg material, whose learned editor described him as a man of great erudition and eloquence.[1]

A year later, in 1596, Hamilton defended a thesis at Würzburg on the invocation of saints, for the degree of *Baccalaureatus Biblicus*. The printed synopsis,[2] dedicated to Whyte, did not omit to mention the latter's theological studies in Rome and his public disputation with the Protestant champion at Ratisbon. Less than a year later Hamilton defended a thesis for the further degree of *Baccalaureatus Formatus*, on the legitimate veneration of saints by sacred images.[3] This was what we would now call post-graduate work, for he was already a priest and was prior, as the title-page in each case declared. The publication of the theses gained Hamilton a place in the history of Benedictine theologians.[4]

A year later the third member of the community, John Stuart, matriculated. Almost certainly the Scots were aiming to fulfil the condition made by Bishop Echter in the deed of foundation, that one monk was to teach theology publicly in the university. It is a fact, however, that all professors in Würzburg university, except in medicine and law, were Jesuits right up to the suppression of the society in 1773. The Jesuits were zealous and learned men but were not inclined to welcome collaborators from outside their ranks. No Scot seems ever to have had a teaching post at Würzburg university. The same appears to be true also of Salzburg university, founded in 1623 by the joint efforts of fifty-seven Benedictine

229

abbeys; no seventeenth-century Scot taught in it, although an occasional Schwarzach monk did so.[5]

The matriculation at Würzburg university of monks who were clearly students is very unevenly distributed. After 1598 there is a gap until the arrival of aspirants from Douai, then there are only two matriculations in the next sixty years. At the end of the century matriculations again increase. It is not a particularly distinguished record, but one has to remember that a number of monks, such as Silvanus Mayne or Ambrose Cook, were graduates of a Scottish university. At the beginning of the century some had followed the Scottish custom of completing their education at a continental university; such were Alexander Baillie at Helmstedt and (probably) Thomas Duff at Braunsberg.[6] Others had studied theology at Rome, like James Brown during the Swedish occupation of Würzburg or, more usually, as students at the Scots college before becoming monks.

There is always danger in trying to equate formal training with scholarship or indeed with any of the fruits of true education. Marianus Irvine, for example, may or may not have studied at a university but there is no doubt about his dedication to the teaching of philosophy and theology. All in all, taking into consideration the letters which the monks wrote and the subjects they wrote about, the notebooks they filled and the texts they transcribed, one gains the impression that the level of education and scholarship was at least adequate. The monastery produced no well-known scholar or writer and aimed at no works of erudition such as the Maurists produced, but the climate of learning at least bears comparison with monasteries today and was probably infinitely better than in sixteenth-century monasteries.

The Würzburg Scots had the inestimable advantage of a good library, and also the particular benefit afforded through the famous scholar Trithemius having lived there. When St James's was secularised in 1803, sixty-eight manuscript volumes were transferred to the university library.[7] Roughly two thirds belong to the sixteenth century or earlier, and of these a fair number are known to have belonged to Trithemius or to have been actually written by him. A catalogue of about 1615, made out on twenty blank leaves of a folio manuscript volume,[8] lists twenty-nine manuscript volumes in the library. Though the library of Trithemius had been broken up before the Scots arrived in 1595, one can surmise that a residue of it formed the nucleus of the monastery's collection of printed books. The catalogue of 1615, the only surviving one from the Würzburg of Julius Echter, lists about three hundred books arranged according to subject, and quite possibly it is not complete.

230

An analysis of the books would be outside the scope of the present work, and the Scots' library has of course been long since broken up, but one can see that they cover the whole period from the fifteenth century to 1615. At least a quarter, probably many more, were published in the twenty years since the coming of the Scots. Scottish writers are included in the list: Sir John Skene, James Gordon the Jesuit, the *Basilikon Doron*. Books published after 1595 were obviously acquired by the Scots, who no doubt acquired earlier books also. Some books were brought from Ratisbon to Würzburg, perhaps by the first pioneer community. One of the previous German administrators had had a stamp with the abbey coat-of-arms made for the covers, which the Scots continued to use until 1620. There is in fact ample evidence, including the catalogue, for the interest taken by Ogilvie's community in the library. Bishop Echter, too, showed his zeal for theological studies. On 1st February 1615 he gave a number of books to the library, and in one of them, a volume of St Cyril of Alexandria, he wrote with his own hand that the gift was made in order that the monks should devote to *lectio sacra* the time left over from their spiritual duties.[9]

When the Swedes came Ogilvie remained in Würzburg and indeed was *persona grata* with them. The library of St James's was spared, with the result that the autograph works of Trithemius, for example, are still in Würzburg today and not in Uppsala. Later abbots added to the library; of Maurus Dixon and Bernard Maxwell the chronicle states expressly that they encouraged study and bought books. The inventory made at Dixon's death in 1679 listed five hundred volumes of some size, excluding small books.[10] The library continued to develop, as we know from various descriptions at the end of the eighteenth century, which was the age of literary 'Journeys'. One of them put the number of books at eight thousand and considered it the most valuable, even though not the largest, collection in Würzburg.[11]

The monastery had other treasures too, for example, the manuscript prayer-book said to have belonged to Mary Queen of Scots.[12] In 1795 the monks had formed the intention of making a gallery of their paintings; possibly the earlier ones were in St James's before the end of the seventeenth century. A list of the most notable portraits was sent to Edinburgh and passed on to the Society of Antiquaries of Scotland in 1788, while in the following decade a Würzburg antiquary also described what he found.[13] There was a Van Dyck portrait of General Alexander Hamilton, who fought under Gustavus Adolphus; one of Mary Stuart, supposed to be an original; busts of James I, II, III and V on wood, thought to be by Holbein; a portrait of James VI and his queen;

portraits of Abbots Trithemius and Asloan. All have disappeared or were destroyed in the air-raids of 1945, except for that of Mary Stuart, which has the execution scene in one corner and is certainly not an original.[14] Some paintings formerly in St. James's may have been by John Alexander, of the well-known Aberdeen family of painters,[15] who died as a young monk of Würzburg in 1682.

Trithemius may have been the only well-known writer belonging to St James's but there were some lesser lights among the Scots. Francis Hamilton can hardly be called a writer, however, for his theses consisted of bald lists of theological statements which he was prepared to defend. In 1612 John Stuart proposed to write a life of Mary Queen of Scots. The German Jesuit historian, James Gretser, commended his proposal and told him where material could be found,[16] but Stuart died two years later without, as far as we know, embarking on the project.

The only printed work certainly written by a Würzburg Scot was a book of religious controversy by Alexander Baillie, published at Würzburg in 1628 and bearing the uncompromising title: *A true information of the unhallowed offspring, progresse and impoisoned fruits of our Scottish-Calvinian gospel and gospellers.* The particular reason for the book was that 'some travelling Scotsmen', having recently come to Würzburg, 'crave earnestly' to be instructed in Catholic teaching. So said Baillie in the dedication to Abbot Ogilvie, and he said something very similar in his Preface to the Reader: that he himself and others had learned to doubt the truth of Calvinism, had come abroad and freely turned Catholic. The book was written in a hurry. Even were there no reference to the 'importunity and haste' of the travelling Scots, the reader would realise this, for the letter *w* is represented by *vu*, while *h* is italic. Half way through, the printer obtained the letters he wanted from Frankfurt. In Würzburg, of course, Gothic type was used for German, while Roman type would only be used for Latin, in which *w* is not found and *h* occurs less frequently than in Scots or English.

The language of the book is basically English, but with enough Scots in it for the Scottish Text Society to have published extracts.[17] Baillie's style is fluent and fairly straightforward, at its best when the subject-matter is homely and concrete. Some pieces of homespun wisdom, which have the appearance of proverbs or folk sayings, are worth quoting: It is good fisching in drumlie waters; fooles are ay faine of flitting; like the bairns of Lesmahagow, who saw never a fairer Abbey nor their owne. For the modern reader, however, the intemperance of Baillie's language in speaking of his opponents becomes tedious. Two examples must suffice: Knox is 'a most pernicious parasite and faithles flatterer', while the devil, 'that great grandfather of Calvine and old enimie of mankind . . . inspired every one of those sacriligious hellshounds (the persons who 'cast doun' the churches in Scotland) with his flaming spirit of malice and blasphemie'.

The book has three parts, one exposing the errors of Protestantism, the next showing Catholicism to be true, and the third dealing with various controverted subjects. The first part takes the reformers in turn, Luther, Zwingli, Calvin and finally Knox; it is the chapters on Knox and Scotland that are the most interesting, if only because of the picture they give of Scottish Catholic attitudes, and to some extent of Scotland itself, in the seventh decade after 1560. Baillie, for instance, admits the harm done to the pre-reformation church by bad pastors and worldly prelates. His interest in Edinburgh is apparent. He laments the downcasting of Holyrood and other churches and gives a detailed description of St Giles's. He imagines Christ 'now entring in at S. Giles', seeing its state and the secular uses to which it was being put, and grieving more than when he ejected the moneylenders from the temple. Baillie also gives a paraphrase, adapted to Edinburgh, of Christ weeping over Jerusalem for its rejection of him. He tells how he himself first gazed sadly on the ruins of Arbroath abbey church, and though he does not say so he evidently knew Edinburgh well and was not afraid to give a contemporary description of it. Surely he had seen it since leaving Scotland in or before 1612; most probably he had returned to Scotland and visited Edinburgh in 1622.

The second part, on the marks of the true church, shows Baillie as a shrewd controversialist with a knowledge of Scotland. He has an interesting comparison between the true church and Edinburgh. Supposing some envious people have built a village nearby and claim that theirs is the true Edinburgh, what should the earnest enquirer do? He should seek the origin of each in the available chronicles, and he should learn the distinguishing marks of the true Edinburgh: the cloven ridge of land running down to the east, one of the fairest streets of Europe, the loch to the north, Arthur Seat to the east, the castle to the west, and so on. Then let him judge whether the old town or the new village fits the description of the real Edinburgh. Baillie makes the most of the struggle of the Kirk with King James. Has the Kirk no head but Christ, as the reformers used to insist against the papists, or is the king its head?

The third and longest part is also the least interesting, for only occasionally does Baillie give glimpses of the Scottish scene. It is still the custom in Scotland for heirs or executors to give a burial-feast for those who accompany the corpse to the grave, the relic (he says) of feeding the poor, who would then pray for the deceased's soul in purgatory, and he supplies a cautionary tale of the man who dared to yoke his plough on yule-day itself and was punished by a mishap, as all Scotland knows.

Baillie dedicated the book to Abbot Ogilvie on St Mungo's day, 13th January 1628. Silvanus Mayne, deputed to act as censor as it was in a foreign language, approved it. Then on 24th May the vicar-general of Würzburg diocese gave an *imprimatur*. It has, as far as one knows, no place in the history of post-reformation controversy. It was not written in reply to any book, nor did it evoke a reply. Perhaps it never circulated in Scotland. But it reveals how Protestant Scots came to Würzburg and were influenced by their Benedictine compatriots, and it shows Alexander Baillie as a writer with a bent for historical work.

There was one monk who produced purely literary work, Thomas Duff, who was making his noviciate at the time of Ogilvie's election in 1615 and remained at Würzburg until after the Swedish occupation. His medium was poetry, and classical Latin poetry at that (in other words, the metre depended on quantity, not on word accent). The impression one gets is that he had a great interest in the possibilities of Latin as a literary medium, but rather to serve a linguistic hobby than as a vehicle for genuine poetry. His verses are notable for ingenuity and not for literary inspiration. Even if the poems themselves did not reveal this, the amount of purely verbal juggling (acrostics, chronograms, and so on) in his autograph book of verse would make one suspect it. Really the medium is everything; there is no poetic vision struggling to find expression in words.

Nevertheless, his poems have much to commend them. They do not fall flat, because Duff did not aim higher than he was able to reach. They convey his meaning adequately, in language which does not jar and is at times felicitous. For instance, the poems addressed to the aged Abbot Whyte (one of them based on the Scots song 'Lowse thy pock, Laurie') successfully create the atmosphere of calm and peace when life's work is over. Much of his work is mere versifying, composed for some occasion such as the feast-day of a fellow monk or the visit of a dignitary or to thank a benefactor. A few poems have a loftier subject, like those to St Andrew; at the other end of the scale are scurrilous verses addressed to Abbot Algeo of Ratisbon. Somewhere in between come such compositions as the ode to the Scots doctor who cured Henry VIII's toothache. After Macarius's body was found, Duff composed a poem asking the saint to reverse his miracle and change the water of his well to wine (the only reference we have anywhere to Macarius's well), so that the Scots can sell it and have money to repair his chapel. One can easily imagine not everyone being pleased by this poem. The lot of a poet could be hard: the book of poems was confiscated by the prior at one point, and there is a poem on the imprisonment he underwent (presumably in the monastery) for prophesying some disaster in 1618.

As Duff's facility for versifying became known beyond the confines of the monastery, he was asked to compose poems or inscriptions in verse to mark events.[18] Thus he provided an inscription with a chronogram for the church of the Conventual Franciscans in Würzburg restored by Julius Echter, and a poem to be recited by a student when Echter's successor was received in the Würzburg seminary. His compositions are valuable not only for the information they provide on his own career and the affairs of St James's but also for the history of religious houses and churches in Würzburg diocese at the time.

In one matter Duff's poems are of much more than local interest. He composed five on the career and death of Alexander Montgomerie, one of the better-known Scots poets, who simply disappears from the records in 1597. The year 1611 has been suggested by scholars as the date of his death. Duff, however, describes Montgomerie, who was born at the latest about 1550, as being cut off in his prime; a date of death as near as possible to 1597 is thus called for. The poems also tell how Montgomerie intended to become a monk at Würzburg but was prevented by his untimely death, and they suggest strongly that he did visit Würzburg at the time of its restoration in 1595. Most interesting of all, however, the poems describe the extraordinary circumstances of Montgomerie's funeral. He was refused burial in consecrated ground by the Calvinist minsters, who had shut their churches and forbidden the bells to be rung. There was general consternation at this, and after a successful appeal to the king the funeral took place under royal escort, with the bells rung after all. Most probably the king was James VI, not yet departed for London. The solution of the problem does not concern the Würzburg Scots, but it seems quite likely that Duff's poems may lead to the discovery of where and when Alexander Montgomerie was buried.[19]

There is another connection between Duff and Montgomerie. In 1631 there was published a Latin translation in hexameters of Montgomerie's long poem, *The Cherrie and the Slae*, the translator being designated by the initials T.D.S.P.M.B.P.P. Students of Scottish literature have not understood that the place of publication, *Arctauni Francorum*, was Würzburg, and the initials have commonly been taken to represent Thomas Dempster. Almost certainly, however, they represent Thomas Duff, who was alive and in Würzburg in 1631 whereas Dempster had died in Italy in 1625. The attribution to Dempster demands that his manuscript was preserved and then published posthumously in another country yet without revealing his identity, even though another of his works was published posthumously at Bologna, where he had lived, and had his name on the title-page. Duff's authorship, on the other hand, is positively supported by his interest in Montgomerie, his passion for Latin versification, and two indirect testimonies: one is that Duff had poems published, yet no publication besides this is known; the other is that a Scottish religious house on the continent was responsible for the translation. We know, too, that Duff had some connection with the 1631 Würzburg translation, since an appendix contains two poems by him. It is thus almost certain that Duff himself translated *The Cherrie and the Slae* into Latin. The initials on the title-page can very plausibly be taken to stand for *Thomas Duff Scotus Poeta Monachus Benedictinus Professus Presbyter,* that is, Thomas Duff, Scotsman and poet, a professed Benedictine monk and a priest.[20]

It is a remarkable work but Duff has hitherto received no credit for it from posterity. One wonders if something similar has happened with another Scots monk, Columbanus Fraser, who was described in the almost contemporary chronicle as having died during Maurus Dixon's abbacy, a native of Buchan, a poet and notable for innocence of life. The necrologies call him a notable poet. In spite of this, not a single composition of his is known.

The field in which the Würzburg Scots produced most of their literary work was Scottish history and what they imagined to be Scottish history, namely, the apocryphal early history of Scotland and the exploits of the Scotic monks. They wrote the history of their own house, as is almost inevitable in a Benedictine monastery, where the monks have taken a vow of stability. Not only are all bound by lasting ties to the same community, but the community is of its nature bound to a particular place. Tradition, in its various senses, is inevitably strong, more so probably than in any remote Highland glen or Hebridean island. When persons or places are mentioned, everyone knows who or what is meant. In the monastery, too, the stones and the documents have, barring some accident, survived from the past, enabling any monk with an antiquarian interest to investigate his community's history.

The Würzburg Scots hardly needed to investigate (or invent) their past history. The learned Trithemius had done it for them, and they had inherited the copy of the *Compendium* written in his own hand. It was certainly in their possession shortly after 1615.[21] The *Compendium* had also been printed in 1604 with a supplement continuing it to 1548. What is surprising is not that the Scots themselves continued the account into the seventeenth century but that they only did so in 1679-80. (If there were earlier additions they have not survived). The *Compendium* begins with the life of

Macarius, puts in various documents and then gives the abbots down to the last Irishman in 1497 and Trithemius himself in 1509. At a time when the Scots were interested in their saint, some editor omitted the documents not directly concerned with Macarius and at once added the finding of his tomb in 1614-15 and a list of miracles worked at his shrine down to 1679. The series of abbots then follows from the death of Macarius to the election and blessing of Bernard Maxwell in 1679-80. This compilation, entitled *Chronicon*, is really two distinct narratives, the life and cultus of Macarius and the history of the monastery. It goes without saying that every remark by Trithemius derogatory to the *Scoti* and every reference to Ireland had been altered in favour of the Scots.

A decade later the two narratives were completely separated. Everything about Macarius except the miracle of wine and water was omitted, leaving a chronicle called *Series Abbatum*. To all appearances this work is independent of the previous *Chronicon*, for the Scottish period is treated quite differently and the miraculous cure of Julius Echter in 1594 appears for the first time. Macarius, too, has become a Benedictine from Iona. The material omitted was made into a *Life of Macarius*, and the two works are found together in a volume dated 1691. The authorship of the *Life* is not important since it is a mere scissors-and-paste compilation from Trithemius and Haim, but the man responsible seems to have been Alan Chisholm,[22] who may well have compiled the *Series Abbatum* also. Of their nature chronicles need bringing up to date, and naturally the cure of the infant Prince of Wales and other divine favours were added to the *Life of Macarius*. The various copies of the chronicle were continued, making the dozen years from 1688 to 1700 one of the best documented periods of the century. Probably what occasioned, or at least stimulated, this activity was preparing for the Maurists a copy bringing the history of St James's up to date to 1690.

Notes

[1] Gropp, I, x.

[2] *De Sanctorum invocatione* . . . (Würzburg, 1596).

[3] *De legitimo Sanctorum cultu per sacras imagines* . . . (Würzburg, 1597).

[4] Dempster, 352; Ziegelbauer, III, 570; IV, 190, 639.

[5] A. Lindner, *Die Schriftsteller* . . . *des Benediktiner-Ordens in Bayern* (Regensburg, 1880), I, 25, 27; Molitor, I, 382-83; Wolff, 307.

[6] Bellesheim, III, 456.

[7] O. Handwerker, "Ueberschau über die fränkischen Handschriften der Würzburger Universitäts-Bibliothek", in *A U*, lxi, 62.

[8] Wz. UB, M.ch.f.130, fo 2-20. Cf. Wieland, 66; Schott, 103-04.

⁹ Schott, 103-04; A. Wendehorst, "Die Dekanatsbibliothek zu Karlstadt am Main", in *Die Mainlande*, v, 11-12.

¹⁰ Wieland, 67.

¹¹ Bundschuh, V, 194.

¹² Wz. UB, M.p.th.d.2. Described in *IR*, xv, 96-97.

¹³ *IR*, vi, 145; *Taschenbuch* (1795), 200-01.

¹⁴ Now in a store-room of the Residenz. One must presume it is the picture formerly in St James's.

¹⁵ *Dict. Nat. Biog.*, s.v. George Jamesone; A. & H. Tayler, *Jacobites of Aberdeenshire and Banffshire in the Forty-Five* (Aberdeen, 1928), 122-23.

¹⁶ Bellesheim, III, 450-51.

¹⁷ *Catholic Tractates*, ed. T. G. Law (1901), 269-78.

¹⁸ Gropp, I, 420, 425 (perhaps also 686, 690, 691).

¹⁹ Edited by M. Dilworth, "New light on Alexander Montgomerie", in *The Bibliotheck*, iv, 230-35. The importance of the poems was shown by H. M. Shire, "Alexander Montgomerie: The opposition of the court to conscience", in *Studies in Scottish Literature*, iii, 144-50. They figure in the same author's *Song, Dance and Poetry of the Court of Scotland under King James VI* (Cambridge, 1969), 82-83, 105-06, 112 ff. and have been translated into Scots in *Akros*, no. 9 (1969, 58-59.

²⁰ M. Dilworth, "The Latin translator of *The Cherrie and the Slae*", in *Studies in Scottish Literature*, v, 77-82.

²¹ Inscription in the volume.

²² Dennistoun, f. 337v.

CHAPTER 19

The Würzburg monastic historians

The first example of historical work on a wider canvas belongs to 1610, when a Würzburg monk prepared a polemical work, evidently for the press though it was never in fact published. It was entitled *Scotia Antiqua et Nova*, Scotland old and new, and consisted almost entirely of two previously published works. The first was George Thomson's work of 1594, simply lifted word for word from the reprint. The other was a Latin translation of Ninian Winzet's *Certane Tractates*, originally published in Scots at Edinburgh in 1562. The compiler put in a Preface of his own and at the end added a hitherto unknown fragment by Winzet giving six reasons why the Catholic faith was eclipsed in Scotland. For good measure he threw in some funeral odes to Winzet by his nephew, James Winzet, who was a monk of Ratisbon.[1]

The Preface is quite valueless, for it treats of the origins of the Scots and Scotland from the sons of Japhet on, and similar fables. The only point of interest is the story of the writer being in the house of one Alexander Paton in Brussels three years before and meeting the aged abbot of Sweetheart, Gilbert Brown, who was exiled about 1605. Viewed merely as polemics, however, the idea was good: to contrast Catholic antiquity with Calvinist modernity, entirely in the favour of the former. George Conn, who had Würzburg connections, was later to do this, and one wonders if he got the idea from the monastic writer. Most likely this was John Stuart, who planned to write on Mary Queen of Scots about that time.

The chief production of Scottish historians at Würzburg was a series of inter-related works written around the middle of the century. The best known are *Germania Christiana* by Boniface Strachan, on the evangelisation of the German lands by Scots, and two volumes by James Brown on the Scottish monasteries on the continent. Both refer in places to earlier historical work by Silvanus Mayne and Alexander Baillie. Mayne has left no writings apart from his appeal for help for the Ratisbon abbey, in which he reveals himself as a historically-minded man who accepted the 'Scottish legend' but was at least aware of Ratisbon archival material. In the Würzburg historical works, however, he appears in very equivocal light. *Germania Christiana* records that he found at Fulda ancient manuscripts in the Scottish language giving St Boniface's birthplace as Rosemarkie in Cromarty. This is surely an invention on someone's part, since they could hardly have been in Scots and Mayne was no Celtic scholar.[2] His discoveries on his journey to Lorraine and France are also cited as evidence for the existence of two Scotic monasteries. One author says he always had great faith in Mayne as a holy and trustworthy man but finds it difficult to reconcile a certain statement of his with other evidence.[3] To the modern reader it is clear that Mayne's testimony is quite worthless, but he cannot be ignored on that account. A tradition of scholarship entails personalities, and Mayne's prestige must have been of value in keeping this alive.

With Baillie we are on much firmer ground since writings by him have survived. When he became abbot of Ratisbon in 1646, his German scribe began to copy documents from the archives into a large folio volume entitled *Codex Privilegiorum et Actorum*. The documents range from the twelfth century to the 1620's, and Baillie himself added guarantees of the accuracy of the transcript; there could scarcely be a better introduction to historical research for a seventeenth-century man. The volume gradually changes character. Baillie's account of Ratisbon during the wars, at first inserted in blank spaces and then filling whole pages, begins to assume greater importance. The second half of the chronicle is his narrative of the Ratisbon abbey after the Swedish invasion, interspersed with the text of relevant documents. Being a first-hand account, it is extremely valuable although somewhat subjective. It continues to 1653, by which time he was writing it partly in English.

Fragments of Baillie's historical compilations have survived through being incorporated in later works. Brown's volumes on Scotic monasteries cite him in evidence for the existence of four ancient and fictitious foundations; apparently Baillie had written a fair amount but his papers were scattered. Brown quotes him verbatim and gives Baillie's sources, which include manuscripts and papers from the Ratisbon abbey and a codex written by an early sixteenth-century Scots abbot of Erfurt named James.[4] This phenomenon of a monk building on the compilations of his forebears is one likely to occur in an institution like a monastery: Brown used Baillie, who used Abbot James, who quite possibly used sources in his monastic library.

Another writer to use Baillie's compilations was Eberhard Wassenberg, who in 1659-61 completed his seven-volume work on the history of Ratisbon diocese, consisting for the most part of extracts lifted bodily from other writers. The fourth volume, *Ratisbona Religiosa*, takes each religious foundation in turn, including the Scots abbey, and it is here that three passages by Baillie are reproduced verbatim.[5] Apparently he had written expressly for Wassenberg. With regard to the Scotic monasteries founded under Charlemagne, Baillie made heroic efforts to harmonise the conflicting sources. In another passage, on the founding of St James's at Ratisbon, he was up against the difficulty of making the fables agree with other authorities placing the foundation around 1100. He concluded that there was a second foundation at the latter date. The third passage carries the narrative from about 1400 to Baillie's own time. He retails the story of how the Irish monks infiltrated and drove out the Scots until the rightful owners were brought back by Leo X in 1515. This was to remain the version of their history accepted by the Scottish monks as long as their monasteries lasted. Baillie then deals briefly with the finances of the abbey during the Scottish period and tells how the Scots improved them. A list of abbots, which is fairly accurate for the years after 1515, concludes Wassenberg's account.

While Baillie was still alive, the chief historical work of the seventeenth-century Würzburg monks had been compiled, although not published. The first intimation is in a letter of Boniface Strachan written at Vienna in November 1641 to Sir John Scot of Scotstarvet, director of the chancery of Scotland.[6] Strachan wrote at the request of John Wood of Largo, of the family of the famous Andrew Wood the sea-captain. Wood carried the letter back to Scotland and presumably delivered it in person to Scot, who was his fairly near neighbour in Fife. Scot, being greatly interested in the cartography of Scotland, helped Jan Blaeu, the celebrated cartographer in Amsterdam, with the Scottish section of his Atlas; or perhaps, with justice, one might call Scot the real author. In 1647 he sent a copy of Strachan's letter to Blaeu, telling him to print it if he wanted. Blaeu did print it, and it appeared in full in various languages and editions of his Atlas. Perhaps it was the hope of recovering the Vienna abbey that stimulated Strachan to plan his work on the Scots in Germany. His letter to Scot is a lengthy document and has two parts: in the first he outlines the provinces of Germany converted to Christianity by Scottish saints, and in the second he gives a list of Scottish monasteries in Germany, including several belonging to remote antiquity as well as the mediaeval Ratisbon group. Then he speaks of his forthcoming work, *Germania Christiana*, in which the first volume will be on the evangelisation of each province, and the second on the monasteries.

In the next two and a half years, before June 1644, Strachan

241

wrote the first volume.[7] The work follows a simple plan: there is a section on Scots who preached the gospel in Germany in the first centuries of the Christian era, then it takes each region of Germany in turn and describes their Scottish apostles. There are long sections on Kilian and Boniface, the apostles of Franconia and Frisia respectively. After the first pages one is inured to shocks, because they tell how the apostle Peter preached the gospel in Scotland and his Scottish converts in their turn at once preached it on the continent. One can sum up by saying that Strachan follows in the footsteps of Dempster and Camerarius, whom he quotes frequently. There is immense erudition in the book, in the sense that a wide range of authors is frequently cited, and a serious discussion of dates can be found side by side with some piece of fantasy.

To this volume of *Germania Christiana* Strachan had added a preface, called *Velitatio* or Skirmish against the Irish. Irish expatriates on the Continent were producing books putting forward their claims that the *Scoti* who evangelised Europe in the early middle ages were in fact Irish. Some refutation of their claims was thus necessary. Strachan produces an impressive array of testimonies from ancient authors, both British and foreign, to back his case, then proceeds to give his own arguments and attack those of the Irish. This seems to be based on a similar procedure in Camerarius but elaborated considerably. Strachan's arguments vary very much in scope and he gives first place to the traditional Franco-Scottish alliance made between Charlemagne and Achaius. The only value in the work is the occasional glimpse of the contemporary scene, in particular when Strachan, who was an amateur philologist, compares the German and Scots languages or speaks about the influence of French on spoken Scots.

Strachan never wrote the second volume on the monasteries. Instead his fellow-monk James Brown (a grand-nephew, incidentally, of Abbot Gilbert Brown)[8] wrote it and made the work into a trilogy by expanding the *Velitatio* into a volume in its own right. Two drafts, made in 1648 and 1652 respectively, have survived of this introductory volume, called *Perspicilium* (or optic glass) to enable one to distinguish Scots from English and Irish. This new work takes all the names for regions of the British Isles found in ancient authors and supplies means of interpreting them correctly. Thus there are sections on Albion, Britannia, Anglia, Hibernia and Scotia, followed by proofs that Scotia can only mean North Britain. The work is almost incredibly bad, a monument of misplaced erudition. The idea behind it was good: one has only to think of the similarity between Alba, the Gaelic name for Scotland, and Albion, used of England, to see the sort of question Brown was trying to resolve. Some explanation is also needed of why

Highlanders spoke a different language and were known to Lowland Scots as Erse or Irish. But if the idea was good, its execution was not. A wide range of authors ancient and modern is cited, although this impressive erudition is found side by side with the most ludicrous traditional fantasies on the early history of Scotland. Not only does Scotia for Brown always denote North Britain but he manages to interpret the other names so that their celebrities are invariably attributed to Scotland. As with Strachan's work the real interest comes from the glimpses it almost unconsciously affords of the contemporary scene, for example, of the Scots expatriates in Ireland.

The volume on the monasteries, now the third of the set, was written shortly before 1652 by Brown, who changed the title either by accident or design to *Germania Sancta*. His list of Scottish abbeys is most interesting. First come the ten belonging to the mediaeval Ratisbon congregation, correctly given; then the two in Cologne supposed to have been founded by Duke William. A list prepared about 1578 contains five names besides the foregoing, then there are four from the papers of Alexander Baillie and two from Dempster. Finally a mixed bag of two in Rome and one each in Strasburg, Lorraine and Ireland brings the total to twenty-eight, though the frontiers of Germany have been considerably extended. Brown concludes with the lives of nine holy men, two of them from printed books and the remainder from some Ratisbon codex.

It is abundantly clear that *Germania Sancta* is a rough draft and in places merely an outline of what Brown intended to do. Even so, one can note the flimsiness of some of his evidence, for instance, the unsupported statements of Silvanus Mayne. The value of the work, on the other hand, comes precisely from its being a mere draft, for the documents used are copied verbatim and not digested. In this way we have an original list of monasteries drawn up for John Lesley with a description of their state at the time, a passage from an Erfurt manuscript used by Alexander Baillie, and long extracts from the codex on the monastic saints. The codex seems to be a mixture of the *Vita Mariani* and the *Libellus*, but makes Irish references into Scottish and quotes Boece (1527). Brown reveals without knowing it that historical work of a sort was done by the sixteenth-century Scottish monks of Ratisbon.

The *Germania Sancta* was merely a draft, and the *Perspicilium* in its final form was never completed. What seems to have happened is that Brown abandoned the trilogy and instead, in 1655, compiled a rather different work entitled the *Indiculus* or short list of Scottish Benedictine monasteries outside Scotland. This dealt in turn with the ancient foundations in various countries and finally with the more recent ones in Germany. There followed a Brief Compendium on the vicissitudes of the monasteries and an epilogue on the observance of the Rule. The new work is clearly derived from *Germania Sancta*, because it contains the same list of monasteries (and an extraordinary assortment they were!) but with three more added. This time, however, they are arranged according to region and date of foundation, while Brown's obvious intention is to indicate where the Scots monks can hope for help and even for the restoration of some of their monasteries. It was also clearly influenced very much by the journeys Brown had made at the beginning of the decade to monasteries lying to the north and west of Würzburg, especially in Lorraine and France, for he often retails his enquiries and discoveries and the conditional offers of help he received in them. He actually composed the work at the Maurist monastery of Jumièges in Normandy. The *Indiculus* is also full of his somewhat unbalanced views on monastic life. He is very critical of the Scots' recent history and is sure that God's blessing is not on them because they do not belong to a reforming, centralised congregation like that of Lorraine. He even thinks it is a sin for monks to wear a habit without a hood. The later copyists wisely left all this out.[9]

Judged merely as history, however, the *Indiculus* is far and away the best work produced by the Würzburg Scots and is outstanding even in comparison with its forerunner, *Germania Sancta*. It has some of the same weaknesses, such as Brown's willingness to rely on the flimsiest of argument or authority, and it is vitiated by the bias, shared by all his fellow-monks and compatriots, which prevented him from allowing the Irish credit for anything connected with the name of Scot except some maladministration in the fifteenth century. Nevertheless its weaknesses are far outweighed by its merits, the chief of which is the division of the monasteries into ancient and more recent foundations. The former are more or less apocryphal, and Brown was unable to see that the connection with Charlemagne was merely legendary, but even here he gives his sources and acknowledges when his information is limited. As for the more recent foundations, the advance he made is revolutionary. Only the Ratisbon group of houses is included in the list; he lists them completely and correctly, so that even today only details need correction; most important of all, he ignores the legendary connection of the Ratisbon foundation with Charlemagne and places the beginnings in the eleventh century. Aventinus, the anti-clerical Bavarian historian, had done this a century and a half before,[10] but it still remains an achievement for Brown, a Scottish monk and thus an interested party, to have been able to do so.

The Brief Compendium outlines the vicissitudes of the Scots monasteries during a thousand years but gives two thirds of the space to the history of the Ratisbon group of houses. Its faults are glaring, chiefly because it deals professedly with the question of the Irish and the decline of the congregation in the fifteenth century. Nevertheless there is reliance on genuine documents, while the period after 1515 is substantially accurate. James Brown, however, has never received credit for his achievements. Nowhere did he give his name, and his authorship has to be worked out from autobiographical references. Boniface Strachan, on the other hand, put his name to the volume of *Germania Christiana* as well as to his letter to Scot of Scotstarvet and has received full credit for what he wrote, and a little more besides.[11]

Brown's work was not limited to the foregoing. He quite often, especially in the *Indiculus*, referred the reader to his other productions, such as *Scoto-Fulda*, in which he apparently made out that the ancient abbey of Fulda was a Scottish monastery.[12] A small work *De Viris Illustribus*, featuring Ninian Winzet among others, had originally been the concluding part of *Germania Sancta*. Years previously, too, he had compiled the *Chronicles* of the Scotic monasteries though he had never completed them. None of these works have survived, as far as we know, but we do have his *Chronologia* of the Scotic abbey in Vienna. Some knowledge of the background of the work is necessary. The Vienna abbey was founded by Irish monks from Ratisbon shortly after 1150 but these were replaced by Austrians in 1418; unsuccessful attempts were subsequently made by the Scots to gain possession of the abbey, notably by John Lesley and Ninian Winzet in the years after 1578. To this day it has remained in the hands of Austrian monks and is the only *Schottenkloster* which is still a monastery.

Brown argues that it was founded for Scots, but Irish monks then supplanted the Scots and were guilty of misconduct, which gave the Austrians an excuse to take over the abbey; but this, says Brown, was an injustice to the Scots who are the rightful owners and want the abbey so as to educate Scots who can then help their poor country. Brown's quarrel is with the Austrian monks who have been in possession since 1418, but he is also arguing the usual Scottish, anti-Irish thesis. The whole question has an air of unreality: Brown is identifying himself, quite wrongly, with one of the parties in an ancient dispute and producing· historical arguments why the Scots should have a monastery which was taken from the Irish by the Austrians two and a half centuries before.

What gives the work its interest is Brown's method. After a short introduction, he announces that he is going to give verbatim the Manifesto produced by the Austrian monks in 1582-83 against the Scottish claimants, and this he does, giving alternately a section of the text and his own comments on it. We thus find preserved a document of whose existence historians have been entirely unaware. It consists of a brief history of the abbey, showing how abuses crept in among the Scotic monks and how they refused to reform and so were replaced by Austrians. In his commentary Brown the historian has renounced all objectivity in favour of undiscriminating polemics. He throws in, too, a fair amount of criticism of Irish fecklessness and barbarism as well as condemnations of German monks in general.

When writing of Vienna in the *Indiculus*, Brown referred to his *Apologia* against the Manifesto.[13] This is in fact the sub-title of the *Chronologia*, which also shows many of Brown's characteristics. Clearly he was the author, though the only known text is in the hand of Alan Chisholm. It was written after 1649, for it refers to the Viennese abbot elected that year,[14] and before 1655, the date of the *Indiculus*. Quite possibly the copyist adapted the work and omitted the year of writing, the autobiographical details and the less acceptable passages as was later done with the *Indiculus*. Brown's right to the title of historian, however, rests not on this work but on the section concerning the Ratisbon group of houses in his *Indiculus*.

It only remains to see what the Würzburg Scots did for the promotion of learning, by helping scholars and in particular by passing on their own historical compositions. Bernard Maxwell's letters show him eager to supply scholars with the books or texts they needed. Francis Fabritius, a Würzburg official who was compiling genealogies of the families of Europe, had read Boece, Lesley, Buchanan and whatever else the Scots could give him, so Maxwell in June 1678 asked Fleming to lend him Dempster's *History* from the Ratisbon library. In the next two years we again find Maxwell obtaining or returning books for him, and during the whole of 1681 he was importuning Fleming on his behalf for the loan of two volumes on old English families. In August 1681 he told Fleming that the rector of the Scots College in Rome had asked if the monks had any material for the continuation of John Lesley's *History*. A second edition of the original work had been brought out shortly before, in 1675, but no continuation was ever published.

Another man for whom Maxwell asked Fleming's help was Dr Christopher Irvine, a Scottish physician and scholar. Maxwell had been with him in Scotland and on returning to Würzburg at the end of 1677 asked for a copy of Winzet's *Velitatio* against George Buchanan to be made for Irvine at Ratisbon. Fleming agreed, and a few months later Maxwell was making a further request for Irvine:

'I pray you minde to send him also the fundations of all the monasteries we have and had formerly in Germany, for he is very desireous to have them, and did speak to me particularly concerning them, desireing they might be sent to him with the booke.'

Evidently what was meant was the foundation deeds and so on. In the National Library of Scotland the volume is still to be found, in the hand of a Ratisbon monk, Andrew Cook, and with four important Ratisbon documents transcribed at the end.[15] At the beginning of 1681 Maxwell, now abbot, wanted to get a book for Fabritius and had written to Dr Irvine about it. Then, in September 1682, being worried about a forthcoming publication by Irvine, he wrote to Fleming:

'Doctor Irwin is puting a peece to the Press wherein he is to treate of our Scots Monasteries here in Germanie and to vindicat them from the Irish, and will also denie that ever the Irish was in any of them, and will also put the bleame of the lost Monasteries of our Nation upon the bad and lewd lives of som of our owne Nation. Your advice is desired in this, and what you thinke best to be said in the affaire, and what excuse you think best to be inserted for the loss of the lost monasteries of our Nation, and as I was always informed the bad economie of the Irish was the occasion of the loss of many of them'.

As far as is known, the piece was never published but this may explain why Fleming had Boniface Strachan's *Germania Christiana* transcribed by Andrew Cook and wrote in it in his own hand 'Written at Ratisbone, and sent to Doctor Irvine by Ab. Fleming for a small token of affectione 1684'.[16]

It was about this time that Fleming sent copies of Ratisbon documents to the Maurists.[17] In June 1681 Maxwell had been asked to supply deeds and a list of abbots for the Maurists and had urged Fleming to do the same. What is interesting is that the documents eventually sent by Fleming included a 'Brief and succinct narration' on the Scotic monasteries in Germany which is no other than an adaptation of Boniface Strachan's letter, taken presumably from Blaeu's Atlas and clearly made at Ratisbon since it stresses the position of the Ratisbon abbot as superior general of the Scots monasteries. Wassenberg, too, had inserted the letter whole from the Atlas into his account of the Ratisbon abbey. The merit of Strachan's list of monasteries is that it is short and so has only four houses besides the Ratisbon group, but its chronology is quite unsound. It is a pity that Fleming did not send James Brown's *Indiculus* to Dr. Irvine and the Maurists instead of Strachan's writings, but seemingly he did not have copies of Brown's works until 1705. What the Würzburg monks for their part sent to the Maurists was their own *Series Abbatum* brought up to date to 1690.

The Maurist *Monasticon Benedictinum* was never published, and the material sent from Ratisbon and Würzburg remained in manuscript. In fact, apart from the life and miracles of Macarius, none of the Würzburg historical compilations have to this day been printed. This is not to say that they have never been used. They must certainly have helped to form the accepted view at Ratisbon and Würzburg (the 'myth', if one prefers) of their monastic past. The various copies which found their way to Scotland may have influenced or provided material for those who read them. Naturally enough, they have been used most by writers dealing explicitly with the Scots monasteries in Germany. Wieland's account of the Würzburg abbey, which has held the field for over a century, relies greatly on the *Series Abbatum*; it could hardly be otherwise.

Probably their greatest effect was to provide material for the eighteenth-century Ratisbon historians, notably Marianus Brockie, whose work has undoubtedly been influential. Brockie forged material when it suited him to do so, with the result that all his work is rightly suspect. In the case of the Scots abbeys, however, he did not need to do so; for Würzburg an account was available in the *Series Abbatum*, while he had the Ratisbon and Erfurt archives at his disposal. He also had the guide-lines for the history of the Ratisbon congregation, with the mythological material discarded, laid down for him in the *Indiculus*. Even if Brockie would have by himself produced a reasonably accurate picture of the Ratisbon group of houses, the fact remains that James Brown had done this a century before him. And lest one be inclined to condemn Brown too strongly for the anti-Irish myth so prominent in his work, one should remember that this was accepted by Scots and Germans into the twentieth century.

Notes

[1] Wz. UB, M.ch.q.58. The Winzet items have been edited in M. Dilworth, "Ninian Winzet: some new material" in IR, xxiv (1973).

[2] "Trilogy", 121 (where references to MSS will be found).

[3] Germ. Sancta, f. 10v, 18v; Indiculus, f. 27v; "Trilogy", 129.

[4] Germ. Sancta, f. 17rv; Indiculus, f. 22v, 23r, 26v.

[5] NLS, Adv. 34.6.1, p. 41-44, 63-65, 87-89. For this manuscript, wrongly attributed to Boniface Strachan, see "Two MSS", 24-28, 32.

[6] NLS, Adv. 17.1.9, f. 225-28; "Two MSS", 26-27.

[7] For the volumes and history of the composite work, their full titles and so on, see "Trilogy".

[8] Indiculus, f. 60r.

[9] See also M. Dilworth, "The original *Indiculus Monasteriorum*" in IR, xxiv (1973).

[10] *Annalium Boiorum Libri Septem*, IV, p. 330; V, p. 553-54.

[11] Ziegelbauer, III, 556; IV, 439; "Two MSS", 24-27; "Trilogy", 140.

[12] Edin. UL, MS Laing III, 201, f. 25v.

[13] Indiculus, f. 38r.

[14] Lindner, 15-16.

[15] NLS, Adv. 31.6.8.

[16] This is NLS, Adv. 33.7.20.

[17] BN, lat. 12,675, f. 219-41; cf. Fleming to Mabillon, 2.3.1684 (BN, fr. 19,652, f. 339-40).

CHAPTER 20

The Scots and Würzburg Life

The part played by the Scots in Würzburg life was influenced greatly by two factors: their antiquity and their geographical position. To understand Würzburg one should picture the Main flowing more or less northwards through a narrow valley, meeting a steep ridge and making a sharp bend of ninety degrees to the west, then making a second turn and resuming its flow northward through an even narrower valley. Just before the river makes its first bend the valley widens; on this flat, hill-surrounded ground on the right bank is built the town of Würzburg, while the ground on the left bank opposite rises steeply from the water's edge to form an imposing hill, a natural site for a fortress. The town on the comparatively flat ground to the east of the river, the fortress-crowned hill towering above to the west of it; these are the two important geographical facts about Würzburg.

The Scots monastery was on the west of the river, on a spur of the fortress hill. It lay slightly to the north, that is, downstream, of the bridge over the Main, while the fortress lay southwards of it. The height on which the monastery was built, called Girberg, had been bare and deserted before the monks came. Gradually it was brought under cultivation, and dwellings were built on the ground that was not too steep.[1] There was a parish church on this left bank, St Burkard's; the people in the Main-quarter, as it was called, were clannish and considered themselves as apart from the Würzburg folk across the river. And there had never been a time in the memory of the people when St James's was not there.

The forged foundation charter of 1140 narrates how Bishop Embricho endowed the Scots with a prebend in the cathedral church to mark the general appreciation of Macarius's miracle in changing wine into water. The forgery could not have been done before the prebend was given, hence we know that the monks were receiving it well before the end of the twelfth century. They were still receiving it in the eighteenth century. It was paid chiefly in kind: daily measures of bread and wine, varying according to the

250

season, with other occasional grants. The wine could be sold if the monks wished, and the price given to them instead. If the abbot attended a meeting of chapter he took precedence over dean and canons, and twice a year a monk of St James's had to sing a Mass in the cathedral.[2]

Another donation to the monks, perhaps the ealiest, was the property of Jobstal; certainly the deed of donation is the earliest genuine document extant. Bishop Embricho in 1142 donated the property to the Scotic monks who were the compatriots of the martyr Kilian. In 1581 Bishop Echter transferred it to the hospital he had founded in Würzburg; then, when the Scots came to St James's they were given the income but not the property itself. In 1631 and 1641 the Scots abbots appealed for their rights according to the donation made to them by Bishop Embricho, and the question was settled in 1650.[3] The point about the cathedral prebend and the Jobstal property is that the Scots were not only looked upon as the compatriots of the mediaeval monks and thus of Macarius and Kilian; they were actually receiving revenues, considered legally theirs, in virtue of donations made half a millenium before.

The properties and incomes of the monastery, being more a matter for the local historian, lie outside the scope of this study except insofar as they affected the life of the Scots. Nevertheless a summary made by one of the monks in 1738, and no doubt in the main valid for the previous century too, gives one a useful insight into their means of support. There was the cathedral prebend, the compensation for the land swallowed up by the fortifications, grain supplied annually by the peasants in several villages, the rent for various properties, and wine from vineyards. Stipends, gifts and alms brought in about 200 *reichsthalers*, and the whole, in cash and kind, came to about 1200 *reichsthalers* or 1800 Rhenish florins. Interest on capital added a little to this.[4] The Scots were poorer than any of the other monastic establishments. In 1613, for instance, the abbot's income was only 126 florins, less than half that of the second-poorest and a fraction of that of the richer prelates.[5]

Probably visitors to the church were generous in the matter of small donations, while the prince-bishops could be expected to supply a princely sum when some pressing need arose. In between came the legacies left by the notables of Würzburg, usually in the form of endowments for Masses to be said for their souls on their anniversary days or oftener. The seventeenth-century monastic necrology records many of these benefactors; the later necrology records at least two such seventeenth-century endowments, and we know of other legacies left to the Scots in 1685 and 1698. By the end of the eighteenth century there were about fifty-five such endowments, and Mass was still being said weekly in virtue of a bequest made in 1167.[6]

When a bishop of Würzburg died the funeral arrangements took into account the antiquity and geographical position of the Scots abbey, which lay on the way down to the bridge from the bishop's fortress residence. Bishop Embricho, the founder, had ordered that his body should lie overnight in St James's, and this was done when he died in 1149. Thereafter it was the custom for the body of each bishop to be brought in procession to the Scots church in the afternoon and to be taken the next day across the river to be buried in the cathedral. Trithemius described the procedure in his history of St James's. The body was carried down from the fortress and met by the incumbents of St Burkard's, who escorted it to the Scots church. The abbot, vested in pontificals, went out to meet the procession, the body was placed in the church and offices of the dead were sung. The next morning the abbot sang Mass and again officiated at the bier. After Vespers the Würzburg clergy came in procession to St James's, sang Vespers of the Dead and took the body to the cathedral. The candles and the precious black cloth which covered the coffin remained with the monks as perquisites.

An account of what actually happened in 1519 has been preserved; it agrees with the foregoing and adds various details, like the little table on which the casket containing the bishop's heart was put, and the lights and coals which had to be provided for those who watched by the coffin all night. The mid-sixteenth century was an unsettled period in Würzburg but we have a record of the body being taken to St James's in 1540.[7] Julius Echter, the reforming bishop, ruled for a long time; when he died in 1617 it was forty-four years at least since the old custom had been observed, and possibly much longer, for St James's was in a ruinous condition before his accession. Probably Echter, having restored the monastery, would have adhered to the ancient custom in any case, but several publications had brought it to public notice: Lorenz Fries's *Chronicle* of Würzburg in 1544,[8] Sebastian Münster's *Cosmography*, which went through at least fifteen editions in four languages between 1544 and 1598,[9] and Trithemius's *Compendium*, printed in 1604. Echter's body lay in the citadel for eighteen days before being brought to the Scots church, where the ancient ceremonies were carried out and a Scots monk preached a panegyric next morning.[10]

The next bishop died at Ratisbon during a Diet and was buried in Bamberg,[11] hence it was not until 1631 that the old custom was followed once more. The ceremonial at the funerals of these episcopal princes of the empire was growing more elaborate. The body was embalmed, the entrails buried in the citadel, and the heart put in a silver vessel. There were the usual protracted offices, with the prince's ministers keeping watch all night. An eye-witness added an extraordinary detail, that he saw the more important personages being given beds covered with bed-clothes so that they could get some rest. Early next morning the Scots abbot sang pontifical Mass (during which a collection was taken up for the monastery) and performed the ceremonies; the body was escorted across the river that morning, while the heart was taken by a grand cavalcade to the monastery of Ebrach.[12]

Presumably this happened at the next funeral in 1642.[13] The following occasion, in 1673, was described by Abbot Dixon, who seems to have had less interest in the ceremonies than in the expense. The suffragan and four mitred abbots, including Dixon, vested and went out together to meet the procession but it was the suffragan who officiated after Vespers. Dixon complained about the officials' parsimony and addressed a note to posterity to the effect that it was not worth it unless the Scots kept the hangings and received compensation for their trouble and for the fuel and food they had to supply.[14]

The two bishops who died during Maxwell's short rule were buried in the customary way.[15] In 1698 the bishop died in the town across the river, and the body therefore did not come to St James's. To mark their traditional role, however, the Scots were invited to sing dead offices beside the coffin. They petitioned to be given the candles and hangings but received a mere hundred florins in compensation instead and were aggrieved at this ignoring of their rights dating back five and a half centuries.[16] In the eighteenth century the magnificent baroque Residence, later described by Napoleon as the grandest presbytery in Europe, was built in Würzburg itself. Henceforth the prince-bishops lived and died there and not in the fortress, and thus ended the age-old custom of taking the bishop's body to the Scots church on its way to burial.

Another liturgical custom resulting partly from the position of the Scots church, partly from its antiquity, was the custom of going there in procession.[17] When the Scots were established under Echter, the people of St Burkard's used to come along the river and climb the hill to St James's on Palm Sunday, the Rogation days and Corpus Christi. In addition to these, presumably liturgical, processions, they came on each Sunday from Easter to Pentecost at an early hour, arriving before six o'clock. On Corpus Christi and the Rogation days groups also came from outlying places and the citadel. On the vigil of St James all the canons of the various churches came in procession to the Scots church, clearly a mark of special distinction as St James was not a local patron nor does any liturgical procession belong to his feast. The procession on the vigil of the Ascension, the last of the Rogation days, was instituted in 1618, and Thomas Duff has left the text of the extempore sermon he preached on the first occasion.[18] A list of processions drawn up at the end of the seventeenth century shows some elaboration;[19] it was evidently a custom to visit one or more monasteries on these days of procession, and one country group had a sung Mass in the chapel of St Macarius in the Scots church.

St James's day was a principal feast for the Scots since he was their titular. They also kept the dedication of the church. The high altar had been consecrated on the feast of St Vitus, 15th June, 1499, after a thorough renovation of the church; in the time of the Scots the dedication was celebrated on the Sunday following St Vitus's day.[20] The dedication of the chapel was also kept in August, on the Sunday after St Laurence. In 1681 Abbot Maxwell was trying to get authorisation from Rome to keep the feasts of Scottish saints and intended to find out more about them from old Scottish breviaries,[21] but nothing came of his plans and at the end of the century the only feasts proper to the abbey were those of St James, the dedication of the church and the chapel, and the two of St Macarius. On the vigil of St James the canons came in procession, while on the feast itself the bishop and other dignitaries could be expected to attend the High Mass, after which they were entertained in the monastery.[22]

It has been made clear that the Scots were integrated into the institutional framework of the Franconian monasteries. On a more personal level, too, they were integrated into the religious life of Würzburg. This is most clearly seen in the position of their abbot, who as a mitred prelate enjoyed a clerical dignity greater than did the officials who regulated his affairs. Often several abbots received their abbatial blessing simultaneously; Asloan, Irvine and Cook, for instance, were blessed with other recently elected German abbots. At these functions the bishop was assisted by two other mitred prelates, among whom one sometimes finds the abbot of St James's. Thus Asloan was present at the blessing of abbots of Neustadt in 1649 and 1660, and on the second occasion he was assistant prelate. Irvine was present at the abbatial election in Neustadt in 1686.[23] Dixon attended the blessing of the prince-abbot of Fulda in 1678, and Ogilvie the consecration of a Cistercian church in 1624.[24] Probably the record of only a fraction of these occasions has survived.

It was the custom in Würzburg for the bishop to invite abbots to be his assistants at episcopal consecrations, and Maurus Dixon was so invited in 1675, while in 1696 Ambrose Cook was actually delegated by the bishop to carry out an abbatial blessing himself.[25] Neither of these two functions would normally be permitted to anyone not a bishop under present law. At the bishops' funerals, at least those in the later seventeenth century, the Scots abbot went with his fellow prelates to the final ceremonies in the cathedral and performed one of the absolutions. Irvine officiated at the funeral of the abbot of Oberzell in 1688. We can be sure that the abbots of St James's were invited to the various special functions or celebrations; such was the consecration of Haug church in 1691 when Cook sang pontifical Mass,[26] or the other occasion the same year when he sang pontifical Mass and afterwards sat next to the prince-bishop at dinner.

Being appointed by the bishop to carry out a visitation (as Asloan and Cook were) can be regarded as something impersonal and juridical. Not so with inclusion in the necrologies of other monasteries. Asloan found a place in that of Neustadt;[27] Dixon, Maxwell and the prior John Stuart, who died in 1614, are in that of St Stephen's; the four abbots from Asloan to Irvine are in the Schwarzach necrology.[28] In November 1679 the monasteries of the dioceses of Würzburg and Bamberg re-established a confraternity for offering prayers for the dead: when a religious died each priest was to say Mass, each religious not a priest to say certain prayers. St James's was among the handful of monasteries represented when the agreement was made; other houses were to join later.[29]

It was commissioners appointed by the bishop who presided over abbatial elections and carried out visitations. For an election the commissioners were received by the monks at the church porch, to the ringing of bells. One of the commissioners addressed the monks, there followed a Mass of the Holy Spirit, and the monks took the oath to elect the man they considered the most suitable. Each wrote the name of his choice on a slip of paper, folded it and dropped it into a chalice. The result was announced, the abbot accepted office, and he was led to the church, where the *Te Deum* was sung. The newly-elect then lay prostrate during the Litany of the Saints. Next he was taken to the abbot's place in choir, where he promised obedience to the bishop and was given authority *in spiritualibus*, and the monks kissed his hand and promised obedience. That done, the abbot was led to the grave of his predecessor and reminded that he too must soon give an account of his stewardship. After a short prayer for the deceased, all repaired to the abbot's quarters. There, when his monks had paid him homage once more (presumably to acknowledge his authority *in temporalibus*), the new abbot was given the administration of monastic property and the keys of the monastery. The result of the election was posted on the church door before it was confirmed by the bishop, and in due time the abbatial blessing was conferred.[30]

At a visitation the commissioners summoned abbot and

community to chapter and presented their credentials. There followed an exhortation from one of the commissioners, after which each monk took an oath to answer truthfully the questions put to him. The answers to the comprehensive questionnaire were recorded in each case.[31] The custom of answering a prepared list of questions under oath, it can be noted, was a recognised legal procedure on the Continent, at any rate in church courts. It was also, perhaps, universal procedure for visitations, unlike modern custom, which is less formal: a historian of the Reformation in England, for example, speaks of the 'traditional routine questions' at visitations. It should be obvious, incidentally, that a balanced view of a religious community cannot be obtained from studying the answers to these questions, which do not seek a judicious assessment of the health of the body but investigate specifically the ailments from which it might be suffering. The same historian calls the study of visitation records the 'pathology' of the religious life.[32]

Würzburg was a university town and a centre of theological studies. Presumably a clerical student could do his divinity either at the university or at the diocesan seminary or in some religious house. Marianus Irvine, we know, taught philosophy and theology in St James's itself. The Scots may also have attended the college for Benedictines which the bishop ordered to be set up in St Stephen's in 1651.[33] Three abbots of St James's held the position of Rector Magnificus of the university: Ogilvie, Asloan and Cook. The Scots abbot is also said to have acted as pro-rector in 1683.[34] Scots names on the matriculation rolls appear to fall into two classes, young students and something more honorific, such as Abbot Ogilvie before his appointment as rector and Abbots Irvine and Cook immediately after their election. Some entries, however, are less easy to evaluate, for instance, Robert Forbes the prior and Thomas Duff the poet in 1629, and Alan Chisholm the senior monk in 1694. It is surely no coincidence that in each case the Scots abbot was Rector at the time. Perhaps they matriculated in order to serve the Rector in some official capacity.

The city of Würzburg, as the residence of a prince-bishop and a seat of learning, naturally attracted foreign travellers. The letters of Abbot Maxwell give an indication of the number of Scots who visited the town and the monastery of their fellow-countrymen. This is not surprising when one considers the great number of Scots on the continent and the liaison which the monks maintained with their homeland. The Irish also came to Würzburg, at least in the middle years of the century. Some matriculated at the university, others were merely visitors, like the friars whom James Brown interrogated about Ireland, or the Vicar General of Ireland and the Bernardine abbot who passed through in 1653-54.[35] During the

Cromwellian persecution the Irish Franciscans who could find no accommodation in Prague wanted to establish a house in Würzburg. They were attracted by the Irish associations of St Kilian's town and by the fact that as a centre of studies it was suitable for their students, but in the event no Irish house was founded. [36]

Some features of Würzburg life were less attractive, at least when viewed three centuries later. The Jews were subject to restrictions. Würzburg was a sort of theocracy inasmuch as the source of spiritual and temporal authority was the prince-bishop, which helps to explain the various enactments against swearing and unchastity in the last third of the century. [37] In one matter Catholic Würzburg's reputation is very black: with Presbyterian Scotland and Puritan New England it shares the unenviable distinction of having persecuted witches with particular vehemence. It is listed as one of the two most notorious German states in this regard. Even if we dismiss some of the figures as fantastic there were 900 persons put to death in Würzburg in the years 1623-31. Abbot Ogilvie at this period was a judge on the bench for reducing clerics accused of witchcraft to the lay state. Nobody was secure: even a relative of the bishop, when he took to a dissolute life, was beheaded for witchcraft. The amount of innocent human suffering was appalling: the accused were tortured until they confessed to anything, then as self-confessed witches or warlocks they were executed. One particularly ingenious and effective torture used in Franconia was to coat the soles of the victim's feet with salt and let a goat lick them. Goats love salt, so the animal's rough tongue soon rubbed off the skin and continued to lick the salt-tasting blood, causing the most exquisite pain. It is to the credit of Archbishop John Philip von Schönborn that he put an end to the senseless carnage. [38]

Since the *Schottenklöster* centred on Ratisbon were almost all founded in the twelth century, the history of their buildings tended to be similar. They were built very near but not in the town, then the town grew and absorbed them within its limits. The Würzburg abbey was different from the others in that it lay across the river from the town, but even so it was in the path of the new city walls, precisely the situation which occasioned the demolition of two Scotic monasteries in the sixteenth century. In 1400 the outer wall of the monastery actually formed part of the city wall. What affected the monastery still more, however, was its proximity to the citadel as the latter's fortifications and defences became more elaborate.

During their occupation of the town and citadel in 1631-34 the Swedes drew up plans which affected St James's. A decade later work began on new fortifications, which took some of the Scots' vineyards and spoiled others for a considerable time. For this they were compensated. From 1653 to 1663 work is recorded on the *Schottenschanz* or Scottish redoubt, which brought the monastery within the fortifications and quite changed its surroundings. As the work continued the Scots again received compensation in 1664 and 1667, including a reduction in their *subsidium charitativum*, the tax paid to the prince-bishop.[39] Inclusion in the fortifications was to cause great inconvenience to the abbey, particularly in the eighteenth century, but it undoubtedly makes its surroundings more picturesque. Even today the visitor comes across high sheer walls and precipitous drops as he walks round the precincts of St James's.

Detailed investigation of the buildings occupied by the Scots is less a matter for the historian than for the local antiquarians, and indeed these have written at length on the subject. All the same, in trying to picture the life led by the Scots in the local setting, it is helpful to know something of their monastery and church. Of the mediaeval monastery nothing survived in the seventeenth century.[40] When German monks were introduced in 1497 the monastery was all but uninhabitable; only the renovations carried out by the bishop, some of them entailing completely new buildings, enabled monastic life to continue. The same pattern of events was repeated not much later. The monastery was in great part burnt down in the Peasants War about 1525 and by Bishop Echter's time was once again uninhabitable. Before the first three Scots could take up residence, Echter had to restore it from the ruins and rebuild it extensively. For all practical purposes, therefore, the monastic buildings dated from the sixteenth century. A plan of the buildings is on page 259.

This monastery consisted of one building at some distance from the east end of the church. It seems fairly clear that little more than the necessary minimum was done before the first three monks arrived in 1595 and that more was planned. References to the buildings are confused and not easy to interpret, and the almost complete destruction of 1945 has removed most of the evidence. Certainly, however, in the seventeenth century new buildings were erected while extensive repairs were carried out on the old ones. The arms of Abbots Asloan and Irvine, with the dates 1652 and 1688 respectively, bear witness to renovations in the old wing.

On St Benedict's day, 1600, Abbot Whyte laid the foundation stone of a new building, and various donations were made by Bishop Echter for the fabric.[41] In 1631, towards the end of Ogilvie's rule, there was mention of a new monastery building, and in 1688 of the old and new monastery buildings. Certainly by the early eighteenth century two other wings had been added, one of which

258

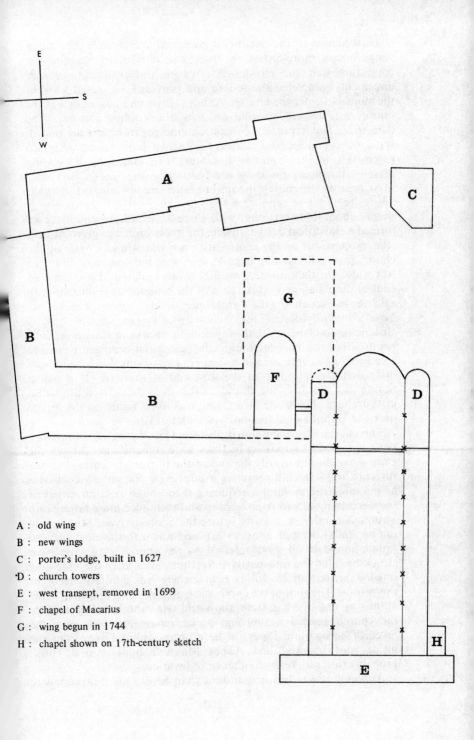

E

S

W

A

C

G

B

B

F

D

D

H

E

A : old wing
B : new wings
C : porter's lodge, built in 1627
D : church towers
E : west transept, removed in 1699
F : chapel of Macarius
G : wing begun in 1744
H : chapel shown on 17th-century sketch

reached almost to the north-east corner of the church. The three wings formed, more or less, the three sides of a square, and one can conjecture that the cloister referred to in seventeenth-century documents completed the square and provided a covered way for the monks to enter the church. Abbot Ogilvie had also added at the outside gate a small building which is still standing and bears the date 1627. The important conclusion emerges from all this that in spite of economic difficulties the Scots built and renovated extensively in the seventeenth century and ended by possessing premises far superior to those of a century before.

As regards the church the uncertainties are less great, for it was always repaired or rebuilt on the same site.[42] It was a basilica in shape, about 140 feet long, with three aisles whose round apses formed a clover-leaf design. Inside, the impression was given of very slim proportions as the centre aisle ran the whole length of the church, had a flat ceiling over 45 feet high, but was only about 25 feet wide. On the outside, two high towers soared above the east ends of the aisles, and on the roof of the rounded apse on the south side aisle squatted the grotesque stone figure called the *Schottenmandl* (dialect for 'Scots dwarf'). The church bore a striking resemblance to that of the Scotic monks in Ratisbon; both had towers over the side aisles to the east, a flat-ceilinged nave and a vaulted choir, with the same slender proportions. Both had a sort of transept with gallery at the west end of the nave. It is worth noting that the surviving church in Ratisbon dates from after that in Würzburg. The stone dwarf, too, was like a figure on the bridge over the Danube at Ratisbon[43] (see Plate 13).

The church was built shortly before 1156. Its basic form and a good many of its surviving features were romanesque, though the choir was rebuilt towards the end of the thirteenth century. In the fifteenth and sixteenth centuries it underwent the same vicissitudes as the monastic buildings, requiring a thorough restoration when the German monks took possession and then once more falling into a ruinous condition. Shortly before the Scots arrived, Mass could not be said at the high altar, so exposed was it to the elements; the foundation deed of 1595 referred to the church as having been struck by lightning and partly burnt out. Even after the extensive repairs carried out by Julius Echter there was constant need for renovation. The roof of the choir was rotten in 1617, and the chapel at the west end in a bad state; snow and rain came in freely in 1625; the church needed a thorough-going repair in 1640 after the Swedish occupation. Later in the century Abbot Dixon had the inside roof renewed and Abbot Maxwell built a new choir; probably this, too, refers to interior renovation.

Although it was less magnificent than before the destruction of the fifteenth and sixteenth centuries, the church of St James's could still be described as one of the most imposing and individualistic churches in Franconia. Its proportions have won praise from architects, and in spite of its vicissitudes it retained not only its early form but a wealth of romanesque and gothic ornament. There were two old chapels, one just outside the north apse, and the other at the west end. The former, the chapel of St James where Macarius was buried, survived until an eighteenth-century extension of the monastery was built on its site. The latter presumably disappeared with the west transept, which was demolished in 1699 as a wall of the fortifications was pressing against it. By that time the church as a whole once more needed repair. It received this in the early eighteenth century, and thereafter remained much as it was until it was gutted in 1945. At present its exterior dimensions remain the same, the towers still stand and one still enters by the early eighteenth-century porch, but the pillars separating the aisles have gone and the nave is a simple rectangle.

In the seventeenth century, then, the Scots had a church of venerable antiquity. The eastward bays of the centre aisle formed the choir and sanctuary; the side aisles too were divided at their east end to form enclosed chapels, one of them used as the sacristy. The details recorded of the altars are confusing, but it can be mentioned that one was dedicated to St Kilian and in 1615 there were six altars in use in the church. At some point, possibly in the eighteenth century, the pillars of the church were covered over with lime or plaster, which hid the frescoes of Kilian and other saints dating from 1504. The chapel of Macarius also had pictures, presumably frescoes, of his miracles made perhaps after the finding of the body. The same is probably true of a picture of Macarius in the church, while another picture showing Bishops Embricho and Echter with Macarius and Abbot Ogilvie clearly commemorates the finding. In the church, besides these and other pictures, were statues, of various dates, of Christ and his mother; above the entrance to the choir stood a crucifixion group. Saints, notably St James, had their statues, including the group of the Madonna, St Benedict and St Macarius. The surviving statue of Macarius is baroque and thus later than its two companions, but may be a replacement of an earlier statue, as we know happened with the crucifixion group. Seventeenth-century churchmen and craftsmen had no hesitation about introducing baroque 'improvements'.

Collection boxes were placed in the chapel of Macarius and at the foot of the steps leading up to the choir. At the top of the steps stood the stone sarcophagus of Macarius, within which was the metal coffin containing his bones. The stone lid, still to be seen in the Marienkapelle, bore the figure of Macarius in Benedictine cowl

261

and hood, of a pattern very like the English Congregation hood of today. On the sides were the arms of Bishop Echter and Abbot Ogilvie. It was the custom to bury abbots in the church and erect monuments to them; one could read the epitaphs of a fourteenth-century Irish abbot as well as of Trithemius and other German abbots. The Scots Ogilvie and Asloan were in their turn given burial and a monument in the church.

In the choir stood the gothic choirstalls presented by Bishop von Bibra about 1500. In the choirstalls were articles not mentioned in guides to the church, namely spittoons; the monks were told that, if one had to spit, it should be done quietly, not while bowing for a *Gloria Patri,* and taking care not to miss the receptacles. [44] This is a reminder that night office in an unheated church during a continental winter had its penitential side. Spittoons, however, were still to be found well into the twentieth century in American monasteries founded from Bavaria. Abbot Ogilvie had an organ built, which was replaced by Abbot Maxwell's new one half a century later. In the south tower was a bell presented by the bishop in 1638, as well as two others blessed in 1657;[45] it was recorded in 1682 that three bells were in this tower, and another in the chapel of Macarius.

One can see from all this that the Scots had more than a little oratory in which to say their choir office far from home. They had a fine church five centuries old, needing constant repair, it is true, but they found the means to supply this. Its furniture and appointments betokened both its venerable past and the present glory of its own saint, Macarius. Its equipment, both the necessary and the ornamental, was being replaced and added to. The chronicle describes most of the seventeenth-century abbots as buying chalices, vestments and so on for the church. Whether this was done out of income or was the result of benefactions — the faithful visiting Macarius's tomb would no doubt express their devotion in a practical way and roughly a sixth of the Scots' revenue in 1738 came from stipends and alms — it seems clear that the sacristy equipment increased. The inventory drawn up in 1688 would seem to indicate that in this Catholic city during the era of Baroque, the Scots were not unaffected by the general process of elaboration in worship. They had half a dozen chalices, at least four sets of Mass vestments of each colour, and all the paraphernalia necessary for pontifical ceremonies.[46]

A Würzburg chalice which has found its way to Scotland is probably not one of these six, as it is a 'travelling' chalice for use by missionaries.[47] On its base are engraved Abbot Maxwell's arms consisting of a saltire cross (for Maxwell), which does not necessarily mean that he was personally entitled to them. Each

Scots abbot would assume the arms of some family of the surname; these he would use either alone or joined to the arms of the monastery. The latter consisted of the scallop-shell of St James, the pilgrim apostle, on two pilgrim staffs crossed saltire-wise. The large seal of the monastery showed St James with pilgrim hat and staff, and scallop-shells on his cloak.[48]

The Scots encouraged the people of Würzburg to visit their church by obtaining papal grants of indulgences. In 1619 Paul V granted several indulgences to the church. Later in the century the Scots sought a plenary indulgence for those who visited the church on the feast of St James. A grant made in 1688 apparently arrived too late but Alan Chisholm asked for it again the following year, and the indulgence was bestowed for seven years in 1690.[49]

Let us consider finally the life led by the monks. We know a certain amount about its externals.[50] The monastery needed employees, and we have a list of them in 1625, but it is not easy to judge which ones were employed full-time: possibly the abbot's manservant, the organist, bailiff, cook, gardener, porter, vinedresser, or at least some of them; hardly, one would think, the washerwoman; and surely not the doctor, surgeon, slater and cooper. The visitation of 1693 laid down that only three men and a boy were to be employed. The habit worn by the monks was the same as that of other Benedictines in the diocese, for not only did the statutes of 1618 lay down regulations for dress but the pictures and statues which survived until recently show the similarity. The only choir books of which we know were those prescribed for use in all Benedictine houses.

The time of rising varied. In 1595 it was 3 o'clock, in 1614 midnight, in 1618 3.45 and an hour earlier on feast-days; in 1665 it was 3.45, in 1692 2 o'clock. Apart from the short period during which they rose at midnight and then returned to bed after Matins, the time must be considered in relation to the habits of the townspeople, who could assemble in procession on Easter Sunday at 5 a.m. In Scotland, too, people rose early. We know the horarium prescribed for the monks by Bishop Echter, while the detailed regulations for daily routine laid down by the synod of 1618 have been preserved through the diligence of the Scot, Thomas Duff, who transcribed them. It is enough to know that the Scots followed the same observance as other monasteries in the diocese.

It is paradoxical that the aspect we know least about is the spiritual life of the monks. This is perhaps inevitable; the history of a university, for example, will say next to nothing about its success in producing the genuine fruits of education, breadth of mind and so on, in its alumni. The synod of 1618 said that priests were to go to confession once a week, and it wanted them to say Mass three times a week or even daily.[51] In 1628 Silvanus Mayne declared that he had said Mass that morning as the custom was to celebrate almost daily.[52] But even this tells us little about the personal spiritual lives of the monks. One has to remember that unless monastic life had broken down completely, as for example during the Swedish occupation, the monks continued to perform their common duties and choir offices and also their private devotional exercises. Day in and day out, whether the observance at the time was such as would satisfy the bishop's officials and edify the later historian or not, this continued. One must presume, except when there is evidence to the contrary, that the monks remained faithful to the essentials of their vows; and in order to do this, the vital spark of spiritual fervour must have been kept alive.

This is putting it at its lowest. We can get some idea of the interest of the monks in spiritual things from the writings which have survived. Even if we dismiss letters, such as those containing Abbot Maxwell's christian sentiments, or works intended for publication, like James Brown's well-meaning hagiography, on the grounds that their purpose was to edify, the notebooks kept by monks surely indicate where their interests lay. Thomas Duff, who filled one volume with poems of his own composition, filled another with prayers, meditations and devotional passages, copied from various authors. He and another monk filled yet another notebook between them with the same sort of thing. James Hegat's scrapbook, containing items on the most diverse subjects, has spiritual topics among them.

Towards the end of the century Bernard Falconer penned a volume of spiritual doctrine and meditations. Augustine Bruce, later to be elected abbot, filled two books with passages on monastic observance. One could perhaps go though all these volumes in detail and examine the source used by the monks and the works they read to nourish their spiritual life. One might even discover that some of what they wrote was their own composition. The point here being made is simpler and more general: that they did read spiritual works assiduously and were interested in spiritual things.

Notes

[1] J. A. Oegg, *Versuch einer Korographie der . . . Stadt Würzburg* (Würzburg, 1808), 761-62; Wieland, 11.

[2] Wz. SA, SB 547, f. 9r-15v; Wieland, 78-80, 88; *Taschenbuch* (1795), 196, 207.

[3] S. Zeissner, "Hofgut Jobstthal", in *AU*, lix, 135-55; Wz. SA, Misc. 5793, catalogue entry; Wieland, 80, 135.

[4] Reg. BOA, Sch. Akten, 322.

[5] *AU*, xliii, 35.

[6] VL, MS Vat. Lat. 10,100; MS Vat. Lat. 11,063, f. 25-30; Reg. BOA, Sch., Akten, 320; Wieland, 58-63.

[7] Wz. SA, SB 547, f. 17r-19r. Gropp, I, 91; III, 77.

[8] Ludewig, 503; cf. *Die Mainlande*, ii, 34-35.

[9] E.g., *Cosmographiae Universalis Libri VI* (Basel, 1572), III, 387, p. 805.

[10] Gropp, I, 91-92, 428-29; III, 365-68.

[11] Gropp, II, 220.

[12] Ser. Abb; Dennistoun, f. 161-62; cf. Gropp, III, 409.

[13] Cf. Gropp, II, 302.

[14] Copialbuch, f. 28-29; Wieland, 55-56; Gropp, IV, 264-69.

[15] Gropp, II, 514-15, 531-32.

[16] Copialbuch, f. 29; Wieland, 56n; Gropp, IV, 308-12.

[17] Wz. SA, SB 547, f. 15v-16r; Wieland, 53-54. Cf. also *AU*, iv, pt. 1, p. 88-89.

[18] Duff, f. 8v.

[19] Dennistoun, f. 336rv.

[20] Wieland, 42. Cf. also Maxwell, 22.6.1681.

[21] Maxwell, 30.8.1681, 5.11.1681.

[22] Dennistoun, f. 336r; Maxwell, 31.7.1680, 23.8.1682.

[23] Weiss, 25, 47, 54; J. A. Kraus, *Die Benediktiner-Abtei Neustadt am Main* (Würzburg, 1856), 186, 187, 189.

[24] Maxwell, 22.6.1678; *AU*, xi, pt. 2, p. 285.

[25] Gropp, II, 537, 508; Dennistoun, f. 334v.

[26] Gropp, II, 210-11, 551; *AU*, xiv, pt.1, p.122.

[27] P. Volk, "Das Necrologium der Benediktiner-Abtei Neustadt am Main", in *WDGB*, vi, 25.

[28] F. X. Wegele, *Zur Literatur und Kritik der fränkischen Necrologien* (Nördlingen, 1864), 51, 55, 5, 10, 36.

[29] Copialbuch, f.205; Wieland, 96; Wolff, 307.

[30] Wieland, 56-57.

[31] Wieland, 58.

[32] P. Hughes, *The Reformation in England* (2nd edn. 1963), II, 236; I, 48.

[33] Gropp, IV, 680.

[34] See Appendix B.

[35] Merkle, 232; "Trilogy", 125; NLS, Adv. 29.7.1, f.41r.

[36] K. McGrath, "The Bruodins in Bohemia", in *IER*, lxxvii, 333-43.

[37] Gropp, IV, 805-07, 759.

[38] Gropp, II, 287-91; H. R. Trevor-Roper, *The European Witch-Craze of the 16th and 17th Centuries* (1969), 81, 83, 87; Merzbacher, passim.

[39] F. Seberich, *Die Stadtbefestigung Würzburgs* (Würzburg, 1962-63), I, 53-56, 214; II, 9-20, 145; Wieland, 17-18; Wz. SA, Urk. 46.136, 9.32.

[40] For the monastery buildings see Wieland, 63-77; F. Mader (ed.), *Die Kunstdenkmäler von Bayern*, III, 12: *Stadt Würzburg* (Munich, 1915), 346; Oegg, 358-61; P. Weissenberger, "Beiträge zur Kunst- und Kulturgeschichte

mainfränkischer . . . Klöster", in *Mainfränkisches Jahrbuch*, iii, 203-04.

[41] VL, MS Vat. Lat. 10,100, f.62r-63v, partly printed in "Necrologies", 194.

[42] For the church and its furnishing see Wieland, 20-49; Mader, 337-46 and the works listed there. Two important studies by F. Oswald have appeared in recent years: "Der Westbau der ehemaligen Schottenkirche in Würzburg", in *Mainfränkisches Jahrbuch*, x, 20-41; *Würzburger Kirchenbauten des 11. und 12. Jahrhunderts* (Würzburg, 1966), 159-86.

[43] B. Hanftmann, "Das Schottenmännchen in Würzburg und seine Sippe", in *AU.* lxx, 323-34.

[44] Wz. UB, M.ch.q.48, f.19r.

[45] *WDGB*, iv, 16.

[46] Dennistoun, f.335v-336r.

[47] D. McRoberts, "Some post-reformation chalices", in *IR*, xviii, 145-46.

[48] Wieland, 11-12.

[49] Wieland, 32, 50n; SCA, ML, Chisholm, 20.5.1689.

[50] Wieland, 49-50, 92-94, 98-99.

[51] Wz. UB, M.ch.q.51, f.137r, 138r.

[52] Brown, 294.

Epilogue

The Scottish monastery in Würzburg remained in being for another hundred years and was not dissolved until the general secularisation shortly after 1800 which put an end to almost every religious community in Germany. It suffered what was perhaps its most serious vicissitude only a few years after the time we have been considering, when in 1703 Abbot Cook was deposed by the prince-bishop for misconduct. Under Augustine Bruce, however, first as administrator and then as abbot, the monastery recovered. After his death two other abbots ruled until 1753. The usual abbatial election did not then take place at once, possibly because numbers were small; instead a prior was appointed, but three years later a monk of Ratisbon, Placid Hamilton, was elected abbot. It was an unfortunate choice: Hamilton was not successful and departed for London in 1763. He was the last abbot of St James's. A prior ruled for three years, then Benedict Mackenzie (the rightful earl of Seaforth in Jacobite eyes) took over the leadership and governed successfully as prior from 1766 until his death in 1785. Thereafter the monastery had priors who each ruled for a short period.

Throughout the century, on the whole, the monastery prospered and recruitment appeared to present no problem. Apart from a period in the 1740s when numbers sank lower, there were always between seven and ten monks, which was probably as many as the revenues could support. At the time of the secularisation in 1803 there were seven priests resident and one missionary in Scotland. As in the previous century, the contribution to the Scottish mission was small but not negligible. One missionary, Placid Shand, led a life of heroic virtue in the bleakest part of habitable Scotland; another, Kilian Pepper, at the end of the century was the first resident priest in Dundee. In the controversy over Jansenism which rent the Scottish mission, a Würzburg monk, Kilian MacGregor, played an active and not too happy part. About the same time Marianus Gordon, a brilliant scholar but unstable, gained notoriety when he was imprisoned in the Marienberg for heresy and hanged himself there.

The Scots became even more dependent on local officials when the administration of their temporalities was given to the diocesan exchequer under Bishop Frederick Charles von Schönborn (1729-

267

46). From then on, their revenues were collected for them, which may have eased their burden but also increased their dependence. The deferring of abbatial elections by the diocesan officials meant a similar loss of dignity for St James's. Nevertheless the system of government by priors worked admirably. The monastery now had superiors who did not attempt to compete with the neighbouring prelates, and in its closing decades it enjoyed peace and stability. In fact the last dozen years of its existence give the impression of timelessness such as one gets in summer evenings in the north when the sun has set but the shadowless light remains. The Scots at this time enjoyed a high reputation for virtue and learning, even among the somewhat anti-clerical supporters of the Enlightenment.

When St James's was secularised and its monks pensioned off, the monastery became a military hospital. The church served as a storehouse but before long the choir was in use as a chapel once more. This was the state of affairs for almost a century until in 1904 the nave too was restored to its original purpose and the whole edifice became a chapel for the garrison and later for the local people. Both the church and the former monastery were devastated in the air-raids of 1945. In September 1945, however, the ruined buildings were taken over by the Salesians of Don Bosco, a modern religious congregation founded for the care of boys. Re-building began and the church was consecrated in 1956. Today all the buildings stand once more on their original foundations and the whole complex is a flourishing home for working boys. The open space outside is still called the *Schottenanger* or Scots meadow.

In the eighteenth century close relations with Ratisbon had been retained but there was no form of common organisation or union. At the secularisation the Würzburg monks made no effort to act in concert with the Ratisbon community (which was not dissolved) for the continuance of Scottish monasticism. Instead they lived privately in or near Würzburg until the last of their number died in 1839. In spite of this, one could argue that the greatest contribution made by the monks of Würzburg to the Benedictine order and the Roman Catholic church was the help they gave to the Ratisbon abbey. In the darkest days after the troubles under Abbot Algeo and the Swedish occupation of Ratisbon, it was Würzburg monks who took charge in Ratisbon and its dependency at Erfurt. It was the Würzburg abbot, Asloan, who saved Ratisbon when the emperor and bishop were trying to expel the Scots, and it was a Würzburg monk, Baillie, who ruled at Ratisbon until 1655. Würzburg monks continued to help the Ratisbon monastery until the election of its great abbot, Placid Fleming.

The achievements of the Ratisbon abbey in the eighteenth century were outstanding: its seminary flourished, its monks played a distinguished part in the cultural life of Bavaria and made a notable contribution to learning, as professors and writers, at Erfurt university. Alone of all the monastic houses of Germany the Scots abbey in Ratisbon was not secularised in the early years of the nineteenth century. It was not dissolved until 1862. Its last monk, Anselm Robertson, having returned to Scotland, took a hand in the founding of the monastery at Fort Augustus in the 1870s. The last student of the seminary, Donald Mackintosh, was a parish priest in the West Highlands until his death in 1927. But without the salvage operations directed from Würzburg it is extremely doubtful if the Ratisbon monastery would have survived into the second half of the seventeenth century. The Würzburg Scots played a vital part in forging the slender link which joins present-day and pre-reformation Scottish monasticism.

Appendix A

Conditions for restoration
accepted by the Scots, 2nd May 1595

(Originals in Wz.SA, Urk. 50.24a, 99.223.
Text taken from the former).

NOS IOANNES IACOBUS ALBUS, DEI et Apostolicae Sedis gratia Abbas Sancti Iacobi apud Scotos Ratisbonae, ordinis Divi Benedicti, et RICHARDUS IREWING Abbas Sancti Iacobi Herbipolensis eiusdem ordinis Notum facimus per praesentes.

Cum temporum iniuria, religionisque Catholicae mutatione, nec non superiorum Abbatum Monasterii Divi Iacobi Herbipolensis negligentia acciderit, Scotorum monachorum ordinis D. Benedicti residentiam in dicto Monasterio Herbipolensi plane abrogari, redditusque ita extenuari, ut nulli vel pauci saltem in eodem ali potuerint, adhaec templum dicti Monasterii caelo tactum magna ex parte conflagrarit, ita ut ob id divina officia longissimo tempore omissa, ac monasterium propemodum desolatum fuerit, adeo ut nisi beneficio atque opera Reverendissimi atque Illustrissimi Principis ac Domini, domini IULII Episcopi Herbipolensis ac Franciae orientalis Ducis restituta fuisset religio, ac restauratum templum, redditusque conservati atque aucti, de Monasterio Scotisque hac in parte actum videretur, Nos praefati Domini Principis atque Episcopi consilio atque consensu, praecedente quoque tractatu nostrorum fratrum Conventualium, eorumque voluntate huic malo praevenire ac in posterum praecavere satagentes, constituimus atque ordinamus, quod in posterum in dicto monasterio S. Iacobi Herbipolensi praeter Abbatem alii quinque Religiosi fratres ordinis (D.) Benedicti genere Scoti resideant, aut si eorum copia haberi nequeat, vel defectus intra semestre tempus non suppleatur, erit liberum praefato Domino Episcopo tanquam ordinario eiusque successoribus ex aliis monasteriis eiusdem ordinis D. Benedicti Dioecesis Herbipolensis alium vel alios Germanae nationis substituere, quo constitutus numerus senarius continuus sit atque perpetuus, ex quo in casu vacationis Abbas legitime eligetur, qui omnium erit aptissimus, sive ille demum sit Scotus sive Germanus.

Ut autem officia divina debito modo persolvantur, novitiorumque ignorantiae subveniatur, curabimus ut omnes sint in ordine Presbiterii aut aliquo ex maioribus constituti, aut intra annum ad id promovendi, qui aliis vita, moribus atque institutione praeesse ac prodesse possint, quorum unus etiam cum laude Theologiam publice atque in Universitate Herbipolensi profiteri debeat.

Adhaec liberum erit praedicto Domino Episcopo ac Principi Herbipolensi eiusque successoribus vi ordinariae Visitationis quotannis praefatum Monasterium, tam quo ad regularem Disciplinam, quam cultum divinum, atque administrationem rerum Ecclesiasticarum per se vel suos Visitatores deputatos visitare, ordinis regulas iuxta praescriptum observari curare, cultum divinum aliquo modo collapsum restituere, regulares personas in nominato Monasterio constitutas iisque cohabitantes examinare, corrigere, debitisque poenis canonicis afficere, transferre ac si opus foret plane removere, ab administrationibus, oeconomis, ac praefectis annuatim pro ut in aliis R.S.C. Dioecesis Monasteriis non absque fructu atque utilitate eorundem observatum ac receptum est, rationes exigere, absque fraude et dolo.

In quorum omnium fidem ac robur has literas nostrae Abbatiae Sigillis communiri fecimus.

Et quia ut praemittitur haec consensu atque authoritate praefati Domini Episcopi ac Principis tanquam Ordinarii, accedente quoque consensu Reverendorum Generosi ac Nobilium DD. Decani et Capituli Cathedralis Ecclesiae a nobis statuta ac in vim iuramenti stipulatione a nobis promissa sunt, hinc ad nos eius rei nomine convincendos, debita humilitate petivimus, ut S.R.C. nec non DD. Decanus ac Capitulum easdem has literas suo ac Capituli Sigillis confirmarent.

Quod nos IULIUS Episcopus Herbipolensis ac Franciae orientalis Dux, qui promissionem praedictam ratione Ecclesiae nostrae acceptavimus, ac constitutiones praedictas tanquam canonibus, ac consuetudini nostrae Dioecesis conformes, ordinaria nostra potestate confirmavimus, ac per praesentes confirmamus atque acceptamus, uti praemittitur requisiti, volentes lubentesque fecimus, atque nostro Sigillo has literas communiri iussimus, Et nos Decanus et Capitulum praedictum ad maiorem huius rei corroborationem nostri Capituli Sigillum his quoque appendi fecimus.

Datas secunda Maii, Anno millesimo quingentesimo Nonagesimo quinto.

Appendix B

Scots matriculating at Würzburg

13 August 1596	Francis Hamilton, prior
5 March 1598	John Stuart
1624[1]	Audomarus John Asloan (Physics)
12 June 1625	James Hegate (Theology)
,, ,, ,,	Richard Tod (Physics)
,, ,, ,,	Andrew Maclean[2] (Physics)
11 August 1628	William Ogilvie, abbot
2 November 1628	William Ogilvie: RECTOR
14 March 1629	Robert Forbes, prior
,, ,, ,,	Thomas Duff, priest
27 November 1641	Maurus Dixon (Logic)
1646	Audomarus John Asloan: RECTOR[3]
18 November 1654	Placid Keith (Logic)
1683	Bernard Maxwell: PRO-RECTOR (?)[4]
28 July 1685	Marianus Irvine[5], abbot elect
September 1686(?)[6]	Augustine Gordon (Theology and Canon Law)
9 August 1690	Ambrose Cook, abbot
1693	Isidore Ogilvie (7)[7]
1694[8]	Ambrose Cook: RECTOR
6 November (?)[9] 1694	Columba Maclennan (Theology)
,, ,, ,,	Maurus Strachan (Metaphysics)
,, ,, ,,	Alan Chisholm
3 February 1695	Joseph Falconer (Theology)
12 March 1695	Gregory Cheyne (Metaphysics)
19 September 1695	Ambrose Cook: RECTOR
19 September 1696	Ambrose Cook: RECTOR

Notes

[1] Undated. The previous dated entry has 3rd March, the next has July.

[2] *Maclenus*, transcribed by Merkle as *Macleus*.

[3] The leaf containing the names for most of 1646 has gone missing (Merkle, 199) but Asloan's rectorship is recorded by an almost contemporary source (Wz. UB, M.ch.f. 260, fos 91v, 95v).

[4] Gropp, II, 195 says the Scots abbot Maurus was pro-rector in 1683, but the date is wrong unless Maxwell is meant. The leaf for 1682-3 is missing (Merkle, 356).

⁵ *Iruin*, transcribed by Merkle as *Frum*.

⁶ No dating in entries for 1686-7.

⁷ The visitation acts of 1693 ordered that he was to do "higher theological studies", but there are no names in the roll for 1693-4.

⁸ No rector is entered for 1694-5 but the 1695 entry refers to Cook's re-election.

⁹ The month is not written. The previous entry has 6th November; the next date given is 14th December.

Appendix C

Students at Scots Colleges

(Information is from the printed Records unless otherwise stated.
The first date is that of entrance to the college.)

Douai College

1581 Alexander Bog	Soldier or monk in Germany, 1598
1587 Francis Hamilton	Monk at Ratisbon, 1598
1588 Adam Simpson	Monk at Ratisbon, 1598
1593 Robert Hill	Monk at Ratisbon, 1598
1594 William Gordon	(Monk at Würzburg)
1595 Alexander Armour	(Monk at Ratisbon)
1596 John Ogilvie	Had been sent to Ratisbon, 1598
1606 George Asloan	Died a monk in Germany
—— John Mayne (?)[1]	(See below)
1620 James Scott	Went to Würzburg, 1623
—— James Hegate	Went to Würzburg, 1623
—— Richard Tod	Went to Würzburg, 1623
1620 James Kinneard	Said to have become a Benedictine in Germany
1621 Edward Maxwell	Went to Würzburg, 1623
1621 Robert Maclean	Went to Würzburg, 1623
1623 George Wedderburn	(See below)
1631 Gilbert Chambers	(See below)
1626, 1632, 1634 Gilbert Gordon	Benedictine for a time in Germany, between 1636 and 1640
1633, 1639 Robert Francis Irvine	Went to Germany to be a monk before returning to Douai in 1639. Monk at Würzburg after May 1643, then became a Capuchin[2].
1641 Alexander Lumsden	At Würzburg for a time, 1644-45
1648 Archibald Alexander	Went to Würzburg, 1649
1657 William Baillie	(See below)
1668 John Brown	Went to Würzburg, 1674

Rome College

1602 Thomas Cuming	Benedictine in Venice[3]
—— Thomas Duff	Benedictine in Germany[4]
1612 Alexander Baillie	Monk at Würzburg
1616 George Asloan	(See above)
1619 John Mayne	Left 1619. Monk at Würzburg
1623 George Wedderburn	Left 1625. Monk at Ratisbon
1633 Henry More	Left 1639[5]. Benedictine in Germany
1634 Robert Strachan	Left 1638[5]. Benedictine in Germany
1635 Gilbert Chambers	Left 1637[5]. Monk at Ratisbon
1645 Alexander Lumsden	(See above)
1653 William Gray	Left 1656. Monk in Germany
1657 William Baillie	Left 1658. Monk at Würzburg
1657 Alexander Gordon	(Left 1658) Benedictine in Germany
1661 William Reid	Left 1661. Benedictine (at Ratisbon)
1661 William Chambers	Left 1661. Monk at Ratisbon
1661 George Colinson	Left 1665. Benedictine (at Ratisbon)

Madrid College

1647 Thomas Johnston	Professed at Ratisbon, 1655

Notes

1 Brockie, *ad* Ratisbon.
2 *Colleges*, 27; Douai Reg., f. 153r, 155r, 156v.
3 VL, Barb. Lat. 8629, f. 26v.
4 VL, Barb. Lat. 8629, f. 26r.
5 For his papal permission to become a monk, see Giblin, 53n.

275

Appendix D

Manuscript Works

(For bibliographical information and further fragments, see "Trilogy", 135-39 and "Two MSS")

Germania Christiana
1. Original in Strachan's hand: Wz.UB, M.ch.q.53. Transcript (1878): Reid, f. 9-54
2. Copy (1678) in Andrew Cook's hand: Mount Stuart library
3. Copy (1684) in Cook's hand: NLS, Adv. 33. 7. 20
4. Copy of preface (1704) in Thomas Ruddiman's hand: NLS, Adv. 34. 2. 6

Perspicilium
1. Original of first draft, in Brown's hand: Oban Cathedral House
2. Original of second draft, in Brown's hand: Edin.UL, Laing MS. III, 201
3. Copy of second draft (1705) by Joseph Falconer, entitled *Lucubrationes, etc:* Glasgow University Library, MS. 1-x.8

Indiculus
1. Original in Brown's hand: Wz.UB, M.ch.q.49/1
2. Copy, 1687 version, in Alan Chisholm's hand: Wz.UB, M.ch.q.49/2
3. Copy, 1687 version, in Chisholm's hand: Dennistoun, f. 1-59
4. Copy, 1687 version, (1691): Wz.UB, M.ch.o.23, f. 39-84. Transcript (1878): Reid, f. 83r-99r
5. Copy (1705) by Gregory Crichton, entitled *Index Monasteriorum:* St. James's library, Ratisbon[1]

Series Abbatum
1. 1690 version, in Chisholm's hand, continued by him to 1699: Wz.UB, M.ch.q.56.
2. 1691 version, continued by Gregory Cheyne(?) to 1716: Wz.UB, M.ch.o.23, f. 8v-36v. Transcript (1878): Reid, f. 74r-83r.

3. 1690 version, sent to the Maurists: BN, lat. 12,675, f. 201-18.
4. Version continued to 1701: in volume *Index Monasteriorum* (see above)
5. Fragment covering 1688-1701, in Fleming's hand: Dennistoun, f.333r-335r.

Vita Macarii

1. 1679 version: Wz.UB, M.ch.o.23, f. 2r-8r. Transcript (1878): Reid, f. 70v-72v.
2. 1679 version, in Chisholm's hand: Dennistoun, f. 315-24.
3. 1679 version, in Fleming's hand, continued to 1689: Dennistoun, f. 337v-342r.
4. Copy in volume *Index Monasteriorum* (see above)

The following volumes written by Scots are in Würzburg University Library:

M.ch.q.48   Praxes monasticae, in hand of Augustine Bruce
     q.51   Thomas Duff's Liber Spiritualium Exercitiorum
     q.52   Statuta O.S.B. Congregationis Anglicanae (1694)
     q.54   James Brown's Germania Sancta
     q.55   Bernard Falconer's Meditationes (1687)
     q.57   'Lavacrum conscientiae', etc.
     q.58   Scotia Antiqua et Nova (1610)
     q.59   'A Spiritual Testament', etc. (17-18 cent.)
     q.60   Liber Orationum, partly in Duff's hand
     q.62   Duff's book of poems
     o.18   James Hegate's Collectanea (1628)
     o.22   Augustine Bruce's Diarium Monasticum (1712-14)

Notes

[1] Not available for examination at the time of writing.

Appendix E

Monks of St James's
by order of profession

The list that follows is intended to be a handy guide. The criterion for inclusion is association with the monastery for a sufficiently long period to have some significance for its history. Where only one forename is known, it is probably the baptismal name in the early period, and from Maurus Dixon on it is the religious name. Among the latter are found the Benedictine saints (chiefly Benedict, Maurus, Placid, Gregory, Bernard) as well as Scottish saints or Scotic missionaries in Germany.

It is impossible in most cases to establish the dates precisely. Normally profession takes place twelve months after reception of the habit, which itself will not usually be long delayed after the arrival of the aspirant, provided he has the requisite age and education. Much of the dating depends on figures given much later at visitations or in obituaries, where the person is described as (say) 20 years professed. It is usually not clear if this means 'in the 20th year' or 'having completed 20 years'; the policy followed in this list is therefore, in general, to subtract 20, which establishes the date within a maximum of twelve months' error. Even this, however, is dependent on the accuracy of the figure 20, and it is obvious that the figures given in visitation records are merely approximate. From 1658 onwards, on the other hand, the order of seniority is accurate (except for Hay and Mackintosh).

In the list, 'before (after) 1620' is to be interpreted as meaning 'in or before (after) 1620'; the date is a terminus. Death can be presumed to have taken place at Würzburg unless there is an indication to the contrary. For all but the later monks, a question mark has been added to the date of death where the only evidence is an unsupported entry in the necrology. Most of the information is found in "Necrologies" (or "Necr.Suppl.") or in Reid, f.112, 117-20, or else it relies on the body of the present work and the sources specifically related there to the monk in question. Source references will only be given if they are in addition to these.

278

1595 *Richard Irvine.* Born at Stackheugh, Dumfries-shire. Professed at Ratisbon after 1580. Abbot of Erfurt 1585-95. Abbot of Würzburg 1595-98. Died after 30th December 1626, presumably at Ratisbon or Kelheim.

1595 *Francis Hamilton.* From Edinburgh. Professed at Ratisbon before 1592. Abbot of Würzburg 1602-05. Died after 1617, presumably at Kirchworbis.

1595 *John Stuart.* Born near Glasgow. Professed at Ratisbon before 1595. Died in May 1614.

1599(?) *William Ogilvie.* Professed at Würzburg. Abbot of Erfurt 1611-17. Abbot of Würzburg 1615-35. Died 17th September 1635.

Before 1609 *William Gordon.* Son of 5th earl of Huntly. Born after 1560. Died at Paris, 14th September 1638.

Before 1611 *Gabriel Wallace.* Was later said to have been a laybrother. Died 1616 (?).

Before 1614 *Robert Forbes.* Ordained priest after 1615. Abbot 1636-37. Died 4th December 1637.

8th September 1616 *Thomas Duff.* Of Maldavit, near Cullen. Born before 1594. Died after 1636.

30th November 1617 *Alexander Baillie.* Of Carnbroe. Born 1590. Administrator of Ratsibon 1634-36. Abbot of Erfurt 1636-46. Abbot of Ratisbon 1646-55. Died 7th April 1655 at Ratisbon.

Before 1624 *Audomarus John Asloan.* Of Garroch, near Dumfries. Born c. 1595. Abbot of Würzburg 1638-61. Abbot of Ratisbon 1639-46(?). Died January 1661.

1620-22 *John Silvanus Mayne.* Born 1583 at Glasgow. Administrator of Ratisbon 1636-39. Died October 1639 at Ratisbon.

Before 1630 *Andrew Urquhart.* The only information about him is his inclusion, with the title of priest, in the necrology under 23rd November 1630.

1624-25 *James Hegate.* Born 1601-02 at Glasgow. Came to Würzburg January 1623. Died in May 1631(?); certainly after 1629 and before September 1635.

1624-25 *Richard Tod.* Came to Würzburg January 1623. Died June 1633(?); certainly before September 1635.

1624-25 *Robert Andrew Maclean.* Born 1604 at Dumfries. Came to Würzburg May 1623. Died before September 1628.

After 1624 *Edward Maxwell.* Born c. 1607 at Conheath, near Dumfries. Came to Würzburg May 1623. Died as prior October 1635.

Before 1631(?) *William Maxwell.* The only information is that he was a deacon and was in Ireland in September 1635. Not in the necrology.

After 1632 *James Brown.* Received the habit 13th July 1631. Not yet ordained priest in November 1636. Died in March 1658(?);

certainly after 1655 and before February 1661.

1638 *Maurus Dixon.*   Born 1618. Ordained priest 1644-45. Abbot 1661-79. Died 16th March 1679.

1639 *Robert Boniface Strachan.*   From Montrose. Left Rome for Würzburg 1638. Ordained priest 1640. Last mentioned in a document in 1645.

After 1639 *George Benedict Asloan.*   Of Garroch, near Dumfries. Ordained a secular priest 1619. Died in November 1656(?); certainly before January 1661.

After 1647 *David Placid Keith.*   Came to Würzburg September 1646. At Würzburg 1654. In Poland 1662(?). Not in necrology.

1659 *William Placid Baillie.*   Of Carphin. Born 1633. Came to Würzburg 1658. Died shortly before June 1680, presumably in Britain.

1st November 1660 *Alexander Macarius Brown.*   Born 1639. Died in England, September 1697.

1st November 1660 *Roland William Dunn.*   Born 1644. Died in Northumberland, 20th August 1675.

1663 *Alan Chisholm.*   From Tweeddale[1]. Born c. 1638[2]. Novice 1662. Died 1703.

1664 *Bernard Maxwell.*   Born 1641. Abbot 1679-85. Died 17th March 1685.

1664-65 *Ninian Graham.*   Born 1639. Died in Scotland shortly before April 1680.

1667-68 *James Blair or Hepburn.*   Died 1st October 1702 at Monte Cassino[3].

1667-68 *Columbanus Fraser.*   From Buchan. Died 1677(?); certainly before 1679.

1668-69 *James Marianus Irvine.*   Of Belty(?). Abbot 1685-88. Died 22nd November 1688.

1669 *John Christian Abercrombie.*   Born 1641. Ordained 1673. Died in Scotland 1714.

Before 1670 *Michael Mackintosh.*   The only information about him is his inclusion, with the title of priest, in the necrology under 29th December 1670. Not in lists of resident community 1661-68.

Before 1673(?) *Benedict Hay.*   Of Dalgety[4]. Is mentioned in no Würzburg document before his transfer to Ratisbon c. 1673(?).

1677 *Gregory Seaton.*   Born 1658. Died before ordination at Ratisbon 13th February 1685.

1678-79 *Kilian Herries.*   Born 1663. Died 30th March 1683.

1678-79 *George Augustine Bruce.*   Born near Edinburgh 1658-59. Came to Würzburg October 1677. Ordained priest shortly before 5th October 1683. Administrator 1703-13, abbot 1713-16. Died 1716.

1678-79 *Boniface Mackie.*   Born 1658-59. Arrived at Würzburg

October 1677. Ordained priest December 1682. Died at Edinburgh 1712.

1680 *Patrick John Alexander.* From Aberdeen. Born 1658. Received the habit December 1679. Died 25th May 1682.

1682 *John Ambrose Cook.* Born at Preston c. 1660. Received the habit July 1681. Ordained priest c. 1685. Abbot 1689-1703. Died at Düsselthal 1727.

1685 *Thomas Joseph Ogilvie.* Received habit as laybrother in May 1684. Still in Würzburg community 1698. Not in necrology.

25th July 1689 *Isidore Ogilvie.* Born 1670. Ordained priest 1694. Died April 1701.

c. 1689 *Placid Crichton.* Of Auchingoul. Died 1730.

c. 1689 *Gregory Cheyne.* From Mar. Born c. 1672. Ordained priest about 1697. Died 1731.

c. 1689-90 *Anselm Gordon.* From Mar. Born 1672. Died 1730.

1691 *Maurus Strachan.* From Buchan. Born c. 1673. Came to Würzburg 1690. Ordained priest 1698. Abbot 1716-37. Died 1737.

Before 1697 *Bernard Douglas.* Died in Bohemia 1703.

Notes

1 SCA, ML, Chisholm, May 1700.
2 SCA, ML, Bruce, 13.4.1698.
3 SCA, ML, Holgher, 2.10.1702.
4 SCA, ML, Fleming, 12.1.1700.

Sources and Bibliography

A. Manuscript

(Abbreviations not in square brackets are those used in the archives.
Some abbreviations which many appear strange are those in use
among German writers.)

Würzburg, Staatsarchiv [Wz.SA]

Material on St James's and Benedictines, in particular one
cartulary, SB 545 (formerly 195) [Copialbuch]
HV: Collection of Würzburg Historischer Verein; HV, q. 17* is
the earliest chronicle compiled by the Scots [Chronicon]
MRA: Archive of the electors of Mainz, relating to the Erfurt
abbey

Würzburg, University Library [Wz.UB]

Original matriculation register. (see Appendix B)
Unpublished thesis (1953): A. Schott, Julius Echter und das Buch
[Schott]
Volumes acquired from St James's, in particular the following:
M.ch.f.126, fo 145-53: Compendium breve fundationis . . .
monasterii Sancti Jacobi [Compendium] (For printed editions see
under Trithemius and Ludewig below)
M.ch.q.49/1: Indiculus Monasteriorum Scotorum Ordinis S.
Benedicti extra Scotiam [Indiculus]
M.ch.q.54: Germania Sancta [Germ.Sancta]
M.ch.q.62: Thomas Duff's book of poems [Duff]
M.ch.q.56, M.ch.o.23: Series Abbatum Monasterii S. Jacobi
Herbipolensis [Ser.Abb.] (This and Chronicon above are the works
referred to as the abbey chronicle.)

Würzburg, Stadtarchiv

Ziegler'scher Nachlass: Schottenkirche St Jakob

Ratisbon (Regensburg), episcopal Ordinariatsarchiv [Reg.BOA]

Bishop's archives relating to Scots monasteries.
Archive of Scots abbey, taken there about 1945 [Sch.] Akten 319,
320 contain correspondence of Abbot Maxwell with the Ratisbon
abbot [Maxwell]

Ratisbon, Seminary Rector's Office [Reg.Regens]

A few documents, apparently belonging to the foregoing archive.

Ratisbon, Library of St James's

MS volumes (to be transferred to the new diocesan library) including the parish register of the abbey [Pfarrbuch]

Ratisbon, Historischer Verein [Reg.HV]

R 91: Scots monasteries in the town.

Ratsibon, Stadtarchiv

Rolls of citizens.
Documents relating to Scots monasteries.

Ratisbon, Staatliche Bibliothek

Rat. Ep.3, Rat. Ep.10: Scots monasteries.

Munich, Hauptstaatsarchiv [Mun.HSA]

Kloster-Urkunden Würzburg, 6470-6494: Early deeds relating to St James's, formerly in the monastic archives.
Kloster-Urkunden St Jakob Regensburg, Fasz.6-9 [KUSJR]
Kloster-Literalien St Jakob Regensburg, 1-13 [KLSJR] Nr.1 is the cartulary and chronicle of Abbot Baillie [Baillie]
HL Regensburg, 43a: Letter-book of the dukes of Bavaria [Letter-book]
Kloster-Urkunden Obermünster, Fasz. 91-115: Scots priory in Ratisbon.
Reichsstadt Regensburg, Urkunden, Fasz. 790: Scots priory in Ratisbon.

Munich, Kreisarchiv [Mun.KA]

GL 3347/30: Scots abbey in Ratisbon.

Munich, Geheimes Staatsarchiv [Mun.GSA]

K.s. 3292: Scots abbey in Ratisbon.

Munich, Staatsbibliothek

Volumes relating to Scottish and Irish monks in Bavaria.

Munich, University Library

U 1924, Nr 8130: D. A. Binchy, Die irischen Benediktinerklöster in Regensburg (unpublished thesis).

Contance, Stadtarchiv [Con.St.]

KS (Literalien), Fasz. 13 and various Urkunden: Scots abbey in the town.

Düsseldorf, Hauptstaatsarchiv

Abtei Werden, III, 19-22: Letter-books of Abbot Colchon, in particular Nr. 19 containing his drafts [Colchon]

Darmstadt, Hessisches Staatsarchiv [Darm.SA]

V.B.3, Konv. 101, Fasz. 6: Original letters sent to Colchon

Erfurt, Domarchiv [Erf.DA]

GG VIe: Archive of former Mainz diocesan chancery in Erfurt, documents relating to Scots

Wiesentheid, Schönborn family archive

Papers of Kurfürst Johann Philipp relating to the Würzburg abbey [KJP]

Münster-Schwarzach Abbey Archives

Felicitas Rediviva: MS chronicle of the Abbey [Fel.Red]

Vienna, archive of the Schottenabtei

Documents relating to Scots monks

St Gallen, Stiftsarchiv [SG]

Material relating to Scots monks

Edinburgh, Scottish Catholic Archives [SCA]

Ratisbon MSS, A1, A4, C6-10: A small but very valuable part of the monastic archives, brought to Scotland in the nineteenth century [Rat.]

Volume (no press mark) containing Catalogus Abbatum Monasterii S. Jacobi Ratisbonae [Cat.Abb.] and Tentamen super vitis et actis Abbatum Monasterii S. Jacobi . . . Erfurti [Erf.Tent.] (The latter is printed in Hammermayer, "Neue Beiträge" below).

Mission Letters: Correspondence of Scottish missionary priests [ML]

Other material relating to the Roman Catholic mission in Scotland.

Edinburgh, National Library of Scotland [NLS]

Adv: Advocates MSS, especially Vol. 10 of the Dennistoun MSS (Adv. 19.2.25), collected by James Dennistoun about 1836 [Dennistoun] Part of this volume, f.265-314, is the sole copy of Chronologia B.M.V. . . . Scotorum Viennae [Chronologia]

Other volumes containing descriptions of Würzburg MSS.

Edinburgh University Library [Edin.UL]

Laing MSS. III, 201

Fort Augustus Abbey Archives [FA]

A small but important collection from the Ràtisbon abbey, in particular Rat. 3, Libellus de fundatione Ecclesiae Consecrati Petri [Libellus]

Rat. 11: copy of Marianus Brockie's Monasticon Scoticum, Tom. I, Pars 3 [Brockie]

Oban, R.C. Cathedral House

Volumes emanating from the Scots abbeys, including one penned by Fr James Blair [Blair]

Rothesay, Mount Stuart Library

Volumes concerning the Scots abbeys, particularly Vol. II of Alexander Reid's Collections [Reid]

Glasgow, University Library

MS. 1-x.8

Kirkconnell House, Dumfries

Papers from the Scots college at Douai, in particular the original Large Register [Douai Reg.]

Dublin, National Library of Ireland

Extensive microfilms of material in continental archives relating to Scots and Irish.

Catalogue of material on Scots and Irish: R. J. Hayes (ed.), *Manuscript Sources for the History of Irish Civilisation* (11 vols. 1965).

London, British Museum [BM]

Occasional MSS relating to Scots abbeys in Germany.

Vatican Archives [VA]

Various repositories, including Nunziatura di Vienna, Processus Canonici [NVPC]

Schedario Garampi, a collection of references made by a former librarian for a projected historical work.

Vatican Library [VL]

MSS Vat.Lat: Volumes brought from Würzburg in the last century.

Barb.Lat: Papers and correspondence of Francesco Barberini, cardinal protector of Scotland.

Rome, Archive of Congregation de propaganda fide [APF]

Acta: Minutes of monthly meetings. (Extracts are printed in Giblin and Tüchle below).

SOCG: Original papers relating to the foregoing.

SC Scozia: Papers relating to Scottish affairs of lesser importance dealt with outside the monthly meetings.

Other minor repositories.

Rome, Archive of Scots College

Papers relating to Scots abbeys.

Rome, Archive of German College

Entries of Scots in sixteenth-century rolls.

Paris, Bibliothèque Nationale [BN]

Fonds Latin, 12,675: Material sent to the Maurists for their projected Monasticon Benedictinum [lat.]

Fonds Français, 19,649 - 19,659: Correspondence of Mabillon [fr.]

Brussels, Bibliothèque Royale de Belgique [BRB]

Material relating to the Scots, in particular MS 8979-82, the Bollandist documents on Macarius.

Brussels, Archives Générales du Royaume [AGR]

Subsidies made to Scots and Irish expatriates by the archdukes.

B.   Printed

The following abbreviations for periodicals and series have been used:

AU	*Archiv des historischen Vereins für Unterfranken und Aschaffenburg*
CRS	Catholic Record Society
IR	*The Innes Review*
IER	*Irish Ecclesiastical Record*
SM	*Studien und Mitteilungen zur Geschichte des Benediktinerordens*
WDGB	*Würzburger Diözesangeschichtsblätter*

This list which follows is select. General works are not listed, while others of more limited scope may be found in individual source references.

Arnold, K., *Johannes Trithemius (1462-1516)* (Würzburg, 1971) [Arnold]

Baillie, A., *A True Information . . . of our Scottish-Calvinian Gospel* (Würzburg, 1628) (S.T.C. 1202)

Bellesheim, A., *History of the Catholic Church of Scotland,* III, IV (Edinburgh, 1889-90) [Bellesheim]

Birt, H.N., *Obit book of the English Benedictines* (1913) [Birt]

Black, G.F., *The Surnames of Scotland* (New York, 1946) [Black]

Brown, W.E., *John Ogilvie* (London, 1925) [Brown]

Bundschuh's *Fränkisches Lexikon,* Bd. 5 (Ulm, 1802), 181-99 [Bundschuh]

Conaeus, G., *De duplici statu religionis apud Scotos* (Rome, 1628) [Conn]

Dempster, T., *Historia Ecclesiastica Gentis Scotorum* (Bannatyne Club, 1829) [Dempster]

Dilworth, M., "Two necrologies of Scottish Benedictine abbeys in Germany", in *IR,* ix, 173-203 ["Necrologies"] (Contains biographical notes on monks. References not usually made to it in text) "Scottish Benedictines at Würzburg: A supplement to the necrology", in *IR,* xv, 171-81 ["Necr. Suppl."] "Benedictine monks of Ratisbon and Würzburg in the 17th and 18th centuries: Emigrés from the Highlands of Scotland", in *Transactions of the Gaelic Society of Inverness,* xliv, 94-110 ["Highland Monks"] "Three Scottish Benedictines", in *The Downside Review,* lxxxii, 233-45 ["Three Scots"] "The first Benedictine mission to Scotland", in *The Downside Review,* lxxxiii, 60-72, 159-68 ["First Mission"] "The Würzburg Scots and the English Congregation", in *The Downside Review,* lxxxv, 39-61 ["Scots and EBC"] "Germania Christiana: A seventeenth-century trilogy", in *IR,* xviii, 118-40 ["Trilogy"] "Two Ratisbon manuscripts in the National Library of Scotland", in *The Bibliotheck,* v, 24-32 ["Two MSS"] "Marianus Scotus: scribe and monastic founder", in *Scottish Gaelic Studies,* x, 125-48 ["Marianus"]

Fischer, T.A., *The Scots in Germany* (Edinburgh, 1902) [Fischer]

Giblin, C., "The *Acta* of Propaganda Archives and the Scottish mission, 1623-1670", in *IR,* v, 39-76 [Giblin]

Gordon, J.F.S., *The Catholic Church in Scotland 1560-1860* (Aberdeen 1874) [Gordon]

Gropp, I., *Collectio Scriptorum et Rerum Wirceburgensium* (Frankfurt, 1741-44) [Gropp, I, II] *Wirtzburgische Chronick* (Würzburg, (1748-50) [Gropp, III, IV]

Gumpelzhaimer, C.G., *Regensburgs Geschichte, Sagen und Merkwürdigkeiten* (Regensburg, 1830-38) [Gumpelzhaimer]

Gwynn, A., "Some notes on the history of Irish and Scottish Benedictine monasteries in Germany", in *IR*, v, 5-27 [Gwynn, "Notes"] "The continuity of the Irish tradition at Würzburg", in *WDGB*, xiv/xv, 57-81 [Gwynn, "Continuity"] "Ireland and Würzburg in the middle ages", in *IER*, lxxviii, 401-11 [Gwynn, "Ireland"]

Haim, M., *Beschreibung der Tugend, Heiligkeit, Leben, Absterben und Wunderwercken Macarii* (Würzburg, 1661) [Haim]

Hammermayer, L., "Deutsche Schottenklöster, schottische Reformation, katholische Reform und Gegenreformation in West- und Mitteleuropa (1560-1580)", in *Zeitschrift für bayerische Landesgeschichte*, xxvi, 131-255 [Hammermayer, "Reformation"] "Restauration und Revolution von oben in Grossbritannien, 1685-1688", in *Historisches Jahrbuch*, lxxxvii, 26-90 [Hammermayer, "Restauration"] "Neue Beiträge zur Geschichte des Schottenklosters St Jacob in Erfurt", in *Jahrbuch für das Bistum Mainz*, viii (1958-60), 205-23.

Hay, M.V., *The Blairs Papers (1603-1660)* (Edinburgh, 1929) [*Blairs Papers*] *Failure in the Far East* (London, 1956) [Hay, *Failure*]

Hay, R.A., *Genealogie of the Hayes of Tweeddale* (Edinburgh, 1835) [Hay, *Genealogie*]

Hübl, A., *Die Wiener Schotten und das Mutterkloster St Jakob in Regensburg* (Vienna, 1914) [Hübl]

Kenney, J.F., *Sources for the early history of Ireland* (2nd ed., 1966) [Kenney]

Lindner, P., *Monasticon Metropolis Salzburgensis antiquae* (Salzburg, 1908) [Lindner]

Ludewig, J.P.ed., *Geschichtschreiber von dem Bischoffthum Wirtzburg* (Frankfurt, 1713) [Ludewig]

McRoberts, D.ed., *Essays on the Scottish Reformation, 1513-1625,* (Glasgow, 1962) [McRoberts]

Merkle, S.ed., *Die Matrikel der Universität Würzburg* (Würzburg, 1922) [Merkle] (See Appendix B)

Merzbacher, F., *Die Hexenprozesse in Franken* (Munich, 1957) [Merzbacher]

Molitor, R., *Aus der Rechtsgeschichte benediktinischer Verbände* (Munster, 1928-33) [Molitor]

Nuntiaturberichte aus Deutschland [*Nuntiaturberichte*]

Oberthür, F., *Taschenbuch für . . . Würzburg,* 1795, p. 195-210
[*Taschenbuch*]

Oegg, J.A., *Entwicklungsgeschichte der Stadt Würzburg* (Würzburg, 1880) [Oegg]

Records of the Scots Colleges (New Spalding Club, 1906) [*Colleges*]
(See Appendix C)

Renz, G.A., "Beiträge zur Geschichte der Schottenabtei St Jakob und des Priorates Weih St Peter (O.S.B.) in Regensburg", in *SM,* xvi-xviii (1895-97) [Renz]

Schmitz, P., *Histoire de l'Ordre de Saint-Benoît* (Maredsous, 1948-56)

Scholle, J., *Das Erfurter Schottenkloster* (Düsseldorf, 1932) [Scholle]

Stamminger J.B., *Die Pfarrei St Burkard in Würzburg* (Würzburg, 1889) [Stamminger]

Trithemius, J., *Opera pia et spiritualia* (Mainz, 1604)

Tüchle, H.ed., *Acta S.C. de Propaganda Fide Germaniam spectantia* (Paderborn, 1962)

Vita B. Mariani, in *Acta Sanctorium,* Feb.tom.2, 365-72 [*Vita Mar.*]

Volk, P., "Abt Leonard Colchon von Seligenstadt (1625-1653) und sein Briefwechsel", in *Historisches Jahrbuch,* lvii, 366-84 [Volk]

Weiss, L.ed., "Ephemeris Neostadiana anno 1631 annotari coepta", in *WDGB,* xxx (1968) [Weiss]

Weldon, B., *English Benedictine Congregation: Chronological Notes* (Worcester, 1881) [Weldon]

Wieland, M., "Das Schottenkloster zu St Jakob in Würzburg", in *AU,* xvi (1863), 1-182 [Wieland] (Summary in Stamminger above)

Winzet, N., *Certain Tractates,* ed.J.K. Hewison (Scottish Text Soc. 1888-90) [Hewison]

Wolff, C., "Die Abtei Münster-Schwarzach in ihren Beziehungen zu anderen Benediktiner-Klöstern im Laufe der Geschichte", in *Lumen Caecis: Festschrift . . . N.Weber* (St Ottilien, 1928), 304 ff. [Wolff]

Ziegelbauer, M., *Historia Rei Literariae Ordinis S. Benedicti* (1754) [Ziegelbauer]

Index

Abbots
  coadjutor, 45–6
  titular, 36
  election of, 113–4, 128, 132, 255
  postulation of, 77–8
  confirmation of, 50
  blessing of, 55, 118, 254
  simony in elections, 53
Abercrombie, John Christian
  (OSB), 103, 280
  journey to Scotland, 108, 113–20
  pass., 184, 186, 187
  on mission, 121, 122, 124, 128,
  130, 190–2, 195–7, 200, 202,
  204–9
Abercromby, John, 88
Aberdeen, 205, 208, 209, 232
Achaius, King, 212, 242
Acta Sanctorum, 220, 221, 227
Adda, d' (nuncio), 132
Alesius (Alane), Alexander, 213
Alexander VII, Pope, 92
Alexander, Patrick John (OSB),
  113, 116, 117, 122, 281
  paintings, 232
Algeo, Peter Benedict (OSB), 57
  abbot, 46–8, 53–5, 80, 167
  later, 69, 70–2, 75, 77, 78
  mission plans, 60, 63, 166
Allen, Cardinal, 35
Alphonsus Liguori, St, 90
Althan, Count von, 63
Amsterdam, 96, 113, 241
Anderson, David, 41–2, 158–9
Anderson, Thomas (OSB), 24, 26
Andrew, St, 19, 234
Arbroath Abbey, 233
Arctaunum, 235

Ardlawhill, 31
Argyll, 15, 218
Armour, Alexander (OSB), 47, 54,
  55, 70, 71, 274
Arundel, earl of, 77
Aschausen, Johann Gottfried von
  (Bishop), 51, 148–9, 235
Asloan, Audomarus John (OSB),
  76, 279
  on mission, 72, 75–6, 168–70
  abbacy, 76–102, 103, 152, 254–5,
  258, 262
  abbot of Ratisbon, 77–83, 88,
  149–51
  mission plans, 171–2, 175
  portrait, 96
  rector of university, 256, 272
  and Macarius, 221, 224
Asloan, George Benedict (OSB),
  76, 88, 96, 274–5, 280
  on mission, 170
Augustinian canons, 200–1
Augustinian friar, 28
Austria, 11, 58, 77, 146, 245–6
Aventinus, 216, 219, 244

Baillie, Alexander (OSB), 51, 55,
  66, 230, 279
  administrator and abbot, 71–2,
  75–82, 86, 88–95
  book, 66, 232–4
  visit to Scotland, 159, 164, 233
  historian, 239–41, 243
Baillie, William Placid (OSB), 96,
  102, 280
  on mission, 103, 109, 113, 176,
  183, 186
  death, 117, 187

293

France
  Scots in, 23, 25, 26, 117, 200, 212
  monks in, 11, 133, 136, 240, 244
  war with, 106–7, 118, 120, 124, 139
  ambassador at Ratisbon, 117, 120, 129, 201
  nuncio in, *see* Paris
  French language, 242
Franciscans, 70, 161, 170, 257
Franconia
  apostle of, *see* Kilian
  dukes of, 18, 35
  plague in, 119
  strategy in, 68
  social status in, 57
  Jews in, 257
  witchcraft in, 66, 257
Frankfurt, 66, 116, 118, 134, 213, 232
Fraser, Columbanus (OSB), 103, 109, 236, 280
Fraser, Mr, 120
Frauenzell Abbey, 56
Fries, Lorenz, 252
Frisia, 242
Fulda Abbey, 88, 240, 245, 254
Fursey, St, 212
Fyvie (castle), 208

Gaelic, 13, 15, 18, 242–3
  in mission work, 161, 177, 181, 189, 190, 195, 204, 208
Gall, St, 34, 213–4
Galloway, 114, 158, 170, 205, 206
Garroch, 76, 279, 280
Gascoigne, Placid (OSB), 91, 94, 99–101, 178
George I, King, 89
Germain, Dom (OSB), 134
Germany
  English monks in, 99
  Scots laymen in, 167
  Protestants and church property in, 36, 64, 85, 147
  German language, 81, 242
Girberg, 250
Glasgow, 41, 56, 58, 279
Goldwell, Thomas (Bishop), 25

Gordon, Alexander, 96, 275
Gordon, Anselm (OSB), 133, 140, 281
Gordon, Augustine (OSB), 129, 134, 272
Gordon, James (SJ), 231
Gordon, Marianus (OSB), 267
Gordon, William (OSB), 50, 58, 274, 279
  on mission, 72, 168–9
Gorizia, 71
Graham, Ninian (OSB), 103, 113, 115, 280
  on mission, 117, 184, 186, 187, 191
Gravesend, 76 169
Gray, William Anthony (OSB), 115–6, 275
  on mission, 182
Great Britain, 101, 171, 175, 184
Gregory XIII, Pope, 23, 25, 27, 157
Gretser, James (SJ), 232
Grünewald, Jerome, 218
Gustavus Adolphus, King, 67, 231
Guthrie, Thomas, 26, 27

Haim, Michael, 97, 221–5, 237
Haliburton, Baillie, 192
Hamburg, 76, 169
Hamilton, Alexander (General), 231
Hamilton, Francis (OSB), 31–2, 41–2, 57, 274, 279
  abbot, 42–3, 48, 52–3
  scholar, 37, 159, 229, 232, 272
Hamilton, John (OSB), 28, 31
Hamilton, John (Sir), 68
Hamilton, Placid (OSB), 267
Hamilton of Stonehouse, 32
Hatzfeld und Gleichen, Francis von (Bishop), 75, 76, 77–9, 86
Hay, Benedict (OSB), 116, 122–3, 278, 280
Hay, John (SJ), 24
Hay, Richard Augustine, 200
Hay, Romanus (OSB), 147
Hegate, James (OSB), 59, 66, 264, 272, 274, 277, 279
Hegate, Robert, 59
Helmstedt University, 55, 230

299